THE REPUBLIC OF
CHINA — MAY 1942

A SHORT HISTORY OF
CHINESE CIVILIZATION

Ten Thousand Nations Paying Homage to China

A Short History of
Chinese Civilization

by TSUI CHI

with a preface by
LAURENCE BINYON

G. P. PUTNAM'S SONS · NEW YORK

DEDICATED TO MY FRIEND

INNES JACKSON

WITHOUT WHOSE COLLABORATION
THIS BOOK WOULD NEVER HAVE
APPEARED IN PRINT

PREFACE

Tennyson crystallized in a line of verse the popular conception of China and China's history prevalent in Victorian England and no doubt in other European countries:

Better fifty years of Europe than a cycle of Cathay.

The hero of *Locksley Hall* was pictured as a young man intoxicated with all the new inventions of science, the triumphs of the machine, which were to lead mankind into a new and glorious era. Contrasted with this Western vision of the nineteenth century, alive with energy and hope, was China, vast and remote, a symbol of stagnation. At that time, it is true, China *was* stagnating. Despising the "barbarians" of the West, living on her past, she hugged her chosen isolation. She believed that the Chinese race was superior to all other races, and wished to have nothing to do with them.

But no country can afford to live in complete isolation; and China had a great contribution with which to enrich the world, if she would but join "the comity of nations." Her most splendid eras in the past, like the Han and the T'ang periods, had been those when she freely and eagerly welcomed into her great cities people from other lands; not only merchants and their merchandise, but ideals, and notably the Buddhist religion. Marco Polo, the first European to bring to the West a knowledge of Chinese civilization, particularly noticed the Chinese courtesy to foreigners. There was no talk then of "foreign devils."

In the mid-nineteenth century the Western nations saw China's contribution to the world solely in terms of her natural riches and commerce. It exasperated them that so magnificent a market should be closed to their enterprise; and as China maintained her policy of disdainful exclusiveness, they resorted to force and guile. Huge but helpless, China resisted in vain. It is a sorry page in the world's history. To the Chinese their own attitude seemed so reasonable; they only asked to be let alone. It was well for China that she should transform her attitude, so that the China of today might be made possible. But that does not excuse the ugly greed of the Western Powers.

What a change has come over our conception of China during the present century! Chinese art, Chinese literature, all the wonderful fabric of Chinese civilization, have been, in part at least, revealed to us. Europeans who have lived in China and come to know the people have always regarded them individually with respect and affection; and these feelings are coming to permeate our public more and more as our knowledge increases. Here is a civilization which has endured far longer than any other in history. And far from being, as Tennyson imagined, stagnant and unchanging, it has in one period after another endured upheavals, wars, calamities, misrule, corruption and conquest. With a marvelous elasticity it has survived them all, and at the present hour discloses hitherto undreamed-of powers within itself. Pacific China has become heroic China. The invading hosts of Japan have united her as she never was united before.

I commend this book to the English reader. There are many books about China written by Europeans. Here is one written by a Chinese, in admirably lucid English. It tells the story of Chinese civilization from remote and half-legendary times, its splendors and miseries, and in fuller detail the story of the recent years, crowded with events which are so near to us in time that they are apt to be confused in our memories or forgotten under the pressure of the momentous upheavals in Europe.

I am glad Mr. Tsui Chi, in the course of his narrative, has given us also a brief but clear account of those wild, turbulent, wandering peoples of Central Asia who, one after another, threatened China with their irruptions, but who even when successful always ended by succumbing to the civilization they came to conquer.

We are apt to associate that civilization too exclusively with Confucius. But while Confucius represents the eminently practical and reasonable side of the Chinese character, there is another side, represented by Laotzu and his followers, which reacted against Confucian formality and infused a kind of romanticism, a revolt from courts and ceremonies, a passion for spiritual freedom. Buddhism came to complete the triple strand of the Chinese tradition and way of life. At the core of this civilization is a great love of nature, whether expressed in the peasant's intimate trust in the "good earth," and his immemorial labor in the fields, or in the Taoist sage's flight from office to the woods and streams, or the Buddhist monk's choice of some lovely mountain-site for his monastery. It is from such a source that the great landscape art of China has sprung. This sensibility to beauty in nature and in everyday things is what gives a special character to Chinese civilization.

It is a very precious gift, all too rare in Europe. I think the author of this book might perhaps have stressed a little more the great importance given to æsthetic considerations in Chinese life and in Chinese history. But this is something no doubt that, as a true Chinese, he took for granted, though it is remarkable to us.

LAURENCE BINYON.

CONTENTS

LIST OF MAPS

List of Maps

FOREWORD

THE AIM OF THIS BOOK is to give, from a Chinese point of view, an account of Chinese history to general readers and students of foreign countries who are interested in Eastern affairs, old as well as new. I have not attempted to be academic and do not pretend that this book presents the unanimous view of my people. Probably there is no such thing as "the unanimous view of a nation"; but I am sure that I am giving a representative viewpoint and one that is shared by a great many of my countrymen.

When the book was first written, it was provided with copious footnotes. On the advice of my friends, and, indeed, after reconsideration on my own part, I suppressed them, for it was against my intention to deter or repel the ordinary reader. The Bibliographical Appendix, however, is retained, partly as an earnest memento of my research, and also for the benefit of serious students. Much of the material has come direct from contemporary Chinese sources or from the colossal standard work—the "Twenty-four Histories," each of which was compiled immediately after the events it records. Memoirs and records of ancient times, which up till now have not been translated into Western languages, have been quoted in this book. With the exception of a few topics such as the archæological, diplomatic, and commercial backgrounds of Chinese history, I have not consulted Western works. Limited space does not allow me to quote every source or enter upon controversies. Nor, for this reason, can I describe every possible aspect of our civilization, as various of my critics would require. Since the publication of this book in England, I have had correspondence with some English scholars and Sinologues, as a result of which I have been able to confirm my viewpoint in many places.

There are some particular characteristics of Chinese history which I might do well to explain here. Through the age-old Official Examination system and, before this, the so-called "Selection and Recommendation" (*hsuan chu*) system, the door was open for the humblest people to enter government service, and thus a certain standard of democracy has existed in China for thousands of years. The repeated

People's Risings, however, which overthrew decadent dynasties and established new ones, aimed more often at effecting a change of government rather than at the assertion of popular rights, or the seizure of political power by any particular class.

Before the penetration of Western capitalism (in the form of foreign manufactured goods) into the interior of China, the Chinese economic system had had its own unique structure in spite of many weaknesses. With the exception of a few periods, such as in the warlike Ch'in and Mongolian dynasties, the Chinese court always adopted a physiocratic policy, and commerce seldom received manifest encouragement from the government. Merchants have never exercised much political power until recent times. It has always been famine, war, heavy taxes, and misrule which have driven the Chinese peasants to revolution. It has always been the first concern of Chinese rulers and ministers, such as, for instance, Wang An-shih of the Sung dynasty, to think out remedies for these evils which rendered intolerable the life of the masses. When famine, war, heavy taxation, and misrule could be avoided, however, the Chinese people lived peaceably, and even happily in their simple way, as, for example, in the days of Emperor Wen of the Han dynasty. It was not without reason that Juan Gonsalez de Mendoza, in the sixteenth century, never saw any poor Chinese beg, and that in the eighteenth century Emperor Ch'ien Lung of China refused to establish commercial relations with the English King George III on the ground that "We possess all things." It was not until the coming of the modern, Western influences that China was compelled to make fundamental changes, because her own old foundations were shaken. The change will bear good fruit in the long run, although at first it was introduced with force and accepted not without pain. We and our friends sometimes look back to our past with nostalgia, but no one should forget that history must develop and progress, and that behind porcelain and embroidery, the philosophy of quietness, and the poetry of beauty, there had always been the toil of the masses, which demanded relief and betterment.

The book contains some legends of prehistoric times, relating to all the races of people who have lived and live in the land of China, and whose different strains have combined to make the modern Chinese. These stories have been quoted not only because they are interesting in themselves, but also because they include some fragment of history which would otherwise be lost. The Flood tradition, for instance, among the people living in "China Proper," was a phenomenon common to the world, and the tradition of a wolf-ancestor shared by the Turks and Mongols may serve to explain that these two great tribes belonged to the same stock. Our legends may, therefore, be noticed in the way as Western historians do the Egyptian and Greek traditions.

I must thank my friend Innes Jackson, author of "China Only Yesterday," without whose help my book would never have been written in its present form—a form to me, at least, that always gives pleasure.

A SHORT HISTORY OF CHINESE CIVILIZATION

I. GENESIS AND DELUGE

In the beginning of the world, says the Chinese legend, there was a great chaos. The sky and the earth were like the white and the yolk of an egg. Primal Man, P'an-ku, was born, and he gave form to the earth and sky. The sky he made from bright and clear elements, the earth from dark, impure ones. P'an-ku transfigured himself nine times a day. The sky became ten feet higher each day, the earth ten feet thicker, and P'an-ku ten feet taller. By the end of his life, which lasted eighteen thousand years, the sky was very high, the earth very thick, and P'an-ku very tall.

When P'an-ku wept, his streaming tears made the Yellow and Yangtzu rivers; he breathed and the wind blew; he spoke and thunder roared; he looked round and lightning glanced from his eyes. The weather would be fine when P'an-ku was in a good temper; dull and cloudy when he was cross. When he died his remains fell apart and formed the Five Sacred Mountains of China. His head became T'ai Mountain in the East; his body Sung Mountain in the center; his right arm Heng Mountain in the North and his left Heng Mountain in the South; his two feet Hua Mountain in the West. His two eyes were transformed into sun and moon, his fat melted into streams and seas, and his hairs took root and covered the earth with plants.

Like the Egyptians, Babylonians, Greeks, and other ancient civilizations, the Chinese have their stock of legends which are supposed to explain the topography of the country—how the mountains, plains, and rivers appeared—as well as how the jungles came to be cleared, wild beasts destroyed, the land made habitable, and civilized usages taught. Handed down originally by oral tradition, many local myths were collected by the great Chinese thinker and teacher Confucius in the first half of the fifth century B.C., and are preserved in his books. Others were recorded by some post-Confucian writers, two or three hundred years B.C. Among the country people, cut off by their circumstances from scientific thought, and especially among the remnants of ancient tribes, these stories are still credited, and their heroes worshiped. The Miao tribe, for instance, which now inhabits the mountains of Kuangsi,

3

is said to have splendid cave buildings where P'an-ku's image is kept and worshiped, as well as images of the "Three Sovereigns."

These three—Lord of Heaven, Lord of Earth, and Lord of Man— were, according to the popular myth, supposed to succeed P'an-ku as rulers of the earth. The Lord of Heaven had twelve heads and ruled for eighteen thousand years in the K'un-lun mountains of Northwest China. These mountains were supposed to be the pillars that upheld the heavens. The Lord of Earth also had twelve heads and ruled for another eighteen thousand years in the Dragon Gate Mountains (probably Honan province). Both had the body of a serpent and the feet of a beast. The Lord of Man had only nine heads, and he ruled for forty-five thousand, six hundred years in a land called "Hsing Ma" (modern Ssuch'uan).

The reign of the Lord of Man forms the first of "Ten Epochs," a period of time mentioned by Ssu-ma Chen, a Chinese historian of the ninth century, quoting a lost book of very ancient sources, but about which very little is recorded except the rulers' names. In the fourth epoch there lived a ruler who tamed the fabulous "flying deer"; in the fifth, one who tamed the "flying unicorn"; another in the sixth who tamed six dragons. This clearly refers to a time when the inhabitants of China were trying to protect themselves from wild animals, probably of species now extinct. In the seventh epoch a ruler taught the people to cover themselves with animal skins, and a certain "Lord Big Nest" taught them to build homes in the branches of trees. The philosopher Mencius (372-289 B.C.) writes of a time when "the waters . . . inundated the Middle Kingdom. Snakes and dragons occupied it. . . . In the low grounds, the people made nests for themselves." This evidently refers to a period of serious floods, when the valley dwellers took to the trees to save themselves from drowning.

In the ninth epoch we hear of three rulers around whom many popular traditions have grown up—T'ai Hao, "Lord Supreme Radiance" (often referred to as Fu Hsi), Queen Nu Wo, and Shen Nung, "Lord Divine Peasant." Lord Supreme Radiance had a human head and the body of a serpent. He invented and taught his people the use of nets for catching fish. He is said to have been the first to establish a marriage ceremonial: two deerskins were to be presented by the man to his intended as a sign of betrothal—a symbolic rite that seems to have been observed at a much later period, as it is found in authentic records.

It is said that one evening as Lord Supreme Radiance sat in thought, and looked first at the starlit sky and after at the earth imprinted with the tracks of animals, he was inspired to design some written forms which should represent the primal features of the world—heaven, earth, fire, water, wind, thunder, marsh, and mountain. These are called the "Eight Trigrams," and were later used as symbols in divination.[1] Some even say they were the actual origin of Chinese writing.

The Queen Nu Wo, who succeeded Lord Supreme Radiance, was no beautiful goddess; like him, she had a human head on a serpent's body. During her reign there were furious quarrels between various petty rulers, and one of them, by name Kung Kung, having been defeated by a rival, is said to have struck his head in mad rage against the "Peak of No-circumference." The shock was so great that the pillars supporting the sky crumbled, and the chains from which the earth was suspended shivered to pieces. Sun, moon, and stars poured down into the Northwest, where the sky became low; rivers, seas, and oceans rushed down to the Southeast, where the earth sank. A great conflagration burst out. Flood raged. Wild beasts and terrible birds made men their prey. The Queen was filled with grief.

In her smelting furnace she cast a five-colored stone, with which she mended the cracked sky. She cut off the four feet of an animal called Ao, and placed one at each of the four corners of the universe to stabilize it. A black dragon was executed. The ashes of the burnt grass she scattered into the floods and dried them up. Thus the sky was made complete forever, the water ebbed, and wild animals were driven away. Peace returned like spring to the earth.

This myth must have grown up to explain in a supernatural way the topography of China, where West and Northwest are mountainous, while the Southeast is low with a network of rivers running towards the sea. The tradition of the grass ashes may have some connection with the quantities of sand, mud, and silt which are brought down to the lower reaches of the Yellow River.

Lord Divine Peasant, the third of these legendary figures, had a human body and the head of an ox. He is said to have been the first to teach people how to till the soil and use the plow. This tradition, together with the Lord's peculiar physiognomy, points to a remote period when agriculture was developed. Market-places were set up under his rule, whither the produce of the fields was brought for sale. He is also said to have discovered herb medicines: with his own stomach for a laboratory, he tested all kinds of herbs and was poisoned seventy times in a day.

The tenth epoch begins with the story of the Yellow Emperor, who

[1] The "Eight Trigrams" are recorded by Confucius in his "Book of Changes" as follows:

conquered the descendants of Lord Divine Peasant. Both he and his Empress are famous figures in Chinese legend, for to their work and ingenuity are credited many of the elements of civilized society. The Emperor is even called the "Grandfather of the Chinese Race."

According to tradition, the Emperor had to fight a formidable rival from the South, by name of Chih-yu, soon after his accession. Chih-yu is said to have been armed with bronze weapons, which doubtless gave rise to a strange tradition that this warrior had a bronze skull and iron forehead.[1] Chih-yu, runs the legend, also had the gods of wind and rain on his side, and with their help he conjured up a thick fog to mislead the Emperor's forces. But though the latter were armed with only bows and arrows, the Emperor had provided them with a sophisticated instrument of warfare—the compass! By this discovery of his, he was able to direct his men through the fog. Chih-yu was defeated and lost his life.

The raising of the fog easily finds a rational explanation. The climate of South China is often wet and misty; that of the North, dry and clear. A southern army invading the North would be at an advantage if they planned an attack during some unexpected spell of bad weather. It is not unlikely, therefore, that this event had its historical existence in some very remote time.

Under the Yellow Emperor's rule, the arts of living developed widely. Houses, palaces, and temples were constructed; land was surveyed, and the country divided up into provinces and districts. His Empress was the first to rear the silkworm in China, and she taught her people to weave the silk and make silk garments for themselves, thus laying the foundation of China's greatest and oldest industry. The Emperor himself designed the fashions of clothing, and made strict regulations whereby the different ranks of society might be distinguished by their dress. The imperial robes were black, with yellow trousers, embroidered with pheasants and flowers. One of his officials invented an early form of writing; another made the first calendar. Coins were introduced. Canoes, chariots, and beasts of burden were employed.

The Yellow Emperor may have been an historical figure, but more probably he is the symbolic personification of an era, covering some hundreds of years, during which many of the foundations of modern Chinese civilization were laid. After him, the next two rulers to emerge are the much-revered Yao and Shun, and though their existence has

[1] According to the writer Jen Fang of the sixth century, Chih-yu's grave was excavated, and the bronze skull and iron forehead actually unearthed!

not yet been proved by scientific research, they seem to be real people.
Confucius and his followers refer to them with high approbation, pointing them out as ideal Emperors, who despised worldly power and
cared only for their people's well-being.

"Oh, great was Yao as a king!" wrote Confucius, "Nothing is greater
than Heaven, but Yao corresponded to it! How vast was his virtue, the
people could find no name for it!"

The years of their rule were looked back upon with nostalgia—they
were the "good old days" when virtue governed the deeds of all men.

But though men's hearts were right in the time of Yao, the country
suffered many natural calamities. "Nowhere on the earth was there
order," recorded Mencius gloomily. "Vast torrents overflowed their
channels and flooded the lands. Forests and undergrowth sprang up
in the cultivated lands. Droves of wild animals ranged abroad, and
many kinds of grain would not grow."

The tender-hearted and virtuous Yao was so distressed at the condition of his people that he went in search of some good man to share
his power and alleviate his anxieties. It is said that he first visited a
hermit by name of Hsu Yu and imparted his idea to him.

"Pshaw!" said the hermit, "share your power? Don't pollute me!"
And he hurried to a stream to wash his ears. At the stream another
hermit was watering his cow, and he asked what Hsu Yu was doing.
Being told the story, he hastened his animal away lest the wretched
news about the throne should make it sick.

The story is intended to show how little the people cared for worldly
power in those days. But Yao was determined to find a worthy man
who would share the responsibilities of government with him, and
succeed him after his death. He called a conference of his ministers and
asked them to make a recommendation. One of them said, "There is a
young bachelor among the people, whose name is Shun. He is the son
of a blind old man and an obstinate woman, and the elder brother of
a haughty boy. Such is his filial piety and brotherliness, that he is able
to get the better of all these domestic difficulties."

"I should like to try him," said the Emperor, and he sent Shun oxen,
sheep, and grain, and gave him the rank of "city-forming Prince." He
gave Shun his two daughters for wives, and told them to watch his
conduct—whether he deserved his reputation. They told Yao that he
deserved it.

How great must have been Shun's need of forbearance is shown by
the treatment he received from his family after his promotion by Yao.
When they heard of his good fortune, they were jealous and angry,

and plotted to kill him. First they commanded him to repair a granary, and when he had climbed into the loft, they took away the ladder and set fire to the building. But Shun jumped from the loft and escaped without injury. Another time they made him dig a well, and when he had dug down very deep, they shoveled the earth back upon him, and went away, thinking he would be buried alive. But by some means, miraculous or natural, Shun escaped again. So magnanimous was he that the younger brother who had instigated these crimes was not only pardoned, but given the rank of prince with lands to administer when Shun became Emperor. And so long as his parents lived, he loved and feared them as if he were a young boy.

The Emperor Yao made trial of Shun in all kinds of difficult enterprises. Success crowned each of them. He was sent on dangerous expeditions into every part of the kingdom to observe and improve the conditions of the people—to mountains, jungles, marshes, and rivers in flood—and in spite of terrible tempests and storms, he fulfilled each mission faithfully. Yao then gave him increased power to deal with the disorders of the times, and provided him with four subordinates. The first of these, Yih, set fire to the trees and bushes that had overrun the mountains and fields, and had turned them into homes for predatory animals, rendering them useless for cultivation. Yih's men also drove away the wild animals from the neighborhood of the people's dwellings. The second of Shun's subordinates, "Prince Millet" as he is traditionally called, taught the people to sow and reap, and cultivate five kinds of grain, in the parts Yih had cleared for them. In this way the people were able to support themselves and enjoy a comfortable existence.

The third was an educationist. He taught the Five Principles to the people. These principles are: probity between the sovereign and his ministers; affection between parents and children; proper division between the functions of husband and wife; proper order between the old and young; and fidelity between friends.

The Great Yu was the fourth delegate. His chief work during Shun's lifetime was his mastering of the floods, and after Shun's death he succeeded to the throne. In the course of time, Yao died, and Shun became Emperor.

Some stories say that Shun had two astronomers, Hsi-ho and Shang-i. Hsi-ho's duty was to observe the sun, Shang-i the moon. Whether astronomy was known as a science to the Chinese of those very remote times cannot be verified, and in some famous poems of the fourth century B.C., in the anthology *Ch'u Tzu,* the two "astronomers" have become god of the sun and goddess of the moon. There are also many beautiful myths about these two, and we do not know whether two human beings living many thousands of years ago discovered some elements of astronomy, and so gave rise to myths among later generations, or whether a more sophisticated age tried to rationalize the myths. In the great wilderness of the West, runs one of them, there was a mountain called the Mountain of the Sun and Moon. It formed the gate of Heaven, and the sun and moon came and went through it. A girl bathed the moon there; she was Shang-i, Shun's Empress, who had given birth to twelve moons. Beyond the Eastern sea, by the river Sweetness, was a country called Hsi-ho. A girl named Hsi-ho bathed the suns there in the deep Pool of Sweetness. She also was the wife of Emperor Shun, and had given birth to ten suns. Nine of the suns lived under the Great Mulberry Tree, but the tenth lived above it in the Heavens. While Yao was still reigning, ten suns appeared at once and scorched people to death. Yi, a great archer, was sent to shoot them, and he brought down nine, all of which were transformed into ravens as soon as they fell to earth.[1]

After a long and beneficial reign, Shun is said to have died while on a tour to the Mountains of the Nine Doubts in the wilderness of Ts'ang Wu. His two wives mourned over him, and shed tears which fell like pearls on to the bamboo groves and never dried. At their death, they became the goddesses of the river Hsiang. Now there grows in a part of Hunan province a special kind of bamboo that is particularly valued by Chinese flute makers. According to present-day tradition, the purple rings on the bamboo stems are the teardrops of Shun's two Empresses, and the plaintive music of the flutes seems to its hearers like a wind that mourns over the flowing waters of Hsiang.

Shun's successor was Yu, who is supposed to have founded a dynasty called Hsia. Neither his nor his dynasty's existence has yet been proved by historical research, but they seem to be facts, although many of Yu's heroic deeds have been magnified to the dimension of legends. Some say, for instance, that he sent two subordinates to measure the earth, and that they walked from the North Pole to the South Pole, and from the East to the West, and found both times that the space was 233,500 *li* and 75 *pu* (about 84,000 miles). He himself traveled over the whole Empire, runs another tradition, marked the positions of the mountains and

---

[1] For the myths, reference has been made to the *Shan Hai Ching*, "The Book of Mountains and Seas," believed written in the period of the "Warring States" (5th–3rd century B.C.), and to other early records. The appearance of the nine suns probably represents a heat-wave: the ravens may originate in the observance of sunspots.

rivers, cut down the forests that impeded his journey, and had roads constructed. All these events probably point to the fact that during Yu's administration, many parts of the country were surveyed, some of the wild parts brought under cultivation, and communications built. Elsewhere it is recorded that he divided the country into nine provinces, appointed governors to them, and made certain demands of tribute from them. Silk and lacquer are among the offerings mentioned. He sent for all the lords to attend his Court and swear allegiance. Ten thousand—a general figure implying a very great number—came, bringing presents of jade and precious silks.

But Yu's greatest work, and with which he is usually associated, is his stemming of the Great Flood. Before Yu came into power, his father Kun had been appointed by the Emperor Shun to control the ravaging waters, but had been unsuccessful. He worked for nine years building dikes to prevent the inundations, but they were swept away before the force of the deluge. Finally Shun exiled him to the Mountain of Feathers, where he died, and was transformed into a yellow turtle with only three legs (or, according to some versions, a yellow dragon or a yellow bear), upon which it would have to limp about in the Pool of Feathers for all time. Another legend says that Kun's body was cut open three years after his death, and that Yu was brought out of it.

Yu, at all events, was more successful than his unfortunate father. Instead of building dikes, he cleared and deepened channels for the waters, and so brought them down in order to the sea. He cleared passages for all the rivers and streams: the four great rivers of China —Yellow, Yangtzu, Han, and Huai—were formed out of the general deluge. He worked unremittingly for thirteen years to accomplish this great task, and in the course of it he passed three times by his own home but did not enter it. On one early occasion, his wife was giving birth to a son, and the child's cry could be heard in the doorway: still Yu did not go in, so engrossed was he upon this work of saving the people from perpetual flood.

There seems to be historical fact behind the story of Yu the Flood-queller—that some ruler, or even some less important personage, with an engineering talent, deepened and cleared silted-up river channels, and so averted inundations from melted snows and spring rains. But many legends have accumulated round it, whose origins are difficult to trace. Besides the legend of Kun, the three-legged turtle, there is a very well-known one related about Yu himself. The author of *"Huai Nan Tzu"*—a writer of the second century B.C.—describes how Yu during his work of regulating the waters used to be transformed into

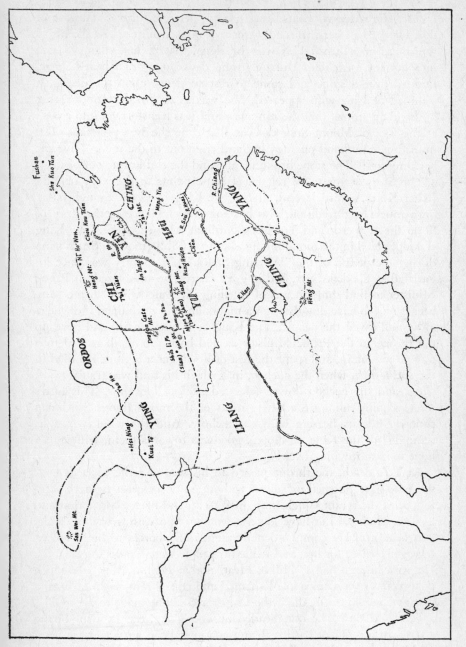

LEGENDARY AND TRADITIONAL PERIODS, I

a bear. His wife, who sometimes used to bring food, was unaware of this, for she had been warned never to approach him unless she heard the sound of a drum. This was the signal that he had changed back into human form. Unfortunately, one day, Yu, still in bear's shape, jumped over a stone and came to rest suddenly upon the drum! It sounded and his wife appeared. She was so ashamed at finding her husband an animal that she ran away and was transformed into a rock at the foot of Mount Sungkao. At that time she was pregnant. The unfortunate husband pursued her and cried out to the rock, "Give me back my son!" The stone broke silently and the child came out of it.

This story seems to be related at some points to the story of Yu's father Kun. A third legend, that of the King of Hope, though based on a much later tradition, also has some resemblance to the story of Shun the Emperor and Yu, his subordinate and successor. The King of Hope ruled in the mountainous country of Shu (modern Ssuch'uan) during the period of the "Warring States." His country was once inundated by flooded rivers, and in great distress he authorized his Prime Minister to find some means of quelling the waters. The Prime Minister is said to have dug through a mountain, and so drained the waters away and saved the people. The King kept his bargain, and gave up the throne to the Prime Minister as had been promised, retired to a remote mountain, and spent the rest of his life as a hermit. He died in the springtime, when the cuckoo, into which his soul was transformed, sings, and the cuckoo flower (the red azalea) blossoms. This bird's song, echoing among the lonely rocks of the mountainous Ssuch'uan country, fills its hearers with melancholy. And the country people, reminded of the King of Hope's goodness towards them, will say, "I hope to have my king back!"

At Yu's death, the throne passed to his son, and the Hsia dynasty seems to have pursued its course without any very great figure emerging, until the tyrant Chieh brought it to an end by his corruption and avarice. He is said to have loved a woman who was as vicious as she was beautiful. He commanded thousands of laborers to build an extravagant palace for her, and while his people were almost starving, the Emperor himself had a "Hill of Meat" and a "Pool of Wine" on which boats could sail! The people lamented and cursed him, saying, "O sun, sink: we would gladly die if the Emperor could be made to die too!"

A revolution broke out, headed by one T'ang, the Lord of Shang (Yin). In a series of battles, T'ang conquered the armies of Emperor Chieh, and took him prisoner, thus bringing the dynasty to an end. With the Shang dynasty which was then founded, we leave the period of legend and conjecture for one of historical certainty, based on excavations and records.

As for any conclusions that may be drawn from this collection of traditions—part legend, part truth—about the earliest eras of Chinese history, we may assert with some confidence that the civilization had its first development in the great plain of the Yellow River, which now constitutes Northern China. According to traditions, all the capitals of the earliest Emperors and Lords, beginning from Fu Hsi, "Lord Supreme Radiance," have been in this area—the modern provinces of Shansi, Honan, Hopei, and Shantung. Archæological discoveries relating to the pre-Shang period, imperfect though they are up till now, have been found in the same part of the country.

As for the character of the civilization, we can presume that it was agricultural from a very early time, that there were large villages and probably some markets to which agricultural produce was brought from a group of surrounding villages. Whether a more highly developed administrative unit, corresponding to a "province," also appeared in these times is doubtful, although the Yellow Emperor is said to have divided his Empire up in this way. The cultivation of silk seems to have been one of the arts of this primitive community, and it is possible that silk clothing was substituted for the animal skins in which the first Chinese settlers dressed themselves. A primitive form of writing as well as some kind of coins seem to have been invented before the Shang dynasty.

I am not here presuming to decide which, if any, of the great figures of early tradition—the Yellow Emperor, Yao, Shun, Yu, and so on— have lived and died as individual human beings, though I have indicated in the foregoing pages two or three who seem to have been living persons, although some of the acts attributed to them have the appearance of legend. If modern historical criticism has been directed against the real existence of such persons as Buddha and Jesus, casting doubts upon whether they have lived at all, or are only symbolical representations of a certain age in the civilizations to which they belong, how much less can we expect to find credence for the "reality" of people like the blessed Yao and Shun, the records of whose lives are far more dubious than those of Buddha and Jesus?

But to prove or disprove whether these personages have actually lived is of little importance to a history of Chinese civilization. We can be content with saying that they epitomized successive historical periods, and we can relate to each of them a stage of development in Chinese civilization rather than the traits of human existence.

II. THE STONE AGE IN CHINA

FROM THE RICH TREASURY of legend and fable by means of which the Chinese are accustomed to picture for themselves the lives of their earliest ancestors, it has been possible to piece together, with aid of imagination and conjecture, the primitive life of the Chinese race in the misty years before the existence of written records. But there are other instruments—the excavator's pick and shovel—which have drawn out of the earth little bits of bone, human teeth, scraps of colored pottery, a necklace that may have added glamour to the face of a Stone Age beauty but serves now only as a pathetic *memento mori,* a primitive hoe, a wild pig's tusk—all of which are able, with the scientific research that has been spent upon them, to depict this same primitive civilization with more accuracy, though perhaps with a little less color. It is with these dramatic discoveries that this chapter is concerned. Although it is not possible to find a scientific parallel to all the legends surrounding the birth of the Chinese civilization, it will be seen that there are sufficient points of similarity between the evidence of the excavators and the traditional legends.

In recent years, in a place called "Chicken-bone Hill," some thirty miles from Peking, bones and skeletons of many birds, which the local inhabitants believed to be the bones of chickens devoured by foxes that had previously infested those parts, have been excavated. This was how the hill had been given its name—or so everybody in the district had always been told: it seemed there could be no doubt about it. Archæologists, however, were very skeptical, and after a close examination of the bones under the microscope, found them to be the fossil bones of ancient birds and rodents, as well as of some beasts of prey!

Further excavations were carried out at the "Chicken-bone Hill" and its vicinity (the district as a whole is known as *Chou K'ou Tien*) and these later discoveries included the molar of a creature resembling a human being. This interesting tooth now suggested to our archæologists that in a lower stratum of that district there was a hope of discovering human remains.

Accordingly a large party of excavators was formed, including members of the Geological Survey from Peking, and it repaired to the "Chicken-bone Hill" in April of 1927. During the first two years of the excavations, about six thousand cubic meters of cave deposits were hewn and examined: a thousand trunks full of fossils were transported to Peking to be analyzed and studied. Human teeth, jawbones, and even pieces of skull were discovered among them. By 1934 fragments of twenty-five different "persons" had been dug out of *Chou K'ou Tien*.

But in 1929, one of the greatest events in modern archæology had taken place; an event more sensational than the discovery of all the previous bones and molars. The complete cranium of P'an-ku—the Primal Man whom legend called the child of earth and sky, and whose dead body was said to have been transformed into mountains and seas, the sun and the moon—was dug up! To speak more plainly, the cranium of the so-called "Peking Man," younger brother of the erect ape-man of Java, and elder brother of the Piltdown Man of England— the Chinese Primal Man and the essential link in the chain of human evolution—was dug up. He is thought to have lived in the early part of the Old Stone Age.

Many scientists worked upon this famous cranium. They tried to estimate the degree of "humanity" and intelligence to which this earliest of Chinese had attained, and whether he appeared to have some relation in racial type to the people now called "Chinese." They also examined carefully all traces of human and animal life excavated from the same district and stratum, thereby building up a sufficiently reliable picture of "Peking Man's" environment and habits.

It has been ascertained by medical authorities that his endocranial capacity was as great as 964.4 c.c., only a little less than the 1,000 c.c. which is the low limit of cranial capacity in normal modern man. More interesting still is the deduction from careful study of the third inferior frontal convolution, Broca's speech area,—that the "Peking Man" may have had the power of articulate speech.

Medical study of the cranium went on, and they paid special attention to the teeth and jaws. It had been noticed that the upper front teeth and canines had what is called a "shovel" shape—the shape that is an acknowledged characteristic of Mongolian, Eskimo, Chinese, and Japanese teeth, but not the teeth of Negroes or any white races. Further, a formation called by modern scientists the "mandibular torus" was found behind the lower front molars, and this was found also on jawbones of Chinese Stone-Bronze Age people, belonging to a later stage of development than the "Peking Man." With some modifications, the same formation is to be observed in Chinese of the present day. The conclusion is that "Peking Man" had a direct kinship with modern Mongolian races, to which the modern Chinese belong.

Some of "Peking Man's" activities, besides speech and thought, have been deduced from various fragments of evidence embedded in the same stratum. For instance, animal bones were dug up which bore traces of burning. Little piles of dark yellow ashes were also found, and thought to be the ashes of charcoal. This primitive man and his fellows had evidently mastered fire. In the same site, some 3,000 bones were found which showed signs of having been worked upon by human hands. The method of workmanship upon each showed points of similarity, and archæologists concluded that although the exact use to which these bones were put could only be imagined, they did in fact represent some form of local "industry." Many thousand pieces of quartz and other stones were also dug up, most of which had evidently been worked on by powerful strokes; some had even been retouched, pointing to the existence of certain standards of workmanship.

"Peking Man's" environment can, to some extent, be imagined from the fauna discovered in the same site. The co-existence of very different types of animals, such as otters and buffaloes, some kinds of deer and carnivorous beasts, tells us that varied types of scenery, swamps and lakes, mountains and woods, were to be found in that part of the earth at that time. The presence of the buffalo, an animal more common to the south of the continent than the north, suggests a climate warmer and damper than the present climate of North China.

Close to the site we have discussed, still in the same *Chou K'ou Tien* district, a special site was discovered and called by the excavators the "Upper Cave." Its contents though comparatively small in number proved to be of the greatest interest, for they formed a link between the earliest Stone Age culture and the discoveries at *Ordos* (or *Ho T'ao*), the second important archæological site in China. The objects and implements excavated from the "Upper Cave" suggest that primitive man of this period had some feeling for beauty. Besides bone implements which had been ornamented with a kind of red coloring, some bone-made pendants were found, and within a square foot of ground twenty-eight animal teeth were unearthed. These latter, the excavators concluded, could only have formed a necklace, the soft string of which must have rotted and perished altogether. Other significant discoveries in the "Upper Cave" were fragments of iron ore (hematites) which had evidently served some useful function in that primitive society, but the material of which was not of native origin. There must, therefore, at that very early age, have been intercourse and exchange of goods with other countries!

Discoveries at the *Ordos* site still belong to the period known as the "Old Stone Age," though they reflect a form of society more highly developed than that of the "Peking Man," and probably at a similar stage to that of the *Chou K'ou Tien* "Upper Cave" culture. In one of the sites, together with many stone implements, excavators found bits of charcoal apparently from the campfires of some very ancient people, and interesting remains of their fantastic meals—bits of bone from the Mongolian desert ass, rhinoceros, hyena, antelope, cows, and buffaloes, as well as bits of egg-shell from the now extinct giant ostrich! From another site, the remains of freshwater mollusks and a variety of water fauna were dug up, from which it was deduced that there had once been a plentiful water supply in this district, and hence a possibility of pasture land. The presence of water and wild game would, it would seem, render the place favorable for human habitation, but to the disappointment of archæologists, a single ancient tooth is so far the only trace of humanity.

Up to the present, the sequence of Chinese pre-history is unfortunately still incomplete. No true link has been found to connect the "Old" Stone Age (represented by the *Ordos* finds) with the New, and in fact, evidences of the early "New Stone Age" culture are entirely missing. Of the later stages, or what we may call the "Stone-Bronze Age," many sites have been discovered, and the culture they reveal is often called the "Yang Shao Culture," Yang Shao being the name of a village in Honan in the fields of which pottery fragments were first found in 1921. Other investigations of the Stone-Bronze Age culture, especially at the Sha Kuo T'un Cave in Liaoning Province and in various parts of Kansu Province, soon followed.

In October of 1921, a band of excavators from the Peking Geological Survey worked in Yang Shao for three months. The complete site of an ancient village was unearthed, measuring 960 meters from north to south and 480 meters from east to west—evidently a large settlement with a considerable population. Certain large stone instruments have the shape of hoes or mattocks and must have been used for tilling the soil, while the frequently discovered perforated disks of clay or stone were obviously some form of spinning-wheel and point to the cultivation of a textile plant. There were, besides, some woven patterns clearly impressed on many clay vessels found in the Yang Shao village, and some basket designs on gray-ware pottery found at one of the Kansu sites, which prove beyond doubt that some textile, probably hemp, was cultivated by these ancient Chinese. Agriculture was, therefore, one of their occupations.

Some form of spinning may have been devised by these people. The Yang Shao site disclosed many likely instruments, mostly pointed and made of bone or horn. There were also some small dainty sewing needles with neatly cut holes which show a remarkable advance in skilled workmanship.

It is clear that the Stone-Bronze Age people had learned to tame the pig and keep it for their use. Nearly all the animal bones found at the Yang Shao site belong to this animal, and they are far too numerous to have been the relics of wild boar killed in the hunt. It is worth commenting that pork is still the staple meat of the Chinese.

Since they had tamed the pig for their food, it is likely that these people kept other domestic animals. We do not know whether they rode horses or harnessed them to carriages for travel and transport, but although no trace has yet been found of anything resembling a wheeled vehicle, we know that the wheel design was familiar to them. Vessels found in one of the Kansu sites are ornamented with wheel-like designs, and it is obvious from the form of the pottery in all Stone-Bronze Age sites that the potter's wheel was one of their possessions. It is not impossible that the Yang Shao villagers constructed carriages.

These examples of pottery which have been dug up in considerable quantity from all the sites of this period, at Yang Shao, at Sha Kuo T'un Cave, and in Kansu, not only demonstrate by their abundance a great advance in the pottery industry, but by the grace and variety of their forms a far more highly developed sense of artistry. There are pots with collar and handles decorated with beautiful impressed patterns; thin-walled and high-collared vases of elegant shape, some with large handles; small vessels with wide mouths and high-seated handles; large unpainted urns with saddle-shaped mouths, and so on through a large range of patterns. Among the designs painted on them are drawings of men, birds, dogs, and horses, and abstract patterns of meanders, triangles, horizontal zones, and vertical lines, as well as the wheel-like pattern already described. In coloring, the vessels are gray, grayish-yellow, black, and violet. Most of the decorated pottery is red with black designs; a few are monochrome. In addition to all these examples of a fairly advanced art, a few small cut and engraved objects have astonished the archæologists. The little figure of an animal, probably a cat, about three millimeters high, and engraved with considerable skill, was one of the remarkable finds in these sites. Some jade rings found in one of the Kansu burial grounds also amazed the discoverers, the material being so hard that it is difficult to imagine how a people apparently lacking metal instruments could possibly have cut such thin and delicate objects. In the rather later sites at Kansu, certainly, a few copper articles were picked up, among them one having a knife-shape. Winged arrowheads of copper were also found.

Much conjecture has been raised as to whether the Stone-Bronze Age people had yet invented any form of writing. Nothing conclusive has been discovered, but among some grave furniture in a Kansu tomb a collection of bone objects was found. These small rectangular bone plates, some smooth, some incised, were grouped together in such a way as to suggest that they represented a very early form of writing; that is, they were the visible expression of some abstract idea connected with the dead.

Until very recent times, funeral ceremonies have held a place of the utmost importance in the minds of the Chinese. Rites for the dead formed a large section in Confucius' moral code—a code that was faithfully followed by the bulk of the community at least until the third decade of the present century, when modern Western thought and literature swept through China in a manner comparable only with the Renaissance in Europe. It is interesting, therefore, and significant, that the earliest approach to writing which the scientists have been able to discover in China was found in a tomb.

These people of the Stone-Bronze Age had apparently set a precedent for elaborate and careful funeral ceremonies. Archæologists have been able to deduce some definite rules connected with burial. The dead were often buried in high ground that offered a commanding view over valleys or rivers; and in order to be honored in this way, the bodies were sometimes carried as far as five miles from the nearest human habitations. The custom of burying in high ground is still maintained by some Chinese of the present day. The skeletons of these ancient people were found with the head invariably facing the southwest, contrary to the modern custom of causing the head of the dead to face north.

At every major site in Kansu where burial grounds were discovered, and in many of the Yang Shao graves, bones were found covered with a bright red pigment. The significance of this is not understood, but it is common to graves of both the Old and New Stone Ages throughout Europe. More interesting than the red bones are certain vessels found in many of the Kansu graves. They bear a variety of designs, but one design in particular occurs with striking persistency. It consists of a red band bordered by very narrow bolts which are left unpainted, outside which are black bands from which saw-like dentations project towards the central red band. As this motive recurs so frequently in funeral urns of the period, and never in household pottery, it suggests a kind of "death pattern" specially connected with funeral rites.

Whether these New Stone Age people were the descendants of the "Peking Man" and his Old Stone Age companions, and the ancestors of the modern "Chinese," are questions both interesting and complex. This much, however, can be asserted: the skeletal remains from Kansu, comprising about 120 different people, men and women, have characteristics which identify them with the so-called Mongoloid division of mankind, and any human remains that have been found at Yang Shao and Sha Kuo T'un are broadly of the same physical type. They all conform in general character with the modern type of "Northern Chinese" (whom the scientists call *Homo Asiatic proprius*). It can therefore be conjectured with little doubt that the people who founded the "Yang Shao" or "Stone-Bronze Age" culture are the ancestors of the modern Chinese race.

How many thousands of years ago these people lived is another problem for the scientists. Some rough dates can be arrived at from the nature of the excavations. For instance, the red pottery ornamented with black designs characteristic of the Yang Shao finds belongs, according to Chinese ceramics experts' opinion, to the same family as the Late New Stone Age pottery found at many sites in the Near East, such as that of Babylonia (3500 B.C.), Asia Minor (2500-2000 B.C), Thessaly (2000-1200 B.C.), and others. Having regard to the absence of any metal finds at Yang Shao (the bronze and copper at Kansu came from sites which indicate a slight advancement on the original Yang Shao culture), the date for the Yang Shao culture was given as not later than 2500-2000 B.C.

When the finds at all the sites in Kansu had been compared with discoveries of the "Young Stone Age" in Europe, the Kansu finds were dated "between 3500 and 1700 B.C."

Finally, the existence and dates of the Shang dynasty (see next chapter) have been established, and the excavations from the "Mounds of Yin" give evidence of a more advanced culture than the one we are discussing now. They have brought to light a form of picture-writing, and also richly decorated bronze vessels and ivory carvings of a degree of skilled workmanship to which none of the Yang Shao people had attained. No pottery from the Yang Shao sites shows any indication of real writing, and no bronze objects so far discovered at Kansu bear any decorative design comparable with the ivory carving from the "Mounds of Yin," which in the year 1401 B.C. became the capital of the Shang dynasty. The conclusion may therefore be drawn that even the most recent of the Kansu sites is earlier than the Shang dynasty. The Chinese dynasty, known as the Hsia, and to which the great Yu and Chieh "the murderer" are supposed to have belonged, is commonly thought to fall within the New Stone Age period.

III. THE SHELLS AND BONES OF YIN

In the modern town of Anyang, in the province of Honan, north of the Yellow River, are "the Mounds of Yin." In the year 1079 a fierce storm caused a part of the ground to fall away and reveal one of the tombs of the Shang sovereigns. The local inhabitants found some bronze vessels in the earth, and being of a practical turn of mind, sold them in the market, probably without realizing their significance. A contemporary archæologist recorded these finds in a book written in 1092, and that, apparently, ended the matter for many hundreds of years. Some time in the fourteenth century a village was built directly over the site where the vessels had been found, and the feet of its population tramped heedlessly over the bones of those ancient emperors.

Towards the end of the nineteenth century, however, some inscribed turtle shells and animal bones were unearthed and sold to the local chemist as "dragon bones." They were doubtlessly judged to be of the highest efficacy in curing ailments.

News of the "dragon bones" must have spread, for we read of a Chinese merchant, whose profession it was to collect curios, buying large quantities of them and presenting them to one of the Court ministers. For this gracious act the merchant was rewarded by the minister at the rate of two and a half taels of silver per inscribed character. By this time, 1899, the "dragon bones" were evidently recognized as being some ancient and valuable examples of Chinese written records. Moreover, the merchant must have made a comfortable fortune. Two Westerners, an Englishman and an American, traveled to his village and bought from him very considerable quantities of the bones and shells, which they subsequently presented to the British, the Scottish, and the Chicago Museums. The first publications on the inscriptions were brought out by Lo Chen-yu, a Chinese collector, who, in 1911, took impressions of shell and bone inscriptions from the "Mounds of Yin" "on wintry nights by the fire side," and published the reproductions in a book, thus bringing this intensely interesting discovery to the notice of the Chinese reading public. Three years later a Canadian gentleman arrived at Anyang in search of the Yin bones. He became a familiar and picturesque sight to the people of the locality, for he used to ride an old white horse, and to wander day after day along the bank of the stream which winds past the Mounds of Yin. During these romantic-seeming excursions he collected more than fifty thousand pieces of inscribed shell and bone, and acquired a great many more from a small farmer who lived nearby and had dug them out of his vegetable garden. It was not until after the second Revolution of 1927 that the Chinese government began to take the Mounds under their protection. A government institution, the Central Research Academy (*Academia sinica*), then organized excavations, and private collectors were no longer allowed to take their pick. These finds have been exhibited in almost all the great museums of the world, and numbers of books written about them: their authenticity is beyond doubt.

Why should these bits of animal bone and pieces of shell from the bellies of turtles have caused such a sensation? Because, in the first place, they represent the earliest examples of Chinese writing, and in the second, they are the most ancient written records of the Chinese people, telling us much about their occupations and beliefs in the middle of the second millennium before Christ. They bring us into the realm of authentic history.

The Shang dynasty (or Yin, as it was also called since 1401 B.C.) is thought to have followed the semi-historical Hsia dynasty about the year 1766 B.C., although the date cannot be verified beyond dispute. The Yin is, however, the first dynasty whose existence is indubitable, and about which we have real information, based on these primitive records.

The people of Shang evidently practiced divination by the tortoise on every possible occasion, and to this practice we are indebted for our knowledge. For these pieces of shell and bone dug up from the "Mounds of Yin" are all records of questions put before the "oracle" and the oracular answers which were delivered. Every kind of problem, religious and secular, questions concerning the worship of gods and ancestors, journeys, hunting and fishing, the raising of battle, doubts about the harvest and the weather, sickness, dreams, queries on the fate and fortunes of an individual or group—all these were brought to the turtle-shell oracles; and from the answers, later ages have learned much about the Chinese "civilization" in those far-off times.

The whole method of procedure is now known to us. The turtles were caught in autumn by the fishermen and offered to the government. The back shell was discarded and only the shell of the belly kept for divination. This would be scraped smooth and polished when an oracle was to be consulted. Careful incisions were then made on the surface so as to weaken the shell at various points, and red-hot sticks were applied at the vulnerable places. The cracks which resulted constituted the oracular utterance, and their arrangement, shape, and direction were interpreted according to fixed rules. This "utterance" was then scratched on the shell, which was apparently buried. Animal bones, frequently the shoulder blades of ox, goat, sheep, or deer, seem also to have been used for the same purpose, and to have been treated in a very similar way. Examples so far discovered, however, are less numerous than those of the turtle shells.

From the shell and bone inscriptions we learn that the people of Shang lived by hunting, fishing, and farming; also that they had some primitive handicrafts. And thanks to the nature of the writing, we know a good deal about the manner in which they carried on these activities. The engraved characters are more or less pictorial symbols, and on this account are doubly valuable. For instance, we know from the appearance of the characters for "fish" and "to fish" that the Shang people used pole and line, bait and net:

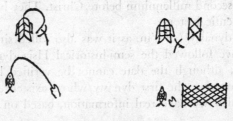

Yu (fishing)

Similarly we know from the varying forms of the character for "hunting" that arrows and double-headed spears were the instruments of the chase. Some of the characters show a bird pierced by an arrow, others a wild animal in similar predicament, others a double-headed spear piercing an animal. That snares and traps were employed for catching deer, rabbits, monkeys, pheasant, and wild boars is another conclusion justified by the written characters.

From the study of a very considerable number of hunting records, archæologists have drawn conclusions about the kinds of wild animals and game that most abounded in the North China of the Shang people. They found that both deer and wild boar were very plentiful, though the deer were hunted more frequently. Wolves were a little less abundant, and the rhinoceros came next. Rabbits and pheasant, the mild food of more sophisticated ages, were evidently far less popular. The taking of a tiger is once recorded. Even more interesting is a record which reads, "Tonight it will rain, and an elephant is to be caught." This, supported by the fact that many ivory tools and tusks

Shou (game, hunting)

were discovered in the Yin site, indicates that elephants trumpeted through the forests of the Yellow River at this time, and hence that the climate of North China was warmer—more like the South. This bears out the conclusion we have already reached about the climate in the Stone Age, judging from the evidence of animal remains.

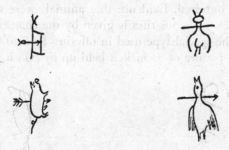

Lieh (hunting)

Additional evidence about the elephant, if any were needed, is provided by the symbolic character for "working" or "doing." This is represented by what appears to be the drawing of an elephant, from which we can only conclude that the Shang people caught and tamed this animal for work on the land! Besides the tame elephant, we know that these people kept horses, oxen, sheep, cocks and hens, dogs, and pigs.

The horses, and probably again the elephant, were used for drawing chariots. The symbol for "driving" is represented by a man with upraised whip at a road junction, apparently wondering which road he should take. The animals to whose backs he applies the whip are usually, though not always, omitted.

Although the other tame animals must have been kept chiefly for consumption, the gods and ancestors seem to have demanded very heavy tribute. The number of animals sacrificed varies, according to

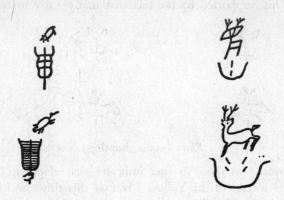

Pi (snaring a boar)   *Ching* (trapping a deer)

the records, from one to a hundred at a time, and occasionally rose to three or four hundred. Evidence that animals were the chief form of sacrifice in these religious rites is given by the character *Yi*, signifying a tripod of the special type used in offering food to the gods. This is formed by the picture of a chicken held up by two hands.

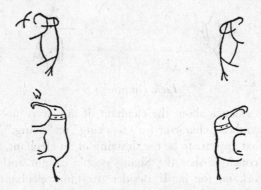

Wei (doing, working)

A primitive plow and some kind of sharp-ended tool were evidently used for agriculture. The symbol for "plow" was later modified in form, and given the more general meaning of "strength." The word for "male" was then represented by a combination of the symbols for "strength" and "field," or, if we refer to the earlier form, the symbols for "plow" and "field," thus giving us a hint that the principal male occupation of those times may have been plowing—the cultivation of the land.

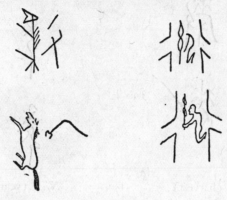

Yu (driving)

The symbol for "harvest" seems to describe the act of threshing. One hand holds a bundle of wheat, while the other beats it with a stick. The word "year" is symbolized by the figure of a man wearing on his head a bunch of wheat. This suggests that harvest time, when the grain was gathered, was felt to be the crown of the year. The symbols for grain include corn, millet, and rice; mulberries were also cultivated.

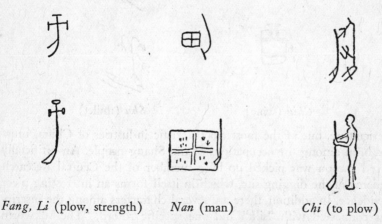

Fang, Li (plow, strength)   *Nan* (man)   *Chi* (to plow)

There can be little doubt that a wine-making industry was in existence: we know that the last Shang Emperor lost his throne through drunkenness and other attendant vices. Moreover, the preponderance of wine goblets over other vessels discovered at the Yin site leaves us in no doubt that at least some of the Shang Emperors were addicted to wine, and serves as a melancholy reminder of how a great dynasty

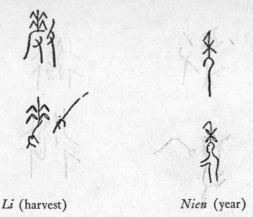

Li (harvest)   *Nien* (year)

decayed. The symbol for "wine" found on the shells and bones shows liquid overflowing from the brim of a jar, while the symbol for "millet" depicts grain being tipped into liquid, indicating that the chief use of millet was for brewing.

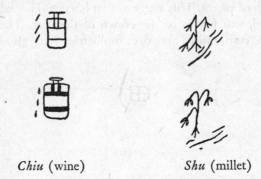

Chiu (wine)   *Shu* (millet)

Sericulture, one of the most characteristic industries of China, must have been among the occupations of the Shang people. An artificially pierced cocoon was picked up by a member of the Central Research Academy at the digging site, which in itself forms an interesting piece of evidence. In addition, there are several characters among the inscriptions connected with "silk" and one specific record, "The silkworm sacrificial offering, three cattle, the Eighth Moon." From this we see that the cultivation of the silkworm was a matter of some importance.

It seems that even at this very ancient time some kind of fine small hair brush, such as the modern Chinese use for writing and painting, must have been invented, though it may have taken the form of the tail of a mouse or some other tiny animal. Nothing but a hair brush could have painted the delicate designs on some of the Yin earthenware, while some characters on the polished shells and bones were not incised and must also have been drawn by brush. Indelible ink, too, must have been invented, since these inscriptions, made with a black or bright red liquid, have been almost perfectly preserved for several thousand years.

The Shang people made earthenware and bronze vessels. Some of the earthenware was evidently enameled with glaze, indicating that a great degree of heat must have been mastered. Decorative designs of wavy lines are frequently seen on the mouth of vessels, which are delicately round in shape. No vessels with big ears or long necks, such as were found at the Yang Shao sites, have yet been discovered.

A very great number of bronze articles have been unearthed from the Yin Mounds, and scholars are confident that they were given their form by casting. It is astonishing that such a mastery of metal work could have been reached in those very early times. The barb of an arrow, for example, on being analyzed was found to be composed of copper, tin, iron, silver, and lead!

Among their other civilized habits, the Shang people evidently elaborated a religious system, and this might be called the characteristic feature of the dynasty. Sacrificial vessels and oracle bones, which have been dug up in thousands from the Mounds, and which far outnumber the practical instruments of living, such as tools and household pottery, point to the all-important part which religion must have played in their lives. Yet in spite of this wealth of material, the exact form of their religious rites is not known, nor can the Shang pantheon be enumerated. However, the deities seem to have been somewhat intimate ones, chiefly ancestors who lived in "heaven" but who would participate in human actions, helping or hindering according to whether they received the proper sacrifices. A god who is familiarly termed "Emperor" and seems to be a sort of First Ancestor of the race is frequently mentioned on the shell and bone inscriptions: every kind of trouble, great or small, private disasters and the fortunes of war, are all brought before him. In addition there are gods of agriculture, mountains and rivers, and natural elements, though it is likely that these too were identified with ancestors, for we read one interesting record which says, "Pray for rain from Grandmother Yi."

As for rites of worship, we know that burnt offerings of animals were sacrificed, and probably wine offered in the libation cups. In the procession to the place of sacrifice, music was made, and this consisted in the playing of flutes, the beating of drums, the clinking of sonorous gems, and the ringing of large bells. Ceremonial dances also formed a part of the rites, and the singing of sacrificial odes. Six of these Odes of Shang are preserved to the present day in the classic "Book of Poetry" compiled by Confucius. One of them, called "Hsuan Niao" ("The Mystic Swallow"), ascribes the founding of the Shang Empire to divine ordinance:

> *Heaven sent the Mystic Swallow down to earth,*
> *From Whom sprang the ancestor of Shang,*
> *Who chose his dwelling in the land of Yin.*
> *By Heaven's will, his grandson, glorious T'ang,*
> *Assigned each State its formal boundary . . .*

So run the opening lines.

Who, then, were these "Shang people" who prayed to Grandmother Yi for rain, used elephants to cultivate their land, and tortoise shells to find out their fate, who seem to have invented the Chinese writing and to have written with animals' tails, and who claimed a swallow for their first ancestor?

They are the successors of the Stone-Bronze Age people of China. The dynasty, called "Shang" or "Yin," was founded by the "glorious T'ang" of the ode, and who is described by Mencius as the man who rescued the people from their wretched Hsia ruler, Chieh "the murderer." He attacked eleven princes of the surrounding states, says Mencius, and met no opposition. People groaning under their own tyrant rulers longed for T'ang's coming as they did for rain in a time of drought. And when his troops marched "the frequenters of the market stopped not, and those engaged in the fields made no change in their occupation," for they expected no danger but only freedom at his approach. And so T'ang completed his victories by overthrowing the Hsia empire which had been built up by the great Yu.

The Shang or Yin Empire covered a huge territory, from the borders of modern Ssuch'uan, Hunan and Hupei, to the eastern seashore, probably including a part of Korea. It had two formidable rivals—the people of Chou, and a branch of the people then called Demons, and in later history the Huns or Hsiung-nu. Battles against the Demons were not infrequent, and during the reign of the Emperor Kao Tsung "the High," one of the outstanding characters of the dynasty, a war against these western barbarians was waged for three years and brought to a victorious end. Among the records of these battles we read of one

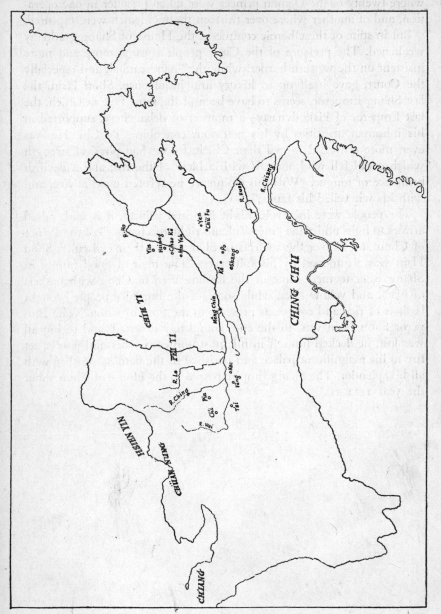

LEGENDARY AND TRADITIONAL PERIODS, 2

where twenty of the Demon princes were taken prisoner in one operation, and of another where over thirteen thousand men were captured.

But in spite of these heroic conquests, the House of Shang gradually weakened. The pressure of the Chou people became more and more insistent on the western border, while the Shang capital, and especially the Court, gave itself up to luxury and indulgence. Shou Hsin, the last Shang Emperor, seems to have been of the same type as Chieh, the last Emperor of Hsia dynasty—a monster of debauchery, supported in his inhuman atrocities by his notorious concubine Ta Chi. He was even more powerful in evil than Chieh, for he had physical strength which could fell wild animals with a blow of the fist, and a devilish brilliance of tongue. "With his eloquence he refuted good advice, and with his wit veiled his faults."

The people were in revolt. Eight hundred princes, it is said, raised armies to fight under the "merciful and righteous banner" of the Prince of Chou and deliver the subjects of Shang from their evil ruler. Shou Hsin was abandoned by his followers. "The men of good family in Shang went to meet some of the leading men of Chou with baskets of black and yellow silks, while some of the humbler people brought baskets of rice and congee as presents to the poor of Chou." The Emperor Shou Hsin was, in the end, completely deserted, and seeing all was lost, he decked himself in his most gorgeous robes and jewels, set fire to his magnificent palace and perished in the flames, together with all his splendor. The Shang Empire passed to the House of Chou about the year 1122 B.C.

IV. THE CHOU DYNASTY AND THE
FEUDAL SYSTEM

An ANCIENT STORY about the origin of the Chou House tells how a
woman in far-off times prayed to Heaven for a child. She made her
sacrificial offerings and trod upon a footprint supposedly left on earth
by a giant god. Immediately, as she rested, the child moved in her
womb. Of her Prince Millet was born, and grew up skilled in
husbandry.

> His peas and beans grow plump and high,
> His rows of rice are beautiful to see,
> His hemp and wheat wave luxuriantly,
> His gourd and melon plants bear glorious fruit.

So runs an ode in the "Book of Poetry"—a collection of popular ballads
from the earliest times.

This happened in the reign of the blessed Emperor Shun, who
employed the young man to teach his people husbandry, and rewarded
him for his services by creating him Prince of T'ai. In the time of his
great-grandson, Duke Liu, so the story continues, the Chou household
had multiplied to such an extent that T'ai was too small to hold them.
The Duke ordered that the harvest should be gathered in, all the
grain and dried meats packed and loaded for transport, all weapons
—bows, arrows, shields, spears, axes of all kinds—made ready. Then,
marching at their head, he led his people towards the East in search
of a new settlement. They wound through valleys and plains, and
scaled lofty mountains from whose peaks the Duke could survey the
surrounding land. At last he came to Pin. There he found a hundred
springs gushing, and looking round saw only a bright and ample
plain, up to the horizon's verge.

A great feast was prepared to celebrate the settlement. Afterwards
the streams and springs were carefully surveyed, and each plain and
marsh measured. A system of field cultivation was initiated, and cottages built for the peasants and farmers. Three armies were raised to
protect the settlers. Some were sent farther afield across the river Wei

to bring back iron and whetstones for implements. The population thrived and multiplied until all the valleys of Pin were filled with the toiling Chou people.

Years passed. Then in the reign of King T'ai, the Chou kingdom —as it had become—was constantly harassed by the inroads of one of the "Demon" tribes (the Huns or Hsiung-nu of later history). The King tried to pacify them with offerings of skins and silks, dogs and horses, pearls and precious jewels—but in vain. Finally, he resolved to move his kingdom yet farther to the East, and led his people across the mountains of Liang, with his wife, the lady Chiang, riding behind him in the saddle.

> *He came with the morning, spurring his horses,*
> *Along the river banks from the West*
> *Till he reached the foot of Mount Ch'i.*
> *And there, by the side of his lady Chiang*
> *He looks down on their future homeland.*

At Ch'i he settled, and his people swarmed after him "as if they were hastening to the market." There they built a lofty palace for the King, stately altars to the spirits of the land, and comfortable homes for themselves. The same ode in the "Book of Poetry" describes the busy industry of the Chou settlers at Ch'i:

> *Here thronging workmen pile the earth in baskets,*
> *With rapid movements empty them again.*
> *The clang of tools echoes to their strokes,*
> *And frequent paring makes the building sound.*

The story we have just related of the Chou House, leading up to its conquest of the Shang dynasty, after which it became the ruling House of China, is compounded largely of fact and partly of fiction. The various removes, the energy with which they were carried out, and the industry of the subsequent settlements, we have every reason to believe are true, but the attempt to father the race upon the legendary Prince Millet, and to link him with the ancient Chinese Emperor Shun, can only symbolize the profound esteem with which the later Chou people regarded their rulers. The Chou were not, in fact, of the same stock as the Shang, and possibly not of the characteristic "Central China" blood. The writer Mencius calls King Wen, father of the first Emperor of the Chou dynasty, a "Western Yi (foreigners)," while according to a history of the period, the "Tso Chuan," the Chou people addressed the Shangs (Yins) also as "Yi" (foreigners). It may well

be that this influx of new blood and new ideas brought about the remarkable development which followed.

After the initial overthrow of the Shang Emperor, and the entry of
the Chou leader into the capital, the Chou troops proceeded to smash
all the remaining Shang influence with the system and thoroughness
which is characteristic of all their behavior. For three years they fought
against fifty tributary States which lay to the east, and subjugated
every one. They also—so says Mencius—drove away the tigers, leopards, rhinoceroses, and elephants from the "Middle Lands." The Empire became, in fact as well as in theory, "civilized."

Partly to consolidate these gains and to preserve the Empire from
attack on any of its borders, Emperor Wu, who succeeded King Wen,
nominated a large body of noblemen to serve as "screen and fence"
to the Empire. The nominees were either members of the imperial
family or meritorious ministers, and some sixteen hundred were appointed to various ranks. A great event in the administration of the
"Middle Kingdom" now took place: a feudal system was born.

Of the workings of this system, many records have survived, but
they are not always consistent. For the purpose of this book, we have
chosen the most reliable. It is also difficult to tell from these ancient
documents whether the reforms were spread over a long or short period: we can only give a picture of the completed system. It appears
that five ranks were created: duke, marquis, earl, viscount, and baron.
A duke or marquis was allotted territory of a hundred square *li* (each
li is equal to about a third of an English mile), an earl seventy
square *li,* and a viscount or baron fifty square *li* each. In addition to
this division of territory among the ruling classes, the country districts
were divided into groups, and officials were appointed to inspect their
administration. The inspector of five districts was called a *"chang"*
("head"), of ten districts a *"shuai"* ("marshal"), of thirty districts a
"cheng" ("chief"), and of two hundred and ten districts a *"po"* ("superior"). All these officials were subject to the supervision of certain
elder statesmen who lived at Court, acted as the Emperor's advisers,
and accompanied him on his tours of inspection.

The establishment of a feudal system, which was one of the great
Chou achievements, served a much more important purpose than the
mere protection of territory against invasion. The basic principle of
feudalism—the care of the feudal lord for his vassals, and the fidelity
of these to him, is one which, though open to abuse, is able to effect
solid government and a good measure of human content. The real
strength of the Chou rule proved to lie in the closely knit relationships

welded between every branch and class of society. The early Chou rulers, too, were remarkable for the humanity they showed towards their subjects. By personal supervision, they made sure that the feudal lords exercised their power with justice and kindness.

At frequent intervals, the nobles were required to attend Court and give an account of their stewardship, while every five years the Emperor himself made a tour of his kingdom. He left the capital at the second moon in spring, and traveled eastward to the Eastern Sacred Mountain, to the spirit of which he offered sacrifices, and where he summoned the lords of the East to consult with him. He traveled to the Southern Sacred Mountain in summer at the fifth moon; to the Sacred Mountain of the West in autumn at the eighth moon, and to the Northern Sacred Mountain in the eleventh moon in mid-winter. Wherever he went he offered sacrifices and interviewed his feudal lords.

In all the places he visited, he inquired specially about the aged people—men and women of a hundred years or more. If any were living, he humbly called upon them to present his felicitations, and also to ask advice about the government of the Kingdom. From this we see how deep-seated and ancient is the traditional Chinese respect for old age. He also sent for specimens of goods which were being offered for sale in the market of each district, so that he might learn the special products of each place. Finally, he asked the people to repeat, in the presence of his Court musicians, their local folk ballads, so that they might be set to music and played before him. The Emperor believed that from these spontaneous expressions of the common people's emotion—the description of their life, work, needs, pleasures—he could construct a truer picture of their conditions than any overlord could describe for him. To the great good fortune of posterity, Confucius later collected many of these folk ballads in the "Book of Poetry," good translations of which now exist in most European languages. The reader may thus discover for himself, in a form clear, bright, and charming, the manner of life, the social conditions, the desires, fears, and loves of the ordinary Chinese people living about three thousand years ago!

During his spring visits to the countryside, the Emperor would examine the plowing and supply any deficiency of seed: in autumn he examined the reaping and ordered help to be given if any crops had failed. Whenever he entered a State and found that new ground had been reclaimed and put under cultivation, that the old fields had been well tended, that the aged were provided with food, the deserving recognized, and the men of intellect given office, then the feudal lord to whom the State belonged would be rewarded with additional territory or higher rank. Failure to perform all these worthy acts would incur punishment or loss. After his Empire-wide tour, the Emperor returned to the capital, offered sacrifices at his ancestral temple, and gave a full report to his dead ancestors, probably in token of his faithfulness to their teaching.

The organization of the land under the Chou feudal system, if we are to believe the records of early historians and disciples of Confucius, embodies a very remarkable conception, mathematically exact, and calculated both to draw the maximum produce from the soil and to give every peasant equal opportunity for living. It was called the "well-field system." The name is derived from the ancient Chinese character for well (井), which roughly depicts eight squares grouped round a ninth. Under this system, all the cultivable land was to be divided into units of nine hundred square *mou* (a *mou* is equal to six thousand Chinese square feet), which was in turn divided up into nine squares of a hundred *mou* each, grouped as in the "well" character. The eight outer fields were assigned to eight families, and were called their "private" fields. It is interesting to note that the Chinese character for "private" (私) is composed of the symbols for a bunch of wheat and for "self-interest"—an obvious relic from the time of the well-field. The ninth and central field had to be cultivated by each of the families in turn for the benefit of the lord to whom all the land belonged, and only after this, the "public" field, had been cared for, did the peasants dare look after their own. One of the long poems in the "Book of Poetry" while describing the rainy season gives vent to the peasants' grievances in the lines,

> *First must the rain fall on our public fields;*
> *The private fields receive it afterwards!*

Certain laws of cultivation were enforced in order to draw the biggest possible yield from the soil. No trees must be grown in the fields lest they reduced the output of grain. Mulberry trees and vegetables could be planted round the homesteads; melons and fruit trees along the borders of the foot-paths. It was forbidden to sow only one kind of grain, so that if one crop failed, there would be others to fall back on, and thus famine—one of the terrors of the Chinese—might be averted. As for animals and poultry, each family must keep at least five brood hens and two brood sows.

There would always be certain lands unfit for crops, or which, for one reason or another, would not be divided among the peasantry.

Upon these also the lord's peasants were obliged to work. We know that they had to hew timber on the mountains and in the forests, that they collected weeds and reeds from the marshes, firewood from the scrub-land, fish and salt from the sea coast and inland lakes. According to another poem in the "Book of Poetry" which gives a detailed description of peasant life in Central China under the feudal system, the peasants, besides working in the fields, had to hunt foxes and wild cats to make winter robes for the young lords. In the snowy weather they must hunt wild boar. In the spring, continues the poem, when the warm days began and the oriels were singing, the young peasant women gathered mulberry leaves in the lonely paths. When the shrike's notes sounded shrilly in the seventh moon they began to twist hemp and weave fabrics, black, or yellow, or brilliant red, to make robes for the young noblemen. During the slack season, after the harvest had been gathered, they still could not rest. They had to go to the towns and put the noblemen's houses in order. When they were not so employed, they would spend the day gathering reeds, and twist them into ropes at night.

According to these poems, which we suppose are the records and complaints of the people themselves, the feudal system seems to have brought nothing but hard work to the lower classes, and abundant riches to the overlord, who had "innumerable stacks rising like islands from the land, thousands of granaries, and carts in myriads."

> *The sorghum, millet, rice, and maize are stored:*
> *The peasants rest at last content and thankful!*

Nevertheless, it brought with it a certain degree of security. Every able man between the ages of twenty and sixty was provided with land and obliged to till it, but when he reached sixty he returned the land to the State, was freed of obligations, and became himself the government's responsibility. The orphans and the aged, the deaf and the dumb, the crippled and the insane were all cared for or pensioned by the government.

Besides the promotion of agriculture, which was then, as now, the main occupation of the Chinese, there seems to have been a great development of crafts and trading under the Chou rulers. We read one record of there being seven kinds of wood craftsmen, six kinds of workers in metal, five in leather, five types of dyer, five types of refiner, and two kinds of workers in earthenware. The crafts seem to have been a family affair, the special technique of each being handed down from father to son. This we learn from the surnames which frequently occur in old records, such as T'ao, Chen, Chiang, Tzu-yu, and Tuan, which mean maker of earthenware, mason, woodcraftsman, sedan-chair maker, and blacksmith.

Under the feudal system, the power of the ruling House and the nobles became paramount, and as a natural consequence the period was marked by a great development of city life. City and Court gave rise not only to a refinement in art and manners, but to the growth of an influential merchant class. Copper coins, lengths of silk, gold nuggets, pearls, and gems were all used as money, and trading seems to have enjoyed a prosperity hitherto unknown. The heyday of the Chou dynasty was undoubtedly a time of richness and splendor, of social advance, of material productivity; but all this was balanced upon dangerous foundations. It depended on the character of the ruling class, and especially on the personality of the Emperor. If his hold upon the nobles weakened, or if they or he became corrupt, then industry must give place to civil broil and tyranny; which did indeed happen. The feudal lords began to offer a menace to the throne, and grew jealous of one another. Then the cleavage between town and country became one of rich and poor; the rival nobles' demand for money to support their armies led to a sharp increase in trading, and to the greater power of the merchant class, many members of which became political intriguants.

But before we pass to the melancholy and final break-up of the Chou House, we may evoke a few of those great personalities who, gorgeous in their golden imperial robes, and even more splendid in their intellectual gifts of statesmanship, maintained for a time an equilibrium in Chinese social and political development.

The founder of the Chou dynasty, King Wen, together with his two sons Fa (who succeeded him as Emperor Wu) and Tan (the "Duke of Chou" to whom so many virtues are attributed), form an almost sacred triumvirate in Chinese history. In the dark days of the declining Shang dynasty, when King Wen was only the ruler of a western State, the eyes of the unhappy Chinese turned to him as a savior. And from all we read, he was not merely a leader of military skill, but a man of honor, pure in motive, humane, and, in the best sense, good. The complete picture of him remains shadowy, partly because later tradition has surrounded him with an aura of unnatural virtue, but he seems to have been a ruler whom people could both fear and love.

Here it may be interesting to note a fundamental social change which although initiated in earlier times was fully developed and applied by the early Chou rulers. It played an important part in stabilizing the dynasty, besides altering, profoundly and permanently, the whole social structure of society.

Under the Shang system, the younger brother of the Emperor was his legal successor, and only when he had no brother did his son become heir to the throne. This arrangement was a great source of treason and insecurity: brother plotted against brother, and all kind of trouble was stirred up among the population. King Wen and his sons laid down the law, which has been preserved with very few lapses until the Empire itself ended in 1911, by which the succession was restricted from father to son. It applied not only to the Royal House but to the domains of the nobility and even to the poorest families in the Empire. This system, with a number of subsidiary decrees which grew up round it, resulted in the Great Family or "Tsung Fa" system, for which the Chinese have been famous for thousands of years, and which is responsible for many of the characteristics of Chinese society.

The founder of an Empire, a State, or a Family was called "Tsu," "the Originator," and was worshiped with the highest honors. His eldest son became his heir, and was called "Ta Tsung" (or "Tsung"), "the Great Honorable One." If one of his brothers shared a portion of the inheritance or started a branch-line of the family, he was called "Hsiao Tsung," "the Little Honorable One."

The eldest son and heir held a place of importance and responsibility in the family: the well-being of the household lay in his hands. Whenever the family interest was affected, or its honor offended, the "Ta Tsung" had to assume full responsibility, and any action he decided to take would be supported unquestioned by the whole family. In the home, he was obliged to maintain any of his relatives who were in financial straits. In return, he and his wife were treated with particular respect by them all. If his younger brothers became high court officials, or gained riches for themselves in one way or another, they would not dare parade their rank or wealth before the "Ta Tsung." If they came to call upon him with a huge retinue of attendants, chariots, and horses, as befitted their rank, they must leave the bulk of it at the outer gate, and enter with only a handful of attendants, to show that their acquired honors were not comparable with the position held by right of inheritance by the "Great Honorable One." In case the latter were poor and went about in shabby clothes, his richer relatives must present him with new garments. Or else they must enter his presence in even shabbier ones.

All these regulations, together with others of a similar kind, and many moral injunctions relating to family life—the ties, the proper standing, and the mutual responsibilities of all its members pronounced by the moralist Confucius in the later years of the dynasty—laid the foundations of Chinese family life for all time.

The good King Wen was succeeded, in conformity with the new law, by his eldest son Emperor Wu. "Wen" has the meaning of "civilized" and "Wu" of "martial," from which we may judge the contrasting character of the two rulers. It appears that Emperor Wu consolidated his father's conquests by many sanguinary battles. The divinity that hedged the sovereigns of that dynasty prevented historians from censuring any of his conduct, but Confucius, who could be both sly and enigmatic when questioned on certain risky subjects, said on one occasion that the music with which Emperor Wu celebrated his victories, "though perfectly beautiful, was not perfectly good," while the music of the ancient Emperor Shun (the "blessed" Shun, supposedly of the ancient pre-Hsia period) was "both perfectly beautiful and perfectly good." Confucius does not explain whether he intended "good" in a technical or a moral sense, but it is reasonable to assume that he was making a subtle criticism of Emperor Wu's taste for battle.

When he died, his eldest son was still a young boy, and Wu entrusted him to the guardianship of his own younger brother, the Duke Tan of Chou.

"The Duke of Chou," as he is usually called, is one of the most outstanding figures in Chinese history. Even Confucius the critical calls him "a man of talent and charm" and declares that with him as guide and teacher, the people were "broadminded, generous, gentle, and good." Already in the reign of his elder brother, Emperor Wu, he seems to have acted as faithful Minister, advancing ideas, supervising their application, pacifying the surrounding States, and, in general, bringing good order into society. All this he performed with modesty, giving all the glory to the "Son of Heaven," the reigning Emperor. Probably the well-field system was his device; certainly it was he who supervised the division of the territory and advised the Emperor on the appointment of nobles, upon whom the working of the system depended. It seems that the whole administrative organization of the Chinese Empire, which in its essentials remained a pattern for thousands of years, was planned by this remarkable man. Ritual and ceremony, characteristic features of the Chinese way of life, and ones with which the Chou dynasty writers and thinkers were particularly concerned, were to a large extent initiated by the Duke, and though the book known as the "Chou Ritual" was not actually written

by him, the institutions it records are certainly mostly his work. Like
the Great Family or "Tsung Fa" system, they helped to bring order
and grace into the lives of the whole population. It is also said that
he taught the people music.

At the death of his elder brother, Wu, the Duke might have brushed
aside his young nephew and declared himself Emperor. Instead, he
respected the new law of succession and acted as regent to the young
boy, bringing him up and educating him discreetly in the arts of state-
craft. To this attitude he remained faithful till he died.

In the history of the Chou House, there are no other figures to
stand beside these three—Wen, Wu, and "the Duke." The fifth Emperor, Mu "the Solemn," is said to have been a great traveler. Popular
tradition tells how with eight highly bred horses he traveled to the
West for ten thousand miles (*li*) and feasted the Hsi Wang Mu—
the "Western Queen Mother"—on the banks of the Green-Jasper
Pond on the Cluster-of-Jade Mountains. We do not know who this
lady was, but we suspect her name is the Chinese rendering of a tribal
name, and that the Emperor journeyed beyond the western confines
of his Empire.

From Mu onwards, the Chou rulers became steadily more decadent,
until the twelfth, Emperor Yu "the Gloomy," practically brought the
dynasty to an end. Yu was completely dominated by a beautiful and
willful concubine. One of her chief pleasures, it is said, was the sound
of tearing silk: whole pieces of rich silk were torn up to amuse her.
They must have been a gloomy pair, for the lady, so they say, had
never smiled in her life until the doting Emperor bethought himself
of a device that eventually cost him his throne. He ordered all the
beacon fires to be lit. This was the signal for the feudal lords to hasten
to the capital with their armies to resist the Western barbarians (the
"Demons" of Shang period who were still quarrelsome neighbors).
The barons with their men, arms, and horses rushed up, and when
they found the whole affair was a hoax their expressions struck the
lady as so irresistibly funny that she burst into peals of laughter. Yu
was delighted, but the sword of Damocles already hung over his head.
The father of the rightful queen joined with the "Demons" and did
in fact invade the Emperor's capital. Now the beacons were lit in
vain: not a man came to the Emperor's help. The capital fell, the beautiful lady was carried off, and Yu "the Gloomy" killed by the sword.
"A smile of Beauty overturned an Empire" runs the song. This happened in 771 B.C.

The son and heir of the murdered Emperor, called P'ing "the Peace-

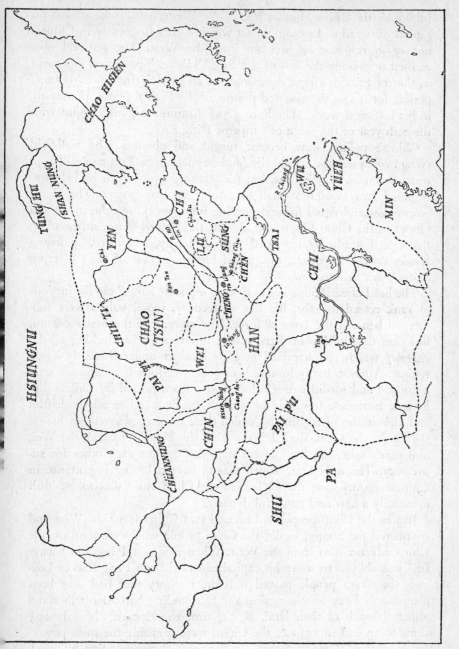

THE PERIOD OF WARRING STATES (*cir.* 333 B.C.)

ful," took the throne, but in fear of the Western tribes he moved his capital eastward to Loyang, an act which occurs frequently in Chinese history in response to pressure from the West. The removal now seemed to presage the fall of the Royal House. The period is known as that of Eastern Chou, sometimes called the "Spring and Autumn" period, for it saw the rise and decline of the Feudal States. Confucius, in his historical work "The Spring and Autumn Annals," begins with the 49th year of the reign of Emperor P'ing.

Chinese politics now become turgid and obscure. The well-field system collapsed and so did the feudal system. The Emperor still kept court at Loyang for a time, but the territory over which he held un-disputed sway was too small to assure him any power. The Court ceremonies and ritual formed nothing but a mocking echo to the old glories of the Chou House. Meanwhile the Feudal States surrounding the capital gradually increased their authority, supported by strong armies until, in 479 B.C., the period known as that of the "Warring States" was ushered in.

The head of each State began to style himself "King," old distinctions of rank ceased to exist, life lost all security, moral values were sub-merged beneath the laws of force. The records of the States contain little but descriptions of wars, savage in character and lacking all the chivalry which characterized people's conduct under the early Chou regime. After so many hundreds of years, we look back and see only a tangled and sordid struggle for power, accompanied by endless dip-lomatic intrigues. It would be of little profit to relate all the battles and vicissitudes of fortune by which these numerous sovereign States, the Ch'in, the Ch'u, the Ch'i, the Yen, the Han, the Chao, the Wei, and many other smaller powers struggled against each other for su-premacy. The only State which was to have a lasting importance in Chinese history was the Ch'in, for the Ch'in ruler was to establish eventually a new and powerful dynasty.

Just as the Chou people had pressed into China from the West and conquered the Shang, so did the Ch'in people who were soon to rule China advance also from the West. When Emperor P'ing "the Peace-ful" was obliged to move his capital eastward from Feng-Kao to Loy-ang, the Ch'in people moved into the territory that had thus been abandoned. They fought against the surrounding barbarian tribes and annexed much of their land. By the time the Eastern Chou dynasty came to an end in 249 B.C., the Ch'ins were probably the most power-ful of all the "Warring States." In the years of struggle that followed, we see the Ch'in State steadily growing in importance and strength;

we see six other large States at first fighting each other, but at length forming a mutually protective alliance against the menacing power of the Ch'ins. But so corrupt and shortsighted were the rulers of these States that the Ch'in diplomats were able to beguile each of them in turn, either by false promises or threats, so that they abandoned the alliance, offered pieces of their territory to the Ch'ins for propitiation, and were swallowed up one by one for their foolishness. "To give away land to appease the Ch'ins is like putting out a fire by piling wood on it. The greedy fire will not die down till the last piece of wood has burned." So runs the popular saying.

The chief good which emerged from this turbulent period of East Chou and the "Warring States" was in the form of philosophy and literature. Bitterness of life often proves the spur to imagination, and from these years come the great moral treatises of Confucius, the eloquent essays of Mencius, and the brilliant philosophical studies of Chuang Tzu, full of humor and imagination. The "Book of Poetry," an anthology of anonymous lyrics and occasional poems compiled by Confucius, represents the poetry of the Northern plains, and laid the foundations for Chinese poetry in all the later ages, while the long lyric poem *"Li Sao"* ("Encountering Sorrow") by the Southern poet Ch'u Yuan is one of the glories of Chinese literature.

Ch'u Yuan, a wise and loyal minister to the Prince of Ch'u State, had been sent into exile for advising his master against friendship with the treacherous Ch'ins. In gloom and disappointment the poet drowned himself. The poem is one of passionate beauty and sadness. Flowers and gods, beautiful girls and strange monsters crowd the pages, and in hauntingly melodious language. The lovely objects of the poet's desire are thought to symbolize the Prince of Ch'u, and the fragrant flowers and herbs, the virtues which should attend a ruler. Ch'u Yuan's immortal appeal was as little regarded by the Prince as his more direct counsel. Ch'u State, in common with the five other foolish powers, was defeated, and in 221 B.C. the Ch'in dynasty was established to rule over the whole Chinese Empire.

V. CONFUCIUS AND HIS WRITINGS

THE NAME "CONFUCIUS," with its somewhat Latin appearance, is the Western form of the Chinese K'ung Fu-tzu, and simply means "a certain gentleman Con." Like eminent persons all over the world, the Sage was known by his surname only, and as a mark of respect the title given to a teacher or scholar was added. K'ung Fu-tzu may perhaps be rendered best as "the Master, K'ung."

He came of a very respectable family that could trace its origins to the ancient royal house of Shang, and the immediate ancestors of the philosopher had all been soldiers or politicians—men of worth, honor, and reputation. His father, the elder K'ung, is described by historians as a soldier of extreme daring, courage, and prowess. He had already begotten nine daughters when Confucius was conceived, and many strange events, dreams, and portents are associated with the birth of this much-desired boy. It is told, for instance, that when her time drew near, the mother betook herself to the cave of a neighboring hill, which had been revealed to her in a dream as the appropriate birthplace. In this same story, the baby Confucius is described as having a miraculous appearance, "with a mouth like the sea, ox lips, and the back of a dragon." All the myths surrounding his conception and birth, however, contain so many elements of common Chinese folk tales that they command no credence. They have evidently gathered about the figure of the philosopher in the years after his death, but at least they serve to mark the reverence in which he was held by even the uneducated masses of later generations. It has been established with some certainty that the birth took place in the year 551 B.C. in the State of Lu (in the modern town of Ch'u Fu, Shantung province).

Few authentic facts are known about his boyhood. He must have been a solemn child, for it is said that his favorite amusement was to play at "Sage Emperors," performing the ancient rites, arranging the sacrificial vessels, and making the ceremonial postures. At the age of seventeen, he had won a reputation among his fellows for learning, but as his father had died some years before, and the family suffered from respectable poverty, he was unable at first to follow the path of pure scholarship.

He began his career as a granary overseer in his native district, and in his year of service all was in perfect order. The following year he was put in charge of the public fields in the same district, and under his supervision the cattle were strong and healthy.

Meanwhile, his ability was evidently attracting the attention of the great. He had married the year before his first appointment, and at the birth of a son, the reigning Duke of Lu State had sent him a couple of carp in congratulation. To commemorate the gift, Confucius named his son Li "the Carp," and gave him the second name of Po-yu, "Fish Primus"!

At the age of twenty-two, he abandoned public employment and became a teacher. He opened his doors to all young men with a thirst for ancient learning. None was too poor or too humble to be welcomed. The only qualifications were eagerness and intelligence, and the only entrance fee a bunch of dried meats, according to the custom of the time. From the many recorded sayings, we can form a clear picture of Confucius the Teacher. One of his favorite students described "the Master" to a fellow-student as being "unpretentious, good, courteous, temperate, and complaisant," and the general impression one has of him is of an austere, almost ascetic gentleman, grudging of praise, stern of judgment, unwearied in learning and teaching, intolerant of both stupidity and laziness.

"A scholar who is searching for the truth and yet is ashamed of shabby clothes and bad food isn't worth speaking to," he declared on one occasion, and again, when one of his students had been caught dozing in the daytime, the Master remarked acidly, "Rotten wood cannot be carved, nor a wall of foul earth be plastered. This Yu fellow —what is the use of scolding him?"

"To him who has no enthusiasm I shall not open up the truth, and I shall not help anyone who cannot express his ideas. If I have explained one side of a problem to someone, and he cannot deduce the other three sides, I shall not teach him any more," is another characteristic utterance.

Partly to gratify his own thirst for research and study, and partly to provide systematic textbooks for his students, Confucius now began to compile those volumes of history, rites, music, and poetry which were to rank as the greatest classics in the Chinese language, and were to mold the thought and conduct of countless generations of his countrymen.

above his soul, or thought that good government lay entirely in the proper observance of ceremony, but that the society he knew was so lawless and graceless that he did not believe a powerful Chinese Empire could be reborn without the new regulation of public and private behavior from top to bottom.

Lover, as he admits himself to be, of the ancients, it was to the ceremonies of the past dynasties that he turned, and for his spiritual guide he chose that social reformer and model of rectitude from the early Chou dynasty—the Duke of Chou.

The story is told of how during the early days of his teaching he visited the capital of the Chou empire, mainly to speak with the venerable philosopher Laotzu, but also to observe the relics of lost imperial greatness. As he examined the places reserved for the great sacrifices to Heaven and Earth, and the Hall of Light where the loyal princes used to be received in audience, noted the arrangements of the Court and the ancestral temple of the royal House, he was profoundly impressed. "Now," he remarked with a sigh, "I understand the wisdom of the Duke of Chou, and how the Chou House attained to the imperial sway!" Round the walls of the Hall of Light were painted the portraits of the ancient kings, beginning with the Sage-Emperors Yao and Shun, and including a picture of the Duke of Chou, with his baby nephew, to whom he had acted as Regent, sitting on his knees, and giving audience to all the princes of the Empire. The power and dignity of the faces, and the whole conception of the Hall, evidently the work of the Duke, filled Confucius, we are told, with awe and delight, so that he exclaimed to his companions, "Here you see how the Chou House became so great. As we use a mirror to examine the forms of things, so should we study antiquity in order to understand the present!"

A memory of the Duke of Chou's great personality evidently continued to inspire Confucius in all his later works. The "Book of Rites," which was a recension of the "three hundred principles of ritual, and three thousand kinds of ceremony" collected by the Duke, was a very proper tribute to his wisdom and took its place beside the Books of Poetry and History for the training and enlightenment of the intelligentsia. Among the recorded sayings of Confucius is the pathetic cry, when fortune was evidently forsaking him, "I'm going to the dogs! I never dream now of meeting the Duke of Chou, as I always used to do!" It was as much as to say,

The god Hercules whom Antony lov'd,
Now leaves him . . .

From 530 till 500 B.C., Confucius persevered in research and teaching and declined to hold office in the government of his State. Lu State was then ruled by three powerful families, each struggling against the other two for supremacy, and each being betrayed and weakened by its own scurrilous vassals. Confucius, the lover of order and dignity, was disgusted at this condition. About the year 500 B.C., however, he consented to become chief magistrate of the State capital, and in a short time, we read, he had brought such order into the city that it became the envy of all the neighboring States. Appropriate foods were assigned to the young and old, and proper burdens to the strong and weak; men and women walked apart from each other in the streets. Merchants selling lambs and pigs charged no exorbitant prices; lost property was returned voluntarily to the owner. Travelers from all parts of the Empire felt at ease and at home when they came to the Lu capital. Presently he was promoted to the position of acting prime minister.

It is clear that Confucius was not merely a philosopher and scholar: he was also a very practical man of the world. A characteristic incident is recorded of his accompanying the Duke of Lu to an interview with the Duke of a neighboring State Ch'i. It was proposed to form a friendly alliance, but the chief officer to the Duke of Ch'i, dubbing Confucius a "man of ceremonies without any courage," advised his master to kidnap the Duke of Lu and annex a part of the border territory. Accordingly, after the ceremonies had been concluded, a band of armed dancers—half-savage tribesmen from the eastern sea coast—advanced towards the assembly. Confucius quickly realized the kind of entertainment these ruffians were to present, and stepping forward with an expression of fiery determination, so boldly rebuked the Duke of Ch'i for this lapse of propriety that the dancers were withdrawn and the discomfited Ch'i ruler was obliged to cede territory to his rival.

It was a temporary victory. Confucius was rapidly becoming the popular idol—"he flew in songs through their mouths"—and he had so strengthened the ducal House and undermined the influence of ministers and nobles, that Lu State promised to become leader of the Empire. The people of Ch'i, still smarting from the "man of ceremonies'" rebuke, declared, "With Confucius at the head of its government, Lu will become supreme among the States, and Ch'i, which is nearest to it, will be the first to be swallowed." At the proposal of one of his ministers, the Duke decided to try to form a rift between Confucius and his master, by cunning trickery. Eighty beautiful girls, skilled in dancing and singing, decked out in gaudy costumes, together with a hundred and twenty of the finest piebald horses that could be found, were sent as a present to the Duke of Lu. The latter, quite overcome at the sight of so much loveliness, forgot all his lessons of propriety. For three days no audience was held at the Lu Court. "Master," said one of his favorite students to the Sage, "it is time for you to be going."

It was the end of winter. When spring broke, the great sacrifice to Heaven would be offered. Confucius hoped that the magnitude and solemnity of this service would put a limit to the Duke's frivolity. However, when the time came, the ceremonies were hustled through, and the customary portion of meat from the offerings was not sent round to Confucius. Disappointed and disheartened that his earnestly conceived reforms and persevering labors for the dignity of Lu had been set aside by a bunch of pretty girls, Confucius handed in his resignation. In the companionship of a handful of his students, he shook the dust of Lu State from his feet.

For fourteen years he wandered sorrowfully from State to State, ever searching for a serious-minded ruler who would employ him and allow him to work out his pattern of government. He arrived first in the State of Wei, where his reputation earned him an immediate welcome. The Duke, an even more dissipated and worthless man than the Duke of Lu, received Confucius somewhat charily. A man of austere virtue and a preacher of morality was hardly to his taste, and he was at that time much preoccupied with the beauty and wit of a brilliant concubine. The lady insisted on being granted an interview with the Sage, and as she rose to greet him, her countless pendants of precious stones tinkled like little bells. His students apparently made vexing insinuations to the philosopher about this event, so that he was driven to call Heaven to witness that he had not behaved improperly!

But the lascivious Court of Wei was clearly no place for him. One day, the light-hearted Duke rode through the city in his imperial chariot, with his mistress beside him. Confucius was obliged to drive behind them in the second chariot. The Duke cared nothing for appearances, but laughed and joked to his heart's content, so that the bystanders cried out, "Lust in front: virtue behind!" The comment was inevitable. A short time afterwards, Confucius was conversing with the Duke on serious questions. Presently, some swans appeared on the wing and passed across the sky. The Duke, palpably bored and inattentive, began to stare vacantly at the birds. Confucius, we are told, made haste to leave.

As he traveled from one State to another, he met nothing but rebuff and disappointment. None of the rulers would listen to him. Some were afraid of his power, others jeered at his solemnity. At one time his life was in danger, at another he was for days without food. Once a madman came up to his carriage and cried out, "Oh, phœnix, phœnix, how your virtue has degenerated! Give up, give up your vain pursuit!" But he never despaired utterly. At last, some years after the death of his former patron the Duke of Lu, he was recalled to his native State. He was by now an old man of seventy, and although the young Duke and his ministers applied courteously to him for advice from time to time, he could no longer make his influence felt in government. His last years were spent in study and writing. His four Classics were completed and put into order, and the "Book of Changes" was compiled. This last was his favorite study; with repeated reading, he had thrice worn out the strings that bound his copy together! It is a puzzling and mysterious work, capable of numberless interpretations, and its origins are perhaps more ancient than those of any other book in the world. It is based on the diagrams arranged by the Sage-Emperor Fu Hsi, living about 4000 B.C. To these diagrams, interpretations were given by Good King Wen of the Chou House and his son the Duke of Chou, so greatly loved by Confucius. In his old age, Confucius studied these interpretations more and more, and finally added his own commentary which seeks to explain the general meaning of the whole book. The book purposes to interpret the origin and progress of life by interaction of two principles, the "yin" and "yang"—positive and negative, male and female, and it was later used as an instrument for divination. Nowadays, scholars have divided the material into two components. While a part is thought to consist of pure folk-lore and superstitions, such as the simple prophecies of peasants about the weather, the remainder contains the more enigmatic pronouncements of soothsayers. The two parts are intermingled, and the text gives a mysterious impression of occultism.

In the spring of 480 B.C. during a royal hunt, a strange animal was caught and killed. As no man could give it a name, Confucius was summoned, and to his horror he found it to be a unicorn! This beast was held by tradition to be so harmless and good that it would not even harm an ant. Its appearance was supposed to presage an era of

peace and happiness, and now it had no sooner appeared than ignorant men had slain it! It was as if a sage had come into the world
at the wrong time, and would therefore meet his death. The aged
philosopher was profoundly moved at the sight and cried out, "For
whom have you come? For whom have you come? Alas! my teaching days are over!" The tears flowed down his cheeks!

However, the fates granted him two more years of life, during
which he wrote down the history of his times, known as "The Spring
and Autumn Annals." Nearing the grave, as he knew himself to be,
he no longer cared for the favor or opinion of his contemporaries.
All the evil and vice, the murders and treachery, the covetousness and
bad faith, the ignorance and dissoluteness of those days were recorded
without gloss. Every word the author wrote had been critically
weighed, and praise or blame were firm and steady. The book ended
with the ominous appearance of the unicorn, and it is said that when
the disloyal ministers and unfilial sons read it, they were filled with
terror, for they felt themselves facing the accusing fingers of all the
after generations.

In 478 B.C., at the age of seventy-three, Confucius died. Early one
morning he rose from his couch, and, slowly pacing about beside the
door, he murmured over and over,

> *T'ai Mountain must crumble;*
> *The strong beam must break;*
> *And the wise man wither away.*

One of his most faithful followers heard these words, and quickly
understanding the meaning, hastened to attend him. "No intelligent
ruler appears," complained Confucius to him sadly; "there is no one
in the whole Empire who will make me his master. My time is up."
He returned to his couch and died seven days later.

He was buried near his native town, and many of his students
stayed three years near his tomb to mourn for him. A temple was
raised in his honor, and his followers visited it at every festival and
performed the rites and music he had taught. Some of his robes, hats,
lutes, and books were preserved there for centuries after his death.

By worldly standards, Confucius could not claim to have had a
successful life. Among his own students he was greatly loved, but by
the powerful whom he had constantly hoped to influence for good,
he was avoided as a prosy and pompous "man of ceremonies." He
had not, apparently, been able to halt—except for a brief period, and
in Lu State alone—the movement towards social and political decay

into which he had been born. He was the unicorn that appeared in the world, only to die unrecognized.

But posterity vindicated him unbelievably. Confucianism penetrated every part of the great Empire and every class of people, remaining their chief moral guide for nearly two thousand years! Until the founding of the Republic in 1911, nearly every school had its portrait of the Master hung in the entrance hall, to which the pupils paid their respects and made their offerings on appropriate occasions. The Confucian Classics became the foundation of all education. Writers imitated his style and embedded his sayings in their compositions. There was no road to official preferment save through the Confucian Classics. To be a person of good breeding and culture tacitly implied an intimate knowledge of the Master.

Some of the secret of his success must lie in his practical nature. He founded no religion; he did not even invent a philosophy; but he understood human beings, and provided rules of conduct which, when tested, really proved workable. He was an educator *par excellence*. He even recommended poetry as a teacher of morals rather than the inspirer of æsthetic feeling. Music, to him, was a "civilizing" force.

Even his elaborate system of rites and his constant emphasis upon "propriety" were not personal foibles. These mechanical rules of behavior to some extent replaced the laws by which Western nations, following the Roman example, were able to maintain social order. Confucius' rites and ceremonies were a deliberate attempt to bring order out of the social chaos into which China had fallen at the decay of the Chou House, and the break-up of the old feudal system.

This function remained with them even after the specific confusion of the Later Chou period had passed away. The relations between various units of the family, between ministers and princes, the behavior appropriate to each, the proper observance of solemn occasions, the respect due to a man's ancestors, all these rules have been followed to a greater or lesser degree by a majority of the Chinese people through all the generations that followed. They helped to put order into that vast mass of humanity which, previous to the outbreak of the present war, neither political nor cultural unity alone could weld into an harmonious whole.

It is a common belief in the West that Confucianism is a Chinese religion, while it is, in fact, no more than a system of behavior. There were four subjects, recorded his disciples, on which Confucius would not speak, and "spiritual beings" was one of them. On being asked by a student how the spirits should be served, he declined to answer directly. "While you are not able to serve men," he said, "how can you serve their spirits; and while you do not know life, how can you know about death?" It is a characteristic utterance. We cannot say he denied the existence of a spiritual world, but rather that he felt his message for humanity to be a practical one. He was a Teacher and Thinker, not a Prophet. Much as we should like to know the measure of his personal faith, the references to spiritual matters in the Sayings and records are few and inexplicit. We are told that he attended the sacrificial offerings and performed the rites observed by the ancient Sovereigns. While in sacrificing to the spirits he "felt *as if* they were present," he thought it "wise" to give himself earnestly to the duties due to men, and though respecting spiritual beings, to keep himself aloof from them.

It would not be possible in so brief a sketch to analyze Confucius' moral system. It contained nothing startling or new, for with his acknowledged love of antiquity, he tried to revive the virtues, real or imagined, of a remote age. He was a Conservative in every sense of the word; an upholder of established order. The terms "chun tzu," "gentleman," and "hsiao jen," "the little man," were used by the people of his times to classify nobles and men of the lower classes. Confucius used them frequently in his utterances, giving all the praise to the "chun tzu" and nothing but contempt to the "hsiao jen." "The mind of the chun tzu is occupied with virtuous thoughts," he said, "and that of the hsiao jen with gain." According to his doctrine, Emperor, feudal lords and their subordinates, "gentlemen," peasants, and workers should keep to their appointed station: any attempt to rise from it meant the creation of disorder. Good government prevails "when the prince is prince, and the minister is minister; when the father is father, and the son is son."

He did not, however, believe in a despotic, high-handed rule. That man who is in power should himself be a pattern to those beneath him, and should influence them by example and persuasion rather than punishment. "The virtue of the 'chun tzu' is like the wind, and that of the 'hsiao jen' like grass. When the wind blows, the grass bends in the same direction." The perfect virtue towards which the "chun tzu" and ruler should aim was what Confucius called "jen," and though capable of many varied translations, seems to denote something akin to the Christian conception of "Love."

Confucius was not an isolated voice crying in the wilderness. His system gave rise to innumerable "Schools" of moral philosophy, and some of his followers themselves became renowned philosophers. Chief of these was the philosopher Mencius (371-298 B.C.).

Compared with his predecessor Confucius, who often despaired of rectifying human conduct, Mencius was an optimist. The two Confucian virtues of "Jen" ("love") and "I" ("goodness") occupied him especially, and it was his belief that the nature of man inclines him to goodness and kindliness as surely as the nature of water compels it to flow downwards. "Now, if a man suddenly sees a child about to fall into a well," he said, "he will certainly experience a feeling of alarm and distress. (If he rescues the child) it is not in the expectation of finding favor with the child's parents, nor that he is looking for praise among his neighbors and friends." In direct opposition to Mencius is the gloomy philosopher Hsun-tzu, who declared that man is born with an evilly inclined nature, and that only by education and moral training can he become a tolerable member of society.

The period of the Warring States which immediately followed Confucius' death, and during which Mencius lived and wrote, was one of the great ages in Chinese philosophy. During this time, Confucianism of every form developed and flourished. But after the reunification of the Empire under the dictator Ch'in Shih Huang Ti (221-210 B.C.), a great persecution of philosophers, and especially of Confucianists, was initiated. For ordinary citizens to discuss politics or methods of government was an unpardonable offense, thought the Emperor. In the year 213, an imperial edict was issued, that "all owners of the 'Book of Poetry,' the 'Book of History,' and works of the authors of the 'Hundred Schools' (a general term for the numerous Schools of Philosophy then existent) must surrender their volumes to the local officials, who would collect and burn them. Only books on Medicine, Divination, and Husbandry may be retained." Anyone who failed to comply with the edict within thirty days of its proclamation would be tattooed on the face and sent to join the building of the Great Wall—the Chinese equivalent of being "sent to Siberia." Anyone who secretly discussed the "Book of Poetry" or the "Book of History" thereafter would be executed.

After this Emperor's death, there followed a series of civil wars, during which the existence of the edict passed unnoticed. In fact, it was not until 191 B.C., some years after the establishment of the equitable and cultured Han dynasty, that the law against the Confucian books was lifted. The most aged scholars were then summoned from all parts of the Empire—men who had studied Confucius in the days before the great persecution, and might be expected to remember pas-

sages by heart. They were asked to recite all they knew in the presence
of the Court scribes or young scholars sent to them by the government, who noted down the extracts in the form of handwriting characteristic of the period. This was very different from the antique style
practiced in Confucius' own day, and in which his works had been
originally transcribed. For this reason, the Han edition of the Confucian Classics, when it was complete, was known as the "New Character" edition.

Now the revival of Confucianism became quite a fashion. A certain
wealthy prince offered huge rewards in gold and rolls of silk for old
editions of the Classics, and many copies were miraculously forthcoming. Another prince conceived the idea of extending his palace
over the ground where Confucius' house still stood. Some of the building had been broken down when a part of Confucius' library including copies of his works was discovered, hidden in the double walls.
These books were presumed to be originals since they were written
in the old style of writing. Accordingly they were called the "Old
Character" Classics.

The "Old Character" edition was the larger of the two, and there
were numerous textual differences. The controversies which now began to rage between the partisans of the respective editions may well
be imagined. They did not entirely die down through the whole of
the Han dynasty. Teachers of the "New Character" School attacked
those of the "Old Character" School by declaring that their texts were
forgeries fabricated by profit-mongers, with the object of claiming rewards from rich patrons. The "Old Character" adherents in their
turn rebuked their opponents for neglecting the precious relics out of
prejudice and personal vanity.

The Han dynasty, however, was the spring and source of Confucian study: during the reign of the renowned Emperor Wu Ti
(140-87 B.C.) Confucianism was promoted to a place resembling that
of State religion. "Doctors" who should teach the Classics were appointed by imperial command, and the children of the royal family,
high officials, or specially favored young men recommended by the
governors of their provinces, were allowed to study under them. The
first National University was founded in the same dynasty, in A.D. 29,
chiefly for the purpose of teaching the Confucian texts. Seldom was
there an age of more industrious learning. In addition to teachers appointed by the State or serving in the University, private teachers of
Confucianism collected students around them whose numbers ran into
tens of thousands!

In the centuries that followed the fall of the Han dynasty, respect for the Confucian Classics never died out in China. In the course of time, the Sage's words became encrusted and overlaid with learned commentaries, so that his original meaning may, in some places, have been distorted; in others, reduced to cold formula. But until very recent times, when the influx of Western thought appears to have swept them, at least temporarily, from their lofty pedestal, these few great books have exercised a predominant influence upon the life of the whole nation.

VI. LAOISM, MOISM, AND HANFEISM

OUT OF THE PROFUSION of philosophical thought, from the "Hundred Schools" which sprang up towards the end of the East Chou period (770-249 B.C.), time has cast up at least three schools of thought (in addition to the orthodox Confucianism) which had more than a transitory significance, and have even exercised an important influence upon the thoughts and behavior of the Chinese people. They are Laoism, Moism, and Hanfeism.

The first is named after its founder Laotzu—"*lao*" meaning "aged" and "*tzu*," "gentleman"—"the Venerable Gentleman." It is better known, especially in the West, as Taoism, "*Tao*" being the word for "Way," the mystic Path of Righteousness which lies at the core of Laotzu's teaching.

From the scanty records of his life, we cannot discover the date of Laotzu's birth, but we presume him to be a rather older contemporary of Confucius, and believe he may have been a librarian in the imperial household of Chou. There is, at any rate, a well-founded report that Confucius visited him in the Chou State, and parts of the conversation between them are recorded. The meeting between these two men of genius—two of the greatest thinkers in the whole history of Chinese civilization—must have been as momentous as that between Napoleon and Goethe at Weimar many hundreds of years later.

Confucius asked Laotzu's opinion about the ancient rites.

"Their authors' bones are rotten now," replied Laotzu, "merely words remain. I have heard," he continued, "that a good merchant looks as if he had no treasure, and a man of lofty virtue as if he had no wisdom. Get rid of your vehemence, your desires, and artificial manners. They are all worthless to you. That's the sum of my advice!"[1]

After the interview, Confucius, far from feeling snubbed, seems to have been filled with awe and admiration for such magnificent skepticism, since he declared to his students:

"Oh, I know that birds fly, that fish swim, and that beasts run. And the runner I can trap, the swimmer I can hook, and the flyer I can shoot with bow and arrow. But of dragons I have no knowledge—

dragons that soar into the sky mounting on the wind and the clouds. Such a one is Laotzu whom I saw today. He is as mighty as a dragon!"

When the House of Chou fell into decay, Laotzu resigned his office, and had no more to do with society. Practically nothing is known about the rest of his life, but the legend runs that after leaving the Court, he traveled westwards riding on a green cow, contemptuous to the last of "artificial manners." When he reached the Hanku Pass, an officer on guard stopped him and questioned him about his doctrines. Whereupon Laotzu wrote them down in two volumes, which he called the "Tao Teh Ching," the "Way of Virtue."[1] Afterwards he rode away on his cow and was not heard of again, though some say he lived for a hundred and sixty years or more. The whole story of Laotzu is a curious confusion of fact and fiction.

Indeed, so little is recorded of Laotzu that even his existence is called in question, and his book, the "Tao Teh Ching," is held by some to have been assembled like the Bible, by a multiplicity of authors. A few say it is mere moonshine—a collection of meaningless paradoxes. But to many it is the profoundest book that has ever been written, in China or elsewhere. Nobody claims to understand it completely.

The philosophy it contains is primarily a nature philosophy. "Tao" is its fundamental principle—the Way, the cosmic force which is the source of life, and in conformity with which man should aspire to live. Life and death are only phases in the great cosmic life-cycle; the visible world and all it contains are but phantoms that will pass: only Tao remains, eternal, changeless. The whole source of unhappiness, then, lies in man's effort to control his destiny, thereby impeding the natural flow of spontaneous events. Knowledge is useless, action superfluous, desire harmful, wealth, rank, and the whole gamut of sensory pleasures and pains are as empty as dreams.

"A man may dream of indulging himself at a feast," wrote Chuangtzu, a contemporary of Mencius and one of the greatest philosophers of the School of Laotzu, "but find things to mourn over in the daytime. In his dream, a man may have wept, but he wakes to join in the hunt. While he is dreaming, he does not know he dreams: he may even dream of dreaming. There is a great awakening waiting for us all, and only then shall we know that we have dreamed a long dream."

"How do I know," said the same writer, "that my desire to live is

[1] The title as well as the whole contents of the book have been interpreted in a number of different ways: Arthur Waley translates it "The Way and Its Power," while a more free but equally pregnant rendering is "The Way and the Waygoer."

not a delusion, and that my distaste for death is not timidity and forgetfulness of my true home? The daughter of a native of Yeh Feng of Li, when she was carried off to wed the Lord of Tsin, wept and soaked her garments with tears. But when she arrived at her Lord's palace, shared his bed, and dined with him sumptuously at his table, she regretted her tears. How do I know that the dead do not repent their craving for this life?"

While death was nothing fearful, but rather man's return to the source of his Being, life could be brought closest to Tao by ignoring art, science, and education, by having no aspirations, and by letting events carry one along without attempting to control them. In the "Tao Teh Ching," Laotzu describes his Utopia:

"Let the country be a small one, and sparsely populated. Let the people have tens of hundreds of implements, but no need to use them. Make them afraid of danger and refrain from traveling. Let them have boats and carriages but nowhere to go. Let them have all kinds of armor and instruments of war, but no chance to display them. Let them be content merely to count numbers on knotted strings as men did in the distant past. Let them have sweet foods and fine clothing. Let them be comfortable in their houses and feel at ease in their daily habits. Though neighboring States adjoin one another so that the crowing of cocks and barking dogs can be heard across the frontiers, the people on either side of the boundary should never meet each other as long as they live."

Fantastic as this picture seems, it is chiefly the writer's love of paradoxical language which makes it appear so. Chuangtzu, who expressed his philosophy with a fine imagination and literary talent, conjured up a Golden Age which has all the essentials of Laotzu's and yet appears more natural and attracts the mind. "In the days of highest morality," he says, "men moved quietly and gazed steadily. At that time, there was no Pass over the mountains, and no bridge or boat over the streams. All living things were created for their own spheres. Man could lead animals on a rope and play with them, and he could climb up and look into the birds' nests. For at that time man lived with the animals, and all creation was one. Who knew any distinction of good and bad? Since all were equally without knowledge, their virtue could not go astray. Being all equally without desires, they were in a state of natural integrity—the perfection of human existence."

To "do nothing" was, in fact, a cardinal principle of Laoism. "The best ruler of a great kingdom," said Laotzu, "governs it as you would boil a tiny fish": meddle with either and it falls to pieces. Again he declares, "Nothing" is the mother of countless useful things. When you have an empty hoop, you can put thirty spokes into it, and behold! the chariot will move on! If you have made an empty earthenware bowl, you can fill it with any kind of food. When you have carved the door and window of an empty room you can go to live in it. When your mind is not filled with worldly desires, you have room for wisdom.

If we are to describe, in terms of Western thought, the influence of the two great Masters Confucius and Laotzu upon the Chinese people, we may say that Confucius founded the Classical school of thought, Laotzu the Romantic. In its practical application, Laoism taught people to live more in harmony with Nature—to throw off the shackles of society, the bonds of artificial manners. And this in turn contributed to China's rich abundance of Nature poetry and "poetic" or mystic landscape painting. It permeated the lives of people of all classes, encouraged them to let things take their course without interference, to be content with what they had, to be free of ambition, to be fatalists. It discouraged people from inquiring into politics. A story told about Chuangtzu gives a picturesque illustration of the Laoists' dislike of worldly life and cares in comparison with the free life close to Nature. The Duke of Ch'u, having heard of Chuangtzu's intellectual brilliance, sent an envoy to him with gifts, and requested him to be a minister at his Court.

"I have heard about the sacred turtle of Ch'u," replied the Sage, "which died two thousand years ago, and has had its remains preserved with the deepest veneration by the Duke of Ch'u, who keeps them in his ancestral temple, and worships them. Now do you imagine that the turtle would prefer to have its remains kept in the temple and honored, or to be alive and crawling about, wagging its tail in the mud?"

"I should say it would prefer to be alive and crawling," replied the envoy.

"Then return and tell your master that Chuangtzu also prefers to crawl about, wagging his tail in the mud (to being kept and honored in his Court!)"

To do Chuangtzu justice, it was not a turtle-like sloth that caused him so scornfully to reject the responsibilities of a governmental position, but the sincere belief—a belief shared by all Laoists—that the whole machinery of government and education only harmed the people. He has a fable in illustration of this which is picturesque enough to merit quoting:

"Once upon a time, a sea bird alighted in the outskirts of Lu. The Marquis of Lu drove it in his own chariot and feasted it in the royal ancestral temple. The orchestra of Shao played for its entertainment, and the sacrifice of a whole cow was offered to it. The bird began to feel bewildered, distressed, and unhappy. It shrank from touching a morsel of the flesh or a drop of the wine, and after three days it died of starvation."

"The Marquis of Lu," commented Chuangtzu, "had tried to feed the bird with his own instead of birds' food." And he points the moral that all the splendid schemes of great statesmen, educationists, and scientists for improving the conditions of society will affect the common people as did the Marquis' mistaken attentions to the sea bird.

In the course of time, Laoism—or Taoism as it was later called—was transformed from a philosophical system into a religion. The teaching of Laotzu and his followers already had something in common with Buddhism, notably a negation of the pleasures of the world, and it seems to have been the infiltration of Buddhism into China from India during the Han dynasty that stimulated Taoism into becoming a regular religion. Its tenets were drawn chiefly from the "Book of Changes," compiled by Confucius, and the works of Laotzu, Chuangtzu, "Liehtzu," and other Laoist philosophers, to which was added the so-called "magic" learning of the many philosophers and pseudo-philosophers who wrote during the period of the "Warring States." A monastic system grew up, closely modeled upon that of the Buddhists, while the Taoist temples which were erected in great number from the T'ang dynasty onwards, and even some of the images contained in them, can hardly be distinguished from the Buddhist figures and buildings.

Nor was Taoism without its priestly hierarchy. During the Han dynasty, when this religious movement appears to have been initiated, a certain Taoist, Chang Tao-ling, claimed to have magic power over spirits, and to have discovered other mysterious secrets of the spiritual world. He bequeathed his powers to his son and his son's sons, and in later years his descendants were appointed the Popes of Taoism, by imperial edict. In the twelfth century, Chang Tao-ling himself was apotheosized as the "Pearly Emperor," and in folk literature is often confused with the Almighty Ruler of Heaven. The institution of Taoist "Popes" was maintained in later periods of Chinese history. During the Mongolian dynasty of Yuan, when the famous Kublai Khan was Emperor of China, we learn that Chang Sheng-lai, lineal descendant of Chang Tao-ling the "Pearly Emperor," was summoned to Court and formally appointed "Pope of Taoism." The beautiful Dragon-Tiger Mountain in modern Kiangsi province, where Chang Sheng-lai and his descendants lived, became the Taoists' Holy Mountain.

But despite superficial resemblances, the spiritual influence of Buddhism and Taoism is not comparable. While Buddhism has spread over the whole of Asia, and has had probably the largest following of any religion, Taoism has never been practiced outside China, and with the exception of a few comparatively short periods,[1] it has not enjoyed within China the same popularity as either Confucianism or Buddhism. The reason for this is twofold. On the one hand, Taoism in its profoundest aspects remained too much of a philosophy: it was too abstract to give ordinary men and women a guide to life. On the other hand, its more popular aspects were too dependent upon magic and fantasy, and though such fantastic stories had a certain appeal to the uneducated, as we see from their frequent appearance in Chinese folk literature, they could have no serious or lasting influence upon people's hearts. They did not help humanity to endure suffering.

In the books of Chuangtzu and Liehtzu, for instance, fables are written about a man who leaped down terrifying rocks unharmed, one who walked through fire unsinged, another who traveled thousands of miles through the air without material aid, a man who never died, and so on. The philosophers intended these stories to be interpreted metaphorically, but the Taoist teachers adopted them as truth, and seriously tried to discover means of effecting miracles. They tried, for instance, to produce gold from cinnabar, and they claimed to expel evil spirits with charms. Especially did they expend their ingenuity upon the attempt to discover the elixir of life—the secret of immortality. This search had been begun in earlier times by the so-called "Magicians," before the existence of a Taoist Society, encouraged by certain royal patrons, such as Ch'in Shih Huang Ti, who seemed to possess everything the world could give, except the power to enjoy it forever, and had conquered everything but death.

Some of the Taoists tried to find the precious elixir among wild herbs and roots; others sought it in more mystic ways. This latter school believed that to master the secrets of immortal life, a man need

---

[1] One of these periods was the early T'ang dynasty when the Taoists declared that Laotzu, whose family name was Li, was related to the reigning imperial family of the same name. For this reason, the T'ang Emperor Hsuan Tsung (713–755) patronized the Taoist faith, and apotheosized its founder Laotzu—his own remote ancestor—with the extravagant title of "T'ai Shang Hsuan Yuan Huang Ti," "the Mighty, Supreme, High and Lordly Emperor"! Many scholars of this period were converted to Taoism. The Sung dynasty, which followed the T'ang, was an even more prosperous time for the Taoists.

only obtain perfect control over his own body, especially over the three chief powers in it—*"ching"* or essence of life, breath, and spirit. Hence that strange religious practice in which the Taoists indulged—breathing exercises. But the basis of this belief goes far deeper than a mere physical control of breath—it is connected with the *"Yin"* and *"Yang"* principle, which appears extensively in the Taoist bible, the "Tao Teh Ching." "Yang" is the positive, "Yin" the negative element in the Universe, and just as the union of male and female produces life, so "Yin" and "Yang," the contrary elements, are responsible for the coming into being of heaven and earth, and of the life force itself. Then, said the Taoists, if heaven and earth, and the body of man, are both products of Yin and Yang, and if heaven and earth are, as they seem, immortal, there is no fundamental reason why a man who gains control over the powers in his body, so that the spiritual and material elements move together as harmoniously as the movement and intercourse of the sky and the earth, should not equally attain immortality. There were certain times in the day, and certain periods of the month, notably at dawn and at the first appearance of the new moon, when the "yin" influence was in the decline and the "yang" influence in the ascendant, which the Taoists, especially those of the Northern Sung period (960-1126), considered specially propitious for their exercises. At those times it would be possible to create within the bodies of the faithful a sort of internal elixir which should effect their release from mortality.

Beyond doubt, there is a profound meaning and much truth in this Taoist belief—the harmonizing of the body and spirit of a man, and of the whole man with the universe in which he lives, but in its popular application it degenerated into superstition, meaningless formulæ, or pure fantasy. There is, for instance, the interpretation in folk literature of the "internal elixir" as a "flying dagger" which had power to kill anything against which it was directed, even at a distance of ten thousand miles. The man who achieved such a power was called the "Immortal of the Dagger." At his wish he could open his mouth and out would fly the dagger, in the shape of a flash of light, and bury itself in the heart of anyone whom he wished to kill! The most famous Immortal of the Dagger in Chinese literature is the Lady Red Thread, a lady in attendance on a certain military leader in the T'ang dynasty. One night she appeared in the private chamber of an enemy Governor, and stole a golden box as a sign that the Dagger Lady had been there. This Governor was so terrified of assassination that he immediately abandoned his plan of attacking Lady Red Thread's patron, who was thus saved from battle.

Abusus optimi pessimus. Thus was the means of obtaining eternal life transformed into an instrument of death, and in such ways, through failure on the part of ordinary people to comprehend its deep meaning, through the outcrop of superstition, and through elaborations and distortions put upon it by men of letters who used it purely as a source of the picturesque, Taoism fell into disrepute after the Sung dynasty. But Laotzu and the "Tao Teh Ching" have not shared in its downfall; they remain brilliant stars in the firmament of Chinese thought.

A second great name among the philosophers of the Eastern Chou period is that of Motzu. The name itself, to be sure, is not very complimentary, its literal meaning being "the Tattooed Gentleman." Most people hold that *"Mo,"* "tattoo," is simply a family name, with no literal significance. "Tattooing," however, was one of the punishments imposed on Chinese criminals in ancient times, and it is not impossible that Mo was a nickname given by contemporaries to the philosopher and his disciples, the Moists, because of the extremely ascetic life which they led, and which formed part of the Moist doctrine. The story is cited of a prominent Moist in Ch'in State whose son pleaded guilty to a charge of murder, and who therefore awaited the death penalty. The King of Ch'in was willing to spare the young man for the sake of his father, who was a respectable aged man and had no other children. "No," said the father, "according to the Moist law the punishment for a murderer is death, and a man who injures another should be tortured. . . . I will not spare my son at the expense of violating my law!" He had his son put to death.

Such an action would not be very remarkable among the Romans, or the Greeks of certain periods, but it is alien to the Chinese mentality, where humanity and family love are intensely powerful elements. On this, and at almost every other point, Motzu came into conflict with Confucius, who was probably a rather older contemporary of his. Confucius had a system of family devotion and loyalty, while Motzu insisted that love for one's fellow men should be universal, without favor or prejudice. "Treat your friends as you would yourself," he said, "and treat their parents as you would your own. . . . If you see a friend hungry, give him food; if cold, give him clothing; if sick, attend him; if he dies, bury him." According to the teaching of Motzu, love was not so much a natural instinct as a religious duty. Indeed Moism is more a religion than a philosophy; possibly closer to the general conception of a religion than any of the other sects and faiths native to China. It may well be that its failure to win popularity among the masses at any time is due to this very fact, for the Chinese as a race, while being possessed of a strong moral sense and some degree of superstition, are not naturally "religious."

Confucius, as we have already seen, paid almost exaggerated importance to ritual. Motzu was on the one hand too much of a utilitarian to advocate anything that would drain the people's purses unnecessarily, and had, on the other, too deep a sense of the spiritual world to allow much consequence to the material one. A king dies, said Motzu, and we are supposed to mourn over him for three years. Then we have to go into mourning for another three years when each of our parents dies. We have also to spend months and years of mourning when our wives, our children, our uncles, brothers, aunts, sisters, nephews, nieces, maternal uncles, and all the rest of the relatives die. And according to the rites, we have to do our best to hollow our cheeks, to make our ears deaf, our eyes dim, and our limbs rotten. If a ruler thinks he can bring prosperity to the people in this way, he might as well finish them off with his dagger, declaring at the same time, "I am lengthening their days!"

The art of music, which Confucius believed to have so salutary an influence upon the human mind, was to Motzu like a red rag to a bull. The use of ceremonial music caused him the extreme of irritation. "Boats are useful for traveling by water," he wrote, "and carriages by land. . . . I have nothing against their being built at the people's expense. . . . And I should have had no objection to the making of musical instruments had their utility been in any way comparable with that of boats and carriages. . . . But the people have three great afflictions: the hungry go without food, the shivering lack clothes, and the overworked get no rest. Could you provide clothes and food for them by striking the curfew, sounding the drum, playing the pipe and flute? Or when the great power attacks the feeble, and the big family the small; when the strong rob the weak, and the many oppress the few; when the crafty cheat the credulous, and the noblemen treat their serfs arrogantly; when the thieves and robbers abound and cannot be restrained by law—could you by striking the curfew, sounding the drum, playing on the lute and harp, pipe and flute, and performing the spear dance—could you restore order in the world? You certainly could not. And therefore I say, music is entirely useless!" He despised the whole Confucianist system with its ceremony, ritual, and sacrifices. To Motzu, this behavior seemed as senseless as "providing entertainment to which no guest came, and making nets when no fish were to be caught."

When Christianity came to China, many drew comparisons between it and Moism. Undoubtedly there are similarities, especially in the Moist doctrine of universal love, and in the importance it gave to "spirit" above "ritual." It is also true that both Christ and Motzu blessed the peacemakers. Motzu, a lonely voice among Chinese thinkers, advocated disarmament and preached peace. In war, he said, the bamboo-wood arrows, the be-feathered flags, the tents, suits of armor, and shields fall in pieces; spears and daggers are destroyed. Oxen and horses go out to the battle strong and fat—either they return thin or they don't return at all. By forced marches, on the battle front, by disease or treacherous slaughter, the whole army is destroyed. You will have lost so much that you cannot count your gain.

The third school of this period which deserves mention is that of Hanfei. Like the Moists, the followers of Hanfei believed in a strict adherence to law, and in the equality of all men before the law. To them is also due the idea of Statute Law—a new process of thinking in China, and for this they were dubbed "the Legists." "If you wait to find a naturally straight arrow-shaft," wrote Hanfei, "you will have no arrow for a hundred generations. If you wait to find a naturally round piece of wood, you will have no wheel for a thousand generations. . . . But all the world over, men drive chariots and shoot game: how is it? Because they have the tools to force them into shape." And so he draws the analogy: it is only by means of the law, which encourages by the promise of rewards, and dissuades by the threat of torture, that men will become good, and order will be established in society.

Hanfei was undoubtedly a "modern" thinker in his day, and openly professed a fine contempt for tradition: his criticism of the Confucianists with their worship of the "blessed Yao and Shun" is far from complimentary. "In the time of Hsia, a man would be laughed at . . . if he built a nest for himself in the trees, or made a fire by rubbing a chisel against a piece of flint. In Shang and Chou times, a man would be jeered at . . . if he declared he was setting out to regulate a flood. Nowadays, if someone pours out all his admiration on Yao, Shun, Yu, T'ang, and Wu, he will seem just as ridiculous!"

Elsewhere he tells the story of a certain farmer of Sung who once discovered a dead rabbit under an old decaying tree. The farmer was overjoyed to think that here was a tree against which rabbits would always scamper and stun themselves to death. Accordingly he gave up all his work on the farm, and just waited under the tree for the easily caught rabbits. All he gained was that his lands ran to waste! "At the present time," he concludes, "if you want to rule the people by the old administration, you are just as bad as the farmer watching by his dead tree!"

Apart from the novelty of his ideas, Hanfei was a talented writer, and a man of bold and fearless personality. He was for some time patronized by Ch'in Shih Huang Ti, then King of Ch'in, but fell a victim to intrigue, and died tragically. He was thrown into prison and there poisoned by order of the jealous and powerful minister, Li Ssu, before the King could rescue him.

VII. THE EMPEROR CH'IN SHIH HUANG TI AND THE GREAT WALL

WHILE THE NUMEROUS sovereign States that sprang up in the decay of the Chou dynasty wasted their substance and reduced their people to conditions of profoundest misery, the Ch'in State in the Northwest was steadily preparing itself for a great destiny. It was to reunite all the lands of China under one Emperor, an Emperor whose descendants should rule for ten thousand generations. Such was the dream of the Ch'in leader.

Even before the final conquest, the Ch'ins were laying the foundations of a new type of government within their still limited domains. In contrast with the human, kindly Chou system it was mechanical, cold, and soulless. The fact that almost all the politicians responsible for its functioning met an unnatural death—assassination, murder, or suicide—offers sufficient comment. The machine continued to work though the men who had set it in motion perished violently. It is hardly necessary to point the parallel between this type of political structure and some totalitarian regimes of our own day.

In place of the well-field system of agriculture, devised by the Chou rulers, and which, despite the labor it entailed, had the virtues of a communal life, with mutual rights and responsibilities, in the Ch'in State land was divided into districts under the charge of officials. Although the peasants were split into groups, and made to supervise each other, each family had to live apart, and families which had more than two male members must separate, or face the impossible alternative of double taxation. Every male was liable to life-long military service, and army officials had better treatment than any other class. Laws were stern, and punishment frequent. There was no longer a system of rank, with power dispersed among the nobles and their subordinates: all power came from the Head of the State.

As a result of these new laws, Ch'in became extremely wealthy and prosperous, and the martial spirit of her people was roused to such an extent that an outlet had eventually to be found in large-scale military adventures. How the six other sovereign States recognized the growing menace of the Ch'ins, how at first they allied to protect themselves from attack, but were one by one wooed away from the alliance, cheated by false promises, conquered and absorbed until in 221 B.C. the Ch'ins were masters of all China, has already been related. It remains to be told how the Ch'in leader organized his empire.

He is described by one of his officials as "a man with a high-bridged nose, long narrow eyes, the breast of a bird of prey and the voice of a jackal; of an ungrateful disposition and the mind of a tiger or wolf. Usually he behaved decently to his men, but in the intoxication of success he only made them his victims." His arrogance was beyond all bounds, and his aim was to master all of the then known world.

His first act was to declare himself "Ch'in Shih Huang Ti," that is "The First Emperor, coming from the House of Ch'in." By this he wanted to wipe out all the history of the past, and stand as the Originator of Chinese civilization. The very words which he chose to designate "Emperor," "Huang Ti," expressed the combination of virtues of all the ancient Sage-Emperors, and connoted divinity: *Huang Ti* is almost an exact equivalent of the Roman *Divus Augustus,* "the Divine August One."

In order to destroy all memory of the former States who had struggled with him for supremacy, he issued an order for the famous "Burning of the Books." This was not an indiscriminate destruction of literature, but the systematic seizure and burning of State records and any historical literature that did not concern the Ch'in State. It included most of the Confucian classics; among them, the "Book of Poetry." In this way, education became the monopoly of the government. Private teachers like Confucius, and the bands of intellectuals who in the "Warring States" period opened their homes to students, and became centers of free and enlightened thought, were no longer allowed to exist. And posterity must be made to believe that Chinese history only dawned when Ch'in Shih Huang Ti rose upon the horizon.

How to form an intellectual barrier against the past evidently stood high in Ch'in Shih Huang Ti's thoughts. The formation of a physical barrier against uncivilized hordes on the imperial borders offered an equally serious problem. Since the earliest recorded history, the "Demons" or "Huns" of the Northwest had destroyed the peace of Chinese rulers, marauding, thieving, and whenever the chance arose, filching territory. The building of the Great Wall was Ch'in Shih Huang Ti's solution.

After thousands of years of human invention, the "Great Wall of

China" still ranks among the Seven Wonders of the World. Parts of it built originally by pre-Ch'in States, and much of it repaired from time to time, especially in the sixteenth and seventeenth centuries, it still stands today, stretching for some sixteen hundred miles from the heart of the Western mountains to the sea, climbing precipitous slopes, and descending unbroken into the valleys, a monument to the huge conception and boundless egotism of one of the greatest tyrants in the history of the world. The Chinese call it "the Long Wall of Ten Thousand Miles," and the great pillar which completes it to the East, whose base is washed by the tides of the sea, "the Pillar-Bridge of Heaven."

It must be admitted that the conception of wall-building as a protective barrier is an age-old one, and that in the period immediately preceding the Ch'in dynasty, there was plenty of activity of this sort. The Ch'i State built a wall against the Lu State, the Wei against the Ch'in and the Han, the Yen against the "Demons" and the Ch'i, the Chao against the Wei; every State in fact seemed to be passionately engaged in building a long wall to shut out its neighbors. But it was left for Ch'in Shih Huang Ti to conceive of a single wall, hundreds of miles long—the longest wall ever built in ancient times—which should form a northern frontier to the whole of his united Empire. Ch'in Shih Huang Ti liked everything large. He believed that size meant power, and had no patience with half measures.

Accordingly he ordered the old stretches of wall to be reconstructed, linked, and augmented. The whole was to form a vast artificial barrier against the constant and irritating pressure of the "Demons" or Hsiung-nu. Huge as the enterprise was, it must be quickly completed, declared the Emperor. Three hundred thousand soldiers who had been victorious in battles over other States and the "Demons" were rewarded by being sent to build the Great Wall. In addition, criminals were made to do forced labor on it, also civil servants who had fallen short of their duty, and scholars who had failed to surrender to the flames any books banned by the imperial censor.

The work went on for years. Citadels and watch towers were built on the rocky heights, and garrisons by the river banks. In winter, those northern parts were intensely cold, with savage winds blowing from the plains of Siberia; in summer, the air was parched, burning, and dusty. The Chinese mind is easily given to nostalgia, and there are many poems which describe the homesickness of men laboring on the Wall, and the yearning of their wives, left in distant homes. The ballad from Han times called "Watering my pony in the pools beneath the Great Wall," with its slow, sad movement,

Oh green, green are the grasses on the river banks,
And far, far goes my heart along the road the traveler treads, . . .

is probably the earliest example which has survived, and has provided the *motif* for many similar poems in later periods. There is also a famous folk tale describing the grief of a lady whose husband died at this work. Her name was the Lady Meng-chiang, and her husband had been summoned to work on the Wall, "ten thousand miles" from his home. Presently she heard that he had died—as many thousands of them died, so hard was the tremendous work. As the Chinese believe the spirits of the dead cannot rest unless the body is given honorable burial, the Lady Meng-chiang started on the wearisome journey of "ten thousand miles" to find her husband's bones. But when she reached the Wall at last, she saw only the mountains, the plains, and the stones, and did not know where to look for her husband's body. She wept. She laid herself down by the Wall and wept for days and nights. At last, even the senseless Wall was touched at her grief, and a part of it collapsed, to reveal her husband's remains, which she reverently and thankfully recovered and brought back to the ancestral burial ground. From unmistakable evidence, we know that this story was current among the people at least a thousand years ago.

When the Wall was completed, at the expense of so much blood and tears, there is no doubt it served a useful purpose for a time. But the pressure from the North was a natural movement, encouraged by Nature, which is in the long run stronger than man. For the boundary marked by the Great Wall marks also the edge of the fertile plain of the Yellow River. North of it are bleak mountains and steppes. It was inevitable that whenever the defensive power of China weakened, a downward movement of the inhabitants of these dreary lands towards the fruitful, pleasant plain was bound to take place. Such a movement could be checked for a time by human-built fortifications, but never finally held. Now the Wall no longer marks the frontier of China: it is contained within her territory, for the last Chinese reigning House, the Ch'ing (Manchus), came from north of the Wall. It remains, substantially complete, the record of much human misery, but also of a huge human will.

The splendor with which Ch'in Shih Huang Ti surrounded himself is worthy of the most romantic ideas of an oriental ruler. His palace buildings must have covered several miles. Whenever his victorious troops entered the capital of a former rival State, the Emperor commanded the design of the palace to be brought to him, a replica of which would forthwith be erected near his own, and linked up by corridors. Thus, at the completion of his conquests, Ch'in Shih Huang Ti had model palaces of all six defeated States attached to his own, and just as he had gathered all their lands under his rule, so had he epitomized, in an ostentatious, material way, his sovereignty over them all.

At a little distance from the capital was the Emperor's royal park, called "His Majesty's Forest," and in it his summer residence. This magnificent palace, the Palace of A-Fang, on the banks of the river Wei, backed by the beautiful Black Horse Hills, had taken the labor of seven hundred thousand prisoners to build! The stones were brought from the Northern mountains, and the wood from forests in the far distant South. Altogether within some two hundred *li* (about seventy miles) radius from the capital there were two hundred and seventy extravagant royal residences! Pretty girls, musicians, and gorgeous furniture had been brought from the conquered States to satisfy the Emperor's vanity. It is said that when a revolution broke out at the fall of the dynasty, the capital was taken and the palaces set on fire; three months elapsed before the flames entirely died away!

Ch'in Shih Huang Ti was fond of travel. He liked to tour the empire and feast his eyes upon the huge tracts of land and the millions of toiling people that belonged entirely to him—their First Emperor! For this purpose, he had constructed the famous "royal roads" throughout the Yellow River district and the Yangtzu valley, in order that "all the scenery of the rivers, the lakes, and the sea might unroll before his eyes." These were also called "the racing roads" or "the straight roads," for, characteristically, the Emperor commanded that mountains were to be leveled and valleys filled in to avoid meanders. No compromise was allowed, even with Nature. The roads were said to be fifty *pu* broad (one *pu* is about five feet) and were shaded by avenues of pine trees. The common people were not, of course, allowed to pollute them with their feet, but must drag their merchandise and make their journeys over roughly made tracks.

However vain and overbearing was Ch'in Shih Huang Ti's character, there are some great achievements which must be credited to him. It is not without reason that the name "China," by which our great Eastern Empire has been known for hundreds of years to the people of the West, is derived from the "Ch'in" dynasty. This powerful despot was the first to rule a united Chinese Empire, and by the irresistible power of his conquering armies he brought new lands under his sway from all the four quarters. To the North his boundary ran by the far shore of the Yellow River; to the South it reached as far as those lands "where the great heat made people build their houses with windows facing the North"—that is, to part of the modern provinces of Kuang-tung and Kuangsi, and the State of Annam; to the East it reached the sea, and included Korea; and to the West it touched the high mountain barriers of the interior. The map of modern China Proper is based on the Empire of Ch'in Shih Huang Ti.

As in his former State of Ch'in, the Emperor completely reorganized the administration. The feudal system had long ceased to exist, and in its place was instituted the system of Provinces, with all power invested in the ruler at the center. The country was divided into thirty-six provinces, to which four were later added, and each was supervised by officials directly chosen by the Emperor. The land was no longer apportioned among the aristocracy—every foot of it belonged directly to the Emperor. So long as that Emperor remained powerful, the administration of the country under this system would be uniform as well as united, and uniformity—standardization—characterized the reign in every respect. The official control of education and literature was calculated to standardize thought, and even that great instrument of education, writing, was made uniform. Previously, the form of writing known as the "Great Seal" was used in royal proclamations and official documents, while the writing current among the scholars varied, sometimes fundamentally, from State to State. To Ch'in Shih Huang Ti's Prime Minister Li Ssu is credited the invention of the "Small Seal" form of Chinese writing—a simplification of the "Great Seal," and a uniform script which became current through the whole Empire. Upon it is based the modern Chinese script in use at the present day, after it had passed through a number of intermediate changes.

Many other elements in public life were made uniform, including the system of weights and measures, agricultural implements, and the gauges of wagon wheels; local customs and usages were strictly repressed. As a precaution against any rebellion on the part of his subjects, all arms owned by the people were confiscated and sent to the imperial capital. There the metal was melted down and cast into bells, and also into twelve colossal images, each weighing a thousand *shih* (one *shih* is equal to about 150 lb.). These were set up in the royal palaces.

Such was the work of Ch'in Shih Huang Ti—one of the strongest tyrants of ancient Chinese history. At his death in 210 B.C. he left an empire of complaining subjects to his son, "the Second Emperor." He was buried in the Ninth Moon of that year, among the Black Horse Hills. In the tomb were placed many priceless jewels and treasures.

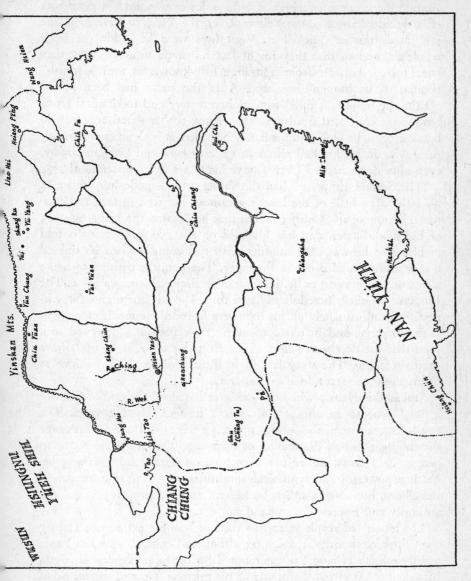

WU SUN

HSIUNGNU
YUEH SHIH

Yinshan Mts.

Liao Hsi

Wang Hsien

Hsiang P'ing

Chih Fu

Chu Chi

Min Chung

Ch'in Yüan
Yün Chung
Tai
Shang Ku
Yü Yang

T'ai Yüan

Chiu Chiang

Ch'angsha

Nanhai

Lung Hsi

Shang Chün

R.Ching

Hsien Yang

Hanchung

R. Wei

R. T'ao
Lin T'ao

Shu
(Chêng Tu)

Pa

Hsiang Chün

CHIANG
CHUNG

NAN YÜEH

THE CH'IN PERIOD (cir. 221 B.C.)

Among the precious offerings of curious device was the vast panorama of "a hundred streams, the Yellow River, the Yangtzu River, and the sea" made out of quicksilver. Vigil fires were lit inside the huge sepulcher, and so that they might last for some time to come, they were fueled with fat from a strange fish known as the "Man-fish" because of its human-like shape. After the coffin had been placed within, the tomb was lined with molten copper and mechanical crossbows were concealed nearby, so that if any robber dared approach to break it open, he would immediately be killed. It is significant that this ruler who all his life had relied on force to gain and keep an empire, even after death needed force to save his bones from desecration!

"The Second Emperor" had the vanity and despotic intolerance of his father, but little of the latter's greatness. He was, in fact, so dominated by one of the Court eunuchs that he became the laughing-stock of his subordinates, and lost his hold on the people. A story is told of him that he was once hunting with this eunuch when he sighted a deer and pointed it out to the latter. The eunuch, wishing to make a fool of him in sport as he did in politics, declared it was a horse. The Emperor laughed incredulously and turned to his attendants for witness. But unfortunately all his followers feared the eunuch more than their Emperor, and in terror of losing their positions, protested to a man that the deer was a horse! The Emperor thought he must have been dreaming. The story is a good illustration of the conditions at Court under the second Ch'in Emperor.

And so the dynasty which was to have lasted till the end of Chinese history came to an abrupt end after a meager fourteen years. The royal descendants of the former sovereign States still pined to revenge the subjugation and destruction of their countries, while the common people, held down under too stern an iron hand, and groaning beneath a powerful and tyrannical administration, were ripe for revolt. Rebellions, one after another, broke out, and the Emperor lacked the authority and respect to command support.

The leaders of revolt were two men of humble extraction, Hsiang Yu, "lifter of the tripod weighing a thousand catties," and Liu Pang, a petty official. Hsiang Yu was reputed for his huge physical strength, his talent for strategy, the beauty of his mistress Yu, and the mettle of "Tsui," his dapple-gray horse. With the powerful support of Hsiang's armies, Liu Pang, whom destiny had chosen as the first Emperor of a new and glorious dynasty, the Han, marched into the Ch'in capital in 206 B.C. The Ch'in Emperor was assassinated, and his successor surrendered. The great palaces disappeared in flames, and the Ch'in dynasty, founded on such high hopes but such inhuman laws, perished in the palace fires.

A brief period of storm followed this cataclysm. Hsiang Yu, claiming all credit for the great victory, entitled himself "Conqueror," and nominated Liu Pang as mere "Prince of Han." Hostilities soon broke out between them, and after a series of successes, fate turned against the "Conqueror." One night, conscious of the approaching end, he ordered a banquet to be served in his camp, and while his beautiful mistress danced before him, he sang a song of his own invention:

> *My strength can heave down mountains,*
> *And I look contemptuously on the world.*
> *Alas! my hour will never strike.*
> *No more shall Tsui my horse gallop,*
> *Ah, no more! What shall I do?*
> *Oh Yu, Yu, how can I leave you here?*

In the depths of her sorrow, the lovely Yu took her own life before her lover's eyes. The Conqueror then mounted his beloved horse and made a last brave sortie. In the ensuing battle he was mortally wounded, and rather than be taken prisoner, killed himself. This heroic story of love and war is not unlike that of the great figures in Roman history, Antony and Cleopatra. With the conquest and death of his rival, Liu Pang now proclaimed himself Emperor of China.

VIII. THE HAN DYNASTY: POLITICS AND LIFE

THE CH'IN DYNASTY, short and violent as it was, had fulfilled its destiny: it destroyed an old world in order that a new might be founded. The Han dynasty which followed was one of the brilliant periods in China's history, and one which left an imperishable mark upon her institutions. It foreshadowed so many of the permanent elements in Chinese life that the Chinese sometimes call themselves "Sons of Han."

Liu Pang, the people's leader, who rallied the rebellious subjects of the Ch'in Emperor, overthrew him, and in 206 B.C. founded the Han dynasty, came of plain peasant stock. Gratified as he must have been at winning the throne of all China, it surely seemed to him shocking that so magnificent an empire as the Ch'in could have been brought to ashes by simple subjects, under a peasant leader. Having become, by right of force, the father of a royal line, he was determined that such an event should not occur again. A major cause he concluded lay in the abolition of the feudal system. As long as a system of rank was steadily upheld, and the nobles kept their power, a People's Revolution would be impossible. Accordingly he tried to restore the old feudalism in a modified form. He distributed land among his relatives, friends, partisans, and meritorious ministers, while officials were appointed from the Court to control their administration. The result could be foreseen. To overlay an old system with an even older one could not possibly come to good. The feudal tenures soon grew strong and plotted against their benefactor, having lost the sense of dignified loyalty with which the Chou dynasty nobles had supported their rulers. This situation came to a head in the reign of Emperor Ching "the Radiant," when in 154 B.C. seven powerful princes joined to start a rebellion against the throne. The chief of these princes, Wu-wang, who had conspired against the Emperor for thirty years, was evidently a formidable person: he is said to have owned a bronze mine, from which he minted his own coins, and to have managed a flourishing salt industry on the sea coast. The imperial troops were able only with difficulty to put down the insurrection, and from this time on the feudal system was gradually liquidated. Finally, under Emperor Wu

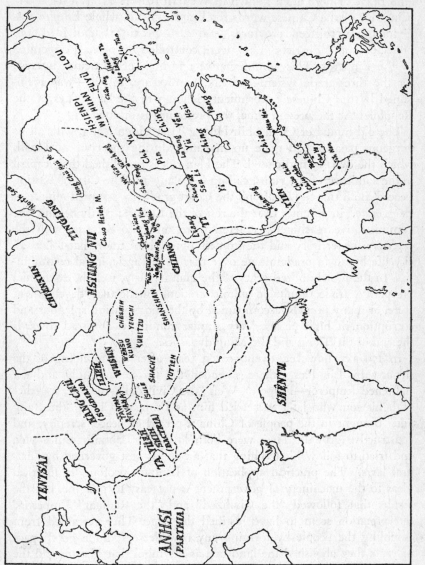

The Former Han Period (*cir.* 100 B.C.)

"the Brave" (more often known to Western readers as "Wu Ti," "Ti" being one of the Chinese words for Emperor), the whole Empire was divided into thirteen provinces, and each province subdivided into prefectures and districts. They were controlled by officials appointed by the Emperor. This administrative reform is of particular interest, for the three-grade system—province, prefecture, district—was maintained by the Chinese government right up to the early days of the Republic! At the present time, the prefecture is omitted.

The old capital of Ch'in Shih Huang Ti at Hsien Yang, with all its gorgeous palaces, had gone up in flames during the civil wars with which the dynasty had closed. The Han rulers established their capital to the southeast of the ruins, calling it Ch'ang-an, "the City of Lasting Peace." Both this city itself and the Court gradually assumed a place of exaggerated importance over the rest of the Empire; partly because the administrative machinery centered there, and also because, with the extension of territory and the immense growth of trade that followed, city life began to predominate over that of the agricultural communities. In the four hundred years of the Han dynasty, wealth, expansion, prosperity, trade, equitable administration, intellectual development were, at many periods, accompanied by the most glaring splendor and corruption in high places. Very similar conditions recurred towards the end of the T'ang and the Ming dynasties.

In 179 B.C., however, twenty-seven years after the founding of the dynasty by Liu Pang, there ascended the throne a kindly and enlightened Emperor—Emperor Wen "the Civilized"—and he, together with his son who later succeeded him as Emperor Ching "the Radiant," brought to the people of China a period of peace, serenity, and constructive growth. They were both lovers of Laotzu's philosophy, and tried to follow his teaching that a State is best governed by "natural laws." The practical application of Laotzu's profoundly mystical ideas to the machinery of government is not easy to imagine, but the results that followed "the Civilized" and "the Radiant" Emperors' interpretation seem to have justified the Sage. They refrained from troubling the people by forming any new decrees; for a good space of years they abolished the land tax, as a symbol that Nature and the Earth belonged to all men, and not crowned heads. They abolished the tortures devised by ancient rulers, and they appeased the perpetual enemy—the "Demons"—by sending treasures and royal princesses as wives for their chieftains. Thus they avoided bloodshed.

In their own lives they spurned the sophisticated luxuriance of the Court, believing that the happiness of all men, even monarchs, lay in keeping free from worldly entanglements, and in imitating the simplicity of Nature. It is reported that "the Civilized" Emperor, in all his twenty-three years of rule, never had a palace built or a park laid out, and that he bought neither chariots nor horses nor rich robes for his own pleasure. Once, it is told, he thought of having a new balcony added to one of the old palace buildings. "How much will it cost?" he asked. "A hundred pieces of gold" was the reply. "A hundred pieces of gold!" exclaimed the frugal Emperor—"why, that is as much as the whole property of ten middle-class families! I have always felt ashamed of the great fortune I inherited from my father. Who am I to build a balcony for myself at the expense of my people?" And he gave up the project.

Records say that this Emperor wore only robes of common black silk, and that even his most beloved concubine was given no expensive flowing gowns. No embroidered curtains hung on his palace. The imperial tomb which, according to custom, was built during the Emperor's lifetime was furnished with no gold, silver, or bronze vessels, but only with some pots and urns of cheap earthenware.

At the end of the reign of this good king and his son, the country was as rich and the people as contented as they had ever been in their history. Official and private barns and granaries throughout the country overflowed with grain; the imperial coffers and the provincial treasuries were loaded with more money than ever before. At the capital so much money had accumulated that the strings on which the coins were threaded rotted away, and the number of coins could not be counted. In the imperial granaries, corn was so plentiful that a part of this, too, rotted. Even the poorer people kept horses, and cattle crowded the foot-paths between the fields. A man was despised as a penniless "country cousin" if he turned up at some public assembly mounted on a cow or buffalo, as was the habit in the past. To "keep a horse" was the patent of gentility, like "keeping a carriage" in the England of Jane Austen. Even the village handymen fed on the best kind of rice and a variety of meats, instead of the rough unpolished rice with a few bits of vegetable, which had been their staple food in the old days. For nearly seventy years, except for an occasional famine due to flood or drought or a disease of the crops, the Chinese people lived in plenty.

The successor to these two good kings was Emperor Wu "the Brave." This Emperor seems to have been one of those dynamic, energetic characters, full of impulses and intolerances, with high ambitions and huge visions. In the course of his reign from 140 to 87 B.C. he exhausted all the riches of the country which "the Civilized" and "the Radiant" Emperors had accumulated, and brought the peasants down to their former level of indigence, though the merchants prospered. This was the price he paid for territorial conquests which stretched to Mongolia in the North, Chinese Turkestan in the West, Canton and Annam in the South, and Fukien in the Southeast. It is for these huge military expeditions, the scientific voyages of discovery and the opening of trade routes which followed, that the Han dynasty is justly famous. They made China the Great Power of the East. Emperor Wu's reign is looked on as one of the Golden Ages of Chinese history, although the price of this expansion was so high that the dynasty itself began to totter, and the common people lost their happiness.

> *Like flocks of birds and shoals of fish,*
> *Precious curios pour in from every land,*

wrote a poet of the time. According to another contemporary record, the capital of Ch'ang-an was decked out with every conceivable splendor, sent as tribute by the conquered countries, or brought by merchants who traded in the newly discovered lands. Bright pearls, streaked tortoiseshell, rhinoceros horn, and the brilliant plumage of exotic birds, it is said, were some of the tributes sent to adorn the imperial harem. Mettlesome horses of extraordinary description, having "dragon veins," "rush stripes," "fish eyes," or "that sweated blood," were sent to the imperial stables. In the royal park were huge elephants, lions, fearful dogs, and gorgeous birds among other dangerous or curious beasts. The envoys and tribute bearers from these far countries were entertained with "pools of wine and forests of meat," with circus shows, acting, wrestling matches, and dancing.

The Emperor's palaces were furnished with every rarity, and stuffed with riches. One of them was constructed from sweet-scented cassia wood, so that whenever a breeze rose from the lake waters beside which the palace was built, and swept through the chambers, it stirred up an intense perfume. Not far away stood the royal "Pavilion for the Reception of Angels," whose door screens were said to be woven from kingfisher feathers and unicorn hair! Tribute from Central Asian tribes included such fantastic gifts as the "Horse-liver Stone," a small piece of which when eaten would safeguard a man against hunger and thirst for a whole year, and which also had the magic property of turning white hairs dark! An aviary of small birds once arrived at Ch'ang-an, "each as big as a large fly, with the appearance of parrots and the voice of swans." These quaint birds soon escaped from their jade cages, but would return to the palace from time to time, alighting on the curtains or slipping into the silken sleeves of Court ladies, whence they became known as love talismen.

Apparently appetites increased by what they fed on. Chinese adventurers in their turn set out in search of strange lands and rare merchandise. The most famous of them was Chang Ch'ien, whose far-distant journeys inspired the legend that he had sailed on a log down the Milky Way—called by the Chinese the "Silver River." In actual fact, he penetrated very far into the West, to Bactria, Yavanas, and Sogdiana, all still ruled by Greek kings; to the Tarim basin and the Pamir districts, which had been the conquests of Alexander. At one of the markets in a Bactrian city he came upon some linen material made of hemp, and a strange kind of bamboo, both of which were foreign to China, and which, he was told, were Indian products. On hearing of this, Emperor Wu sent other delegates to find a route to India. Chang Ch'ien was thus the initiator of communications between those two great Eastern nations, which a little later were fully developed, and along which Buddhism, with all its spiritual æsthetic, and moral influence, was destined to flow.

Chang Ch'ien's penetration of Central Asia forged an even more remarkable link than that between China and India: it led to a kind of indirect intercourse between Ch'ang-an and Rome! The record stands that in the year A.D. 166, some two hundred and eighty-eight years after Chang Ch'ien had made his adventurous journeys, the Chinese Emperor Huan received a message from Emperor "An Tun" of "Great Ch'in" who had gifts of ivory, rhinoceros horn, and chelonian shells to be presented through the channel of the Annam government. "Great Ch'in" is the ancient Chinese name for Rome, and "An Tun" is thought to stand for the Roman Emperor Marcus Aurelius Antoninus (A.D. 121-180). Spices, pearls, and gems are said to have been brought to China from Rome, while Chinese silks were sent in great quantity to the Roman markets. An interesting indication of this is found in the name "Serica," "the Silk Country," by which the Romans called China. It seems to have originated in the Chinese word "Ssu" (pronounced "Se") meaning "silk." Chinese silk was also known to the Greeks, who called China "Seres." Some even think that Ch'ang-an is the city which Ptolemy calls "Sera metropolis," "the Silk City," and which he describes as being the resort of Greek merchants.

During the Han dynasty, then, and especially in the reign of Emperor Wu, the barrier that lay between the great civilizations of the East and the West was lifted, and not only merchandise, but conceptions of the human mind were interchanged, having repercussions we cannot measure. The barrier was to fall again, and China to return to her self-appointed isolation, but Emperor Wu's example sowed seed for the mingling of East and West which has become so important a feature of the modern world.

After Emperor Wu's death, there was no similar powerful Emperor to take over the reins. Court scandals and intrigue weakened authority, while the conditions of the people became progressively painful. The time was ripe for revolution, and this took an unexpected form. A certain member of the Empress' family called Wang Mang, who seems to have had a talent for collecting supporters, poisoned the reigning Emperor and set up a young boy in his stead, proclaiming himself "Regent." He pictured himself as another "Duke of Chou" who still remained the model of kingly virtue in the Chinese mind. However, the temptation to wear the kingly crown was too great for Wang Mang, and in 9 B.C. he made himself Emperor of China, and founded a dynasty which he called "Hsin"—"the New Dynasty."

True to the title of his dynasty, Wang Mang determined that the whole administration of the country should be reformed and made new. By this time the cleavage between rich and poor had greatly widened: "when the foot-paths of the rich ran across every field, and the benefits from streams and mountains were monopolized by them, the poor hadn't enough ground on which to rest the end of an awl," declared a contemporary. Wang Mang, in devotion to his hero the Duke of Chou, decided to return to the communal well-field system of those ancient times, and accordingly confiscated the lands and redistributed them. In his passion for antiquity, he even restored the old coins and shell money. Industrious and well-meaning, he worked incessantly on his schemes, but he was, in fact, a dreamer with no sense of practical politics. He did not realize that social reform could never be effected by an arbitrary return to more primitive times; that any schemes must be based on a study of actual conditions; that society was evolutionary and must go forward, one stage growing out of another; that the Han administrative machinery was already far too complex to admit of a superimposed simplicity. It is not surprising, therefore, that both he and his dynasty fell before the revolutionary army of a Prince of Han. Wang Mang was killed and the Han prince, having removed the capital from Ch'ang-an to Loyang, founded a new branch of the Han dynasty which was known as the Eastern or Later Han. This happened in A.D. 25 and the new Emperor was called Kuang Wu "the Bright and Brave."

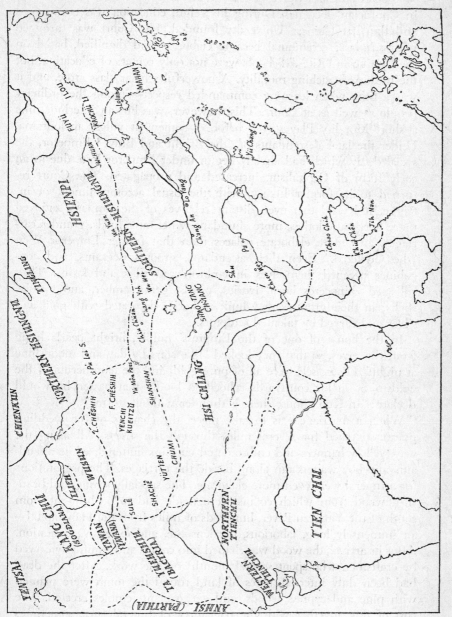

The Later Han Period (*cir.* A.D. 100)

"The Bright and Brave" Emperor was a learned man deeply versed in Confucian doctrines. During his reign, education was encouraged and the first Chinese University founded. His Court was thronged with scholars; ceremonial became elaborate and dignified, based on the Confucian "Rites." Schools were not only centers of education, but the means of teaching morality. A powerful scholar class arose, and it was a time when learning commanded respect—among the ordinary people as well as at Court. This, however, was but an interlude, like a short Morality Play staged before a somewhat vulgar melodrama. Under the later descendants of "the Bright and Brave" Emperor, the social decay which had already begun under Emperor Wu, due to an early form of Capitalism, increased and propagated. The Court returned to its former luxury, with the usual accompaniment of intrigue. It is said that even distant relatives of the Emperor enjoyed more gorgeous clothes, more abundant wine, rarer foods, grander carriages, and more elaborate palaces than that former Emperor Wen "the Civilized." Even their attendants, grooms, servants, and concubines preened themselves in embroidered silks and satins. They collected rhinoceros horn, ivories, pearls, gems, amber, and tortoise shells; in their grounds they built rockeries decorated with gold and silver and carved by talented sculptors.

In the house of one of the Empress' family, bright pearls hung from the   ves, so that they looked "like stars by day and moonshine at night. His vessels were all of pure gold, and the hammering of the goldsmiths in his courtyards echoed so loudly that passers-by would declare: "In Kuo's house there is thunder without storm!"

When a marriage was to take place, the chariots of the wedding guests stretched for several miles through the streets. All along the way, yellow banners and embroidered curtains fluttered, while attendants and boy waiters ran along beside the carriages. The preparations for a funeral were even more elaborate. The specially strong and beautiful wood from which coffins were made had to be brought from south of the Yangtzu River, hundreds of miles from the Han capital— an immensely long, laborious, burdensome, and expensive operation. After its arrival, the wood was shaped into coffins and cunningly carved by craftsmen who spent several months on the work. After the dead had been duly interred, acres of land round the tomb were planted with pine and cypress woods, and extravagant temples erected. The cost of this, together with the pageantry of funeral rites, sometimes devoured the whole fortune of a family.

While the aristocracy enjoyed this extravagant life, the Han merchants became increasingly rich and powerful. Many of the peasants abandoned the land and came to the big cities to make their fortunes. Agricultural economy which had prospered so wonderfully under the Chou rulers began to break down completely. The streets of the capital were thronged with the oxen, horses, and chariots of wealthy traders.

Trading had been facilitated during the Han period, not only by geographic expansion and the exploration of many foreign lands, but by the remarkable development of communications within the Empire. We have already heard of the splendid roads built by Ch'in Shih Huang Ti, and it is probable that others were constructed over the newly won territory of the Han rulers. Along these roads, public inns called *"t'ing"* (literally "pavilions") were built at a distance of ten *li* apart for the convenience of travelers. Rich and poor, noble and peasant, men and women, could use them freely, and already in the early part of the Han period we read of there being nearly thirty thousand such "pavilions" in the length and breadth of the country. There were also more luxurious inns where rooms might be rented and merchandise discharged. "From every point of the compass (literally, "from the eight directions") imperial delegates and private travelers crowded along the roads," writes one historian; "there were inns in plenty, providing warm shelter in winter and cool shade in the summer days. Fodder was stacked in piles for the animals, and there was no lack of furnishings."

It is interesting to learn that "Post Offices" were known to the Chinese many years before Christ. In Han times, office buildings were set up every five *li* along the main roads; letters were carried by officials on horseback from one office to the next, and so were brought great distances by relays of riders. Travelers could find lodging at these post offices too, if they pleased, as well as at the public inns.

Some of the more enlightened Han rulers recognized in the exaggerated growth of trade a danger to the whole social system, and attempted to discredit the merchant class and bring men back to agriculture. At the beginning of the dynasty, an order was issued prohibiting merchants from wearing silk or owning carriages, and very heavy taxes were levied on them. Later, the restrictions imposed on them seem to have been somewhat relaxed when social order was relatively restored, but the merchants and their children were still forbidden to hold any government office. Later still the ownership of land was withheld from them. But despite all these deterrents, the merchant class continued to expand and prosper, nor were the laws strictly held against them towards the end of the dynasty.

It will be readily recognized, therefore, that in this greedy clamor for riches, and neglect of agriculture, lay a powerful seed of decay for the Han dynasty. Another lay in conditions at Loyang Court. Scholars who, under Emperor Kuang Wu "the Bright and Brave," had so powerfully influenced the life of Court and nation, now became a target for spiteful attacks on the part of imperial eunuchs. As the Emperors grew feebler, so did these eunuchs take it upon themselves to control the administration, and they prevailed on their masters to persecute any persons or communities who seemed obnoxious to them. More than one hundred scholars of high reputation lost their lives for criticizing the eunuchs, and about seven hundred more were imprisoned. This happened in A.D. 169. The general feeling of social unrest became manifest. Branches of the royal family, especially the Empress' relatives, exercised a rival influence with the eunuchs, and in the course of the intrigues between these two parties, the Han dynasty fell.

The immediate cause of the disaster was a plot by one of the Empress' relatives to have the eunuchs murdered. In the confusion that accompanied the conspiracy, a fat and powerful general named Tung Cho kidnaped and carried off the Emperor, having first sacked and looted the capital! He planned to set up a new empire at the old Western capital of Ch'ang-an, but before this could be achieved, he was murdered by his own soldiers. A second general named Ts'ao Ts'ao, notorious in fact and fiction as the type of cunning traitor, succeeded in capturing the Emperor, and appointed himself Prime Minister. Ts'ao Ts'ao hoped to be conqueror of the whole Chinese Empire, but there were rival forces mustering in the South. At a naval engagement fought at the famous Red Cliff of the Yangtzu River in A.D. 208, his great fleet was destroyed, and he had to content himself with ruling a kingdom which stretched north of the Yangtzu. After his death, his son actually usurped the throne and created the Kingdom of Wei. South and west of the river was established the Kingdom of Shu, governed by a relative of the last Han Emperor. The southeastern portion became the Kingdom of Wu. The whole period between the downfall of the Han dynasty and the reunification of the Empire under the short-lived Tsin dynasty in A.D. 265 is known as "The Three Kingdoms," and its history is a continuous tale of conflict. Wu and Shu first contracted an alliance, then Wu passed into the partial control of Wei. Wei, extending its power, annexed Shu, and, finally, its throne was usurped by a minister, who became the first King of Tsin and annexed Wu. The leading generals in these battles became figures of romance to later ages, and their exploits are eagerly read by Chi-

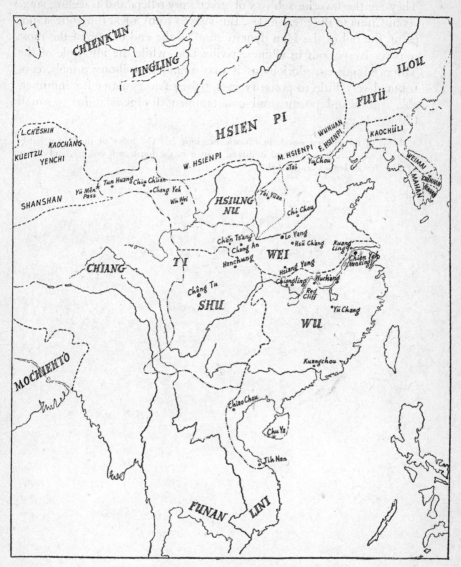

THE PERIOD OF THREE KINGDOMS (*cir.* A.D. 220)

nese children,[1] rather as the Robin Hood stories are read in England. They are the favorite subjects of street story-tellers and traveling singers in China to the present day. But viewed from a less romantic standpoint, the fall of the Han dynasty marked the end of one of the most constructive periods in Chinese civilization, while the interlude of the Three Kingdoms, glorious as it may sound in military annals, contributed very little to posterity except the subject matter for innumerable stories and poems, and entertainment for generations of small Chinese boys.

[1] One of the greatest novels in Chinese literature is "The Story of the Three Kingdoms," a narrative based on oral tradition, written in the fourteenth century, and where all these heroic battles are related.

IX. THE HAN DYNASTY: THE HSIUNG-NU AND THE "WESTERN REGIONS"

MENTION HAS BEEN MADE in the last chapter of the Han exploration towards the West, and of the relations the Han Emperors entertained with the Hsiung-nu or "Demons" who lived north of the Great Wall. So romantic is the story of these peoples—the westward repulse of the Hsiung-nu which directly or indirectly precipitated the Huns into Europe, and the conquest of the "Western Regions" which for a brief time brought China into contact with the Empire of Rome—that it may be worth while to examine their history in a little more detail.

The conflict between the Chinese and the Hsiung-nu was age old, even before Ch'in Shih Huang Ti built the Wall against them, or the Han Emperors seriously tackled the problem. And no doubt geography was the prime cause: the Chinese inhabited a fruitful, well-irrigated plain, while the Hsiung-nu were obliged to scrape an existence from the bleak plateau of the North, with its savage climate, and the rugged mountains of the Northwest. At any rate, we hear of battles between the two as far back as historical records exist, and even farther than authentic history, in the reign of the semi-fabulous "Yellow Emperor." During the Shang dynasty, the Hsiung-nu appear as "the Demons," and apparently caused much distress to those early people by raiding excursions and, at times, more menacing pressure. The Chou people who succeeded the Shang were driven eastward from their original home by those restless and battle-loving barbarians, and after the Chou leaders had become rulers of China, the "Demon" pressure again compelled them to migrate: the capital was removed from Feng-Kao to Loyang and the "Eastern Chou" period began. Ch'in Shih Huang Ti, the obstinate tyrant who succeeded the last Chou ruler and founded a new dynasty, was the first Chinese Emperor to measure his will against the "Demons"; he built the Great Wall along the whole northern border of his empire and had it fortified and manned. This restrained the barbarians for a while. But even this was only a defensive measure, and could not indefinitely hold back such an enemy.

During the Han dynasty which followed the Ch'in, battle was constantly and bitterly renewed, but this time some of the Han Emperors realized the necessity of carrying war into the enemy territory, and of beating the "Demons" away from their borders. It was this significant phase in the relations of Chinese and Hsiung-nu—as the "Demons" were then called—which had repercussions on world history.

"The Huns" is a general name for the wandering, predatory hordes who inhabited Central Asia, and who in the first century A.D. began their westward movement towards Europe. There can be no doubt that the expansion of the Han Empire, and the aggressive policy which Emperor Wu "the Brave" especially adopted against the Hsiung-nu and all the western border tribes, turned the movement of these warlike nomads from an eastward to a westward one. There were, no doubt, other contributory causes, such as the decay of the Roman Empire, but the fact remains that it was the power of China in those early centuries after Christ which goaded into action that gigantic movement of peoples ending in the conquests of Attila.

We are not concerned here with the history of the Hun invasion into the Western world, but only with the Hsiung-nu tribes in their relation to China. What sort of people were they, how did they live, and how were they governed? Their racial origin is obscure, but a theory which seems plausible assumes them to have been a heterogeneous collection of Mongol, Tungus, Turkic, and perhaps even Finnish hordes, under a Mongol military leadership. We know that they were nomads, who kept horses, oxen, sheep, camels, and other animals; that they built no townships, nor agricultural settlements, but pastured their animals wherever they found good land, and lived chiefly on animal flesh. The skins they made into clothing. It is said they used to put pieces of raw meat under their saddles, and after riding on them for a day, would eat them, uncooked! They were great riders and great huntsmen. The little Hsiung-nu boy would mount a sheep and hunt birds and rats with bow and arrows. As soon as he grew up, he would ride on horseback and shoot foxes and rabbits, as well as the more savage animals. Most of them were trained for fighting, and became mounted soldiers. According to Chinese records, they reached the peak of their expansion towards the end of the third century B.C—at the opening of the Han dynasty. At this time the lands which they controlled extended from the Great Wall of China to the Caspian Sea.

The Hsiung-nu chieftain was called the "Ch'an Yu," and he had a number of princes to administer the lands he owned. In the first moon of each year the princes came to the Ch'an Yu's Court, to offer sacrifice to the ancestors. Other sacrifices were offered in the fifth moon to the spirits of heaven and earth, while in the autumn, when the pastures were lush from the late summer rains, and their horses were fat, there was a great and jubilant meeting to count up the men and cattle.

We do not know much about their beliefs, but like most primitive peoples they seem to have been greatly governed by superstitions, and especially by astrology. They always made marauding attacks when the moon was full, and withdrew when it waned. The gains in battle were shared among the captors, and prisoners were made their slaves. This bait of personal booty made the Hsiung-nu into furious fighters.

Originally, it appears, they were divided into small clans, each of which had its own chieftain. In the general confusion, fire, and slaughter that accompanied the fall of Ch'in Shih Huang Ti's dynasty, they poured into Northern China, occuying land south of the Yellow River, and offered a menace to all the northern provinces. Liu Pang, who restored order to China and founded the Han dynasty, was in no position at first to oppose them, and was obliged, after suffering defeat in a short engagement, to make peace on terms favorable to the enemy. At this time, the Hsiung-nu clans united and were rapidly growing into a formidable power.

The early Han Emperors followed an unfortunate policy of appeasement towards the Hsiung-nu—a policy which only increased the power of the latter. They were influenced by the teachings of Laotzu, the "laissez-faire" philosopher, and believed that in avoiding bloodshed they were doing their subjects a service. It must be admitted that the country was weary of fighting, and was only too thankful for a respite. To keep on good terms with the enemy, the Chinese rulers contracted marriages between Han princesses and the Ch'an Yus of the barbarians. Valuable silks, choice food, and barrels of wine were sent as peace-offerings, and vows of "brotherhood" were exchanged—but all in vain: the Hsiung-nu continued to attack the Han frontiers even while they were receiving gifts.

It was Emperor Wu "the Brave" who saw the futility of such a policy. He determined not only to repulse the invaders, but to drive them far back from the Chinese borders and to occupy the territory they left, sending his own subjects to colonize it. There were three great campaigns. In 127 B.C. Han armies first crossed the frontier and challenged Prince "White Sheep" of the Hsiung-nu at a point south of the Yellow River. The engagement was successful: "thousands of the Hsiung-nu were killed and millions of head of horses and cattle were taken."

The second great battle was fought six years later, in 121. This time the Han general led his army in a northwesterly direction as far as the Ch'i Lien mountains (on the borders of modern Kansu province). This ended in a rout of the Hsiung-nu; their most precious possession —the golden image which they worshiped—was carried off, and forty thousand men surrendered. The territory thus acquired was divided into four districts, and officials were appointed by Emperor Wu to govern them. Chinese families settled there, bringing with them the Chinese culture and manners. After this victory "the right arm of the enemy was cut off," and henceforth the way lay open to the western border countries, known as "the Western Regions." Travel and trade followed. The third battle, in 119, succeeded in breaking the power of the Hsiung-nu completely. The Ch'an Yu himself was put to flight, and the whole people was forced to retreat and find fresh land for itself farther to the West. To this new piece of the Empire too, the Han Emperor sent his officials: the ground was brought under cultivation, and irrigation systems installed.

Now, ever since the way had been opened up to the Northwest, the Han rulers began to exploit those small, half-civilized border countries, called collectively by Chinese historians "the Western Regions," and comprising, roughly, modern Chinese Turkestan. Some of these people were, like the Hsiung-nu, nomads; they were called "the wandering nations." Others who settled and formed agricultural communities were "the staying nations," and it was with these that the Han rulers were chiefly concerned. Most of them had been attacked by the Hsiung-nu at one time or another, for the latter could never resist plundering a weaker people than itself. Emperor Wu conceived the idea of contracting military alliances with them against the common enemy.

Among these potential allies were the Yueh Shih, a people who originally bordered on the Han Empire, but who had been driven by the bullying Hsiung-nu westward as far as Bactria. They had left their homes angrily and bent on revenge, all the more because the Hsiung-nu had killed their ruler and made his skull into a wine-cup for their own Ch'an Yu. These, thought Emperor Wu, would be ideal confederates. An envoy plenipotentiary Chang Ch'ien was sent, who with the utmost pains and after the passage of several years, during which time he had endured every sort of adventure, including capture by the Hsiung-nu, and had even fathered a child on a Hsiung-nu woman, arrived in Bactria. But to his dismay, the envoy found that time had blunted the edge of vengeance. The Yueh Shih were very comfortable in Bactria; the soil was easy and fruitful; they had no more taste for military adventures. The envoy had to return empty-handed, and even suffer a second captivity by the Hsiung-nu on his way back to the Han capital.

But though the mission had been a failure diplomatically, it had brought new countries into the vision of the energetic Emperor. One of these, through which the envoy had passed on his way to Bactria, was the country called Ta Wan (Yavanas). Here, he reported, the wealthy rode a wonderful breed of horse, so mettlesome that they sweated blood! Emperor Wu was a great lover of horses, and nothing would satisfy him but that he should have a specimen for the royal stables. He sent another envoy with a thousand gold pieces and the model of a horse made from pure gold, to strike a bargain with the King of Ta Wan. The envoy made the long and dangerous journey only to have his bargain rejected by the proud king. He justifiably lost his temper, and threw down the golden model he had brought with him, smashing it to pieces on the palace floor. This contempt of majesty was not allowed to remain unpunished; on his return journey, the envoy was ambushed and murdered. As might be expected, war was immediately declared by the Han Emperor on the King of Ta Wan. A general was dispatched with a hundred thousand invading troops, and after three years of fighting, the gates of the capital were reached. The citizens, apparently afraid of the fate that might await them, in a cowardly and disloyal manner rose against their king, murdered him, and obsequiously offered three thousand blood-sweating horses to the conqueror. The Han general and his forces, together with the three thousand steeds, made a jubilant victory march of their return journey, and so impressed the small countries through which they passed, that many of them spontaneously offered to form an alliance with the Emperor Wu. Thus quite by chance the Han Emperors became masters of a great part of the "Western Regions."

The westerly boundary of the Han Empire was now very strongly held, with many of the smaller countries cowed into allegiance, and the Hsiung-nu dislodged and driven towards Central Asia. Nevertheless, the latter had caused such discomfort to the Chinese in past history that the Han rulers were still on their guard against possible advances. They worked on the "divide and rule" principle, and by this means, with the aid of good fortune, so broke the inner strength of the enemy that for very many years the invasion menace was destroyed. This is how it came about.

Among the "Western Regions" was a tribe called the Wu Sun, whose people are described as having "blue eyes, red beards, and the general appearance of monkeys!" These people of such strange physiognomy had tried to avoid the risk of conflict by forming an alliance with the Hsiung-nu and at the same time accepting friendship from the Han Court in the shape of royal marriages. When this came to the ears of the Hsiung-nu Ch'an Yu, the furious demand was made—"Surrender your Han princess or we make war on you!" The Wu Sun immediately called on the Han Emperor for assistance, and war broke out in 73 B.C. The Han army together with the Wu Sun forces succeeded in dealing the enemy a smashing blow: forty thousand were killed, including many generals and members of the ruling family, and more than seven hundred thousand head of horses, oxen, sheep, mules, and camels were taken. That winter the Hsiung-nu launched an avenging attack, and had some small success, but as they retreated with their booty they were caught in a terrible snowstorm, and about ninety per cent of their troops were frozen to death. This disaster was the beginning of evils for the Hsiung-nu: their many enemies took advantage of it to attack from all sides. A ghastly slaughter followed. That winter, either by famine or war, thirty per cent of the whole population perished, and half their cattle.

From that time, civil war raged among them; many rival princes laid claim to the leadership, and so great were their domestic distresses that the Han boundaries were safe from attack. This condition lasted until about 54 B.C.—nearly twenty years. It is significant of the Han policy that when once the Hsiung-nu had united again under a single ruler in 54 B.C., and had begun their old marauding policy with an attack on the monkey-like people with the red beards, the Han Emperor promptly sent an army against them, killed the ruler, and besieged his capital. The new Ch'an Yu hurriedly offered good terms to the Emperor, and asked for the honor of a Han princess in marriage. Chao Chun—"the Lady Bright"—was sent to be his wife, and her story is one which has caught the imagination of generation after generation of Chinese poets. It is worth relating, for it throws a very human light upon the actions of men and women in China, in days even before the Christian era.

The Lady Bright was one of the imperial concubines at the Han Court. She lived in the women's apartments at the palace, together with some hundreds of other beautiful girls of noble family, waiting for the Emperor's favor to shine upon them. The Emperor himself never visited them, but merely commanded the Court painter to make their portraits, and from these he chose his new favorite. The Court painter at the time of our Lady Bright was a certain Mao, a gentleman certainly not above corruption. The ladies bribed him to the utmost of their means to paint them more ravishing even than they were in life. Only the Lady Bright, though more lovely than them all, had also greater integrity of character. She disdained to bribe the painter, or to seek to appear more beautiful than she really was. The painter, in his anger, made the likeness of an ugly woman and sent it to the Emperor as the portrait of the Lady Bright. The Emperor never summoned her. In her lonely, remote building, deep in the palace, the years passed. As she watched the seasons change—the petals falling and the yellow leaves driven from the trees in autumn, she realized that her youth and beauty must pass too, unseen and unloved. Then came the demand of the Hsiung-nu chieftain for a wife from the Han palace, in order to cement the friendship between their two countries. All the beautiful princesses and palace maidens shrank from the ordeal of leaving their country to marry a barbarian chief. Only the Lady Bright offered to sacrifice herself for her country's sake. The Emperor, believing her to be the plainest of all his harem, was delighted, and gave his consent. But when she was brought out and presented to him before beginning her journey, and he saw her shining in natural and exquisite beauty, he grew pale with anger. Mao was brought to judgment and executed, but the Lady Bright had been promised to the Hsiung-nu and was bound to go. Many poets and dramatists have pictured her melancholy journey as she left her fatherland forever, and crossed the dreary desert to the wild western country. They tell how her attendants tried to comfort her, in vain, with the music of guitars—a musical instrument of the Hsiung-nu which was introduced to China about that time. They describe the "ever green grave" on the wild desert sands in which she was finally buried, a scene to remind travelers of the warm South whence the lady had come.

Peaceful relations between the Hsiung-nu and the Han Empire, beginning from the marriage of the Lady Bright, lasted for almost half a century. They lasted, in fact, as long as the Han Emperors were strong enough to keep their neighbors in awe of them. But with the break-up of the Western Han dynasty, and amid the internal confusion that accompanied the short-lived "New" dynasty of Wang

Mang and the subsequent founding of the Eastern Han,[1] the
Hsiung-nu returned to their evil ways, and even drew away from the
Han alliance many of the dutiful "Western Region" countries. Punishment descended on them in the form of a plague of locusts which
devastated the greater part of their pasture land, but it did not check
their exploits.

The old story of battle and defeat began all over again. In A.D. 73,
in 89, and again in 91, the Han armies engaged their traditional
enemy. In each battle the Hsiung-nu suffered an increasingly bitter
defeat, and were driven farther and farther westward. The third
battle was fought five thousand *li* (about sixteen hundred miles) from
the Han frontier, and ended in a complete rout—the Hsiung-nu flee-
ing to "no one knows where." It was then that the movement of
"Huns" across Asia to Europe was given a new impetus, and the
Hsiung-nu menace to China was permanently destroyed.

It now remained only to win back the "Western Regions" to their
former friendly relationship, and in this process a very talented and
shrewd diplomat called Pan Ch'ao played a leading part. He seems to
have had the temperament of a Robinson Crusoe, and to have been
born with an ardent desire to travel and to engage in heroic adventures. In his youth he was apprenticed as a clerk in one of the government offices, but found the work of perpetual copying irksome and
dull. "Alas!" he would often sigh, throwing down his writing brush,
"if only I had the chance, I could make a name for myself on the
frontier districts, as did Chang Ch'ien and Fu Chieh-tzu.[2] Why
should a man like me wear himself out forever over a miserable
brush and ink?" Fired by his dreams and ambitions, he visited a
physiognomist, and asked to have his future predicted. "Sir," declared
the latter, "humble as you now appear to be, you will be created a
marquis and govern remote countries, ten thousand miles away! You
have the jaw of a swallow and the neck of a tiger. That means you are
to make a journey, and dine on fine meats like an aristocrat!" Con-
firmed in his own beliefs by the fortune-teller, Pan Ch'ao gave up his
office work and joined the army that was about to cross the borders
and attack the Hsiung-nu (this was the battle of A.D. 73). In this first
of the three final encounters between Han troops and Hsiung-nu, Pan
Ch'ao so distinguished himself that the general in command sent him

[1] See Chapter VIII.
[2] Fu Chieh-tzu was one of those early Han travelers to the "Western Region"
countries. In 77 B.C. he had succeeded in assassinating the rebellious King of Lou Lan.

on a delicate mission to the "Western Regions." He was to visit the
country of Shan Shan and persuade the King to break off relations
with the Hsiung-nu and make an alliance with the Han Emperor.
Here was the chance of which the young man dreamed.

The King of Shan Shan received him graciously at first, but one
day the courtesies changed to coldness, and Pan Ch'ao discovered that
a Hsiung-nu delegation had arrived and was quickly winning favor
with the King! What was he to do? Crafty, resourceful, and determined not to fail in his first appointment, he summoned the members
of his own delegation, and after plying the wine cup repeatedly among
them so that their blood was heated to the point of recklessness, ex-
pounded a scheme by which the Hsiung-nu delegation should be
destroyed! "You can't catch the tiger cub," he declared, "unless you
dare venture right into the cave of the great beast!"

At dead of night, Pan Ch'ao sent ten of his men with drums to
conceal themselves behind the house in which the enemy delegation
was quartered. The remaining twenty-six he sent armed with bows
and arrows to lie in ambush in front of the building. He himself
went boldly up to the house and set it on fire. It was a stormy night.
The wind blew furiously; the flames roared and spread; the drums
began to beat a wild tattoo. Panic seized the sleepers: some of them
rushed out of the house, only to be shot down by the armed ambush.
Pan Ch'ao himself killed three with his sword. The remainder—about
a hundred men—perished in the burning house.

The King of Shan Shan was dumbfounded when the news reached
him. Never had he known such summary methods in diplomacy.
He was impressed and also intimidated. He swore everlasting friendship with the Han Emperor, and on the crest of his glory Pan Ch'ao
departed to look for other diplomatic conquests.

Next he came to the country named Yu T'ien. Here the King's
most influential adviser was a certain witch who apparently resented
any advances from the Han Emperor. She thrust herself into the
presence of Pan Ch'ao and demanded a horse "with a yellow body
and black snout" to be sacrificed to the local god as the essential
preliminary to diplomatic conversations. Pan Ch'ao gravely agreed to
the request, but asked that a representative of the god should come to
his lodging and fetch the horse. When the witch herself as the "representative" appeared, she was seized and put to death, and her head
sent to the King. The latter, like the King of Shan Shan, was considerably impressed by Pan Ch'ao's methods. He reproached himself
for having allowed the woman to insult a Han delegate with such

nonsense, and as a token of his repentance, had all the Hsiung-nu envoys in the country put to death, and promised faithful friendship to the Emperor of China.

Using similar high-handed tactics, Pan Ch'ao soon brought most of the "Western Regions" into line. His reputation can well be imagined. It is related that while staying in Yu T'ien he was recalled to the Han court. The King, his host, was so distressed at the prospect of losing him that, royal person as he was, he rushed out from the palace and clasped Pan Ch'ao's horse by the leg! The popular envoy was obliged to remain. Eventually the whole of the "Western Regions" was united under his banner, and communications were opened up more and more with the Chinese Empire. The Emperor dubbed him "the Marquis for Pacifying Far Countries," and thus the fortune-teller's prophecy was fulfilled.

At the age of sixty-nine, when he had served for nearly thirty years in the "Western Regions," and "no hair of his head was still black, nor could he walk without a staff," Pan Ch'ao asked to be allowed to resign and return to his homeland. He reached Loyang in A.D. 102 and died almost immediately after. So ended a remarkable career, and one of the strangest and ablest personalities passed out of Chinese history.

After Pan Ch'ao's death, the Han rulers maintained their power over the "Western Regions" for some time, but as the administration of the dynasty again grew weak through the intrigues of disreputable ministers and eunuchs, imperial control over the Northwest began to loosen, and was finally disrupted altogether. The western movement of the Hsiung-nu, having once been set in motion by the Han armies, was never reversed, but as the dynasty drew to an end, some branches of these barbarians who had surrendered and become subject to the Han Empire grew audacious and moved south, over the Wall. After the fall of the Han dynasty, they were powerful enough to overthrow Western Tsin which succeeded it, and to drive the Chinese rulers south of the Yangtzu River, leaving North China in foreign hands, and in great chaos.

Although a huge empire had fallen to pieces, the exploits of men like Pan Ch'ao, the sacrifice of the Lady Bright, the vision of rulers like Emperor Wu, had not been in vain. For something like three hundred years, and through the labors and sufferings of such men and women, China had stamped her will and her civilization upon a large part of the continent of Asia. How much of this endured in the centuries that followed, no one can estimate.

X. THE SIX DYNASTIES: HARASSING BY THE FIVE HU; "THE FAMOUS SCHOLARS" AND "THE HONORABLE FAMILIES"

Rain drizzles on the Yangtzu River,
The water reeds seem to be neatly cut.
The glory of the Six Dynasties passes like a dream,
And only birds remain, chirping sorrowfully.

Ungrateful are the green willows
Shading the Terrace City,
They flourish now as of old on the ten-mile dyke
Swaying in the mist.

SUCH WAS THE ROMANTIC melancholy that a poet of a later day spread over the palace ruins at Nanking, once splendid home of the royal Houses of Wu, East Tsin, Sung, Ch'i, Liang, and Ch'en, who succeeded one another in rapid succession between the years A.D. 222 and 581 and are known in Chinese history as the "Six Dynasties." His can only have been a literary nostalgia, for it was a period of constant wars and oppressions, of barbarian incursions and civil conflict. Indeed, the removal of the capital from the North, where it had been maintained for many hundreds of years, to Nanking in the South was evidence of the powerful inroads made by bordering tribes. But Nanking soon began to emulate the ancient glories of Ch'ang-an and Loyang. Beautifully set in a circle of hills, named from their coloring at sunset "the Purple-and-Golden Hills," and bordered by the broad, meandering Yangtzu River which connects the city with the snowy Himalayas to the West, and the strangely blue water of the Pacific to the East, Nanking now became the seat of imperial splendor, though also the pivot of political intrigue and civil broils. Noble and fashionable families, hangers-on of the Court, politicians, poets, artists, philosophers all flocked to the new capital. "When the sleeves of the passers-by fluttered, a gale of wind rose in the street. When the red dust was stirred by their trampling, it darkened the sky. When they sweated, it was as if rain fell and made the ground muddy. . . . On the river, the slow creak of oars sang, and on land the carriage-wheels chanted, at dawn and dusk and all the day long. . . . The houses of the rich filled whole streets. Their clothes were made of pearls and they feasted on precious jewels. . . ." Such was the poet's impression of Nanking during the first of the "Six Dynasties."

But although Nanking seems to have been a city of delights, the center of a thronging populace and thriving trade, of a rich and sensual life, history has little of value to record about the six royal Houses who ruled from it. Some few of the Emperors were not without personal virtues, as, for example, Emperor Wu of Liang, the fifth dynasty, who was a sincere practicing Buddhist, and displayed much piety though little statesmanship. On the whole, they were weak and ineffective, unable to hold the throne for their descendants or to better the lives of those they attempted to govern.

Meanwhile, north of the Yangtzu River, other races, more primitive, but also more virile, were pouring in, sending new blood coursing through the enfeebled limbs of the vast Chinese Empire. These tribes, five in number, and of Turkic, Mongolian, and Tibetan stock, are called by historians the "Five Hu" (foreigners), and the period during which, in their various branches, they occupied Northern China and set up independent States, that of the "Sixteen Kingdoms." In time, a single tribe, the To Pa, grew strong enough to unite all these States, thus bringing to an end the "harassing of the Middle Kingdom by the Five Hu." Five "foreign" dynasties now followed each other in the North, almost contemporaneously with those "Chinese" dynasties of the South—Northern, Eastern, and Western Wei, Northern Ch'i and Northern Chou, so that this whole period of history is also known as the time of the "Southern and Northern Dynasties."

The invaders, like the so-called conquerors of China throughout her long history, were conquered in their turn by the Chinese culture and manners. By intermarriage, but also through submission to the civilization they found in their new home, they became indistinguishable from the Chinese, though not without having made valuable contributions of their own. They inspired a fresh and vigorous strain in literature, with entirely new images and subject matter; painting owed the same kind of debt to them, while in the realm of religious sculpture, the "foreign" dynasty of Northern Wei produced some of the noblest and most sublime Buddhist images that have ever been carved.

It may be remembered that after the fall of the great and long-lived Han dynasty in A.D. 220 China was divided into three Kingdoms

—Wei in the North, Wu in the South, and Shu to the West, and that a minister of Wei, after usurping the throne, proceeded to subjugate Wu, having already conquered Shu before. This powerful upstart then founded a new dynasty, which he called the Tsin, and for a brief period of years, from 265 until 316, China was united. Profiting from the melancholy fate which had overtaken his former sovereign, the last King of Wei, the Tsin Emperor now attempted to restore the old feudal system, thus imitating the policy of Liu Pang, founder of the Han dynasty. He had remarked that as his plot to usurp the throne developed, no loyal aristocracy stepped in to forestall it. Nobody had appeared to care much whether the Wei House stood or fell. With the hope, therefore, of establishing his own dynasty on surer foundations, he endowed the members of his family with titles and lands, allowed them to build up armies of their own, and to appoint administrators in their own locality. They were intended to serve as "screen and fence" to the royal House, ready to spring to arms at the head of their followers whenever the Emperor was endangered.

In practice, however, the "screen and fence" proved as disastrous in the Tsin dynasty as it had in the Han. It was a revival in form only, not in spirit, of a social order which had worked admirably so long as the sovereigns were great enough to exact spontaneous loyalty from their nobles. But under these Tsin Emperors of a later day, the nobles merely took advantage of their power to further their own ends. The time of chivalry had passed. The situation came to a head between the years 299 and 306 when, a notorious and ambitious queen having murdered the Crown Prince, the eight most powerful nobles sought with all their vigor to get control of the administration. Civil war broke out, during which the queen was put to death. The eight nobles then fell upon one another, and from the ferocious battles that followed, only one of them survived. The Tsin Empire was now in chaos, and the Northern "barbarians" took advantage of its weakness to pour over the border and drive the Emperor and his followers out of North China. The latter established his new capital at Nanking, and the dynasty, henceforward known as Eastern Tsin, the second of the "Six Dynasties," was maintained there for over a hundred years, from 317 till 420.

The North was now in the hands of the barbarians, and remained so until the reunification of the whole Empire by the Sui dynasty in 589. The first of the "Five Hu" was a branch of China's traditional enemy, the Hsiung-nu. The old Han policy of appeasement, supported by the marriages of royal princesses to Hsiung-nu chieftains, gave the present leader an excuse to proclaim himself a descendant of the Han dynasty, and a legitimate ruler of China. He adopted the family name of the Han Emperors, and already during the period of the "Three Kingdoms" the Hsiung-nu people had made incursions over the Great Wall and settled in the center of North China round the capital city of Wei Kingdom. During the subsequent Tsin dynasty, and especially in the civil wars with which the period closed, these Hsiung-nu made pillaging raids upon Tsin territory. In 311 they sacked Loyang, then capital of Tsin, and in 316 Ch'ang-an, the second capital. On each occasion a Tsin Emperor was captured and put to death, after suffering shameful indignities. The Hsiung-nu chieftain, who now called himself "King of Han," had the two Emperors dressed in green, like slaves, and ordered them to wait upon his victorious generals at the banquet. When innumerable cups of wine had heated his blood and roused his ferocity, the Han King ordered them to be executed before his eyes. This bloodthirsty sovereign met the fate he deserved, being murdered by one of his ministers. His kingdom was divided between his nephew and the chieftain of another branch of Hsiung-nu, called the Chieh tribe. The Chieh, second of the "Five Hu," presently usurped the whole territory, but their king was in his turn driven from the throne by a Chinese general who during a short-lived reign instituted so thorough a racial purge that the power of the Hsiung-nu in China was weakened once and for all.

Southwest of the Chinese borders, in part of the territory we now call Ch'ing-hai, Ssuch'uan, and Tibet, lay the home of the Ch'iang tribe, third of the "Five Hu." They claimed to be descended from a very ancient western tribe, the San-miao, who were said to have battled with the semi-mythical Chinese Emperor Shun in the beginning of Chinese history. During the Chou period they were on good terms with the Chinese, for their chieftain had shot a terrible white tiger that had molested one of the Chou States. In gratitude, the reigning duke of that State (the Ch'in) made the somewhat curious vow that "if the people of Ch'in do any harm to the people of Ch'iang, they shall recompense their victim with a pair of yellow dragons, but if the Ch'iang do any harm to the Ch'in, they will be fined only a cup of clean wine."

During the subsequent Han period, relations between the two were at first disturbed by Hsiung-nu intervention in the Northwest, but later the armed forces of Han re-established Chinese domination in that area, and trade was briskly plied between the Ch'iang tribe and

the Han Empire. When the latter fell, and civil wars broke out, the
Ch'iang, in common with the other bordering tribes, poured over into
Chinese territory.

A branch of this Ch'iang tribe, known as the "Ti," and described
by Chinese historians as the fourth of the "Five Hu," set up a kingdom in the Northwest about the year 351. The first ancestor of these
invaders, so the legend told, had grown an enormous rush plant in
his pond, fifty feet tall, and with joints like a giant bamboo. This was
said to be an auspicious sign, and he gave his family forthwith the
name of "Rush." Whether the giant rush or their own strong arms
stood them now in good stead, cannot be revealed, but at all events the
kingdom they founded in North China, and which they called Ch'in,
gradually spread north, south, and east, until in 376 the "Rush" tribe
claimed to hold sway over "seventy per cent of all the lands under
Heaven!" This grandiose boast may be interpreted to mean that they
governed more than half of China and its border States. It is on
record that sixty-two of the States to the East and in the "Western
Regions" sent envoys to the Ch'in Court to present gifts and declare
their allegiance. Eventually the Ch'in ruler was tempted to conquer
the rest of China and to pit his strength against the Emperor of East
Tsin, the Chinese dynasty with its capital at Nanking.

The soldiers were massed and set in motion for the great enterprise
—"from a thousand miles away the banners could be seen and the
roll of drums heard as the huge army began to march." The two
armies met, and after a preliminary skirmish, struck camp for the
night on the banks of the River Fei. In the evening, the "Rush" King
climbed a small hill to survey the enemy's tents and try to judge the
number of the opposing force. Deceived by distance and the evening
mists, he mistook the indistinct forms of waving trees and grasses for
men, and was disheartened at the apparent number. As dawn broke
next day, battle was joined, but the "Rush" leaders had no spirit for
the encounter, and when early in the fighting the commander-in-chief
was accidentally thrown from his horse and killed, the King wheeled
round and fled from the field. Thereupon panic and confusion filled
the army; it broke up and retreated in the utmost disorder. It is said
that the soldiers' terror was so great that "the whistling wind, the cry
of cranes from the clouds, and the murmuring of grass and trees"
seemed to be the shouts of their pursuers. In this disastrous retreat
thousands were killed or died of exhaustion so that their bodies
"strewed the plain and piled up in the mountain valleys."

This battle, perhaps made decisive by one man's strange hallucination, marks a turning-point in Chinese history. Had the "Rush" armies been victorious, the whole of China would have been conquered by the Northern hordes, as she was in much later days by the Mongols and Manchus. The glorious page of the T'ang dynasty might never have been written. As it was, Chinese influence was now the more firmly established in the South, and the dangerous "Rush" tribe with its huge Northern Kingdom fell to pieces. A period of great confusion followed in the North: many short-lived States had an ephemeral existence, then disappeared forever. Emerging from them and surviving to become a strong power are the Hsien Pi hordes, who form the fifth of the "Five Hu" in Chinese history.

The Hsien Pi belonged to the Tungus tribe, one of the great tribes of Asia. They occupied the vast mountainous wastes of Eastern Siberia, to the north of the Hsiung-nu domain. In the Han dynasty, which was the heyday of the Hsiung-nu, the Hsien Pi were subject to them, but when eventually the Hsiung-nu Kingdom was split into North and South by the forces of Han, and lost much of its power and independence, the Hsien Pi transferred their allegiance to the Han Empire. The Chinese Emperors then employed them to defend their northeastern frontiers in exchange for a large annual subsidy. When the Hsiung-nu were finally driven out of their eastern homes in the third century, and retreated across Central Asia, their old neighbors, the Hsien Pi, moved into the lands they had thus abandoned, and the tribe grew exceedingly strong.

The first family of Hsien Pi to settle south of the Great Wall and to found a dynasty on Chinese soil was given the name of "Mu Yung." Taking advantage of the declining Chinese influence in the North, they established themselves in the Northeast, in the district which is now Peking. The fashionable headdress of the ladies in those parts was a hat stuck over with artificial flowers, the flowers being attached by little coils of silver wire. As the lady walked, her little flowers would bob and dance, and so the headdress had the name of "Pu-yao" —"Dancing with Every Step." Now the Hsien Pi intruders were fascinated by this fashion, and the ladies lost no time in adopting it. Their fellow tribesmen nicknamed them the "Pu Yaos," and by a mispronunciation of the Chinese this was later modified to "Mu Yung." And so this whole branch of the Hsien Pi tribe goes down in history as the Mu Yung! They grew powerful, and established many kingdoms in North China after the downfall of the "Rush" tribe.

The "Dancing with Every Step" Hsien Pi, together with all the States and kingdoms that had been set up in the North, were gradu-

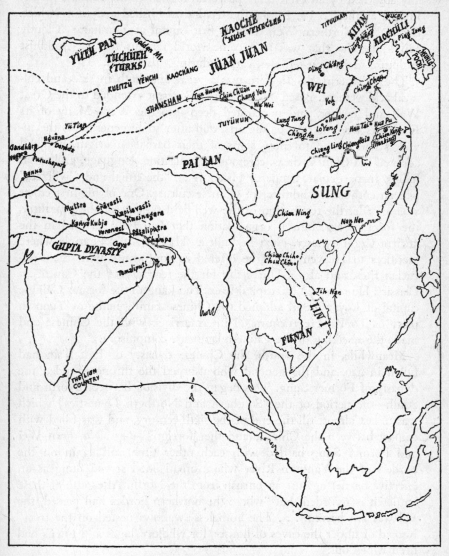

The "Six Dynasties" Period (*cir.* A.D. 439)

ally absorbed by an even more powerful branch of the Hsien Pi tribe, known as the To Pa. In 386 the To Pa established a dynasty which they called Northern Wei, with its first capital at Yun-kang "Cloudy Hill"—the city that was to become world famous for the Buddhist sculpture in its cave-temples, carved during this period.

The Northern Wei Empire was a great one, both in size and cultural achievement. Based on the Yellow River, it extended to the Great Wall and farther, and penetrated deep into the West. Many of its Emperors were patrons of the arts, and after some generations the invaders had ceased to show signs of their barbarian origin, but had adopted the Chinese dress, ceremonies, education, language, and social habits. In particular, Emperor Hsiao Wen, "the Filial and Civilized," was an enthusiastic admirer of Chinese culture. One of his first edicts was to order the restoration of the well-field system for the peasantry, the form of agricultural organization that had been devised in the ancient Chou dynasty. Next he built a "Hall of Light" temple where sacrifices to Heaven might be offered in conformity with the Confucian rites, and also a University for the teaching of the Confucian Classics. He removed the capital from Yun-kang to the former Chinese capital of Loyang, and adopted the Chinese family name of Yuan in place of To Pa. He encouraged intermarriage with the Chinese and made the speaking of the Chinese language compulsory.

Meanwhile, in the South, the Chinese dynasty of East Tsin had fallen in 420, and the general who usurped the throne founded the dynasty of Former Sung. This began the division between North and South—the period of the "Southern and Northern Dynasties" which was to last almost till the end of the sixth century, and was filled with conflict between the Chinese and the "foreign" rulers. Northern Wei and Former Sung battled with each other time and again on the borders of the Yangtzu River whose broad flood served Sung as an effective barrier against an onrush from the North. After one of these battles it is recorded that "where the northern hordes had passed, the soil was left barren. . . . The homeless swallows nested on the trees" instead of under the eaves of houses, for whole villages and towns had been wiped out.

It seems that the Sung Emperors were not strong enough to withstand these tireless attacks. In 479, after less than sixty years of existence, the dynasty fell; a military leader seized the throne, and founded a dynasty of Ch'i. The struggle continued, and Ch'i disappeared from history even more abruptly than Sung. In 502 the self-appointed Emperor's successor abdicated and presented his throne to one of his able generals. The new dynasty took the title of Liang, the first Emperor of which was that famous Liang Wu Ti, "the Brave Monarch," renowned for his devotion to Buddhism.

Wu Ti's devoutness grew with the years, and he made repeated attempts to abdicate and enter a monastery: he was held upon the throne only by the earnest pleadings of his ministers. At the same time, in the "foreign" empire of Northern Wei, Buddhism also enjoyed royal patronage. Emperor Hsuan Wu "the Shining and Brave" would preach Gautama's doctrines in the temple as if he were an abbot, while his successor sent envoys to India for copies of the Buddhist scriptures. And still Buddhism, one of whose great teachings is mercy and compassion, by no means hindered the pious Emperors of North and South from waging murderous wars against each other.

As the sixth century proceeded, the lives of the royal families both North and South grew increasingly troubled. In the North, the Wei Emperor had been deposed in the year 529, and for six unhappy years the great Wei Empire was broken by civil war. Eventually it was divided into West Wei with its capital at Ch'ang-an, and East Wei with its capital at Loyang. Still there was no peace. East Wei and West Wei fought each other continuously until in 550 a general of the former usurped the throne and established yet another dynasty, Northern Ch'i. Six years later the Prime Minister of West Wei also succeeded in deposing his sovereign and in founding a dynasty which he called Chou. In 557 he achieved the conquest of his eastern neighbor and enemy, Northern Ch'i, and thus united the whole of North China once more.

In the South, the Liang dynasty had been succeeded in 557 by the Ch'en, the last of the short-lived "Six Dynasties." After some thirty years of uneasy reign, it was vanquished by a minister of Northern Chou who achieved at last the reunification of the Chinese Empire in 589. The royal House which was founded on so many and such great ruins was the dynasty of Sui, forerunner of the famous and glorious T'ang.

These centuries of wars between the people of China and the foreign tribes, between neighboring States, and between sovereigns and ministers, thrust a deep vein of pessimism—and also of anarchy—into the intellectual life of the times. Confucianism, in its origins an energetic and virile ethical system, now grew formal and lifeless. It was upheld by the Court and the officials, who found its ceremony and ritual a convenient mask for many an act of disloyalty, usurpation, and misgovernment. For this reason it was shunned by the true scholars and thinkers, many of whom banded themselves together into coteries of somewhat cynical free-thinkers. They despised ritual; they extolled wine, Nature, and poetry; they condemned restraint; they declined to sully their speech with politics or current affairs and earned the name of "the School of Pure Speech." The most famous group of poets and philosophers was the "Seven Sages of the Bamboo Grove," whose leader, Yuan Chi, attacked with both venom and humor the Confucianists and politicians. So powerful was his intellect and so wide his influence that he was feared rather than persecuted by the Court. One of the usurping Emperors even tried to win his support by an offer of marriage into the Royal Family. Yuan Chi's only response was to get so drunk for ten days in succession that the imperial go-betweens were forced to abandon the project! The following extract from one of his essays exemplifies both his attitude to life and his manner as a writer.

"A man wrote a letter to a Philosopher [1] in which he declared, 'There is no one in this world of more worth than your perfect gentleman, who dresses with propriety, looks about him with propriety, talks and behaves with propriety. . . .' The Philosopher heaved a deep sigh and replied to the man from his lofty and remote seat, 'Have you ever heard of the lice that live in trousers? The louse takes sanctuary in the depths of the seams, and makes a home for itself in ragged cotton, thinking itself wonderfully lucky. When it takes a walk, it carefully keeps to the edge of the seam. When it moves about, it never ventures beyond the confines of the seat and believes it is behaving with proper etiquette. When it is hungry it feeds on flesh, and is confident it can never starve. But when the trousers are taken to be boiled and pressed, the towns and cities of the lice are scorched and destroyed. It dies with all its tribe in the trousers, unable to escape! Is not your "perfect gentleman" who confines himself to the visible world like the lice who would live forever in the trousers?'" The author then goes on to explain the nature of the true Philosopher, to whose fullness of spiritual and intellectual life all these "Free-thinkers" were aspiring. "We Philosophers," says the imaginary figure, "have a life in common with the Creator, and its duration is as the duration of heaven and earth. We live at ease and are made perfect according to a natural Law. We are constantly changing and never confine ourselves to a definite form of life. Earth and sky bound the finite world, but their illumination shines beyond them. The constancy and solidity of the Universe is beyond the understanding of common man!"

[1] In this, as in the following quotation, the Chinese term means literally "Great Man and Teacher."

Another writer of this group describes his particular vision of the ideal Philosopher in less transcendent terms than Yuan Chi, and the conceptions are very typical of the times. They combine the mystical Nature philosophy of Laotzu and his followers with a cynical and slyly humorous note. "The Philosopher," he writes, "treats the life of earth and sky as a single day, and a thousand decades as a single moment. Sun and moon are his door and window, and all the points of the compass make his courtyards and paths. He moves about without leaving the trace of a wheel. He lives without building. He makes the sky his tent and the earth his mat and he wanders at will. When he rests he clutches wine-cups and vessels, and when he moves on he bears them with him. He loves wine—that is all he knows.

"An aristocratic youth and a gentleman heard about him and began to rail against him. They turned up their sleeves and unbuttoned their jackets (as if preparing to fight); they glared at him furiously, gnashed their teeth, and endeavored to tell him what was propriety and what not. All the time the Philosopher was holding his wine jar in both hands, putting the cup to his lips, savoring the liquor, blowing his beard out of the way, and sitting at ease, his legs wide apart. He made cakes of yeast his pillow, and malt dregs his sheet. Not a thought, not a worry disturbed him. He sank into bliss. He became unconscious with drink. Presently he awoke. He listened attentively but not even thunder reached his ears. He gazed around keenly but not even the great T'ai mountain had any shape for him. He felt neither the cold of winter nor the heat of summer, neither was he enslaved by profit or desire. He looked on all the manifold objects in the world as if on troubled duckweeds, floating on the quivering ripples of the rivers and sea. (Under the transmuting influence of his vision), the aristocratic youth and the gentleman simply disappeared."

It is interesting to notice how the thought of these writers has been permeated not only by the Nature mysticism of Laotzu and Chuang-tzu, but also the Nihilism and contempt for the world which are especially associated with the Buddhist faith. It is also very characteristic of the writings in this period that the freedom from worldly cares and desires towards which the Buddhists strove was to be attained, not by prayer and meditation, but by unlimited wine-bibbing amid the beauties of mountain and stream, far from the dust and intrigue of the cities!

The persecution of these "Free-thinkers" by the orthodox Confucianist officials, and the general wretchedness of the times with their needless slaughter, their lack of any true morality, their instability in human affairs, drove writers to skepticism. "Death is yours," writes one of the most talented anonymous philosophers of the Six Dynasties,[1] "whether you live for ten years or a hundred years, whether you are a virtuous man or a sage, a notorious rascal or a fool. Behave as perfectly as Yao and Shun all your life, you still become a rotting carcass when you die. Live as evilly as Chieh and Shou-Hsin, and you still become no more than a rotting carcass afterwards. Everyone on earth will become a rotting carcass in the days to come, so what is the difference between one man and another?"

As the turbulent days of the Six Dynasties passed, and Chinese history emerged into sunshine and fruitfulness, the pessimistic skeptical note in literature was replaced by one of affirmation, and if melancholy remained, it was a milder, more sentimental kind. But from those dark days a few writers and thinkers stand out in the unmistakable garments of immortality. Greatest of all, perhaps, is the poet T'ao Ch'ien, whose poetic essay on "The Peach-blossom Fountain" is among the best-known works in Chinese literature. "In the T'ai Yuan period of Tsin," it begins, "a man from Wu-ling, who was a fisherman by calling, rowed one day along the bank of a stream. He quite forgot how far he had wandered when he found himself amid a forest of peach-blossom. For a hundred yards on both sides of the stream there was no other tree to be seen but peach. The grass was deliciously fresh: petals showered down from the branches. The fisherman experienced a strange sensation, and rowed on to make for the other end of the forest. The cutting through the forest brought him to the stream's source. Before him rose a hill, in which he noticed a crack, with a ray of light stealing through it. The fisherman fastened up his boat and began to walk in through the crack. At first, it was only wide enough to allow one man to pass. After he had advanced a few yards, a whole world opened before him.

"The scene extended to a great distance. Cottages and homesteads lay spread before his eyes. There were fertile fields, ample ponds, mulberry trees and bamboo groves. Foot-paths through the fields led in all directions. The sounds of cock-crowing and the barking of dogs could be heard on every side. Men and women were dressed and worked just like people in the outside world. The old men with their yellowing hair, and the children with their plaited tufts falling from their foreheads, looked perfectly happy in each other's company.

"The people showed astonishment at the sight of the fisherman, and

---

[1] This is ascribed to the writer Yang Chu of the "Warring States," but according to modern scholars it actually belongs to the "Six Dynasties" period.

demanded to know where he had come from. He told them, and some of them invited him to their homes where he was entertained with wine and chicken. When all the villagers heard the news, they came and paid their respects to the fisherman. They told him that their ancestors had escaped from the troubled world at the end of the Ch'in dynasty, to this uninhabited land. They had never tried to leave, and so they had lost contact with the outer world.

"Then they asked the fisherman what the world was like now. They knew nothing about the Han dynasty, not to mention Wei and Tsin. The fisherman described everything, and they were deeply shocked at all the changes. He was invited to other families and entertained with wine and meat. After several days, he asked that he might return home, and the people made him promise to tell his experience to no one.

"When he emerged from the mountain, he found his boat and returned the way he had come. As he went, he marked the roads. As soon as he reached his home town, he went to the magistrate and told him about his adventures. The magistrate, Liu Hsin, sent an official to find the spot, but no one could ever find it again."

This simply but beautifully told story is not only a subtle indictment of the times in which the poet lived; it is an imaginative picture of the "world remote from the world" which the poets and philosophers tried to create for themselves in their mountain retreats, and where they managed to forget or ignore the slaughter and corruption going on around them.

In the whole Six Dynasties period, there was no poet to compare in stature with T'ao Ch'ien, but there were, nevertheless, some interesting literary developments. The Northern tribesmen who invaded North China and settled there brought with them no highly developed culture, but they breathed a fresh, young, and wild spirit into Chinese forms that were already growing conventional. These people were mostly nomads, who had endured hard lives in the deserts of Mongolia and Eastern Siberia. Their warlike spirit infused new blood into Chinese literature, which now divided into Northern and Southern Schools, corresponding with the political division of Northern and Southern dynasties. While the poets of the South, living in a mild and fruitful climate, amid the exquisite scenery of towns like Suchou and Hangchou (a Chinese saying runs, "Paradise above; Su and Hang below!"), chose, on the whole, to write pure love songs—descriptions of pretty girls gathering lotus seeds on flowery lakes and so on—the northerners preferred such themes as warriors fighting on horseback, battle tales, and descriptions of desolate scenery in the wind-swept barren plains. This vigorous strain was not lost when China was once more united under a Chinese Emperor. It survived into the T'ang dynasty and was taken up by some of that era's most brilliant poets.

While the penetration of the Chinese civilization by those barbarian tribes sent a fresh strain into the native arts, it also provoked a reaction of quite another sort—the rise of a Chinese aristocracy, or as Chinese historians call it, "The Honorable Families." The feudal nobility of Chou times had disappeared in the political evolution of later periods, and successive attempts to revive it artificially had failed. Now it seemed that changed historical conditions favored the growth of a new type.

In the "Three Kingdoms" period immediately preceding the "Six Dynasties," a system of official promotion had been evolved which was maintained for nearly three hundred and fifty years, until the beginning of the Sui dynasty. Men of ability were to be selected from every part of the country by local officials, called "the Great Balancer" or "the Small Balancer," classified into nine grades, and on the bases of these, promoted to government positions.

In practice, however, this system merely resulted in the promotion of influential families. Relatives and friends of the "Balancer," together with those families which, profiting by the current political unrest, had acquired large estates, found themselves in the upper grades, while scholars of humble origin, whatever their talents, could never rise above the lower ranks. Gradually, power passed from the central government into the hands of the new aristocracy.

A spirit of exclusiveness was born. Members of the "Honorable Families" held themselves strictly aloof from the rest of the population, and intermarried within such narrow limits that an imperial prohibition had eventually to be issued early in the T'ang dynasty. And it was just this tendency that the entry of foreign tribes into North China naturally accentuated. Although the newcomers ruled over a great part of the Chinese terrain, and in time became cultured and "civilized," the somewhat upstart aristocracy of the South continued to regard them as barbarians. The fact that marriages were constantly being contracted between these "barbarians" and the Chinese caused the "Honorable Families" to guard their blue blood even more jealously, and this condition did not change until the system of appointment by official examination was introduced in the T'ang dynasty. The prestige of the "Honorable Families" then declined gradually, and personal merit became the proper key to advancement.

XI. BUDDHISM IN CHINA

CONFUCIANISM GAVE THE CHINESE a good pattern for living, but it did not satisfy the common human craving for worship. Confucius, as we know, expressly refused to speak of a spiritual world. "Until you have learned how to serve men, how can you serve the spirits?" he asked one of his students, and "While you are still ignorant about life, how can you understand anything of death?" Buddhism, a very ancient and a very noble religion, originating in India, and introduced to China sometime during the Han dynasty, offered a response to that craving for spiritual food.

In the succeeding periods of Chinese history, the power of Buddhism waxed and waned, responding both to the people's needs—for in times of social unrest they sought relief for their suffering in its doctrines—and also to imperial patronage or persecution. Gradually, although it was not a native religion, the Chinese so modified it by their own cultural traditions and modes of thought that it assumed a kind of Chinese dress, and eventually claimed more adherents in the land of its adoption than in the land of its birth.

Buddhism in its earliest form was a very practical faith. It was not, like Christianity, an ethical religion, concerned with the origins of good and evil, with sin and redemption: it centered round the problem of human suffering. Its founder Gautama Buddha (?—about 480 B.C.?), an Indian prince, so moved by all the forms of human misery with which he saw the world to be filled that he renounced his possessions and wandered among men as a beggar, came at last to believe that the prime cause of suffering is desire. He preached, therefore, a renouncement of the world, in order to rid oneself of suffering. If a man can but reach that state of mind in which wealth, food, comfortable living, fame, beauty, love no longer seem desirable, then he will find rest for his soul and deliverance from all the ills this flesh is heir to. This state of mind the Buddhists called "Nirvana." To attain "Nirvana" was like entering, in the Christian faith, the Kingdom of God on earth.

In the perfect quietness and peace of Nirvana, the faithful are made partakers of the Great Wisdom, and share the omniscience of Buddha himself. No worldly troubles will disturb them, for they know all worldly phenomena are passing shadows. One of the great teachers of Buddhism in China uses the golden image of a lion to express the relation of the Buddhist believer to the world. He compares the mind of man to the golden *substance,* and the appearance of things as they are reflected in the mind's eye he compares with the lion *form* into which the metal has been wrought. When the image is destroyed, the lion form disappears, but the gold substance is unaltered. For the time being, however, the existence of the lion image is true, but it has no permanency. It is made *with* the gold, but the latter could equally well form other objects such as a tiger or a cat, or it could simply remain unaltered, as a lump of gold. It is only *"Yuan"* ("Chance") that gives birth to one thing or another, and while the mind recognizes the existence of phenomena, there is no other relation between them. The mind is constant; the objects and affairs of the world have a temporary existence and then pass into nothingness.

A man, therefore, who has attained the Great Wisdom makes his mind like a bright mirror. Worldly phenomena appear in it simultaneously and successively, but the mirror remains constant with its brightness (its wisdom) for all time. It is neither bewildered by the presence of numerous things, nor does it retain any impression of them after they are gone. To choose another image, the man of Great Wisdom makes his mind like the vast surface of the sea. Over it, the waves rise here and there, but the general level is everywhere constant.

Those fortunate beings who reach this state of grace, and are no longer troubled by the world, are possessed not only of the Great Wisdom of Buddha, but also of his Great Mercy. He was the All-Compassionate as well as the All-Wise. Those who had become his representatives on earth were required to teach and deliver their fellow-sufferers from the entanglement of worldly troubles. As he was the Enlightened One, so must they offer enlightenment to suffering humanity.

When and how Buddhism was first introduced to China from India are not certain, though there are many stories and theories. We can, however, affirm that it arrived very early in the Christian era. We also know that it had penetrated Central Asia long before China received it, and many imagine that hints and traces filtered through from the border tribes many years before Chinese envoys traveled to India for the Scriptures or Indian monks arrived at Ch'ang-an.

As far back as 121 B.C., for instance, in the reign of Emperor Wu "the Brave" of the Han dynasty, a certain general, leading his victorious army in pursuit of the Hsiung-nu tribesmen, and tracking them deep into the desert of Turkestan, came upon various huge golden images, worshiped by these barbarians, many of which he carried back to the Han capital as booty. The images were mostly ten feet high, and the Emperor took a fancy to these "tall men," as he thought they were nearer Heaven. He had them set up in the palace, where incense was burned before them. He put golden plates in their hands to catch the sweet dew from Heaven, by drinking which, His Majesty hoped to win eternal life. Some historians think that they were Buddhist images, the first to appear in China.

Nearly two hundred years later, in A.D. 65, we read of the famous dream that came to Emperor Ming "the Bright" of the Later Han period. He dreamed of a golden man from whose body flowed streams of light, and who seemed to float about the palace hall. The Emperor consulted his ministers, who assured him that he had seen the Buddha. Forthwith he sent a delegation to the "Western Regions" to bring back the teachings of Buddha. Some forty-two chapters of Buddhist sacred writings and a portrait of Sakyamuni were obtained, carried to the capital on a white horse, and honorably lodged in one of the palace buildings. Some Indian monks who had accompanied them also lived there and translated the texts into Chinese. A Buddhist monastery was consecrated in their honor, and "The White Horse Monastery" was thus the first to be established in China.

After the fall of the Han dynasty, when China was divided into three Kingdoms, Buddhism first became an authorized religion. During the reign of Emperor Fei who governed Wei Kingdom—in the Yellow River valley (A.D. 240–253)—an Indian monk came to Court bringing Chinese translations of Buddhist law. By imperial edict, Chinese monks were now compelled to conform with it; novices, besides shaving off their hair and learning to chant the Buddhist scriptures, must pass through certain stringent tests and ceremonies. A Chinese pupil of this same Indian monk, named Chu Shih-hsing, traveled as far as Chinese Turkestan, where Buddhism was already flourishing, and brought back many ancient editions of Buddhist texts.

The period of the Six Dynasties, which followed that of the Three Kingdoms, saw a great propagation of the Buddhist creed throughout China. Some of the Emperors became monks, and the whole of public life was so permeated with Buddhist thought that China then might almost have been called Buddhist in the same sense as Europe was Christian. It was perhaps the most troubled period in Chinese history. The mighty Han Empire with its limbs stretching far into the West, its trade routes penetrating the whole Continent of Asia, had utterly decayed. Internal unity fell apart; independent States rose up, each striving for mastery, so that futile warfare replaced social development. At the same time relations with Central and Western Asia were broken off, and China, thrown back upon her own resources, suffered economic dislocation with all the attendant miseries of famines and burdensome taxation. It is not surprising, therefore, that the people tried to find relief in abstract thought. The Nihilism of the Buddhist faith attracted them—its rejection of the world. It was at this time that the doctrine of the Pure Land developed—a Heaven to which the souls of the faithful would be transported after death. The importance of attaining Nirvana while on earth diminished. Kwan Yin, the Goddess of Mercy, corresponding in many ways to the Blessed Virgin in the Catholic faith, became the object of popular supplication.[1] Buddhism, in fact, took on a form which appealed to the masses as well as to pious scholars, and was able to give them comfort.

From time to time, the jealousy of the Taoists or the malignance of evil rulers brought about severe persecutions. The first of these took place in the reign of T'ai Wu "the Great Brave One," Emperor of Northern Wei dynasty (424–451). Under the influence of a Taoist minister, T'ai Wu issued an edict commanding that "all gods from 'the foreign land' should be wiped out, and no trace left. Anyone who dared to worship these gods or build images of bronze or clay to them should be put to death with all his family. All pictures of Buddha and all Buddhist texts must be destroyed or burned. All monks, young or old, were to be buried alive." We do not know what atrocities followed this brutal proclamation, but it cannot have been carried out literally, and certainly it was unable to stamp out Buddhism in Wei. About fifty years later, when the prohibition had been raised, Buddhist monks flocked into the new capital of Loyang so that from every part of the city was heard the sound of their chants. "A full third of the private houses were converted into temples. Not a street was without them: they crowded within the city walls and were even found adjoining the market, near the butchers and wine shops. . . . Chanting in Sanscrit and sounds of slaughter echoed all along the eaves. Round the shrines of the holy image floated the smell of meat, and speculation was drenched in passion. Dissenters mingled with the true believers so that it was impossible to distinguish them." Such was the con-

[1] Kwan Yin was originally a male deity, attendant upon Buddha. Later, in folk-lore, the figure appeared as a woman, having those gentle and compassionate female qualities which appeal to the poor and humble.

demnation of a Wei officer of the time, and we learn from other official documents that during the Northern Wei period the number of monks and nuns in that State amounted at one time to two million, and that there were at least thirty thousand temples.

During this period of internal disruption, when there was a major division between North and South China, Buddhism, which enjoyed the patronage of both Northern and Southern dynasties, followed the political trend and split into two schools, each with its characteristic forms. Almost contemporaneously with the growth of Buddhism in Northern Wei, a Southern dynasty called Liang opened its arms to the religion from the "foreign land." Emperor Wu "the Brave" of Liang (502–549) worshiped devoutly in the Buddhist temples, studied the sacred texts, and wrote commentaries upon them. In his personal life he imitated the asceticism of Sakyamuni himself, the prince who chose to live as a beggar. He took only one meal a day, and never touched meat or garlic. Because the Buddhists abhor the killing of any living thing, Emperor Wu forbade the customary offering of animals at the sacrifices. Instead, the figures of animals were formed out of flour and offered to the gods! He even prohibited the embroidering of human figures and animals upon silks and brocades, as such an act seemed to destroy life. When criminals were doomed to death, the compassionate Emperor would have mercy on them, and with tears of pity set them free. Harboring no evil intentions against any man, he naturally failed to make any military preparations, and this weakness was a temptation to his less pious enemies.

A treacherous general, Hou Ching, suggested to the Emperor then ruling in the North that he should kidnap Emperor Wu and, after carrying him to the Northern capital, install him as abbot of the Buddhist Temple of Peace. All his territory might then be annexed. After his first attack on Liang, the general feigned surrender, and the merciful Wu pardoned him and set him free. The Northern general then mustered his men, and when Liang was entirely off its guard, attacked the capital and took the Emperor prisoner. An abbot's hat would doubtless have made Wu happier than a temporal crown, but his captors deprived him even of this comfort. Broken-hearted and ill, he died in captivity.

It was during the reign of the devout Wu that the famous Indian monk Bodhidharma (in Chinese Ta-mo) arrived in China from India and spread the Buddhist doctrine of meditation. As a result of his teaching, the *Ch'an* ("Meditation") School of Buddhism was later founded and claimed many adherents. It centers round the belief that

Enlightenment may be achieved through stillness and contemplation rather than by a study of the scriptures, the worship of images, or the performance of elaborate ritual. Bodhidharma wandered over a great part of China, and did much to pave the way for the rapprochement of Northern and Southern schools.

Towards the close of this troubled period, there were many forces working towards unification, and among them may certainly be ranked the wide acceptance of Buddhism by every form and class of society: by the people of North and South, by the imperial family and the humble peasantry, by the intellectuals and the illiterate. Moreover, it tended to disgust people with the sordid internecine strife with which the past two hundred years had been filled. It contributed to that fusion of political currents which culminated in the glorious T'ang dynasty.

In the three hundred years of T'ang rule, China enjoyed a fullness of creative and intellectual life unparalleled in her history, before or since. It is not surprising that Buddhism too flourished as never before, despite the bitter attacks made upon it by Confucian scholars. This was the time of the great translations of Buddhist texts from Sanscrit; of the adaptation of the doctrines to the Chinese mentality; of the famous pilgrimage to India of the Buddhist monk Hsuan-chuang. It was the time when Buddhist art rose to its highest perfection, particularly in the realm of sculpture, lovely examples of which, together with a few from earlier dynasties, still survive and bear witness to a grave and deep spirituality that later periods could never emulate.

The journeys of Hsuan-chuang must have greatly advanced the faith, for he is said to have brought back more than six hundred and fifty texts, a part of which he and his pupils faithfully translated into Chinese, producing more than a thousand volumes of the sacred word. This intrepid and pious pilgrim set out from Ch'ang-an in the year A.D. 629 and plunged alone into the Gobi Desert, known to the Chinese as *Liu-Sha*—"the River of Sand." He proceeded painfully through the wastes of Central Asia, over mountains and glaciers, past Tashkand and Samarkand, then inhabited by fire-worshipers, until he reached the Oxus valley and passed into India.

He traveled much in that vast country, visiting many famous sites of Buddhist and ancient Indian history, including Sravasti, Kapilavastu, and Nalanda. At the last-named, the most renowned monastery and college in India had been set up, adorned by the gifts of successive kings. Hsuan-chuang remained there for nearly two years, mastering Sanscrit and the Buddhist philosophy. Fifteen years after the start of his lonely pilgrimage, he returned through the desert, carrying with him a great collection of books, precious images, and relics. In April 645, he was received at the Chinese capital, with both imperial and public acclamation.

This bold expedition and the reports, true and imaginary, of the adventures he encountered, provided meat for Chinese ballad-mongers and street story-tellers, as did the monsters and strange events in Shakespearean England.

In later years, these scraps of verse and story were collected together by a talented writer, and Hsuan-chuang comes down to posterity as the hero of a witty but good-natured and exceedingly popular tale. He is described as being companioned in the hazardous journey by three pupils—a converted monkey,[1] a pig, and a water monster of miraculous powers. In all his ten lives, so the author says (the Buddhists believe in transmigration), he had never touched a woman or tasted meat, and now the monsters, bugbears, and goblins, whose several homes were the mountains, rivers, and forests, sought to ensnare him, as he passed through their domains, into either of these sins, or to swallow him up. Anyone who succeeded would be rewarded with immortality. Eighty-one cunningly devised temptations and dangerous battles are described, and from each the faithful monk emerges unsullied and unhurt through the brave and loyal conduct of his companions, and even more through his own unshakable faith in Buddha. At last he reaches the Western Heaven, pays homage to Sakyamuni, the Great and Wise God, and returns to his Emperor, laden with the sacred texts.

By now, Buddhism was far from being a uniform religion. Besides the split into Northern and Southern schools which had occurred in the Six Dynasties period, and had never been entirely healed, the T'ang period produced a medley of sects all at variance with each other. Nor were persecutions unknown, notably at the close of the dynasty when yet another Emperor Wu issued an edict in 845 calling in all the bronze and copper images to be melted down, and ordering the wholesale destruction of temples and monasteries. However, it was a period of such intellectual animation, such experiment and exploration, that this religious wrangling did not result in skepticism. Buddhism only weakened and lost hold on popular imagination when China herself declined and the stream of intellectual life grew sluggish.

In the Sung dynasty, which followed the T'ang, Buddhism per-

---

[1] He apparently corresponds to Hanuman, the Monkey God, in the great Indian classical epic, "Ramayana."

meated the intellectual life perhaps more deeply and thoroughly than at any other time. It was a period of sophisticated thought, of metaphysics, of philosophical poets and poetic philosophers. Different branches of thought mingled with each other. Both Buddhism in its Chinese form, and Taoism, acted upon Confucianism and produced a highly characteristic form of religion—neo-Confucianism. It was the old moral system of Confucius overlaid with philosophic and religious conceptions, and gave rise to yet more schools and cults.

At the end of this dynasty, the Mongols poured in from the Northwest and set up a foreign dynasty in China, which they called the Yuan (1277-1367). The old order of society was entirely changed, and for a time at least the conquerors tried to impose their own manners and customs upon the Chinese. As the Mongols were mainly followers of the Lama religion, which was a branch of Buddhism, the Chinese Buddhists enjoyed imperial favor. In the new gradations of society they were ranked third, only one degree below the members of the Emperor's family. Confucianists, on the other hand, since they followed purely Chinese beliefs, were degraded to the ninth rank, one degree above the beggars! In the reign of the great Kublai Khan, the magnificent and victorious Mongol Emperor, over a hundred Buddhist ceremonies were performed by the Emperor every year, costing the imperial treasuries thousands of pounds of flour, vegetable oils, cake fillings, and honey.

However, although the temples and monasteries flourished, and monks enjoyed a welcome freedom from persecution, the ethical and spiritual side of the religion declined. No great Buddhist thinkers or teachers appeared. It may even be said that the Yuan dynasty started a gradual decay in the Buddhist faith in China from which it has never recovered. Just as the Sung dynasty marked the end of the old China and the beginnings of a new Empire, weak and decadent at first, but now at last regaining strength, so did the same period mark the end of Chinese Buddhism as a living religion. At the present day, innumerable monasteries and temples are to be found scattered over the country, some belonging to a Buddhist organization, others to individual monks, who pass on the property to their pupils as they would to their sons. Many of them are set in the mountains amidst beautiful scenery, especially those known as "Ts'ung Lin"—"Forest Temples"—and which serve as inns and resting houses for both secular travelers and pilgrim monks. Not a few Buddhist establishments have been turned into village schools, and the chant of small voices reciting by heart has replaced the deep tones of the monks chanting the sutras. In very recent times, some are even transformed into barracks and billets for the Chinese soldiers in their fight for liberation. Devout, practicing Buddhists still exist, but they are rare, and among the young generation hardly any could be found.

Since its introduction to China at the beginning of the Christian era, until the present day, Buddhism has exercised an immeasurable influence upon Chinese life and action, upon philosophy, art, sculpture, literature and architecture. It has also undergone many and subtle changes of doctrine in conformity with Chinese conceptions of life. For instance, the Indian caste system naturally found its counterpart in the Indian form of Buddhism. Some men were considered so low that they were born without the disposition to attain the Great Wisdom. For all their striving, they could never become Buddhas. And again, the Indian Buddhists held that a man of inferior disposition would have to pass through many reincarnations, and endure many lifetimes of human suffering before reaching the freedom and peace of Nirvana, while a superior man could attain it in a single life. Such a conception was entirely alien to the Chinese, who regarded all men as potentially equal. "Any sort of person can become a Yao or a Shun" runs a saying of the philosopher Mencius. Yao and Shun were the Sage-Emperors of old who were perfectly good and wise and great. And indeed, Chinese history is full of peasants who became Emperors, and simple people who rose to high rank through their learning or unusual talents. Chinese Buddhists, therefore, held that any man could reach Buddhahood, and without passing through numerous lives. The Great Wisdom might sometimes be granted with the immediacy of an inspiration.

Nirvana, according to the Indian Buddhists, is a state of mind of permanent stillness. But to the Chinese, the highest virtue in the universe and in the human mind is permanent activity. "The movement of the heavenly bodies is constant," is an early saying recorded by Confucius in the "Book of Changes," "and the perfect man, learning from their example, seeks to improve himself without rest." Arriving at a compromise between Confucius and Buddha as the Indians interpreted him, the Chinese Buddhists formed the conception of "stillness which is in constant activity, and activity which is in constant stillness." The mind which is possessed of the Great Wisdom is like a mirror held up to the world. In itself the mirror remains still and unaffected by all the varied images that fall upon its surface, but these images, these forms and colors and movements, are unceasingly active in it.

Another interesting compromise was made over the nature of the Great Void. The Indian Buddhists held that in the understanding of those who have been made wise, who have freed themselves from Desire, the visible world is an illusion, a fiction of the imagination; it is unreal, empty, the Great Void. Now, the schools of Chinese philosophy existing before Buddhism took root in China were all in favor of realism. They postulated the existence of an objective world, co-existing with man's own subjective idea of it. Thus the Chinese converts to Buddhism accepted the teaching of Indian monks that the outer world was an "emptiness," a Void, but insisted that it had a kind of illusory substantiality. It was, in short, like the form of a human being which a stage magician produces "by magic." Such a being does not, of course, really exist, but it seems to walk and go through the actions of a real person; it can be seen by the audience, and for the time being it has a kind of existence. In this way, the Chinese clung to the "reality" of the world which, as people of common sense and with no appetite for mysteries, they cherished.

The influence of Buddhism upon Chinese painting and sculpture cannot be measured. The art of representing human form in sculpture, for instance, was introduced to China in the wake of Buddhism, and it is certain that some elements of Greek art traditions came with it after they had penetrated India. The Northern Wei period of the Six Dynasties produced the first, and in many ways the finest flower of Buddhist sculpture in China. The most famous figures are to be found cut into the rock face at Yun-kang "the Cloudy Hills," and Lung-men "the Dragon Gate," in the present provinces of Shansi and Honan. The Cloudy Hills are somewhat smooth and round in shape, and are strewn with huge rocks: figures which were carved there out of the face of the living rock were as much as sixty or seventy feet high. The Dragon Gate Hills are jagged and rough, with steep faces. Parts are honeycombed with small grottoes, one above the other, each with its group of Buddhist figures, mostly on a small scale. But great or small, the carving of these statues symbolizes a deep religious emotion—a desire to link the worship of Buddha with the most permanent of all natural forms—the rocks of earth itself. The finest examples of this period have a high æsthetic value, as if the sculptors' hands had been strengthened by the force of their belief, while from the expressions of the statues shines that passionless spiritual calm which is the very essence of Buddhism. T'ang and Sung sculptors added their carving to the Dragon Gate grottoes, most of which still survive, so that the hills present a somber pageant of Buddhist faith through the ages.

During the T'ang dynasty, Buddhist sculpture reached a high peak. Although the art of the Six Dynasties showed a devoutness, depth, and simple grandeur which later periods failed to recapture, æsthetically the T'ang carving was many degrees nearer perfection. At that time, Buddhist sculpture ceased to imitate the conventional Central Asia forms; and just as the Buddhist faith itself was adapted to conform with Chinese modes of thought, so did the sculpture begin to show a marked individuality. Naturalism replaced convention: the Buddha heads, instead of reflecting an impersonal, spiritual idea, a conception which Epstein has worked out in his great Biblical statues "Ecce Homo" and "Genesis," now became individual portraits. Buddha was represented as a living being.

There are still many lovely examples of Buddhist sculpture in the later periods of Chinese art, skillfully and artistically executed, but in spiritual feeling they did not approach the masterpieces of T'ang and Six Dynasties. The stage was being set for the introduction of a totally different culture—the art of Europe.

Upon the art of painting in China, the advent of Buddhism exercised an even more extensive influence, both in manner and methods. Fresco painting, for example, although an ancient Chinese form, received a great impetus from India, and was now employed purely for religious subjects. Stories from the life of Sakyamuni and illustrations of the Buddhist texts were painted round the temple walls, and from the Six Dynasties until the Sung dynasty this form employed the talents of many painters of genius. As far back as the third century A.D. a Chinese painter named Ts'ao Hsing, following the instructions of an Indian monk, used to depict Buddhist scenes on gauze five hundred feet long. It is told of that greatest of T'ang painters, Wu Tao-tzu, whose wild and powerful strokes were said to resemble storm and thunder, that he once painted a scene of hell on a temple wall with such terrifying realism that many butchers and fishmongers repented of their slaughter and changed their trade!

Portrait and figure painting also profited from the example of Buddhist art. It is doubtful whether any figures had been represented in Chinese painting before the arrival of these sacred pictures from India. The representation in Chinese painting of tiny human figures against a vast background of landscape is said to be of Buddhist inspiration: Ku K'ai-chih, the famous figure painter of the Six Dynasties, examples of whose work are to the present day in the possession of the British Museum, was in the first instance a painter of Buddhist frescoes.

Indian methods of painting, the choice of coloring, Indian images and symbols, undoubtedly found their way into Chinese art through Buddhism, but deeper and more important was the influence in feeling and spirit. Quietness, serenity, calm, peace, contemplation—these are characteristics in almost the whole field of Chinese painting, and they permeate especially that great glory of Chinese art, the schools of Landscape. It may justly be claimed that the Buddhist faith brought these elements not only into the limited domain of art, but into Chinese life itself. It taught people to endure hardships patiently, and even to grow unaware of them. It made them philosophical about disasters, and if it also made them too fatalistic and over-tolerant of bad forms of government, it gave them hope, without which it is hard for any man to go on living.

XII. THE SUI DYNASTY: EMPEROR YANG
AND THE GRAND CANAL

FOR NEARLY FOUR HUNDRED YEARS, China had been torn from north to south and from east to west by civil wars and the rival ambition of selfish rulers who cared nothing for the happiness of their people. The whole country was bankrupt, not only of wealth, but of peace and those spiritual riches which accompany it. The time had come when a kind of inner compulsion forced China towards unification and rest. This was accomplished by a prime minister of Chou, the last of the Northern dynasties, who having seized power from his own king, and in 581 made himself king of a new dynasty which he called Sui, gradually conquered all the surrounding petty kingdoms and brought the whole Chinese Empire under his sovereignty by 589. He was not in any way a great man, and he met an inglorious end, being murdered by his own son Yang "the Shady."

Emperor Yang, who now mounted the throne of all China, was eccentric and deplorably extravagant. He built vast palaces and ships, had the Grand Canal constructed, and organized imperial pageantry on a scale hitherto undreamed of. He undertook dubious military exploits, notably against Korea, spending huge sums for very minor successes. And he met the end he deserved. Extortionate taxes eventually raised the people against him, and a governor of one of the northern prefectures organized the rebellion. The "Shady" Emperor fled from his capital, and a year later was murdered by the furious mob. The energetic governor proclaimed himself Emperor in 618, and thus ushered in the great T'ang dynasty—a dynasty that was to rank with the Chou and the Han as one of the lofty peaks in the growth of Chinese civilization; that was to produce poets, artists, statesmen, and men of action almost without peer in the whole of Chinese history.

The Sui dynasty had thus lasted only thirty-six years. It seemed as if history had used it to clear away the debris of the past, and to prepare the way for the real Masters of China—the T'ang Emperors. It was also, in a limited way, a period of development. Although the

"Shady" Emperor only schemed for his own glory, he was, in fact, constructing instead of destroying; he built more than he fought. Moreover, the building of the Grand Canal was an event of immense commercial and cultural importance, for it linked the North and South through the centuries before railways were thought of, or roads constructed on any large scale. As an architectural achievement it almost parallels the building of the Great Wall. A record of its construction has been made by an unknown writer, possibly of the T'ang period, which brilliantly brings to life the splendor and tyranny of those times.

The writer relates that, at the beginning of the Emperor's reign, an ominous mist appeared over the southeast of the Empire. According to tradition this portended the existence of a rival to the throne in that district, and the danger could be averted only by the presence there of the Emperor himself.

As the news was being hurried to Court, the Emperor was enjoying a few hours' leisure in his "Magnolia Palace," while an imperial singing-girl sang to him "The Willow Song." On the wall facing him was a landscape painting of the beautiful Kuang-ling district of Southeast China. The Emperor was lost in admiration at the loveliness of the girl, the charm of her song, and the beauty of the landscape on the wall. He gazed with speechless delight first on the girl and then on the painting.

The Empress, surprised at his unusual manner, asked, "What has so rapt the attention of our omnipotent Emperor?" "The picture!" he replied. "Not that artistically it is so remarkable, but it reminds me of my bygone days." He went over to the Empress and leaning on her shoulder pointed out the hills and streams, the cottages, the peasants, and fishermen in the painting. "When I was a prince and governing Kuang-ling," he said, "I had time to enjoy beautiful scenery. Now I am so occupied by affairs of State that I can no more indulge my love of Nature!" Next day, he announced in Court that he was leaving the capital to make a tour of inspection ending at Kuang-ling.

Meanwhile, news had been brought of the portent—the cloud of mist in the southeast. The Emperor's desire to revisit the lovely scenery of his youth aptly coincided with the necessity of removing a possible usurper. But to execute the plan was no simple affair: the Emperor would have to sail down the Yellow River to the hazardous seas of the China coast, at a season when the waters were wildest. Then one of the Court officials came forward with an ingenious plan. At the time of Ch'in Shih Huang Ti, he recalled, a similar mist had appeared above Nanking. The Emperor on that occasion had, characteristically, com-

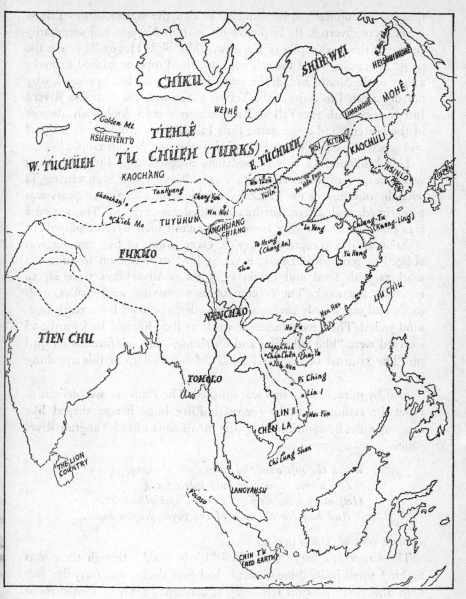

THE SUI PERIOD (*cir.* A.D. 610)

manded a mountain to be tunneled so that the waters of the Yellow River were diverted. By imposing his will on Nature, and summarily changing the topography of a region, Ch'in Shih Huang Ti broke the spell! Now, continued the official, since the Emperor wished to make a tour to the South, and, at the same time, the mist had appeared, why not dig a canal to connect the Yellow River with the Yangtzu River? Interference with the Yellow River waters would doubtlessly dispose of the portent, and at the same time His Majesty would have a direct and peaceful passage from the capital to the south of his empire!

This brilliant idea was immediately adopted, and Emperor Yang was as impatient for its completion as had been Ch'in Shih Huang Ti over the building of the Wall. Every able man over fifteen years was conscripted, and severe penalties attended any evasion. The recorder says that three million six hundred thousand men were employed. In addition to this compulsory service, every group of five families was obliged to send an old man, a young boy, or a woman to serve the workers with food and drink. Fifty thousand soldiers were set to supervise the work. The column of men arriving with spades, mattocks, and other tools, declares the recorder, stretched for several thousand miles! Their movements at work as they hurried backward and forward were "like lightning and hurricane," and reinforcements sped up "like swarms of bees and ants." Many died from this appalling labor.

As if by miracle, the canal was finished. The Emperor was delighted. Now the retinue must be prepared. Fifty huge barges shaped like dragons must be contributed by the inhabitants of the Yangtzu River valley.

> *When the soft winds of spring are blowing,*
> *The whole country is busy cutting silk,*
> *Half are for saddle-flaps of the imperial cavalry,*
> *And half for the sails of the royal dragon boats,*

wrote a poet of T'ang period.

The Emperor's barge was called "Little Red,"[1] though there was nothing small in its dimensions: it had four decks, was forty-five feet high and two thousand feet long. It contained a lavish throne room as well as a miniature private palace and two immense halls of East and West. On the two lower decks were a hundred and twenty sumptuous cabins for the royal attendants, all decorated with gold and jade.

[1] Red is a symbol of good luck in China.

The Empress had a barge to herself in similar style, named "Flying Yellow Dragon." A series of nine barges following these had the name of "Floating Landscapes," and the imagination is left to picture their appearance. The rest of the fifty brought up the rear—"Shimmering Light," "Crimson Bird," "White Tiger," "Seven Stars," "Flying Feathers," "Green Sheldrake," and a host more, every one as gorgeously adorned as the wit of man could devise, and manned by diplomats and merchants, monks and nuns, princes and princesses, the imperial concubines, ministers and officials. The royal progress in these dragon boats must have been as dazzling as any of Egyptian Cleopatra's on her river Nile.

Thousands of men, dressed in silk, drew the barges along with ropes, while hundreds of young girls, specially chosen for their beauty, mingled with the barge men and pulled on brightly colored cords. Lambs frisked beside them to add to the charm. On both sides of the canal stood rows of willow trees to protect the girls and men from the scorching sun. The Emperor had previously issued a proclamation to the effect that anyone who presented a willow plant should be rewarded with a forty-foot length of silk. Forthwith, young willow trees poured in, and in a short time the whole length from the capital to Kuang-ling was planted with weeping willows.

When the fleet started out at last, it stretched over the waters of the canal for "nearly a thousand *li*"! Horsemen galloped along both banks, waving their banners, and the onlookers crowding the way were dazzled at the array and the splendor. After the fleet had passed, perfumes lingered on the air for tens of miles.

Such was the result of an Emperor's caprice. The total length of the canal was more than three thousand *li*, that is, about a thousand miles! It was built without machinery, and in the space of a few years.[1] The work must have cost unspeakable suffering, not only to the thousands of forced laborers, but to the whole community whose taxes were multiplied in order to pay for it. But for more than a thousand years it was of inestimable service to the people of China, forming a great vein of communication for trade and education between the north and south extremes of the Empire.

The canal seems to have been the chief delight of Emperor Yang.

[1] The three canals forming the Grand Canal were Emperor Yang's work. The chief and longest one was the T'ung Chi Ch'u; the other two were the Chiang Nan Ho and the Jung Chi Ch'u. Like the Great Wall, the Grand Canal was due to the conception of one man. Small stretches of canal had been built in previous dynasties, but it was Emperor Yang of Sui who joined them and made one huge waterway. Additions and alterations were made in later times.

He was constantly improving it by building palaces and parks along its banks. Of these extravagant constructions, the Imperial Western Park, at the capital, Loyang, where the canal began, was perhaps the most brilliant. A T'ang writer has devoted the whole of a small volume to descriptions of Emperor Yang's parks and palaces, and from him we can read poetic and first-hand stories of a tyrannical, extravagant, pleasure-loving, but artistic sovereign who ruled China fourteen centuries ago.

Between the park and the palace, begins the narrator, were the Imperial Walks. Tall pine trees and giant willows bordered them. In spring, every path and lane was deep in the drifting petals of peach and plum blossom, while green shadows fell coolly across them in intricate pattern. There were flocks of "golden monkeys and purple deer." When autumn and winter approached, and flower and leaf began to wither, silks in every color of the rainbow were cut into the shapes of foliage and blossoms, and attached to the bare twigs. Whenever they faded they were quickly replaced.

In the great park itself, a huge lake of forty square *li* was dug. It was called "the Northern Sea" and was dotted with islands modeled on the imaginary forms of islands where the Immortals dwelt, in the "Sea of Heaven." The waters were adorned with lilies and lotus flowers of every color; with water caltrop, algæ, and duckweed. On the banks were sixteen mansions, each of them inhabited by twenty girls of astonishing beauty. Sometimes the Emperor would visit one of the mansions and allow himself to be feasted on rare foods and entertained by the ravishing inmates; at other times he would have them all mounted on ponies and would gallop with them along the Imperial Walks in the bright moonlight. On still, starlit nights he liked to row with them on the lake, enjoying the softness of the night wind and the quietness of the calm waters. Those who had voices sang him the lovely song, "Wandering in the Clear Night."

Such were the tastes of Emperor Yang "the Shady." Extravagance and love of ostentation marked every enterprise. There is a description, for instance, of how a Turkic ruler from the northern borders paid a diplomatic visit to Emperor Yang in 607. The "barbarian" king was so overwhelmed by the splendor of the entertainment provided that he even begged permission to wear Chinese robes at ceremonial meetings, as a token of his admiration and a symbol of his humble friendship! On the return visit in the same year, the Emperor surpassed himself by ordering a "Traveling Palace" and a "Traveling Town" to be built. These two vast constructions were mounted on wheels and drawn for hundreds of miles. The "Traveling Palace" held hundreds of imperial bodyguards, while the "Traveling Town," when it was unveiled before the astonished eyes of the Emperor's host, was declared the Wonder of the Age. The people thought that only the Immortals could have made it!

The Emperor's reputation for splendor, though not for military power, grew from year to year. Envoys came to offer obeisance at his Court; from Japan, from Siam, from the Liukiu (Liuch'iu) Islands as well as from many countries of the "Western Regions." But his ill-starred expeditions against Korea in 611 and 614 cost him the throne. He ordered repeated attacks, and led them several times in person. His men died in thousands, without any decisive victory being achieved. Moreover, the imperial coffers were emptying, and the taxes for a futile campaign laid such insufferable burdens on the people that the inevitable rebellion broke out. The Emperor himself was assassinated in his Kuang-ling palace.

Although Emperor Yang had wasted the whole wealth of the Empire on his pleasures, and had won only a cheap reputation for his country by a ludicrous degree of ostentation, he was not an altogether hateful character. His sincere love of Nature, his appreciation of beauty, his affection for the countryside where he had spent his youth, redeem him from inhumanity.

XIII. THE T'ANG DYNASTY: POLITICS
AND CULTURE

JUST AS THE CHINESE sometimes call themselves "Sons of Han," regarding the Han period as the true origin of their civilization, so, among the Pacific Islands, the Chinese are still called "The People of T'ang." To the world outside the Chinese borders, the T'ang period shines more gloriously than any other in its history, and even after the inevitable political decay had begun to shake the throne, intellectual life, painting, poetry, prose, music, continued to flow, borne on an irresistible current. The careers of Emperors and their ministers belong to the past and the history books, but the lovely T'ang sculpture, as simple and living as the Grecian marbles, the poems of Li Po, Tu Fu, and Po Chu-i translated into all the great languages of the world, the pieces of strong and vivid calligraphy, and the few paintings that have survived, tender in color, clear and "classic" in form, remain for the world's admiration. To Westerners, the Chinese may well be called "The People of T'ang," for it is in the relics of this time, in the museums, art galleries, and libraries of the Western nations, that the best concrete symbols of Chinese culture and civilization appear.

The political history of the T'ang dynasty is less remarkable than its intellectual and artistic life, though some of it is highly colored. Like so many Chinese dynasties, it began brilliantly under the rule of an outstanding personality, and ended, as so many others had ended, in corruption, strike, and rebellion.

The governor of a northern prefecture, T'ai-yuan, who had overthrown the preceding Sui dynasty and made himself first Emperor of the T'ang, presently resigned the throne to his talented son Li Shihmin, who became Emperor T'ai Tsung "the Great." The name was apt: T'ai Tsung, the virtual founder of this famous Chinese dynasty, was perhaps the greatest of its rulers. All the border tribes gave allegiance to him, looking to him as their Grand Khan. And in the interior administration of the country, he made very significant reforms. The Emperor of Sui dynasty had already initiated the Chinese examination system for official appointments, which lasted almost without alteration until the end of the last century, and completely reorganized the methods of government. The Sui Emperors had recognized the constant menace to the throne offered by a strong hereditary nobility, and had conceived the idea of appointing governors and high officials by merit, through a system of examinations. The dynasty was too short for the reform to be carried through thoroughly, and the perfecting of it was largely due to Emperor T'ai Tsung of T'ang. As a result, the power of the aristocracy gave place to a kind of intellectual hierarchy.

A candidate for the highest office had to pass through successive stages. Success in the first examinations only enabled the candidate to take up a position in his local government, and he mounted the ladder to imperial honor through increasingly severe tests. The subjects of the earlier examinations were partly scientific—mathematics, law, history, calligraphy, and so on, but these practical subjects gave way to the Confucian Classics, as the candidate mounted higher, while the "Advanced Scholars," who were honored above every other class of society, must compose poetry, and write essays in a prescribed elegant, subtle, and elaborate style. "Welcome the Advanced Scholars with burnt incense, but regard the Scholars of the Classics with indifferent eyes," ran a popular saying of the time. From this we see the high regard in which literature, especially poetry, was held in the T'ang days, and one reason for the great flood of poetry that poured out, richer and more beautiful than at any time before or since.

Many of the early T'ang Emperors were themselves writers and patrons of poetry. T'ai Tsung "the Great" instituted a Salon for his literary friends, and he joined them from time to time in academic discussions. The men who were lucky enough to belong to this company were called by their fellows "Men of the Immortal Island"! Another Emperor, Chung Tsung, used to hold a kind of literary festival once a year, beginning on the fifteenth day of the first moon. At that time, all the provincial officials, and as many of the Emperor's subjects as were wealthy enough, flocked to the capital to enjoy the pageantry. A great procession wound through the streets, headed by the imperial family, and including people from every class of society. On gaily bedecked ponies, the royal princesses played musical instruments to entertain the onlookers, while anyone with a talent for poetry hastened to write memorial verses on the scene. On the thirtieth day, the Emperor would order an ornamental tower to be set up in the palace courtyard and hung with silk embroideries. Here an imperial reception and feast were held, and every Court official had to compose a poem in praise of the event.

Emperor Hsuan Tsung, whose love of women and song brought disaster on the imperial T'ang House, was himself a poet of talent. In his royal orchard, called "The Pear Tree Garden," talented musicians used to assemble, and young students of music were tutored by the Emperor himself. The days passed in music and poetry, and some even say that the prototype of the Chinese drama, which like the great drama of European countries is in verse, and is also set to music, was originated by this beauty-loving Emperor. At all events, Chinese actors and actresses of the present day are still called "Students from the Pear Tree Garden."

Love of women and love of poetry seem to have gone hand in hand in T'ang times. From the young unmarried girls shut up in their remote boudoirs overlooking a garden of willows and flowers, to the sing-song girls who lived in their "zigzag railing mansions," every one learned to recite poems. The little sing-song girls vied with each other in winning the love of poets, and there are many beautiful and romantic stories about such loves.

It is not surprising, therefore, that while on the one hand Chinese poetry reached its golden age, the political structure was weakened and finally smashed largely through the influence of women. "A hen crowing to herald the dawn portends the destruction of a family" wrote the philosopher Confucius, quoting a prince of ancient times. Such a crowing hen was the Empress Wu, wife of Emperor Kao Tsung, son of T'ai Tsung and one of the strongest and most glorious sovereigns of the T'ang House. No sooner had he breathed his last than the Empress seized the throne and threw her son, the legitimate heir, into prison. Her triumph, however, was short lived: loyal supporters of the imprisoned heir rose and overthrew her. But now the new Emperor faced a fresh danger—his wife, the Empress Wei, nursed the same ambition as her late mother-in-law. She would listen to the discussions of State counselors, concealing herself behind the embroidered curtains, and on the basis of what she overheard would start political intrigues. She stirred up untold mischief among the rival Court officials, but when, further emboldened, she began to plot against her husband's life, the conspiracy was discovered and Empress Wei went to her death.

Next appeared the Princess T'ai-p'ing. This lady had helped to put down the conspiracy of Empress Wei, but now in her turn organized a plot to poison the Crown Prince! This too was discovered in time,

The Tʻang Period (*cir.* A.D. 660)

and the Princess was imprisoned and executed. It was this Crown Prince who became, in the course of time, Emperor Hsuan Tsung, the Emperor of the "Pear Tree Garden," whose disastrous passion for the beautiful imperial concubine Yang Kuei-fei began the downfall of the T'ang House. The story is not without its beauty and pathos, and has stirred the imagination of a host of Chinese poets, painters, and dramatists in later generations.

Kuei-fei, or Yu Huan—"Jade Ring"—was originally the wife of a prince, and later entered a nunnery. But her beauty could not remain hidden: she was brought to the palace where she became the Emperor's most beloved concubine. Not only did Hsuan Tsung heap riches on her and forget all the responsibilities of government in order to wanton with her, but he loaded her relatives with honors and wealth. Her three sisters, who are described as "fit and handsome, clever and full of humor," and her two brothers, lived like emperors and empresses. In a suburb of the capital, on the Black Horse Hills, where the Emperor had his summer residence, these three sisters and two brothers had their palaces too. Whenever the Emperor held a banquet they attended; whenever he went in procession, their chariots followed his. All the members of their respective families also joined the imperial progress, and in their brilliant robes they looked, so it is said, "like hundreds of moving flowers." After they had passed, "golden and silver head ornaments, embroidered shoes, pearls and precious gems would be found strewn on the ground." Some onlooker who dared to peep into one of the ladies' carriages could smell the perfume for three days afterwards!

Such foolish extravagance, such favoritism, and such neglect of government could only end in disaster. What the poet Po Chu-i in an immortal poem has called "the Long Woe" befell China in the form of An Lu Shan's rebellion.

An Lu Shan was the governor of a northern prefecture, and under his ruthless leadership a great rebellion broke out. The force was irresistible. The eastern capital of the Empire was seized and An Lu Shan declared himself Emperor. Hsuan Tsung fled to the West towards Shu. The road was rough and Shu was a district among rugged mountains whose repellent, barren nature was very apt to rouse homesickness in men who traveled there. The imperial guards murmured among themselves and refused to go on. In that lonely place, even they turned traitor. They attacked the relatives of "Jade Ring" and killed a brother and two sisters. Then, excited by their bloody deeds, they demanded the life of "Jade Ring" herself—the cause of a whole

Empire's misery. She was forced to hang herself from a tree with a piece of white silk before the anguished eyes of her royal lover. After this dire act, the march proceeded into the lonely mountains.

> *In the valleys of O-mei Mountain*
> *Travelers are few.*
> *The banners flapped sadly*
> *In the rays of a sinking sun. . . .*
>
> *When the moon rose above the traveling palace*
> *It looked down in grief;*
> *When the animals' bells were shaken by night raindrops*
> *They tinkled with a heartbroken sound.*

The broken-hearted Emperor abdicated and passed the rest of his life in sad seclusion. The rebels meanwhile made their way up the Yellow River valley, plundering and laying waste. They were checked at last at a town called Sui-yang. There the garrison held out for many weeks until the besieged armies were at the point of starvation. They kept alive on the bark of trees, grass roots, rats, and sparrows. When even these were exhausted, they ate horses and the bodies of their dead comrades. But at last their heroic resistance was broken, the town fell, and the inhabitants were massacred. All this time, however, loyal troops, led by the old Emperor's son, had been attacking in the rear of the rebels. Benefiting by the enemy's preoccupation at the siege of Sui-yang, they recaptured all the northern towns, and finally, coming up from behind, defeated the rebel army.

The rightful heir was proclaimed Emperor, but the glory of T'ang was never renewed. The short period of recovery before the dynasty itself came to an end was like the gleam of a setting sun. Nor have the Chinese people ever known such a glory again. Tu Fu, perhaps the greatest of all Chinese poets, stood at the junction and sorrowed at the changes. Thus he wrote:

> *I remember the golden days of K'ai Yuan,*[1]
> *When a small town was thronged with ten thousand families;*
> *The rice grains bulged with fatness and the maize was white,*
> *Imperial and private granaries overflowed.*
> *No jackals or tigers were to be seen on any road in the Empire,*
> *And every day was favorable for the traveler.*
> *Gauze from Ch'i, silks of Lu, came in creaking carts.*
> *Men plowed and women span; they worked in harmony.*

[1] This period covered the first thirty years of the forty-four years' reign of Emperor Hsuan Tsung, from 713 till 756.

In the palace, the Sage-King enjoyed the song of "Cloud Gate," [1]
And from every corner under the sky, the people lived in friendship.
No disaster happened for a hundred years.
The rites and music of Shu-shun, and the laws of Hsiao Ho were carefully
    followed.
Whoever heard then of a piece of silk costing ten thousand coins,
Or of fields meant for cultivation overflowing in blood?
Now the palaces of Loyang are reduced to ashes;
Foxes and rabbits make their homes in the imperial temples.
I am sorrowful and dare not question the elders,
Lest the moment they open their mouths they speak of the troubles. . . .

All the poetry of this time reflects a whispering sadness, a nostalgia for the past, and describes the misfortunes of the people, in contrast with the poems of the golden age before the An Lu Shan rebellion. These are chiefly concerned on the one hand with battles successfully won and triumphant journeys to far lands, and on the other with love and music and wine. The favorite titles of those happy days were "Marching off to the Frontier," "Drinking under the Moon," and "Love-longing in the Boudoir." There were also eulogies of courtiers and bold imaginative descriptions of scenery. In Tu Fu and other poets of the declining years, Nature was but the background for man's bitter toil.

The weakness of the later T'ang Emperors was largely due to the growing power of the war-lords—an evil from which China has suffered ever since. Under the T'ang military system, the standing army was divided into something over six hundred units, each containing from eight hundred to a thousand soldiers. A third of them were normally stationed in the capital and the surrounding districts, and in this way the authority of the Court was maintained over the local officials. But unfortunately, after the An Lu Shan rebellion, this large imperial army came under the control of ambitious eunuchs, who ever after menaced the throne and did not stop short at murder to keep their power. And meanwhile, military commanders stationed at some distance from the capital, especially those entrusted with the pacification of border districts, enjoyed a great deal of administrative independence. Gradually, as the central authority weakened, autocratic military leaders made strongholds for themselves and resisted all efforts on the part of the imperial officials to control them. They appointed their own successors, and even turned the position into an

[1] The name of a song traditionally composed by the ancient Sage-King "Yellow Emperor."

hereditary one, refusing to recognize the new commander sent by the central government. These war-lords thus became petty princes in their own districts, fought each other, and annexed each other's territory. The ties binding the whole Empire to the throne fell apart through their disloyalty. After the An Lu Shan rebellion their number greatly increased, for such positions were lavishly bestowed on meritorious generals of the loyalist party as well as on surrendered rebel chiefs. The development proved an even greater evil than the old hereditary nobility.

Under such conditions the dynasty could not long survive: it went down in confusion and blood. The disaster was heralded by another rebellion, the rebellion of Huang Ch'ao (875-884), even more terrible than that of An Lu Shan, and one of the greatest devastations in Chinese history. A famine had driven the inhabitants of Huang Ch'ao's native place to the brink of desperation. The people became bandits to thieve and rob wherever they could find plunder, and they raised Huang Ch'ao, a wealthy salt merchant, at their head. It is said of him that "he wrote with style, spoke with refinement, rode with extreme skill, and fought cunningly with a dagger." Now he declared himself the People's Savior, and a relentless enemy of the officials and war-lords.

Local banditry soon changed to full-scale rebellion. Huang Ch'ao and his followers fought their way all along the eastern seaboard to the southern provinces and then fought back towards the North, dev-astating the West as they went. In the end they had seized both Ch'ang-an and Loyang, the eastern and western capital cities, while the Emperor Hsi Tsung escaped to Shu, the mountainous refuge of his unhappy ancestor Hsuan Tsung. In a huge golden sedan chair at the head of his armies, Huang Ch'ao made a victorious entry into Ch'ang-an, where he was received by the imperial ministers and a thousand maids-of-honor from the palace. He mounted the throne and proclaimed himself the first Emperor of a new dynasty. But his joy was short lived. Two years later, loyal troops of the rightful T'ang Emperor attacked the capital and forced the usurper to flee for his life. He fled to the East, having first set the palaces on fire. On the long march that followed, his men died in hundreds from starvation and his generals deserted. There was nothing left for the once glorious rebel—salt merchant, commander, and king—but to commit suicide. And so the rebellion ended, having accomplished nothing but the useless shedding of blood.

By the time this revolt had been quelled, the whole Empire was in a state of exhaustion, and the end approached, accompanied by further slaughter. Chu Wen, a former general under Huang Ch'ao, who had deserted to the Emperor, was at bitter enmity with the Turkic general Li K'e-yung, and with the all-powerful Court eunuchs. The struggle between them developed into more than a local rivalry, for the eunuchs in the end had practically seized the Emperor's person and were governing in his place. Chu Wen succeeded in releasing him and in exterminating the eunuchs, but, in keeping with the reckless abandonment of moral behavior in those last years of the dynasty, he himself murdered the Emperor, had all the royal princes strangled at a banquet, and the leading supporters of the T'ang House murdered in one night! So ended the great dynasty.

Another period of confusion was ushered in, and lasted for more than fifty years. Chu Wen himself founded a dynasty which he called the "Later Liang," but the other war-lords refused to recognize his authority. One after another the more powerful among them rose against the self-appointed "Emperors" and overthrew their "dynasties." Within those fifty years, five such "dynasties" followed each other: Later Liang, Later T'ang, Later Tsin, Later Han, and Later Chou, and the period is sometimes called by historians the "Later Five Dynasties." Each of the Emperors exercised only a local authority, and held it by strength of the sword, while the whole of the southern provinces remained independent under the control of numerous petty warlords. The wealthy classes were pillaged until their wealth melted away. The poor could hardly exist. Fighting never ended. This state of affairs continued until a general of Later Chou with the personality, talent, and following sufficient for the task, usurped the throne and succeeded in bringing the whole Empire under his sole power. This was the first Emperor of Sung dynasty, a worthy successor of the glorious T'ang. China became once more the great leader of the Eastern world.

During all the period of political decay that accompanied and followed the downfall of the T'ang dynasty, intellectual and artistic life flowed on irresistibly. Poetry had an even deeper beauty and an added strength from the undercurrent of sorrow and despair, while the disgust felt by sensitive men at the corruption of worldly affairs threw them even more readily on Nature. Thus there grew up that great volume of closely observed, somewhat emotional Nature poetry which is so characteristic of our Chinese poetic genius.

All the important schools of painting also trace their origin to the T'ang dynasty, when there lived such famous painters as Wu Tao-tzu,

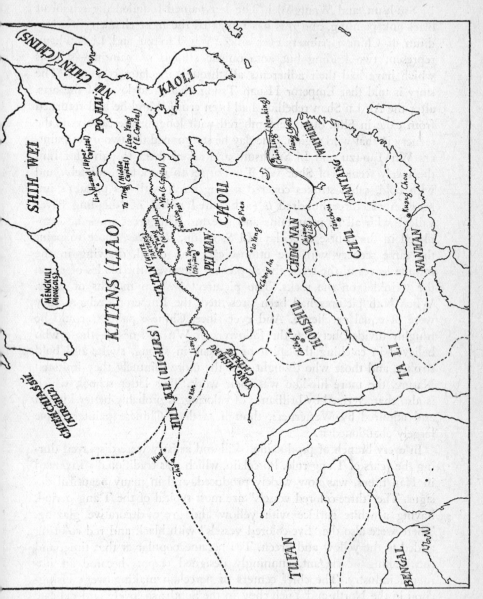

The Period of Five Dynasties (*cir.* A.D. 995)

Li Ssu-hsun, and Wang Wei. The last named founded the school of black ink painting, and this has remained the most characteristic medium of Chinese painters ever since. Wu Tao-tzu and Li Ssu-hsun represent two leading but antagonistic schools of painting—schools which have had their adherents all through the later centuries. The story is told that Emperor Hsuan Tsung, that great lover of the arts, after the An Lu Shan rebellion had been crushed and he had returned from exile in Shu, often remembered with longing the beauty of the scenery in that wild region. One day he summoned the two great painters Wu Tao-tzu and Li Ssu-hsun, and asked them to paint for him the lovely scenery of Shu. Wu Tao-tzu set to work immediately, and with bold, rapid strokes covered a long scroll with his painter's impression of "three hundred *li* (a hundred miles) of Chia-ling River valley" with all its mountains and streams. This great work he completed in the course of a day! Li Ssu-hsun, however, chose to paint the same scenery with the utmost care and detail, drawing in the minute leaves of the trees, the ripples on the river, the blades of grass, the wrinkles on the rocks. The picture took him months of labor. When both pictures had been presented, the Emperor declared they were of equal excellence. And ever since, Chinese painters could be roughly divided between the followers of Wu and of Li—those who believed in catching the spirit of a scene in strong, swift, and bold strokes, and those who thought that the more minutely they imitated Nature, the more life-like was their work. This latter school, which is also characterized by brilliance of coloring, is probably better known and admired by Westerners, though modern Chinese painters have largely abandoned it.

In every branch of production, skill and artistry were displayed during the years of T'ang rule. Porcelain, which was traditionally invented in Han times, was now widely produced, and in many beautiful designs. The "three-colored vessels" are most typical of the T'ang period, having a white surface with yellow and green decorative glazing. There were also the "five-colored vessels" with black and red coloring added to the yellow and green. Tea became popular at that time, and the making of elegant, cunningly designed teapots became an immense industry. The chief centers of porcelain making were Hsing-chou in the North and Yueh-chou in the South: so lovely and delicate were their products that a T'ang poet was moved to write poetry about them:

> *The Hsingites and the Yuehites—*
> *Those are the porcelain makers!*

Round as the shape of moon
Shining on the earth, and
Light as the soul of snow
Are their wares. . . .

In the dark days that followed the fall of the T'ang dynasty, the seed of a whole new world was discovered, both for the East and the West. Printing was invented! During the Han dynasty the Confucian Classics had been inscribed on stone tablets, as the Ten Commandments had been inscribed by Moses, for the benefit of posterity. In T'ang times a method of transferring the tablet inscriptions to paper was devised by inking the surface of the stone and applying a sheet of paper to it. The characters then showed white on a black ground. During the "Later Five Dynasties" a certain Feng Tao—a political opportunist and an amateur in the arts, who wrote a eulogy on himself as "the ever gay old man"—suggested the use of wood blocks in place of the large, clumsy, and immovable stone tablets. His suggestion was immediately acted upon, and after some years of labor by the wood engravers, the whole of the Classics had been transferred to wooden blocks. Block printing became popular from this time, and especially in the Sung dynasty, that followed the Later Five Dynasties, the printing of books by this method became one of the great activities. Some beautiful examples of it have survived till the present day. Thanks to this invention, Confucianism could spread through the whole Empire, and the possibility of general education appeared.

In the middle of the eleventh century a certain Pi Sheng invented movable type—an innovation of the very greatest significance. According to a contemporary writer, the characters were carved upon a compound of gum and clay, which was then baked hard and spread on an iron sheet for the printing operation. Towards the end of the fifteenth century, copper replaced the clay and gum type, and thus modern printing emerged. But long before this time the Chinese invention had traveled by trade routes to the West, to be adopted by Gutenberg and other European printers, and to revolutionize the course of human thought.

XIV. THE T'ANG DYNASTY: TURKS, UIGURS, AND TUFANS

THE T'ANG EMPIRE at the height of its power was an even vaster one than the Han. While north and south it comprised all the territory which the Han sovereigns had ruled, to the east it took in new lands, including Korea, over which a successful battle had been fought against Japan. Westward, through the subjugation of Central Asian tribes, the boundary extended immeasurably farther—up to the edge of Persia! The T'ang empire was, in fact, the focusing point for the whole of the Eastern world, in trade, commerce, and especially in intellectual life. Japanese students and scholars were sent to China at that time to study literature, art, philosophy, and science. On this the foundations of Japan's own culture were laid. Their literature, their writing, their painting, almost everything of value in their civilization, are imitations of Chinese culture, dating from the T'ang dynasty.

From the other direction, the art and thought of Central and Western Asia poured in to enrich the native Chinese culture. Chinese travelers reached India and brought back many volumes of Buddhist scriptures: the profound influence of Buddhism, both upon Chinese philosophic conceptions and the Chinese arts, dates from this time. Chinese ships sailed as far as the Persian Gulf, while the Caliph Haroun-al-Raschid sent his envoys to the Emperor of China. There is no doubt that this westward expansion, and the absorption through conquest of many western tribes, were in part responsible for the brilliant renaissance of Chinese culture that took place in the T'ang period.

The history of India, Persia, and Japan has been amply described by numbers of historians, but that of the tribes west of the T'ang empire has had very scant mention. And yet in their relations with China they may well have exercised a more pervasive and lasting influence than these greater nations, whose contact was only spasmodic. This chapter therefore purports to deal chiefly with the Turks, the Uigurs, and the Tufans.

It may be remembered how, in the lands north of the Chinese Empire, the Hsiung-nu had been succeeded by a people called Hsien-pi whose ancestral home was supposedly Siberia. During the Six Dynasties period they invaded North China, became masters of a great part, and established the Northern Wei dynasty. By the time this dynasty had passed away, the Hsien-pi, like so many invaders of China, had completely merged with the Chinese population.

The old territory abandoned by the Hsien-pi was now reoccupied by a tribe having the curious nickname of "High Vehicles." It seems they were chiefly remarkable for the huge wheels of their carriages and carts, but of their origin little is known beyond the fact that they were probably related to the Hsiung-nu. A legend is told about them that traces their descent from the union of a wolf with the lovely daughter of a Hsiung-nu chieftain. "This chieftain," so the legend runs, "had two daughters so beautiful that the rest of the tribe worshiped them as divine beings. The chieftain (inordinately proud of his offspring) declared, "How can I match my girls with mere men? They should only be married to Heaven!" He built a high tower in the wild regions to the extreme north of his country and shut his two lovely daughters up in it, saying, "Heaven will take them. . . ." Four years later there came an old wolf, and howled day and night at the foot of the tower. It made itself a cave there, and lived in it for some time. At last, the younger daughter said to her sister, "My father hopes to marry me to Heaven. Can it be that this wolf is a divine animal, sent to me by the desire of Heaven?" . . . And she descended the tower and became the wolf's wife. By him she had many children, whose descendants formed a new tribe. A characteristic of this people is their strange kind of singing, like the howling of a wolf."

The people of the curious nickname and wolf-like songs were conquered presently by tribesmen called the "Juan-juan." [1] "Juan-juan" means literally "the creeping of a worm," and they were so named by an Emperor of Northern Wei, who thought them "as harmless as creeping worms." In the middle of the sixth century, these "harmless worms" were attacked and partly exterminated by the Turks who now occupied all that part north of China formerly the habitation of the Hsiung-nu, as well as a great deal more territory to the west. The survivors of the Juan-juan were driven to find their new home still farther westwards.

The term "Turk," though generally associated with the people who inhabited parts of Asia Minor, is a purely linguistic one, without a racial meaning. It covers all the tribes speaking Turkic languages,

[1] Often identified with the Avars of Roman history.

and includes both a Western and an Eastern group. To the Western belong those races which, in the end of the Middle Ages, were comprised in the vast Ottoman Empire; to the Eastern—about which we are at present concerned—many of the peoples of Turkestan and Central Asia.

It seems that the national name, now so famous, did indeed originate in Eastern Asia. We learn from reliable records that in the year A.D. 433, when the To Pa had founded the Northern Wei dynasty and were ruling in North China, a clan of the Hsiung-nu, disliking the Wei rule, moved north to the protection of the "Juan-juan," whom they served as workers in iron. They lived at the foot of the "Golden Mountains" (i.e. Altai mountains), beside a peak called from its shape "Turk" or "Tu-chueh," meaning a helmet. The name Turk (Tu-chueh) applied to this tribe first appears in Chinese records about a century later.

If we turn from record to legend, we are led to conjecture that this small Hsiung-nu clan, from whose descendants sprang a great eastern empire, had a racial connection with the "High Vehicles." The mythical story of their origin is also concerned with the union of a wolf and a human being. "The ancestors of the Turks," runs the legend, "lived on the right bank of the Western Sea, and were a people descended from a branch of the Hsiung-nu. They were defeated by a neighboring tribe and massacred. . . . The enemy soldiers took pity on a small boy of ten and spared him from death, though they cut off his legs and left him in a marsh. A she-wolf came and fed him with animal flesh. The she-wolf brought him up and he made her his wife. She became pregnant. At that time, news of the boy's escape reached the enemy chieftain, and he sent a man to kill him. The man was to destroy the wolf as well, but she escaped to the North Mountain of Kao-ch'ang (modern Sinkiang). There, from a cave entrance she saw a grassy valley several hundred miles square, securely hemmed in by mountains. She settled in this valley and gave birth to ten boys. The boys grew up, married, and founded ten families. One . . . became prosperous . . . and moved away from the old home. They became subjects of the 'Juan-juan,' lived at the foot of the Golden Mountains, and served as blacksmiths to their masters."

During the Six Dynasties period, this small but rebellious tribe grew increasingly powerful, revolted against its overlords, the "Juan-juan," and crushed them so effectively that they seem to have completely disappeared from history. Now began the first brilliant epoch of the Turkish people. Under its chieftain T'uman, who in 552 proclaimed himself "Khan of the Turks," and his immediate successors, the formerly servile clan became leader of all the Central Asian nomads. Its armies turned to the West and began an amazing series of conquests, so that within a few years its rule extended from the Liao Sea (Manchuria) in the east to the Western Sea (Sea of Aral) in the west, and from the desert in the south to the Northern Sea (Lake Baikal) in the north.

The Turks were now so formidable that the Chinese rulers whose territory bordered on the Khan's kingdom were thoroughly intimidated. These were the Emperors of Western Wei and Northern Ch'i who hastened to send bales of silk and imperial maidens, with the object of winning Turkish friendship and of buying at least a temporary peace. One of the Khans is said to have declared impudently, "Why should we worry about our fortunes so long as our two little boys in the South remain filial?"

During the Sui dynasty which followed upon the Six Dynasties, relations between the Turkish Khan and the Chinese Emperors improved for a time. This came about through a family quarrel in the Khan's household. The Chinese Emperor had given a royal princess in marriage to the Khan's younger brother, and out of some caprice had refused to send a second for the Khan himself. Angry and jealous, the Khan made a murderous attack upon his brother, who then escaped into China and sought protection at the Chinese Court. This young Turk and the Chinese Emperor became fast friends, and upon the Khan's death he returned to claim the succession, supported by a Chinese bodyguard. After this incident the Khan and the Emperor remained on excellent terms, and exchanged visits frequently. At one of these diplomatic exchanges, it is recorded that the Chinese Emperor's envoy brought gifts to the Khan and his Chinese wife which included two golden jars and twenty million pieces of silk. In return the host and hostess presented "tens of millions of oxen, sheep, camels, and horses."

As the short-lived Sui dynasty fell into decline, all the local leaders in China who were quarreling for supremacy courted the friendship and military support of the Turks. This circumstance, combined with the spectacle of an ever-weakening Chinese throne, put the Khan into such a high conceit of himself that the possibility of peaceful relations existing between the two countries came to an end.

Just as the early Han Emperors embarked on a policy of appeasement with their border enemy the Hsiung-nu, so the first Emperors of T'ang dynasty offered friendly gestures to the Turks. They met with exactly the same response: the Turks, like the Hsiung-nu before them, received gifts from the Chinese Emperors with one hand and attacked their frontiers with the other. It became very clear that only military operations could keep them within their own domain.

In 627, Turkish armies, comprising hundreds of thousands of men, plundered and hacked their way as far as the outskirts of Ch'ang-an, the Chinese capital. They encamped on the opposite bank of the river on which the city was built. Emperor T'ai Tsung, "the Great," second Emperor of T'ang dynasty, still hoping to avoid bloodshed, approached in person attended by only six guards, and asked to speak with the Turkish Khan. The two sovereigns met on the bridge which separated the capital from the hostile armies. T'ai Tsung rebuked the Khan for his senseless breaking of the peace, and it is said that the latter was so impressed by the Emperor's nobility and eloquence that he dismounted and humbly saluted him. As this moving scene was being played, thousands of T'ang troops poured into the plain and filled it with their banners, demonstrating the power of the Emperor. A bloody battle was converted into a sworn peace, and the Turkish armies withdrew to their own lands.

Meanwhile, various tribes, including the Uigurs, who were presently to take the place of the Turks as the dominant power in Central Asia, were growing dissatisfied with the Turkish rule, and began to break away. To add to the Turks' difficulties, a disastrous failure of their crops in 627, and heavy losses in cattle after an unusually severe winter, brought widespread famine and death. Their power was failing.

Taking advantage of this state of affairs, the Chinese were wise enough to attack. In 629 the T'ang Emperor sent a hundred thousand men to engage the Turkish armies at the foot of Iron Mountain (now Mongolia) and inflicted a crushing defeat on the Turks. The Khan was taken prisoner and thousands of his subjects, worn out by wars and famine, surrendered to the Chinese and became subjects of the T'ang empire. Others fled to join the Uigurs and other tribes. The end of this eastern branch of the Turks did not come, however, until more than a hundred years later when the Uigurs and Chinese in combination conquered and dispersed all that part of the tribe which bordered on the Chinese Empire. The empire of the Eastern Turks, like that of their predecessors the Hsiung-nu, disappeared from history. Their ruler, who was at that time an Empress Dowager, surrendered, and was created a "duchess" of the T'ang Court by the Emperor Hsuan Tsung, who was also graciously pleased to accord her an annual revenue of two hundred thousand coins for "pin-money!" This event took place in the year 745.

The Chinese government during the T'ang period had followed a policy of supporting factions that were weak or distant against those that were strong and near. Accordingly, during its years of most intense conflict with the Eastern Turks, it had kept on terms of friendship with the western branch. The latter at this time occupied lands west of the Golden Mountains (i.e. the Altai mountains) and their aggressive movements had been directed more against the countries of Western Asia than the Chinese border lands. They had even contracted an alliance with the East Roman Empire against the Persians. In 620 they had become masters of Eastern Persia.

When the great T'ang Emperor T'ai Tsung died, they turned for the first time eastward, and made an assault upon the northwestern borders of China. But their strength was already cracking. Dissensions prevailed among the various tribes of which they were composed. In 657 they suffered a heavy defeat by the T'ang troops, and their Khan was taken prisoner. Not long after, the Chinese were able to declare that they had annexed the whole territory of the Western Turks.

It seems that neither the Turkish occupation of Eastern Asia nor the Chinese annexation of most of these countries was effective. In the hundred years 650-750, possession of them was disputed not only by the Turks and Chinese, but by the Tufans (Tibetans) in the east and the Arabs in the west. We can only assert that between the contending pressure of Chinese and Arabs especially, the broad Kingdom of the Western Turks gradually fell to pieces, and that the whole Turkish race as an integrate body disappeared from Eastern Asia.

They were to some extent replaced by the Uigurs whose authority in Central Asia grew in proportion as the Turks' waned. They seem to have been a nomadic people, descended from the tribe known as the "High Vehicles," and living formerly in small groups, in Northern Mongolia. From the fourth to the eighth centuries their domination extended over a very large part of these wild northern regions, and though they were at one time subject to the Turks, they quickly regained their independence while the latter were involved with the Chinese. Joining with the T'ang armies in the final defeat of the Western Turks, the Uigurs inherited a considerable part of their territory, and though they remained allies of the Chinese, their wildness and savagery were not an unmitigated blessing. During the An Lu Shan rebellion, for instance, the Emperor was assisted by four thousand Uigur troops, who fought with reckless bravery round the capital of Ch'ang-an, and recaptured it from the hands of the rebels in 757. They had the Prince Regent's promise that, should they be successful in battle, they might seize all the girls and treasure they pleased, while leaving the territory in his hands. These half-savage soldiers refrained from looting Ch'ang-an excessively, but when the eastern capital of Loyang fell to them soon after, they plundered the city for three days on end, and were systematically emptying it of every valuable object. The Chinese military and civil authorities were in despair. At last they persuaded their greedy ally to cease this troublesome activity with the bribe of "ten thousand pieces of good silk," which had by some means to be procured from the local inhabitants. It is said that as a result of the bribe, the Emperor's civil servants ran so short of silken materials that they were obliged to appear at Court in paper dresses!

Nor was the Uigurs' friendship less embarrassing to China in peace-time. They compelled the Chinese to trade with them on their own terms, and one of their favorite ruses was to send a broken-winded, lame, or worn-out horse to the Chinese capital, recommending it as a well-bred mettlesome steed, and demanding at least forty pieces of good silk in exchange! Numerous such worthless jades were disposed of, and no one dared refuse to bargain with so ferocious a people. The wealthier among them made their homes at Ch'ang-an, and would drink their heads off and riot in the streets, to the distress of self-respecting, law-abiding Chinese citizens. If the local authorities had the temerity to throw them in jail, their friends would lay siege to the building, break it down if need be, and carry off the prisoners. The government found itself in the awkward situation of being obliged to protect these rude swashbucklers against the resentment of their own mannerly people, and to extenuate their social crimes.

By the beginning of the ninth century, the supremacy of the Uigurs was shattered. Like the Turks, they had been gradually weakened by internal conflicts and by the incursions of neighboring tribes. Their chief opponents, besides the Chinese, were a people called Haka, and these two powers between them broke up, killed, or dispersed the Uigur tribe about 830. A part fled farther west, but a great number of them moved into that part of China which is now Kansu and the neighboring provinces, and there they gradually merged with the native population.

The third power which had important relations with China during the T'ang dynasty was the tribe known as Tufan. The Tufans inhabited Tibet, parts of Kansu, Chinese Turkestan, and Northern India, and were the predecessors of the modern Tibetans. They belonged to the stock of the Ch'iang people, whose history was connected with the Chinese as early as the Chou dynasty, but their ruling class at this time was of North Indian blood. Their king, or "Tsan-p'u" as he was called, had his capital at Lhasa, the present capital of Tibet, and as in modern Tibet, a religious hierarchy seems to have controlled the administration. The national policy was decided by a council of monks.

During the reign of Emperor T'ai Tsung of the T'ang dynasty, the Tufans were attracted by the splendor of the neighboring Chinese Empire, and made tentative overtures at diplomatic relations. The Tsan-p'u, hearing that the Turkish Khan had been given a Chinese princess in marriage, asked that he too might be vouchsafed the hand of a royal Chinese lady. His request was somewhat bluntly refused, and the Tsan-p'u was so furious at the rebuff that he raised an army of two hundred thousand men and attacked China from the west. He had no success and withdrew. Nevertheless, on his sending a second envoy to the T'ang Court to solicit an imperial princess, his prayer was granted. The display of force had achieved what gentle words had failed to elicit.

The Tsan-p'u was overjoyed. In his delight he poured presents on the Emperor T'ai Tsung—five thousand taels of gold and countless other rarities. He built a complete city for his bride, and because the appearance of his people terrified the timid little stranger, he prohibited their custom of tattooing the face with red patterns. He himself put on robes of Chinese silk, and ordered his ministers and subjects to follow his example. Apparently, this Tsan-p'u had a genuine admiration for the Chinese culture: during his rule, many Tufan scholars were sent to the Chinese capital of Ch'ang-an to study the Confucian Classics at the Chinese National University.

But years after the little Chinese princess and her Tufan husband had died, another Tsan-p'u showed no compunction in attacking his former ally when in distress. Profiting by the disturbances in China during the An Lu Shan rebellion, Tufan troops crossed the border in 763, and entering Ch'ang-an just after it had been painfully recovered from the hands of the rebels, completely devastated the city. They retired with their plunder, and with thousands of kidnaped Chinese subjects, whom they carried back with them and caused to marry their own people and become subject to their Tsan-p'u.

Many years later their treachery was rewarded. Beginning from 839, they suffered one disaster after another—earthquakes, landslides, floods, famines, and pestilences, and by these they were irretrievably weakened. When they came to blows with the T'ang armies in 848, they were utterly routed, and were driven out of the eastern part of their lands (Kansu).

Although their territory and influence had been reduced, the Tufans remained a Central Asian power and were never dispersed as the Hsiung-nu, the Turks, and the Uigurs had been. During the Sung dynasty which, after some fifty years of disruption, followed the T'ang dynasty, the Tufans sent envoys to China, and even offered to assist the Sung troops in their combats with other tribes. When the Sung dynasty fell before the irresistible expansion of the Mongol empire, and a Mongol ruler mounted the Chinese throne, the Tufans too became subject to him. They were well treated by the Mongols, who, like them, believed in the Lama religion. But of the relations effected between Tufans and Mongols through the medium of Lamaism, and of how the Lama priesthood swayed the foreign policy of the whole tribe, we shall treat hereafter.

History repeats itself. Just as the ocean tides rise and fall and rise again, to nibble off bits of rock and cliff against which they wash, so has the Chinese civilization acted upon the bordering races which it touched. Like the Hsiung-nu before them, a large proportion of the Turks and Uigurs were driven westward by the Chinese armies, while the remainder moved ever closer to Chinese territory, until they themselves became assimilated by the huge T'ang empire, and in their turn enriched the composition of Chinese blood.

As in Han times, the people of T'ang controlled communications from China to Central Asia, through the Turkic and the Tufan countries. Along this route, Buddhism with its profound and incalculable influences had begun to pass in the early years of Eastern Han. Now in addition came the three "Persian" religions—Nestorianism, Zoroastrianism, and Manichæism,[1] which were welcomed by the T'ang Emperors, and in ways we cannot measure enlarged and diversified the Chinese arts and conceptions. For the space of some three hundred years, by contact with newly risen tribes, and through them with the mighty empires of India and the Caliphs, Chinese civilization was sown with fresh seeds of greatness.

[1] The Chinese called them collectively the "San Hu" or "Three Foreign" religions, but "hu"—"foreigners"—usually referred only to Persia. Although Nestorianism did not originate in Persia, it came in time to be chiefly associated with that country.

XV. THE SUNG DYNASTY: POLITICS
AND THOUGHT

THE SUNG DYNASTY was, in many ways, the end of the Classic Age in China. In the arts and in thought it provided a sequel to and a development of the great creative work of the T'ang period. Painting and poetry became self-conscious and sentimental, subjective and thoughtful; religion and philosophy consisted chiefly in a revaluation of old ideas. Men were already looking backward with veneration to the past, and were basing their ideas, creative and intellectual, upon the old giants. It was the time of the encyclopedias, the catalogues, the academies. In politics, the power of China was on the wane. The western territory was already lost, and in the north the Sung rulers were unable to withstand the downward onrush of alien tribes. Thus the way was laid open for the great Mongol invasion which was to engulf the whole of China at the fall of the Sung dynasty, and so to spread over the greater part of Asia that for some years Mongols rather than Chinese were masters of the continent. In the sphere of internal politics, reform was urgent. After years of strife and civil war, the social and agrarian systems threatened to collapse altogether. The Prime Minister Wang An-shih introduced certain important and even "modern" reforms, but they were neither scrupulously administered nor permanently maintained. In comparison with T'ang times, the internal life of the country was on the decline. China was ready for a new era, and this was to dawn with the Mongol conquest, with the new ideas it brought, and especially with the opening up of relations with the Western world.

The Sung dynasty arose almost by accident. Its founder was a certain general Chao K'uang-yin in the service of a Later Chou dynasty Emperor, who, with his army, was setting out to repel attacks by the Kitans on the northern boundaries. While the troops were on the march, a lieutenant suddenly declared that he saw a second sun rising in the sky beneath the old one. This, he assured his fellow-officers, was the sign of a new Emperor about to appear in China! It was no novel event, for through the whole of the past fifty years Emperors and dynasties had followed each other like puppet kings whose strings were manipulated by capricious war-lords. The present Emperor of Chou was still too young to govern ably, and General Chao K'uang-yin had gained very wide support as the next candidate for imperial honors.

That night in camp, having fallen into a heavy sleep, he woke suddenly to find himself encircled by a cordon of his officers and men. Some of them dragged him to his feet and threw an imperial yellow robe over him. They mounted him on his horse, while an assembly of troops hailed the bewildered warrior with "Long live our King!" In the morning, with the new king at its head, the whole army marched back to the capital. The Emperor of Chou hastily abdicated, and General Chao K'uang-yin became Emperor T'ai Tsu "the Great Originator," founder of the Sung dynasty. Such was the instability of Chinese politics at the end of the Five Dynasties.

This first ruler of Sung was neither a genius nor a scoundrel; but an honest man of practical common sense, with a sincere and orderly mind. He was the type of character particularly suited for the task of reuniting those war-weary fragments into which the Chinese Empire had been broken. After his forces had secured the allegiance of all the scattered States, and China was once more a united Empire, he summoned his leading generals to a banquet. He first handed round the wine goblet, and then in frank and friendly terms asked them to surrender to him their military authority.

"I should like our cordial relations to last forever," he explained. "I should like our descendants to intermarry, and that we should all enjoy as much wealth and power as we do now. There is only one way: you must return your military authority to the State—then we shall be free from any suspicion of each other!" Filled with brotherly feeling by the wine and the Emperor's words, they all agreed to relinquish their posts. In compensation they received lucrative civil positions. The Emperor then seized the opportunity of abolishing the military governors of border districts—a T'ang institution—and thus by peaceful means brought to an end those disturbances, stirred up by ambitious war-lords, which had harassed the whole country for more than two hundred years—since the An Lu Shan rebellion.

Although it was helpful as a unifying factor, and as a means of centralizing the government, this reform alone was not enough to heal the country's wounds, and it carried its own serious disadvantages. The capital was now at Pien (K'aifeng), halfway between the modern cities of Peking and Nanking. It was thus some distance from the northern and western borders, where campaigns were constantly in progress. Delay in the delivery of orders from the capital, together with Court intrigues, must often have impeded the action of generals in the field.

Whether for these or other reasons, the efforts of Sung armies to hold back invaders on the frontiers were a disastrous failure. The Kitans especially, in the North, repulsed one attack after another, inflicting heavy losses, until the Sung Emperors were obliged to let them settle where they willed. The only result of these campaigns for the Chinese citizen was an ever-increased taxation, while the army of the central government was doubled, trebled, and quadrupled, without effect. In the reign of T'ai Tsu, the first Sung Emperor, these troops numbered only 378,000, while a hundred years later they had reached the figure of 1,162,000! It is perhaps understandable that the huge additional forces succeeded in little but in draining the national exchequer. The government had adopted a charitable policy of enlisting peasants at famine times, to save them from starvation, so that the Sung imperial army was not unlike Falstaff's ragged regiment—on a greatly enlarged scale—the rags and tatters of the Empire!

The rulers, in despair at their failure, turned to religion. They desired Heaven's blessing on their efforts, and pleaded that Heaven would grant peace to their much-distressed country. The cost of these prayers also fell on the population, for the Emperors felt bound to offer magnificent sacrifices and to undertake long pilgrimages to the Sacred mountains, attended by an appropriate imperial retinue. The weight of taxation became indeed a painful load.

Various compulsory national services added their burden to the costs of war and prayer under which the peasants labored. They included the arresting of thieves, the supervision of public granaries, and—ironically enough—assistance in the collection of taxes. None of these services received any reward, but failure to carry them out met with heavy punishment.

Meanwhile, a class of big landowners had grown up, to whom the peasants were constantly and necessarily in debt. During the civil wars that had raged in the preceding Five Dynasties, hundreds of peasants and small farmers had been driven from their fields or killed, and much of the land had fallen into disuse. The foot-paths which formerly marked the boundaries of the various properties became overgrown, and there seemed nothing to hinder those farmers who still remained from annexing as much of the surrounding land as they wished. In this way, a wealthy landlord class began to appear. From them, the honest but despairing peasants were obliged to borrow money to save their families from ruin. Groaning both under the government taxes and the usurers' demands, these wretched people were deprived of the ownership of their grain and silk before the men had taken the former from the threshing yard, or the women the latter from their looms.

It was very clear that relief must be forthcoming both for the general population and for the national finances, if the country was to be saved from collapse. A man named Wang An-shih, an energetic, ruthless reformer, a statesman with clear and astonishingly "modern" ideas, came to the rescue of the Sung empire, about a hundred years after the dynasty had been founded—almost contemporaneously with the Norman Conquest of England.

That his reforms were unpopular with the upper classes, and that many of them did not outlast his lifetime, are no discredit to the man or his work. He was possessed of an uncompromising personality, and he never shrank from making enemies. He lacked the power of patient persuasion, while his energy and speed upset the temper of the leisurely State counselors. Many of the most eminent men of the day, including the famous poet Su Shih (Su Tung-p'o), became his bitter opponents; possibly because sudden change and drastic measures are alien to Chinese habits of thought. Wang was often condemned before his proposals had been honestly examined. Eventually the very word "reform" became a party tag, and long after Wang had fallen from power, "reformers" and conservatives tussled with each other in a way that brought no credit either to themselves or the State.

However, so long as Wang An-shih remained Prime Minister (1068-1076), and enjoyed the confidence of his sovereign, very important measures were proposed and carried through with some measure of success. His principles of taxation, for instance, have formed a basis for all later Chinese administrators.

In the first instance, Wang established an official commission, for the purpose of drawing up a national budget of revenue and expenditure. He insisted that the budget be strictly adhered to, and this resulted in an annual saving of almost forty per cent! Next he advised the "green sprout" scheme, which is followed in principle even at the present day. When the green sprouts of the crops began to push up in spring, and small farmers urgently needed money for the employment of extra labor, the purchase of fertilizers, and so on, the government undertook to distribute loans, and thus save them from the usurers' claws. When the grain had been harvested, the loans had to be repaid with twenty per cent "commission." The plan enabled farmers to make an extra outlay and increase the yield of their land: both they and the government profited. At the present day, farmers' banks are established to perform the same service, though at a much lower rate of interest.

Statute labor was also abolished under Wang's reform system. All who had formerly been liable to national service were exempted on condition that they paid a yearly sum of money, proportionate to their means, into a State fund. Officials, women, and members of religious orders, who had previously been exempt from the statute labor, were obliged to contribute to the fund as well. The money thus collected from all sources was properly administered for public works; workmen were regularly engaged, and their salaries paid from the fund.

Another measure of fundamental importance was the institution of a new land survey. Every individual holding was to be measured and its productive capacity assessed. Land taxes would be levied on the basis of the survey.

These were the most important of Wang's financial reforms; his military measures were equally drastic. He began by cutting down the regular army to almost a third, which was then composed of "crack" troops. A part of the rejected troops he enrolled as a territorial force, and the remainder—all those who were really unfit to be soldiers—he disbanded and sent home. In this way the fighting power of the imperial armies was very greatly increased.

His next step was to organize a militia under a system which was called *"Pao-chia."* *"Pao"* stands for "a unit of defense" and *"chia"* means simply "armed." Every group of ten families formed a *"pao,"* every fifty families a "great *pao,"* and five hundred a "head *pao."* Each family with more than two male members sent one to serve in the militia, and the whole force was responsible for public security up and down the country. The head of each "great *pao"* was trained by officers of the regular army—was taught to ride, to shoot, and to use the various weapons of war. When the training was completed, the head men would go back to their own districts and drill their militiamen. The local defenses thus became effective soldiers under Wang's administration; banditry and other social disorders were put down, and the countryside enjoyed a great measure of security.

"Pao-ma" was an adjunct to the *Pao-chia* system, *"ma"* being the Chinese word for "horse." Groups of families, especially in the frontier districts, were intrusted with the upkeep of the army horses in

exchange for a rebate in taxation and the use of the animals in peace-
time. The families were responsible for keeping the horses well fed
and in good condition, and must pay the government for any casualties.[1]

From their appearance Wang's reforms seem practical, advanced,
and comprehensive: they appear to provide a complete machinery for
the ordering of society and the safeguarding of the State. One might
have expected a real recovery in the Sung empire, and an advance
towards what we call a "modern" civilization. In fact, the tide of
invasion from the north and west was stemmed but not checked, and
at home the reforms for the relief of the peasantry were so badly administered by local officials, either from downright bad nature or lack
of understanding, that the people's lot was only slightly alleviated.
Wang's measures were not decisive in rescuing China from the social
and political decay into which she had fallen at the decline of the
T'ang dynasty. On the one hand, they were perhaps not sufficiently
drastic to lift up the people and sweep them forward into a new era:
history proved that total invasion and conquest by the Mongols was
the movement demanded by the times. On the other hand, many of
the measures were in themselves too radical for the diehard statesmen,
and Wang pressed them on with too little regard for the opposition
he was rousing. As a result, many politicians began to attack the
premier's person, instead of passing an honest judgment on his proposals. They accused him of trying to change systems which had been
consecrated by their imperial ancestors; they called him a war-monger
for attempting to resist the invasion of the Hsia tribes from the west,
even compelling him to restore several strategic points that had been
retaken from them, and to buy with this means a temporary and discreditable peace. They called him a profiteer for imposing on farmers
the twenty per cent interest on loans, and for levying service taxes on
the privileged classes.

For many years Wang faced all opponents and held firmly on his
way, but when his measures had been partly nullified by maladminis-
tration, and when, finally, he lost the confidence of his sovereign, dis-
illusioned and disappointed, he resigned from the premiership. He
still kept a following among the younger, more enlightened politicians,
but after the death of the Emperor, and while an Empress Dowager
acted as regent to the youthful heir, the Opposition came into its own,

[1] Technicians were organized by the government under a technical bureau to study
and experiment in improved military equipment. In addition, high rewards were offered
to any member of the general public who would submit a practicable military invention.

and Wang's followers dared not raise their voices. At the Empress Dowager's death in 1094, the Emperor restored the reformists to high positions in the State, but although he and his successor were both in favor of Wang's policy, the statesmen who administered it were both stupid and dishonest. Wang's original conception was distorted and ruined. Meanwhile, as the reformers and conservatives were pursuing their petty quarrels, northern tribesmen called Chin (the "Golden Tribes") took advantage of the government's disunity to invade the Sung empire. They attacked and destroyed the capital city, compelling the Emperor to abdicate. He and his young heir were both carried off to the enemy's land, where they died a tragic death. The Northern Sung dynasty came to an end in the year 1126.

A prince of the imperial blood had, however, made good his escape from the Chin conquerors, and fled southward across the Yangtzu River to set up Court, first at Nanking, but later, after that city was attacked, at Hangchou, even farther south. This was Emperor Kao Tsung "the High," founder of the Southern Sung dynasty.

At the same time a government sponsored by the Chin invaders had been set up in the north, with a "puppet Emperor" at its head. The "puppet," however, proved too weak to check the advances of loyalist troops from the south, and was soon dethroned. The Chin became masters of Northern China. Fighting continued for some time between the two powers, and although the Sung forces were led by the famous general Yueh Fei, no decisive result was achieved. Eventually the Sung cause was betrayed by the intrigues of a prime minister—rival of Yueh Fei—who persuaded Emperor Kao Tsung to sue for peace. A settlement was reached in 1141 by which the frontiers of the two kingdoms were laid down, and it was agreed that the Sung Emperor should address the Chin Emperor as a "nephew" to an "uncle." Further, he should present "gifts" annually to his "uncle" to the value of a hundred thousand taels of silver and a hundred thousand pieces of silk.[1]

The amicable arrangement was not destined to last. The Mongol conquerors were already on the march, and they fell upon the nations in their paths like tigers upon their jungle victims. The Sung politicians made an alliance with them in order to defeat the hated "uncle," a deed which was accomplished in 1234. But no sooner was the Chin empire wiped out than the Mongols broke with their Sung ally and turned their forces against his capital. Beautiful Hangchou

[1] Later the terminology was modified to "Younger Brother" and "Elder Brother."

fell to them in 1276. In three years' time, the Sung forces had been utterly destroyed by the formidable Mongols; crushed—in the expressive words of an historian—as "the Sacred Mountain T'ai would crush an egg!" China was incorporated into the vast Mongol empire.

The story of the Sung dynasty seems to be one of incurable weakness. An inward rot had spread too far to be eradicated. But in the intellectual and creative life of that time there was no sign of decay. It was a period of stocktaking, and also of advance, and the most marked advance was, undoubtedly, in the realm of painting, the finest examples of which may rank beside the masterpieces of the world. The glorious outpouring of Sung art is chiefly characterized by an intensely keen apprehension of natural forms, a fresh understanding of landscape, and its presentation infused with "spirit." It may well be that the confusion and decay which had long abounded in politics turned creative minds away from worldly affairs and sent them to study Nature. We already see a precedent for this in the life and work of Fan K'uan, a master of landscape from the Five Dynasties period. Disgusted with the confusion of the times, he passed many years as a hermit, living in remote mountain valleys, and becoming, as he said, "a student of the Creator." He never wearied of study: deep in the moonlit night, and in the cold snows of winter, he still turned his painter's eye upon the mighty forms of Nature. His landscapes reflect a profound inner experience—the mood of one who has probed Nature's secrets.

All the great Sung painters have, like Fan K'uan, approached Nature rather as mystics and poets than as mere painters. From them we obtain a new vision of the external world and a poetic interpretation of Nature that mirrors the painter's heart. They aimed chiefly at expressing the essence and "spirit" of a scene while ignoring the details. The empty spaces in a picture were as pregnant of meaning as the brush strokes: thoughtfully placed, they might suggest to the discerning onlooker hundreds of miles of water, or valley, or unlimited tracts of cloudy air.

Painting at this time reached such a peak of development that it was included in the subjects for official examinations. The Imperial Academy of Painting was founded, and it ranked above the Academies of Calligraphy, of the Lute, and of Chess. By its establishment, painting traditions were fostered and students were encouraged to study the technique of old Masters. Important as it was, this institution must largely be blamed for the vice of imitation so prevalent

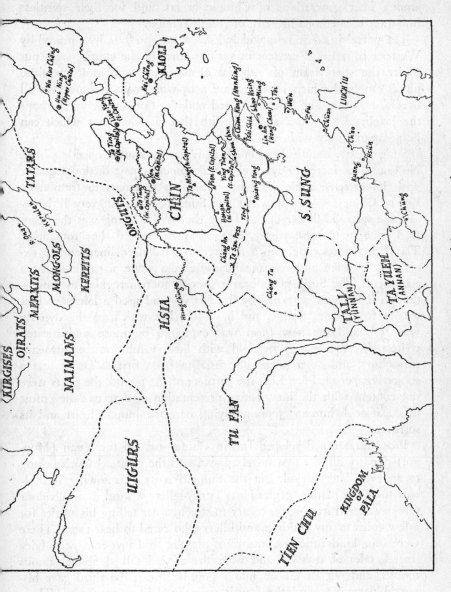

THE SUNG SOUTHERN PERIOD (*cir.* A.D. 1141)

among later generations of Chinese artists, and for their spiritless imitation of methods in place of free invention.

The porcelain of Sung is widely known and profoundly admired by Western countries. Furnaces in various parts of the empire were put under the supervision of imperial officials, and the most exquisite pieces emerged which have become a by-word with connoisseurs all over the world. The "ox-blood" red and the pure white are perhaps the loveliest: the latter suffused with that shadowy tint which can be compared only with moonlight.

Sung poetry, beautiful though it is, is hardly known outside China. No doubt the increasingly allusive and obscure poetic diction together with its extreme subjectivity has proved a deterrent to translators. But to Chinese lovers of poetry the Sung poems rank very little below the splendid flower of the T'ang dynasty. If T'ang was the "classical" age in Chinese poetry, Sung may be termed the "romantic." The T'ang poets caught in a few regular, balanced lines, and in exquisitely delicate and restrained language, a scene, a situation, or a sentiment. The Sung poets beat a longer, more irregular measure— though it too was governed by fixed laws—and used a language that was at first direct, simple, and heart-felt, but which, as the dynasty wore on, and the new form was exploited by more sophisticated writers, became heavily overlaid with literary allusions, extravagant metaphors, and other poetic devices. But from first to last it was a subjective, personal art. Like the painters of the period, the poets were not content with the imaginative presentation of a scene—they must infuse it with human emotion, laying bare the human heart and its sorrows.

Prose literature developed late in China—not till the Yuan (Mongol) dynasty did the first novel appear, and the greatest novels belong to an even later period. But the Sung dynasty was sowing seed. It was the time of the "professional" story-teller—a kind of troubadour who wandered from street-corner to street-corner telling his stories for a few coins to any children and idlers who cared to hear them. There were four kinds: the first and most popular told love-romances, fairy stories, tales of mystery and war; the second talked about famous monks, and put Buddhism into a popular form; the third gave historical narratives, and the fourth specialized in conundrums. These stories, passed from mouth to mouth, were occasionally written down in the rough spoken language of the time. In themselves, they were not "literature," but they were used by the great Chinese novelists of the future in such works as "All Men Are Brothers" *("Shui Hu"),*

"The Romances of the Three Kingdoms" *("San Kuo"),* and "The Western Pilgrimage" *("Hsi Yu Chi").*

No record of the Sung dynasty would be complete without a reference to its intellectual life. The outstanding development here was the formation of a neo-Confucianist school, partly religious, partly philosophic. By the Chinese it is called the School of Li-ism, *"li"* having the original meaning of "the vein in jade" and the extended meaning of the "life principle." Li-ism was a kind of summing-up or recension of the ethics, morals, and beliefs of the past, and as such was perfectly in keeping with the spirit of the times. It contained the principles of Confucianism in a new form, thoroughly fused with both Taoism and Buddhism. Its disciples, like many of the Sung painters and poets, cut themselves away from politics and worldly affairs, and gathered in study groups deep in the country. Small numbers of students would collect round some distinguished scholar, and the little party would strive to understand "li," "the life principle," in a secluded valley, or on the banks of a stream. This development of study circles was quite in conformity with Confucius' own practice, but the idea of holding them in the lap of Nature must have derived from Buddhism. Buddhist monks usually built their monasteries on mountain peaks, very far from the habitations of man.

The "li" round which the neo-Confucianists assembled their metaphysic clearly has some kinship with the "tao" of Taoism—the natural law to which every being, animate and inanimate, should conform if it is not perverted by exterior influences.

The neo-Confucianists—or Li-its—believed that "li," the inner spirit, or life force, of all things, existed before the creation of the world. Before the invention of house-building, boat- or chariot-making, for instance, the principle or idea—the "li"—of house-building and boat- and chariot-making existed, and this "li" was discovered by the wise men who had so attuned themselves to the inner "natural" world that they had discovered its secrets.

The same principle applied to human personality. Much controversy had arisen in the past among the followers of Confucius as to the fundamental nature of man. Hsun-tzu and some of the earliest disciples, filled with gloom and despair about the race, declared that man was essentially evil, and that only by the practice of self-control and attendance to the rites could he regulate his behavior according to the will of Nature. Mencius and other Confucianists, however, asserted that the nature of man must be essentially good. The Li-ists adopted this latter view, saying that the inborn nature of man has a tendency to goodness. They likened the "li" in man to the luster of a pearl. Just as a pearl grows dull when it is covered with dust, so is the inborn goodness of man's nature dulled with worldly passions. All the endeavors of a wise man, therefore, are directed towards freeing himself from the temptations of the passions, and this he learns to do chiefly through an understanding of the world.

On this point there was a divergence of thought among the Li-ists which led subsequently to the formation of two separate schools, the contemplative and the scientific. The leader of the scientific school was Chu Hsi, a great naturalistic philosopher and a brilliant scholar. He held that only by a comprehensive knowledge of all the phenomena of the world could man bring his spirit—the "li" in his nature—into harmony with the great creative spirit of heaven and earth. Knowledge was the keystone to the Perfect Life.

> *The men of old who wished to spread complete virtue*
> *throughout the world*
> *First ordered well their own State.*
> *Wishing to order well their State*
> *They first regulated their families.*
> *Wishing to regulate their families*
> *They first cultivated their own person.*
> *Wishing to cultivate their person*
> *They first rectified their hearts.*
> *Wishing to rectify their hearts*
> *They first tried to be sincere in thought.*
> *Wishing to be sincere in thought*
> *They first extended to the utmost their knowledge.*
> *Such extension of knowledge*
> *Depended on the study of phenomena.*

This quotation from the "Great Learning," a Confucian Classic, with its typically Confucian orderliness and slightly pompous utterance, was more or less adopted by the disciples of Chu Hsi as their motto. They were closer to the teachings of the Master, Confucius, than were the contemplative Li-ists, who were much influenced by Buddhism and Taoism.

Chu Hsi himself was a faithful student of the Sage. He wrote commentaries on most of the important Confucian Classics, and edited the texts; his interpretations were accepted by all scholars until very recent times, as if they had the authority of a Bible. He seems to have emulated the rigorous life which Confucius had chosen. "Rising at dawn," writes his biographer, "he clothed himself decently and paid homage to his ancestors and to Confucius. Then he went to his study and attended to his daily work. Sitting or sleeping he held himself erect: working or resting he behaved according to the model of behavior prescribed by Confucius in his Classics. Everything in his home was permanently in good order, and in this way he lived from youth to old age. He was faithful to his friends and a diligent scholar." Small wonder that many of his disciples called him Chufucius!

The head of the contemplative school was one Lu Chiu-yuan. In accordance with Chu Hsi on most of the fundamental principles of Li-ism, he differed from him on the value of knowledge and learning. While Chu Hsi's disciples were occupied with research and the rational interpretation of ancient philosophy, Lu Chiu-yuan's followers scorned controversy and looked on study with considerable skepticism. They believed in intuitive knowledge, and it was this section especially of the Li-ists who went to the quietness of Nature for enlightenment. In outlook, they owed as much to the meditative (Ch'an or Zen) school of Buddhism and to the original Taoism, before it had been vulgarized by common superstitions, as to the teachings of Confucius.

To illustrate the natural goodness of man's mind, Lu Chiu-yuan was fond of quoting the story from Mencius about the baby crawling towards the edge of a well. A man seeing this will hurry to save the child, he would explain, and he will do this without regard to the gratitude he will have from the parents, or the reputation he will gain from the onlookers or his friends. It is the prompting of "li" in his mind which causes him to act spontaneously without thought or calculation. The man who performed this good action needed no books to prompt him: he acted according to the true nature of his mind, and if all his conduct was in conformity with this action, he would be leading a life of perfect goodness. He would have taken the dust from the pearl, set free the "li" in his nature.

The Li-ist School is the mature fruit of thousands of years of Chinese thought and culture. The spiritual influences that had acted upon China in the past, culture that had been brought from lands far beyond the Chinese borders, are fused and concentrated in this body of thought. Much that is beautiful and significant in Sung painting and poetry derives from it—the calm and quietness, the depth, the profound understanding of Nature, the breadth of conception. But with the fall of this ripe fruit, an era of civilization ended. China began to enter a new world.

XVI. THE SUNG DYNASTY: THE KITANS, THE HSIA, AND THE CHIN TRIBES

THE CHINESE EMPIRE is not a determined geographic entity: the history of China shows a kind of territorial ebb and flow. When strong sovereigns of a powerful ruling house occupied the "Dragon Throne," an expansion of empire was sure to follow. The border tribes would be engaged, conquered, and either incorporated into China or thrust back across the continent of Asia. These events, as we have already seen, took place during the glorious days of the Han and the T'ang dynasties. When, however, the ruling house was weak, this was the signal for the bordering peoples to press down into the fertile plains and dispossess the Chinese of their own lands.

The Sung dynasty was such a period. The inefficiency and weakness of the army, the constant squabbling of the officials, and the political disunity which resulted, offered an invitation to predatory tribes on the northern and western boundaries. The history of those times is one of constant border warfare, especially with the Kitans (i.e. the Ch'i-tans) in the North who occupied part of the lands formerly held by the Turks, and before them by the Hsiung-nu; with the people of Hsia in the Northwest, apparently a branch of the Tibetan tribesmen; and, in the Northeast, with the Chin tribe (i.e. the Golden tribe), ancestors of the Manchus, who conquered China in the seventeenth century and founded the Ch'ing dynasty. These last lived in a part of Northern Manchuria which is called "Long White Mountains and Black Dragon River valley."

The Kitans, a race of warriors and hunters, with a clan organization, began as a small subject tribe of the Turks in the years preceding the T'ang dynasty. The legend of their origin tells how an angel mounted on a white horse floated eastward down a stream, while the heavenly spirit of a maiden mounted on a green ox floated to meet him down a westward-flowing river. At the meeting place of the waters the two united, and it was called "The Mountain of Leaves." Eight sons were born to them, and they founded the eight clans of the Kitan race. The chieftains of each clan elected a grand chieftain of the whole tribe, who was given a flag and drum to symbolize his authority. The Grand Chieftain was responsible for the general well-being of his people, and especially for averting famines and cattle-plagues. If any disaster of this sort befell the tribe, he must resign and give place to a new leader.

When their masters, the Turks, were beaten and dispersed by the T'ang armies, the Kitans grew bolder and sallied out towards the coveted Chinese plains. During the Five Dynasties period which followed the T'ang, they advanced, through a series of battles, to the very edge of the Chinese northern boundary, and settled there, await-ing an opportunity to creep farther south. The Chinese governor of those frontier districts [1] kept the Kitans at bay for a time by starva-tion. Every year, when the frosts began in autumn, he would have all the border grasslands set on fire, so that the Kitan cattle had no fod-der for the winter. The policy was effective. The Kitan chieftains came to modest terms with the governor, bringing him gifts of their best horses as an inducement to neighborly conduct.

The chiefs of the eight clans were, however, dissatisfied with this relationship, and pressed for a more energetic policy. The Grand Chieftain was relieved of his position, and a new ruler was elected of uncompromising character. His first action was to hold a banquet in celebration of the "salt harvest," to which he invited all the clan chief-tains. On their arrival they were, one and all, ambushed and murdered. The murderer proclaimed himself King of the Kitans, bringing the eight clans under his single sovereignty. From that day the power of the Kitans began to grow until they were masters of a large kingdom covering most of the old Hsiung-nu and Turkish empires.

This period in China was one of the deepest political corruption. None of the so-called "Emperors" of the Five Dynasties held author-ity by right or loyalty: they kept their thrones by force and bribes, while "pretenders" sprang up like mushrooms in summer. Such con-ditions were naturally very favorable to the advancing Kitans, who took full advantage of political intrigue to tighten their hold upon Chinese territory. There was, for instance, a rascally general of the Later T'ang empire who hoped with the Kitans' help to make himself king of yet another dynasty. Not only did he servilely agree to address the Kitan ruler as "Father" and "King" and offer him three hundred thousand pieces of silk every year, but he even surrendered to the enemy sixteen prefectures, covering all the strategic points for defense

[1] Liu Jen-kung, governor of Yu-chou—the district round present-day Peking. He was murdered in 914.

in Northern China, including modern Peking. This land the Sung Emperors in later years tried vainly to recover in campaign after campaign.

The Kitan Emperor proved a stern parent to his generous "son." Whenever a birth, marriage, or funeral took place among the members of the Kitan Court, the general (who was now "Emperor of Later Tsin") must send extravagant presents. Huge bribes were freely extorted, not only by the Kitan sovereign, but by any member of his family. At the death of this disreputable character, his son, succeeding to the ill-gotten throne, adopted a sterner attitude. He agreed to call the Kitan ruler "grandfather," but refused him the title of "King." The King of the Kitans, enraged at this lack of respect, sent an envoy post-haste to the unregenerate grandson, demanding apologies and a change of attitude. He was received coldly, and given this message to carry back: "You are asking too much. We are only your grandson— that and no more. If you like, grandfather, you may prepare to fight us. We have a hundred thousand soldiers with swords in their hands, newly sharpened on the whetstones! But beware, grandfather! If you are defeated by your grandson, you will be the laughing stock of the whole world!"

Such a challenge was not to be ignored: the Kitan troops began to march southward. The war lasted for years, and fighting was extremely bitter. At last the capital of the little "empire" fell, the proud "grandson" was taken prisoner, and the Kitans became masters of yet more Chinese lands. After this success the Kitan troops deliberately plundered the peasants along both banks of the Yellow River, stole their cattle and grain, and confiscated silk wherever they found it. Such was the situation when the Sung dynasty began.

For many years the Kitans robbed and plundered the people of Northern China, and the Sung armies could do nothing against them. Every autumn, winter, and early spring they stripped the fields and emptied the granaries of the defenseless peasants. In 979 and 984, Sung armies engaged the Kitan forces, but without success. At last, in 1004, after many indecisive battles had been waged, the two sovereigns met on the battle ground and agreed to terms. In the amicable arrangement that followed, the Emperor of Sung was to pay a hundred thousand taels of silver annually, and two hundred thousand pieces of silk. He was, moreover, to address the Kitan ruler's mother as "Aunt," while the Kitan King addressed the Sung Emperor by the familiar title of "Elder Brother!"

By this treaty, the Kitans had consolidated their position in the

North, but some years later a new enemy rose up—the tribesmen of Chin (i.e. the Golden tribe) on their eastern border. This tribe formed a subject State to the Kitans and had suffered much from its overlords. The King of the Kitans at that time was an enthusiastic huntsman, and as the Chins specialized in breeding a cunning kind of hawk called "the green hawk of the Eastern Sea," nothing would please him but that they should hand over the young birds to him every year. The messengers he sent to collect the hawks behaved disreputably: not only did they demand lavish hospitality during their stay in the country, but insisted on having women to sport with. At last the Chin, under an energetic chieftain, rebelled in defense of their women's honor, and in the years 1125 and 1126 fought ferociously against the Kitan troops. They succeeded in capturing all the eastern provinces of the Kitan empire, and thus began its disintegration.

News of the defeat soon reached the Chinese Emperor, and on the pretext of sending a horse-purchasing commission, he dispatched envoys to Chin to propose concerted attack. Agreement on military co-operations was reached, and hostilities began immediately. The Chin troops battered their way victoriously through one province after another and captured the Kitan Emperor, while the Sung armies, feeble and badly led, were unable even to take the last capital city until they were relieved by their allies. The Kitan empire finally collapsed in 1122. The tribe was utterly dispersed, like so many others in the past who had attempted to settle on the Chinese borders but could not resist the temptation to grab and pillage. One of their generals managed to escape to Samarkand in Central Asia with a following of Kitan tribesmen, and there at Kashgaria founded a new kingdom, which was called the Kingdom of Kara Khitai (i.e. the Western Liao Empire). It was short lived, and fell before the Mongol conquerors.

The early Sung dynasty with its political and military weakness was a fruitful time for the building of new empires near the Chinese frontier, and it was then that the short-lived, but powerful Hsia empire was founded. The Hsia people lived to the northwest of the Sung territory; and so long as they remained an unsophisticated tribe, having no cultural contact with the Chinese, their civilization was of a very primitive sort. They themselves claimed to have descended from monkeys. They were an agricultural community, making a living by tilling land and tending cattle. They dressed in animal skins and roofed their buildings with fur. They lived chiefly on meat. They had no written language and no calendar. When the buds began to break on the trees, they knew it was spring and time for planting; when the leaves fell, they knew autumn was coming and that the crops must be gathered.

The T'ang empire, as it spread its great hands over Asia and gathered a large part of the continent into its grasp, numbered the Hsia tribe among its subject States. And so it remained until the beginning of the Sung dynasty. Over this long period the Hsia people had been assimilating something of the Chinese civilization. The time was ripe for them to proclaim themselves an independent and progressive nation. This happened in the year 1038 when an enlightened chieftain, Yuan Hao, became their tribal leader, proclaimed their territory an empire and himself their first Emperor. Yuan Hao was a very lovable character—a brave soldier, a scholar, and an artist. He painted skillfully, and was well learned in Chinese literature and Buddhism. He worked hard to raise the educational standard of his country, basing it on that of the Chinese. He imitated the Chinese system of administration, the official examination system, the rites and ceremonies. He set up a National University in his capital city, to which there came at one time as many as three thousand students. Some were even sent to China for the purpose of studying Confucian Classics, while Confucius was worshiped by them as "Lord of Education." They were an industrious and diligent race.

The territory over which this first Hsia Emperor ruled was extensive, and covered nearly twenty thousand square *li*. He kept it garrisoned with fifty thousand armed men. From time to time he sent his armies southward to engage the Sung troops, but secured only minor victories at considerable expense. Eventually the two powers came to terms by which the Sung government managed to buy off the Hsia, without loss of "face" to either side. It agreed to send a "gift" of fifty thousand taels of silver, thirty thousand pieces of silk, and twenty thousand catties of tea leaves every year to the Hsia Court. In exchange, the Hsia Emperor consented to be styled "Prince Viceroy" by the Emperor of Sung.

After the death of this enlightened Hsia monarch there were further skirmishes between the two countries, and during the premiership of Wang An-shih, the great Sung politician, the Chinese armies were able to withstand and even temporarily to push back the Hsia invaders in the Northwest. But a little later the old relationship was restored. Finally, when the Chin conquered and annexed the Kitan empire, and had occupied a part of Northern China, the Hsia, whose lands lay between the Kitans and the Chinese, became separated from the latter.

In the end they shared the common fate of all the States and empires of Eastern Asia—they were swallowed up by the Mongols.

The third formidable enemy of the Sung empire were the Kitan's conquerors, the people of Chin. That conquest had been made, it is true, by the allied armies of Chin and Sung, but it was no holy alliance: each power sought territorial aggrandizement for itself, and a rift quickly formed between them. One of the five capitals of the Kitan empire was the city of Yen, now known as Peking, and which had originally formed part of the Sung territory. In the battles with the Kitans this city had fallen to the Chin troops, but at the conclusion of the war the Sung Emperor had required to have possession of it. Negotiations were somewhat acid. At last the city was returned to Sung, but at a very high price—an annual "gift" of two hundred thousand pieces of silk, two hundred thousand taels of silver, and a thousand million coins. This huge subsidy was supposed to represent the taxes which might be collected from the inhabitants of Peking, and which by right should have been paid to the Chin sovereign!

Before long the forced bonds of friendship between Chin and Sung cracked. Chin armies were once more on the march, and this time they laid siege to Pien, the Sung capital city. The first siege, in the year 1125, was withstood, and the enemy troops withdrew, but when the onslaught was renewed the following year, the city fell, and the Emperor himself and three thousand men, women, and children of the imperial household were carried off as prisoners to Chin. Few of them survived: cold, grief, starvation, or the hard labor imposed on them by their conquerors brought about their death.

By this defeat the Northern Sung dynasty came to an end, but a prince of the imperial blood who had managed to evade captivity escaped to the South and established the Southern Sung dynasty. A great part of Northern China was in chaos, and thousands of the Chinese people banded together for guerrilla warfare. Their distinguishing mark was a band of red material round their heads, for which they were called the "Red Turban Corps." Their tactics had some effect for a time, but when the regular troops were unable to help them, they were rounded up and dispersed by the enemy. North China was in the hands of the Chin invader.

The same year, not content with their first success, the Chin armies moved south, one column advancing from the East and another from the West. The Western divisions were checked some hundreds of miles from their objective; those from the East succeeded in capturing Nanking, but were trapped there for forty days by the Sung fleet. This seems to have intimidated them, for when they slipped through the defenses at last, they returned to their own territory and ceased to molest the Chinese.

At this stage Sung took up the offensive. An army under the loyal, brave, and much worshiped general Yueh Fei advanced against Pien. He was about to lay siege to it when the whole campaign was foiled by the disloyalty of an evil politician—Ch'in Kuei. This traitor had been a prisoner of the Chin, but had been released, no doubt on condition that he would influence the Sung Emperor to make peace. As Yueh Fei was about to launch the attack on Pien, Ch'in Kuei, who was now prime minister, and who by every kind of guile had won the Emperor's confidence, commanded him to cease hostilities and to return to Court. In the course of one day he dispatched a summons on twelve successive golden imperial tablets. Yueh Fei had no choice but to abandon the campaign and return. But instead of being treated as an honorable and victorious soldier, he was thrown into prison and there poisoned. An inglorious peace was made the same year with the Chin (1141). The Sung Emperor through his stupidity and credulousness had killed the man who might have restored the dynasty to its former glory. Posterity judged Yueh Fei and Ch'in Kuei. At Hangchou, the beautiful capital of Southern Sung, stands the magnificent tomb of the loyal general. Kneeling abjectly before it are the images in iron of the treacherous prime minister and his wife. A poet of later years wrote an epigram upon it:

> How happy you are, blue mountains,
> To hold the bones of the loyal!
> But you, iron, what is your sin,
> That you should form the image of a traitor?

Another decade passed without hostilities, till a new Chin Emperor Liang determined on becoming master of all China. In 1153 he moved his Court from the extreme north of his domains to the ill-fated Pien in the south. He sent artists to Hangchou that they might show the great Sung city to him in pictures—the palaces which he intended to inhabit, and the beautiful lakes and hills which were to belong to him. In his arrogance, he even composed poems celebrating his future conquests. In 1161 he mustered an army of some six hundred thousand men and proceeded at its head, accompanied by the imperial harem. When he reached the north bank of the Yangtzu River, before attempting the fateful crossing, he had an altar built on which he offered up the sacrifice of a black horse to the god of waters. He himself led the ceremonial procession, dressed in the golden armor of a conqueror.

But his proud hopes were doomed. The Sung fleet, like the Greeks challenged by Darius' armada, fought with the utmost courage and fury. The enemy was defeated on the Yangtzu River, at the foot of Ts'ai-shih Chi—the "Promontory of Rainbow Rocks," just below Nanking. The vain Chin Emperor, in his rage at the failure, ordered the rest of his army to cross the river within three days: any man who failed would be put to death. Mutiny was the only result of this brutal folly. The Emperor was seized and hanged by his own troops, who presently came to terms with Sung and retreated to their own land.

This did not end the wars between the rival powers, but the battles which filled the later years of the twelfth century had no decisive result. The disputes between Chin and Sung were only resolved at the arrival of the Mongols, who like a hurricane swept away every force that withstood them. History repeated itself strangely. These Mongols, a mixed tribe of Tungus, Turks, and Hsiung-nu inhabiting the vast Central Asian country now known as Mongolia, were at first a subject tribe of the Chin, as formerly the Chin had been subject to the Kitans. As the Chin had been oppressed by the Kitans, so had the Mongols by the Chin, and like them revolted in defense of their honor and independence. In 1206, the great Mongol ruler Jenghiz Khan, having subjected all the small countries to the north and south of the Gobi desert, was elected "Grand Khan" of the whole Mongol empire by the local chieftains. Four years later he attacked Chin and was victorious in every battle, but died before the complete conquest of Chin could be effected. In 1226, the city of Pien fell to yet another conqueror: it was taken by Jenghiz Khan's successor. The next year, assisted by the Sung troops, the Mongols took the last great Chin city. The Emperor of Chin burned himself to death amid the ruins and his huge empire perished.

The Mongols showed no gratitude to the Sung Emperor for his help, but very soon engaged him in battle. The Chinese armies, holding their own at first, could eventually do nothing against this tiger. Hangchou, the capital of Sung, fell in 1276, and though two Sung princes escaped and held the tatters of the empire together on the south coast for a time, after three years their tiny forces had been completely destroyed. The Mongols were masters of the largest empire the world had ever known.

XVII. THE MONGOLIAN DYNASTY OF YUAN

THE ORIGIN OF THE NAME "Mongol" is still a matter of conjecture. Some modern European scholars have traced it to the Chinese word *"meng,"* meaning "brave" or "fierce," which seems likely enough until we examine Chinese historical texts and find that none of the various *"meng"* characters so used has this meaning; some scholars say, however, that a Mongolian word *"mong,"* meaning "brave," is the root of this name. All the Chinese characters *"meng,"* we must conclude, appear to have been chosen to represent a certain sound, rather than sense. Chinese writers have a different and a very simple interpretation. Those tribesmen who had overthrown the empire of Northern Sung, and established their own kingdom in North China, called it the "Empire of Chin," meaning "Golden." The Mongols, say these writers, took their present name, which in their own language has the meaning of "Silver," in emulation.

The deserts and pasture lands of Central Asia, including that great tract now known as Mongolia, have been inhabited by successive tribes of nomads since the beginning of history. The Mongols were only one tribe in the long succession. Their first origins are hard to trace, but all Chinese sources agree in naming the "Black Ta-tan"—a branch of Tartars—as their immediate ancestors. The Mongol legend tells of a gray wolf and a pale deer, both of heavenly birth, who journeyed together from a great distance—some versions say the Caspian Sea—to the source of the river Onon in Northern Mongolia. There they united and a son was born to them, from whom sprang the Mongol race. This legend has clearly elements in common with the wolf-origin tale of the Turks, and there are some records which claim a Turkish origin for the Ta-tans. It is very probable that the Mongols who conquered China and a great part of Asia in the twelfth and thirteenth centuries were mixed descendants of the Ta-tan and the Turks.

From Chinese writers of the Sung period, we are able to form some picture of this great conquering people before their invasion of China. Their homes, it is said, were in black wagons or white tents. They lived by hunting and tending herds. They dressed in furs and lived chiefly on meat and milk. They had innumerable wives. Until they subjugated some of the Moslem countries, they had no artisans: their annexation of the Chin empire entitled them to claim perfection in many forms of art. They were cunning, fierce, and savage fighters.

It was to lead these sturdy, brutal, war-loving nomads that Jenghiz Khan was born in the second half of the twelfth century, and under his hand the vastest empire the world had ever known was created. In the West it extended to the borders of Eastern Europe, and in the East to the Yellow Sea. Slaughter and destruction marked the path of the conqueror, but the natural barbarism of the Mongols was manifestly subdued by the refining influence of Chinese manners. Indeed, the descendant of Jenghiz Khan and first Mongol Emperor of China —Kublai Khan—was regarded as the model of a sage and civilized ruler. It was during Kublai's reign that China really became famous to Europeans: it was the time of Marco Polo's visit to "Cathay," and of the introduction to the West of Chinese inventions—paper, printing, the compass, and gunpowder. Not only had the Mongol armies carried their conquests to the edge of the Western world, thus breaking down the barriers that had formerly separated China from Europe, but venturesome travelers who reached the Court of the great Khan in Peking were so well entertained and so astonished at the splendors and the culture they found there, that China for a period became the very center and focusing point of the known world.

Jenghiz Khan, the founder of this immense Asiatic empire, was no man of culture and fine language: he was a man with an unbounded power-lust, to be set beside such conquerors at Attila the Hun. His father Yesukai had been taken prisoner by a neighboring chieftain and sent in chains to the Emperor of Chin, then ruling in North China. The Emperor had him brutally put to death. He was nailed to a wooden ass and left to die in slow agony. Jenghiz, who now became Khan of all the Mongols in the year 1206, was determined to avenge his father. A strange and ominous cradle song, the author of which was unknown, began to pass from lip to lip of the Chin mothers as they put their children to sleep:

> *Ta-ta (Tartar) here,*
> *Ta-ta there,*
> *Our royal House will be left nowhere!*

A sense of doom was beginning to oppress the common people.

The first blow was struck in 1213. Jenghiz Khan, at the head of three armies, overran the heart of the Chin empire. His savage troops poured through North China, from its western borders to the edge of the Pacific Ocean, until the Chin Emperor pleaded for peace, and offered the Khan two princesses, five hundred youths and maidens, and three thousand horses.

It was a patched-up truce, and only a few years later war again broke out between them. This time, Jenghiz was attacked in the rear by the Khan of Khwarizm, an empire in Western Asia which lay south of the Sea of Aral. Still young, and lacking the confidence of an established leader, Jenghiz was unwilling to face so formidable an enemy. He sent envoys immediately to the Khan of Khwarizm, begging him to cease hostilities, and offering the comfortable assurance—"Thou knowest that my country is a magazine of warriors, a mine of silver, and that I have no need of other lands." His enemy, however, replied by beheading his envoy and sending the minor officials back in a humiliating manner without their beards!

Such an insult could not be allowed to pass. Jenghiz now abandoned his legitimate punishment of the Chins, in revenge for his father's murder, and began a conquering drive westwards, thereby making the Mongols notorious to the peoples of the West. In 1219, the invasion of Khwarizm began. Within a short time, Bukhara, the "center of science," was sacked, and Jenghiz Khan, heated with victory, leaped on to an altar, proclaiming an Order of the Day: "The hay is cut; feed your horses!" His troops interpreted it as he had intended: all the great cities of that powerful empire—Bukhara, Merv, Nishapur, Herrat—were laid low beneath the victorious hoofs of the Mongol cavalry. The Mongols pressed on constantly, to the borders of the Caspian Sea and beyond. At Kiev, north of the Black Sea, they halted, and fought a victorious engagement with the Russians. They ravaged Greater Bulgaria, and almost within reach of Constantinople they returned, and retired to Mongolia with their plundered treasures. Europe, after experiencing the ravages of the Huns in the eighth century, had felt once more the fury of the Mongols. She was presently to taste its culture when she sent her traders and travelers to "Cathay"—the name by which China was long known to the West.

In 1223, Jenghiz Khan turned east once more and resumed his attacks on the obstinate Chins. He had made himself master of all the territory north of the Yellow River when, in 1227, "the five planets appeared in a certain conjunction and gave a bad omen." Returning from the battlefield, the Great Khan fell dead just in front of his traveling palace, probably hit by a stray arrow.

The vast Mongolian conquests did not cease, however, with the

Khan's death. His son Ogotai, and his two grandsons Kuyak and Mangu, who became successively Khans of the Mongolian empire, led their forces again into Western Asia and Europe. Under their leadership, the Mongol expansion covered Russia, Poland, and Hungary to the west, and the whole of Northern China to the east. Mangu Khan, the last of the three, died in camp in 1259, while besieging a town of the Sung empire in Western China. He was succeeded by his brother Kublai, who has become a familiar figure to Westerners, partly through the writings of Marco Polo and partly through the English poet Coleridge's great Fragment,

> *In Xanadu did Kubla Khan*
> *A stately pleasure-dome decree,*
> *Where Alph, the sacred river, ran*
> *Through caverns measureless to man*
> *Down to a sunless sea. . . .*

Kublai was the first of the Mongol Emperors to rule in China itself. He moved his capital from Mongolia to the Chinese city named by him "the Great Capital," and which is modern Peking. A few years later he gave his empire the Chinese name of "Yuan," meaning "Greatness," and it is by this adopted title that the Mongol "dynasty" is known in history. By 1279, he had completed the conquest of China, including Korea, Indo-China, and Burma. The Mongol empire had reached the peak of its expansion.

Kublai's reign was one of splendor and success. His Court was the most brilliant in all Asia; his treasuries loaded with wealth from a conquered continent. But from his death the Mongol power began gradually and surely to decline. Kublai had himself sown the seeds of decay, although they did not mature in his lifetime. According to Mongolian custom, each successive ruler should be elected at a general assembly of princes, leading members of the ruling family, and high officials. Kublai Khan, on becoming Emperor of China, abolished the practice without consulting the privy council, and substituted the Chinese custom of hereditary succession, the throne passing regularly from father to eldest son. This measure greatly discomfited the nobles, and especially the princes of high rank, who themselves had pretensions to the throne. Under the powerful Kublai they dared not revolt, but the reigns of his successors were almost all marked by palace intrigues and plots against the throne which gradually weakened the Emperors' authority. Even in Kublai's later years, in Mongolia, Persia, and Russia, then part of the great Mongol empire, independent Khans set up their own regimes and paid no allegiance to the Great Khan in Peking. However, the downfall of the Mongol rule in China was not ultimately brought about by "Pretenders," but by a revolt of the Chinese themselves against the harshness of their foreign rulers.

Under the administration of the last Mongol Emperor, Shun Ti "the Docile," conditions went from bad to worse. Shun Ti himself was a superstitious, lustful, self-indulgent weakling, chiefly influenced by debased Lama monks, who instructed him in all sorts of magic practices and encouraged him in the lowest forms of immorality. Under their supervision, he had a room built, which he called ironically "the Room of Harmlessness," and there practiced unnatural crimes upon his mistresses. His maids-of-honor were taught to perform "the Heavenly Devil's Dance" for his entertainment, the indecency of which may well be imagined. The Lama monks who promoted these evil practices, and who more than his ministers enjoyed the Emperor's confidence, were even said to have kept their own harems.

With such a person on the throne, the true functions of government were entirely neglected, and the people's sufferings increased almost beyond endurance. Peasants already on the verge of starvation after years of famine [1]—years during which no relief had been forthcoming from the administration—were expected to hand over impossible taxes for the satisfaction of a licentious Court. A popular revolution broke out. The disturbances started in the Yangtzu River provinces, and spread like fire through the whole country. Chu Yuan-chang, leader of the most powerful revolutionary group, was himself a farmer's son, and had known hunger and despair. Some of the early uprisings were put down by the government, but as time went on they grew beyond the control of the officials. The farmer's son gradually combined the forces of all the revolutionary leaders under his sole command, and in a victorious march made himself master of the Yangtzu valley. The Mongol Court, far away in the northern capital of Peking, seemed paralyzed. The people were triumphant. In 1368, Chu Yuan-chang proclaimed himself Emperor of a new "Chinese" dynasty—the Ming, or "Brightness"—with his capital at Nanking. In the same year, his armies marched on Peking, capital of the dying Mongol empire. Shun Ti "the Docile" fled back to his home in the desert, whence had come the great conqueror Jenghiz Khan, and the Mongolian domination of China disappeared forever.

[1] Seven years of most intense famine occurred in China in the first half of the fourteenth century; in 1326, 1327, 1334, 1336, 1341, 1342, and 1346.

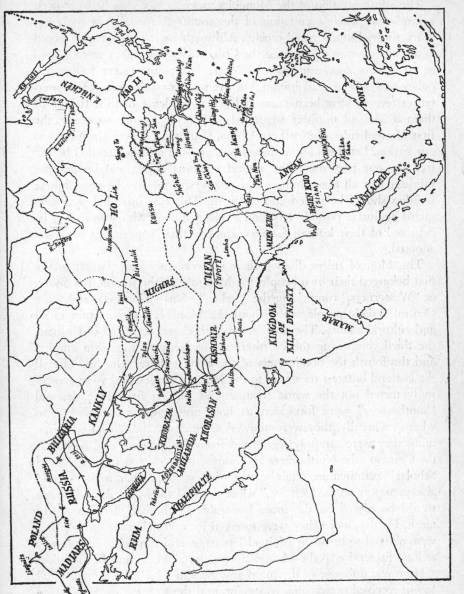

THE YUAN (MONGOLIAN) PERIOD (*cir.* A.D. 1294)

The administration of the Mongol Emperors in China had not been a kind one. Their occupation of the country, especially in the early years, showed unmitigated cruelty. Although we have no special record of atrocities committed against the Chinese, we know they were treated as an inferior race, and that the Mongols to some extent followed a policy not only of exploitation, but even of extermination. Two interesting records have been preserved giving evidence of this. In one of them a Mongol minister suggested to Jenghiz Khan's successor, the first Mongol ruler of Northern China, that "the Chinese are useless to our nation. Let them all be driven out, and the soil they tended be left free for our pastures." The second contains a proposal by another minister that all the members and relatives of the five largest Chinese families should be seized and executed. This was intended as a safeguard against a possible rebellion of the Chinese, who would thus be deprived of their leading families. Luckily these suggestions were not adopted.

The Mongol rulers divided their subjects into four classes: to the first belonged their own people, the Mongols; to the second, the *Se-mu* or "Westerners," comprising the Turks, Tufans (Tibetans), and other Central Asiatic people with whom the Mongols had a certain racial and cultural affinity. The third and fourth classes consisted of Chinese, the third comprising the Northerners, formerly of the Chin empire, and the fourth the Southerners of the Sung empire, who had offered the last and bitterest resistance to the Mongol armies, and were accordingly meted out the worst treatment of all. At first these detested "Southerners" were forbidden to hold any government office, and when, eventually, they were allowed to enter for the official examinations, they were carefully segregated from the Mongols and *Se-mu*. If the Chinese—the Northerners and Southerners—passed the "Advanced Scholar" examination, attaining the highest rank, their names would always appear on the "left list," while those of the Mongols and *Se-mu* would be placed on the more honorable "right list," irrespective of merit. Finally, when they were received into official employment, they were obliged to learn the Mongol language, and compelled also to pay at least lip-service to the Mongolian-sponsored Mohammedan religion.

Here was only one of the many instances in which the Mongols and *Se-mu* received preferential treatment, and the Chinese were subjected to indignities and petty persecution. The most flagrant breaches of justice occurred in the law-courts. In cases of theft, the Chinese were tattooed—on the left arm for the first offense, on the right arm for the second, and on the neck for the third, so that their guilt should be apparent to every passer-by. This inhumanity was never inflicted on the Mongols, who would be let off with a nominal fine. Similarly, if any Chinese was convicted of murder or manslaughter, and the victim was a Mongol or *Se-mu,* the murderer would be put to death, and a handsome fine extorted from his family to defray the victim's funeral expenses. If, however, the positions were reversed, the Mongol accused would always plead that he killed the Chinese in the heat of a quarrel, or in a state of drunkenness, and would, at most, be fined and exiled to the frontier.

Horses kept by the Chinese were liable to confiscation. By an imperial edict of 1337, they were forbidden to hold arms. They were unable to hunt, since even a bow and arrow was prohibited. Mongol garrisons were stationed throughout the country to keep a stern watch on the conquered.

Most illuminating of all the Mongol innovations was their new classification of society. Under the former Chinese administrations, Confucian scholars had ranked second only to royalty, while merchants, traders, soldiers, and artisans were regarded with some contempt. Under the Mongols, however, the Confucianists, as storehouses of ancient Chinese learning and culture, were debased in the social scale to a place only a little above the beggars.[1] Merchants and technicians whose callings had been neglected for centuries now came into the sun of Court favor. Traders who brought luxurious merchandise to the Mongol Court were given traveling facilities from all parts of the country to Peking, being provided with splendid accommodation by the local governors in all the cities through which they passed. Overseas traders received subsidies from the government. A number of ports on the Southeast China coast were opened to them, including Shanghai and Canton, and so rapid was the growth of these cities under the flow of wealth that passed through them, that Marco Polo, disembarking at Ch'uan-chou (Zaiton, or Kaitam), described it as one of the greatest seaports of the world in his time. Whenever a town was captured by the Mongols, any skillful workmen or technicians found there were spared and given both honorable treatment and fair employment. Many so-called Bureaux of Arts were opened, in Peking and in provincial towns, where these artisans were employed in spinning, embroidery, dyeing, the manufacture of blankets and furs, the sculpturing of Bud-

[1] The social classification is given as: 1, High Court officials. 2, Subordinate or local officials. 3, Lama monks. 4, Taoists. 5, Physicians. 6, Workers and artisans. 7, Hunters. 8, Professional people. 9, Confucianists. 10, Beggars.

dhist statues, the carving of amber, jade and lacquer, and the distilling of fragrant oils.

To the Westerner of the modern world, who has grown accustomed to regard the accumulation of wealth as a necessary part of an advanced civilization, and to look upon bankers and business men with at least as much favor as government officials and politicians, the Mongol divisions of society may cause no great surprise. But to the Chinese of the thirteenth century it was somewhat contrary to their noblest traditions. To them, a scholar who knew the Confucian Classics by heart, and who lived according to their precepts, was more valuable and more respected than the ablest general, the wealthiest merchant, or the trader loaded with the most splendid silks and gems. The Chinese ideal of life is one that is lived simply, without ostentation. Much wealth is felt to be vulgar; much busying with worldly affairs a waste of the life force. It may well be that the Mongols' gaudy and comfortable way of living, and their disrespect for learning, prevented the Chinese intellectuals from ever conforming completely with their conquerors.

The Mongols were by nature and inclination fighters rather than administrators. For this reason, some Europeans as well as many *Se-mus* were given high governmental posts by the Mongol rulers. Among these favored foreigners was the famous Italian traveler Marco Polo, whose "Travels," it is said, first inspired Europeans with the fascination of the East, and at least helped to incite those sea adventures of later years which made European history. Marco Polo's career has long ago captured the Western imagination; his book of travels has been translated into almost every European tongue, and his name is familiar to every Western reader. Nevertheless, it may be worth recording here a brief outline of his journeys in the Far East. In the thirteenth century, Venice was one of the great trade centers of the Western world, and Venetian merchants were renowned throughout Europe. Two of them, Maffeo and Nicolo Polo, arrived in Constantinople about the year 1255, with many cases of jewels which they offered for sale at one of those oriental bazaars for which the city was famous. Having struck some good bargains, they proceeded into the adjoining Mongol territory to make further sales. In that land they were invited by an envoy of Kublai Khan to accompany him to Peking, for the Khan loved to collect such jewels as they were offering.

Now that the whole interior of Asia had been knit into one vast empire, it was comparatively easy for Europeans to travel eastward. Accommodation on the road was everywhere provided, and the degree of safety for travelers had never been exceeded before. All this consideration was due to the Mongols' desire to encourage trade within their vast dominions. The two Venetian merchants, therefore, did not hesitate to accompany their Mongol host, and within a reasonable period of time they reached the splendid oriental Court of Kublai Khan. After being well entertained, they returned to Europe with a message from the Khan to the Pope of Rome, head of the Western world as Kublai was head of the East.

Pope Gregory X desired to send a reply to the Eastern sovereign, and there being no other means of communication between Rome and Peking, Nicolo was obliged to make the second journey to China. This time he took with him, not only his brother Maffeo, but his son Marco, then a youth of seventeen. They were honorably received at the Mongol Court, and Marco, who was evidently a lad of unusual intelligence and ability, gained particular favor with the Khan. He was dispatched on many missions to various parts of the empire, to examine the topography, and make reports. Eventually he was appointed Governor of Yangchou, a town of considerable economic importance. During their seventeen years in China, the Polos rendered outstanding service to the Mongol government. In particular, they suggested various modern improvements for the army, such as the use of cannon and catapults, and supervised their construction. The employment of these modern weapons was chiefly instrumental in the Khan's resounding victory over the Chinese garrisons at Hsiangyang in 1273; an event which brought about the collapse of the last Chinese centers of resistance.

But although they enjoyed the most luxurious hospitality in that distant country, they longed to revisit their Venetian home. The Khan responded to their plea, and sent them westward as escorts for a Mongol princess who had been betrothed to a Persian prince. After a sea voyage that lasted eighteen months, the two Venetians and the Mongol lady reached the Persian Gulf. The ship put into port and the princess disembarked; the Polos continued towards Italy by way of Constantinople, arriving in Venice in 1295. The two adventurers were a source of amazement and admiration to their friends and acquaintances, who constantly demanded to hear their story. When Marco insisted that the Khan's revenue was estimated as between ten and fifteen million gold ducats, and that he governed "millions of souls," they laughed at his fantastic figures and nicknamed him "the Millioni." Marco now became involved in the conflicts of his homeland: only a year after his return to Venice, he was taken prisoner in a battle between the Venetians and the Genoese. It was during the captivity which followed that he related the facts of his Eastern adventures to the well-known Medieval writer Rusticien de Pisa, who compiled them into the now famous book, "The Travels of Marco Polo."

The Chinese look back upon the Yuan dynasty by no means as an age of high culture, but rather as one of wealth and vulgarity, during which the old Chinese manners and thought, especially as represented by Confucianism, were either despised or suppressed. There was, however, one branch of the arts which sprang up and flowered as never before. This was the drama. Singing, acting, dancing, the art of elaborate make-up, and the performance on a stage of historical or romantic stories, had long been practiced independently in China; it was in the Yuan dynasty that they were all brought together for the first time and harmonized in a highly artistic unity. Chinese drama of all the later centuries was based upon this surprising development of the Yuan period.

The first actors in China, as in Europe, were jesters, employed by princes or the imperial Court to entertain the Great in their leisure time. Like the Fools of Shakespeare's plays, the Chinese jesters often showed themselves wiser than their royal owners, and there are many stories of tyrannical Emperors receiving a well-deserved and subtle scolding through their humorous allegories. One of these stories tells of an Emperor entertaining a certain provincial governor, notorious for his exploitation of the peasants' lands. Two Court jesters were called in to amuse the guest. One of them pretended to be a governor on visit to an Emperor, while the second accompanied him, rigged out in the guise of the "local god of the soil." The Emperor asked the meaning of the god's appearance. The reply came that the governor had extracted and carried away everything the soil could produce, and that the god had come in person to accompany his possessions! The discomfiture of the rascally governor in the presence of his Emperor can well be imagined. This early form of acting was practiced from a pre-Confucian time, and was maintained right up to the Sung dynasty, just before the Mongol invasion.

The drama which came to be characteristic of the Chinese stage, and which was initiated by the dramatists of the Mongol dynasty, combined singing with acting; and to find a precedent in China for singing as a form of public amusement, one may look to the ancient custom of singing odes and poems from the Confucian "Book of Poetry." These were performed at Court by the imperial musicians on the occasion of diplomatic feasts, suitable poems being selected which might appear to extol the honored guest. From the Han dynasty onwards, music formed an important part in Court life. A "Music Prefecture"—an Academy of Music under royal patronage—was established. In the T'ang period, the great age of the arts, poets sometimes composed the words for songs, which the imperial musicians set to music, although they wrote them more often at the request of the "sing-song girls." In the following dynasty, the Sung, these popular entertainers developed a new and more complex form of art—a combination of singing and dancing. The musical dances fell into various conventional forms, such as "Swirling and Stamping," "the Dagger Dance," and "the Great Songs." Both song and dance expressed some story, and although the dancers were not dressed in elaborate costume, they carried symbols like daggers and flags. Clearly these dancing and singing entertainers were forerunners of the actors and actresses proper. Chinese drama, starting from Yuan times, differs from Western drama not only in its use of singing by all the main characters, but also in its conventional rhythmic movements, very much akin to dancing.

In their early attempts at native drama, the Chinese used neither stage settings nor make-up, and through all the later history of drama, up to the present day, the stage settings are of the simplest—a table and some chairs and a few silk hangings. The stage illusion is created by symbolic actions: the movement of opening and shutting doors takes the place of a stage door, while other movements on the part of the actors denote a journey, a ride on horseback, a battle, and so on. But the make-up of later-day actors is quite alarming: masks of inhuman appearance and gaudy robes of great volume and splendor, huge head-dresses of feathers and flags combine to make the Chinese theater a dazzling and an extravagant spectacle. Curiously enough, this custom originated in real life. In the Six Dynasties period, when there were constant civil wars in China, a certain Northern Ch'i prince, courageous in act, but of somewhat effeminate appearance, conceived the idea of intimidating his enemy on the battlefield by wearing a ferocious mask! This story was retold on the stage, and the prince was represented by an actor in a repulsive mask, wearing a purple robe and carrying a golden whip. This was one of the first Chinese plays in which an actor used make-up, and the particular style he adopted formed a precedent for the actors of later periods.

The Yuan writers employed all these dramatic elements: dialogue, singing, dancing, and make-up. They used stories from ancient history and from contemporary events. They represented striking events in the lives of heroes and heroines known and beloved by the Chinese people. They established certain dramatic rules and conventions; there should be, for instance, only four acts to each play, and in each act only one character, and a leading character, could sing in rhymed verses—the rest of the cast must speak in more prosaic language. A good example is the great play "The Western Chamber" admirably translated into English by S. I. Hsiung. This Yuan type of play came to be known as the "Northern Drama" to distinguish it from the "Southern Drama" which was evolved by Chinese writers in the Ming period, and which followed rather different and freer dramatic conventions.

The Mongol rule in China, though comparatively short lived, and only glorious in material ways, imprinted some few permanent traits upon Chinese civilization. Whenever fresh and "barbaric" blood flowed into Chinese veins, it stimulated new life, especially in the fields of art and thought. We already saw this in the Six Dynasties, and to some extent in the T'ang period; now, under the Yuan Emperors, certain developments stand to the credit of Jenghiz Khan's countrymen. And highest among these must certainly rank the drama. Vernacular literature, so long despised by Chinese men of letters, began to command attention. Novels and plays written in unaffected language now began to appear, forerunners of the great plays and novels of the Ming period.

In painting too, significant changes in subject matter, treatment, and feeling were introduced. The graceful movement and calm spirituality of the Sung pictures gave place to a bold rhythm and strong, fresh strokes. Peaceful landscapes were less popular, while scenes of riding, hunting, and hawking, sports so much beloved by the nomads, were frequently represented. Strong and swift movement appeared in Chinese painting. The Chinese arts had, in fact, been spurred forward into new paths.

XVIII. THE MING DYNASTY

THE MONGOL DYNASTY of Yuan had shown an inpouring of power from the North, and had been a period of immense territorial expansion. The Chinese Ming dynasty which succeeded it marked a swing-over to the South, for the revolutionary bands that eventually proved strong enough to drive out the foreigners all originated from the Yangtzu River valley, and the capital of the first two rulers of the Ming dynasty was set up at Nanking. As the Mongols retreated over the Great Wall and returned to their original home in the steppes of Northern and Central Asia, the old barriers between China and the West fell again. The "Middle Kingdom" was once more hemmed in by hostile tribes and compelled to fight in defense of its frontiers—the Wall in the North and the high border mountains to the West.

The revolt of the Chinese against their Mongol rulers had been a truly national movement, already seething in the early part of the fourteenth century. The first leader of importance was the head of a religious sect known as the "White Lotus." Like so many secret religious societies in China, the White Lotus men were in fact political conspirators sheltering under the cloak of religion. The leader of this group proclaimed that Buddha himself would descend to the world in human form, for the deliverance of the oppressed, and that the present social and political order was about to fall in ruins. To increase his authority, his men declared him a descendant in the eighth generation of one of the Sung Emperors. He gained a great following among the distressed and dissatisfied, and it soon became apparent that he would readily change his role of prophet for that of temporal ruler. In a ceremony of dedication, his partisans first sacrificed a white horse and a black ox to please the god, and afterwards swore loyalty to their leader and proclaimed their desire to set him on the throne of China! Before this ambition could be achieved, however, he was captured and executed by Mongol officers. His son succeeded to the leadership of the party. Establishing a so-called capital in the lower Yangtzu valley, he entitled himself "the Little Bright King," and called his reigning era, beginning with the year 1355, "the Period of the Dragon and the Phœnix."

The Little Bright King was able to mobilize quite a formidable force, known as the "Red Army" from the red turbans worn by its members. In repeated sallies these soldiers devastated a large part of the northern provinces, as far north as the borders of modern Manchuria, and had it not been for the jealous quarrels of his lieutenants, the Little Bright King might have succeeded in overthrowing the Mongol Emperor. But without unity in the military command, the counter-attacks of the Mongols gradually whittled away the huge forces collected by his father. The Little Bright King's empire dissolved before it had properly taken shape.

The disquiet, however, which the rebel leader's activities had aroused spread far and wide, and having once conceived the idea of throwing out the Mongol tyrants, and crowning a ruler of their own race and ancestry, the people sought everywhere to set up revolutionary commanders. All through the Yangtzu River valley such men sprang forward, ready to organize the local rebels into armed bands, and to offer resistance to the government troops. Among them was one Chu Yuan-chang who later became founder of the Ming dynasty and one of the Chinese national heroes. The romantic story of this farmer's son, who by his bravery and intelligence became Emperor of all China, is as well known to Chinese children as the tale of Dick Whittington to English boys and girls, and his figure is surrounded by many a fanciful legend. It is told, for instance, that as a young herdsboy, working for a rich farmer, he killed and ate with his friends one of the oxen under his care. He then planted its tail behind a rock, and assured the farmer that his ox had dived into the earth! The furious farmer, certain that the boy was playing a trick on him, tried to pull the tail out of the ground, but, so runs the legend, the deity did so good a service for the future sovereign, that he held the ox tail fast in the ground, and even imitated the animal's angry groan at having its tail pulled! The story, probably a later invention, is doubtlessly intended to show the daring and resource of Chu Yuan-chang, and also to convince simple listeners of his being helped by an invisible power and appointed by Heaven for his great destiny.

His parents and three brothers died when he was still young, and since he was no more than a peasant boy, without means now of keeping himself alive, he became a monk, and subsequently a mendicant friar. When the uprising sponsored by the Little Bright King reached his district, his naturally active and ambitious spirit led him to join the rebels, and in their company he first began to feel the attraction of personal power. Clearly born for leadership, he soon rose from the ranks, and after a series of promotions, was made the rebel king's second-in-command. When the king's power waned, and he seemed in danger of imprisonment by the Mongols, he naturally fled for protection to Chu Yuan-chang. But he never reached Chu's headquarters: on the journey he was accidentally drowned. Chu could now command so great a following that he stepped into the dead leader's place, adopting the title "King of Wu"—the district which contained most of his supporters.

As "King of Wu" he found himself not without rivals, the most powerful of whom was the fisherman's son Ch'en Yu-liang, who by reason of his early acquaintance with boats had now built and manned a sufficiently formidable fleet of heavy junks. Chu Yuan-chang had only small swift barges with which to meet his enemy, but in a three-day battle on the great lake of P'o-yang, south of the Yangtzu, he out-maneuvered and finally set fire to the imposing fleet. The leader himself was killed by a stray arrow as he was issuing an order on board.

As he was thus destroying his rivals one after another, the future Emperor also sent part of his army northwards "to deliver the suffering people from the fire that would burn and the waters that would drown them"—a euphemistic expression for the persecution of a tyrannical government. His forces met with very little resistance: the people had no confidence in their Emperor, the dissolute weakling Shun Ti; and the leaders, both military and civil, felt that their end was approaching. In 1368, the Mongol capital of Peking was taken, and the Emperor escaped in the darkness back to his Mongolian home. The foreign rule in China collapsed completely. Some remnants of the Mongols still remained on the northwestern borders, and despite the new Emperor's desire to treat them courteously, and live at peace with them, insisted on offering battle year after year; while the exiled Shun Ti still regarded himself as the legitimate ruler of China. Not till some forty years after Chu Yuan-chang had proclaimed himself Emperor of China and first Emperor of the Ming dynasty, did the last Mongol general's resistance break against the advancing Ming troops, and the Mongol Emperors withdrew their claim to the imperial crown, resuming their old title of Khan.

The Chinese people held great expectations of the new "Chinese" dynasty. They had flocked to support it, in their longing to sweep away the hated domination of foreigners, who had no understanding of their culture and who made their lives miserable with every kind of petty tyranny and extortion. Chu Yuan-chang, the bold and talented revolutionary leader, now Emperor T'ai Tsu, founder of an absolute monarchy, proved an uncompromising and powerful ruler. With strongly enforced enactments, he restored order in a turbulent empire: ministers who opposed his policy or who showed an overreaching ambition were summarily executed. Like so many dynasty founders, T'ai Tsu abolished the current political system and substituted a form of feudalism, intending thereby to strengthen the throne. Members of the royal family were nominated to govern the richest and most strategic towns, and were allowed to appoint their own officials, build palaces for themselves, and assemble armies. They lived, in fact, like the rich barons of feudal times in Europe. Inevitably their ambitions grew, and instead of safeguarding the throne, offered the chief menace to it.

On the death of the first Emperor, a grandson Hui Ti, still only a young man, succeeded to the throne. His uncle, the Prince of Peking, commanded by now the strongest army in the Empire, and was clearly casting envious eyes upon the throne. The Emperor's counselors at Court—which at that time was still in Nanking—strongly advised him to check the power of the princes, and the Prince of Peking, hearing of this, forthwith raised his standard and began to march southwards at the head of his vast army. He declared he was acting as a loyal servant of the Emperor, and that he merely intended to make war upon those plotting Court ministers who were bent on disturbing the peace of the realm. He called his campaign the War of *"Ching-lan"*—the "War for Pacifying the Troubles."

The conflict lasted four long years, and ended with the collapse of the Nanking troops. Emperor Hui Ti ordered his gorgeous palace to be set on fire, and some say that he himself perished in the flames, before enemy forces entered the capital. Other stories tell that he escaped through a tunnel and wandered off into the deep mountains of Southwest China, where he ended his days as a Buddhist recluse. Whatever his fate, Hui Ti disappeared from history and the knowledge of men, while his uncle, the Prince of Peking, usurped the throne, becoming Ch'eng Tsu, third Emperor of the Ming dynasty. He removed the capital to Peking, where it remained until the second revolution of 1926.

The glories of Peking had already been foreshadowed in the Yuan dynasty, but it was from the time of Ch'eng Tsu that it steadily developed as the center and epitome of Chinese civilization. If the reader has seen illustrations of the gigantic buildings which have survived from the early Ming period—the walls and palaces of Peking, especially the Purple Forbidden City—a palace so vast that it is almost a city in itself —the tombs of the Ming Emperors, which stretch across whole valleys, and the Great Wall, the present remains of which date mainly from the time of Ch'eng Tsu, he will have some impression of the huge conceptions and love of splendor entertained by the third Ming Emperor.

The removal of the capital to Peking had also a great historical significance. It acted as a stronghold against invasion from North and East, for the threat of conquest was beginning to develop from these two directions: from the still undispersed Mongols and also the Manchus in the North, and from the Japanese in the Northeast. Under Ch'eng Tsu's direction, and with the help of the newly repaired and extended Great Wall, the assaults of Mongol tribesmen were effectively driven off, while attacks by Japanese troops upon the Northeast in a later time were also repelled by the Chinese. In the South the Emperor's armies advanced into the interior of Annam, now Indo-China, and all this time the famous sea expeditions of his envoy Cheng Ho were spreading the glory of China throughout the Pacific Islands and the neighboring lands.

But despite the strong, constructive personality of Ch'eng Tsu; despite the feats of his armies and envoys, Ming politics remained and continued corrupt as the dynasty advanced. This was due to the unfortunate power of the eunuchs, whose evil influence upon the administration is one of the features of the period. Court eunuchs have always played an unlucky part in Chinese politics, at least since the Han dynasty, although one Emperor after another had tried to keep their influence within bounds. The founder of the Ming dynasty was one of those who imposed restrictions on them. He limited their rank, power, and salary, and he caused to be hung from the palace gates iron tablets on which were engraved the prohibition for eunuchs to interfere with politics upon pain of death. When the Prince of Peking's rebellion was raised, eunuchs from the Nanking Court who had suffered under those restrictions escaped from the capital, taking with them valuable military secrets. These they handed over to the Peking military leaders.

When the Prince became Emperor, he rewarded the eunuchs by restoring to them all the power they had enjoyed in former dynasties, believing them to be loyal. The fifth Emperor even allowed them to be educated, though they had never before been permitted to read. Eminent scholars were instructed to teach them in the "Inner Study" of the palace, the sanctum of the Court scholars and poets. The more they learned, the more overbearing and dangerous they became.

One of the most notorious was Wang Chen, a eunuch in the Court of the sixth Ming Emperor. He had been a companion to the Emperor in his boyhood, and continued to influence him all through his reign more than any of his ministers. The Emperor addressed him by the respectful name of "Master" (teacher), while the nobles were obliged to speak to him as "Venerable Father." He was ambitious without prudence, and his rash exploits eventually cost him his life, and caused the Emperor to be captured by an invading horde of Mongols.

The quarrel between these Mongols and the Chinese began from rather ludicrous circumstances. The former had the custom of sending envoys annually to the Ming Court, at first probably on diplomatic missions, but later merely to enjoy the famous imperial hospitality. The delegation gradually grew in number until it totaled as many as three thousand men! Moreover, when the delegates reported their arrival to the Ministry of Rites, which was responsible for their entertainment, they usually doubled their number, so that each might be doubly feasted. When the Ministry discovered the truth, it made preparations for the actual number of guests, and this so discomfited and angered the Mongols that they withdrew and sent instead, in 1448, an invading army.

The Ming troops were unprepared for so formidable an engagement, but disregarding the advice of all the Emperor's ministers, Wang Chen urged his unfortunate sovereign to lead a force against the aggressors. The army, hurriedly mobilized and badly equipped, was constantly thrown into even greater confusion on its northward march by false rumors originating from no one knew where. When at length the real strength of the Mongols became known to him, even Wang Chen quailed, and persuaded the Emperor to turn back. In their disordered retreat, however, the Ming soldiers were overtaken. The source of their water supply was cut by the enemy, so that although they dug twenty feet into the ground, not the smallest trickle rewarded them. The army was by now utterly demoralized, and when the Mongol hordes charged down upon them, they were hardly able to put up any resistance. About a hundred thousand died, or were wounded; Wang Chen was killed and the Emperor carried off by the victorious enemy. Such was the disaster that overtook the Chinese throne when eunuchs were allowed to meddle in politics. Unfortunately, Wang Chen was neither the first nor the last of these dangerous mischief-makers: a long succession of them fills the pages of Ming history. There were some who climbed into royal favor by pandering to an Emperor's love of hounds, horses, and hawks; of music and dancing and wrestling; of racing and hunting; of plays. There were eunuchs who entirely swayed the foreign policy of the country, and always with an eye to their own glory rather than the benefit of China. There were others who, with a privately organized secret police, spent their venom in hunting down political

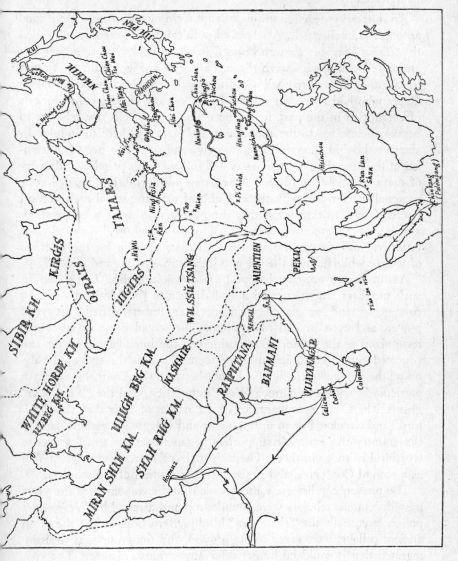

The Ming Period (*cir.* A.D. 1415)

rivals and bringing about from time to time a hideous reign of terror in the capital.

An interesting reaction to this corrupt form of government developed among the intellectuals. A school of political critics was formed, called the *"Tung Lin,"* or "Eastern Forest," to which flocked all those scholars and intellectuals who were dissatisfied with the government. It was founded by a well-reputed Confucianist, formerly a high official at Court who had retired in disgust from political life. At many periods of corruption in the past, it had been the habit of Chinese scholars to betake themselves to the mountains and streams, there to indulge in abstract thought, literature, philosophy, and art. The neo-Confucianists of the preceding Sung dynasty had followed this practice, and many of them had boldly criticized the current administration, regardless of personal danger and with the sole aim of reaching social and political truths. It was in their steps that the *"Tung Lin"* men were treading, and with even greater temerity. "The man of culture," declared their founder, "will condemn him who . . . cares nothing for the interests of society while he lives the life of a hermit by streams and woods."

As time went on, courtiers and scholars joined the *"Tung Lin"* in such numbers that it formed a real danger to the administration. In courageous and outspoken writings, its members defied dictatorial power, and even invited martyrdom. The school came at last to be recognized as the organized opposition of the intelligentsia to the uneducated eunuchs and corrupt statesmen. Towards the end of the dynasty, the inevitable conflict broke out between the Court, headed by a particularly notorious eunuch Wei Chung-hsien, and the *"Tung Lin"* group. The Court sycophants listed the names of their critics as "traitors," and circulated them in the towns and villages. In various parts of the country the eunuch's supporters began to set up temples and to worship his image in them. These shameless flatterers even hailed Wei as a second Confucius, and praised his persecution of the scholars.

The uneven conflict grew more violent and envenomed as the years passed. Famous scholars were rounded up and arrested by Wei's secret police. Eventually the *"Tung Lin"* headquarters, built on the site of an ancient college, were razed to the ground, and the group was so disintegrated that it could no longer offer any serious resistance. The government was left to perish in its own folly.

The closing years of the Ming dynasty were marked, not only by the growing power of unstatesmanlike eunuchs, and their persecution of intellectual critics, but also by threats of invasion from two sides. Inner corruption and assaults from without were combining to overthrow an already effete government. The two sources of attack were the Japanese under their madly ambitious prime minister Hideyoshi, and the newly grown Manchus in the North. Hideyoshi's forces had begun to nibble at Korea, which strategically offered a serious threat to the capital of Peking. His expeditions in this direction were unfruitful in the main, but the campaigns proved all too costly for the impoverished Ming treasury. The Manchu threat was a graver one, for no hazardous sea journey separated their forces from China: only the Wall and the Ming border garrisons.

The last Emperor, I Tsung, inherited a half-shattered empire. War expenditures had laid an unendurable burden upon the people, and a succession of famine years drove thousands of them to become bandits, roaming and plundering wherever they expected to find booty. They started a terrible revolt in the Northwest, and there was hardly a province in the empire which did not suffer devastation. In 1643, a bandit force occupied Peking, and the Emperor who, though not lacking in many amiable qualities, had been too weak to stem the advance, committed suicide. In the confusion and looting that followed, the Manchu forces broke through the border, and with their better equipped and organized armies soon overpowered the irregular bandit troops and captured Peking. The Manchu leader then mounted the throne of China, and in 1644 the new Ch'ing dynasty began—a dynasty of fresh expansions and conquests, though one which, like its predecessor, also perished at last through folly and incompetence.

The three hundred years of Ming rule, from 1368 till 1644, can hardly rank among the most progressive eras of Chinese history. The greatest pages had already been written by the end of the Sung dynasty, and not till the strong winds of revolution swept her in the twentieth century did China show promise of returning to her former glory. Some few of the Ming rulers had been men of remarkable character and administrative talent, but with the exception of Ch'eng Tsu, no one could compare with the giants of the past. Court life was rich and brilliant, but its splendor was tempered with licentiousness, and at some periods with a high degree of political corruption. There was a worm in the bud!

Ming culture is by no means to be underestimated, though here again its most important achievements were made on the somewhat lower slopes of Parnassus. Ceramics and cloisonné, embroidery and tapestry, architecture and carving—forms of art which the Chinese themselves have never rated highly, although they are widely praised by Western connoisseurs, are the outstanding products of the time. The exquisite *Ku* embroideries, so fine that they are also called "painted embroider-

ies"; the *"Ching-tai* blue" enamel vessels so beloved of Western collectors; the Temple of Heaven at Peking, built of pure white marble
and *liuli*; carving in jade, rhinoceros horn, gold, silver, agate, and
bronze—all evince an elegance, refinement, and delicacy of craftsman-
ship. Painting, although it could boast several important figures such as
Tung Ch'i-ch'ang, lacked the creative power of former periods: it was
graceful without strength, and pleasing without intensity. In the field
of letters, novels and plays came into their own. Both forms traced their
origin from the Yuan dynasty and even earlier, but it was in Ming
times that the novel was fully developed in such memorable examples
as *"San Kuo"* and *"Hsi Yu Chi,"* many of which have been translated
into European languages. The Ming dramatists evolved a new type of
play, known as the "Southern Drama" to distinguish it from the
"Northern Drama" of Yuan, having its own rules, and in some districts its own characteristic melodies known as the *"K'un* tunes." [1]
These musical settings are still much appreciated by the Chinese of the
present day, although the classical drama of more recent times uses
the *"Ching* tunes" which are associated with the plays of Peking. But
novels and plays, written as they are in colloquial language, were
hardly recognized as literature by the Chinese until the twentieth century, while poetry and belles-lettres, forms which they have always
regarded as the finest flower of imaginative thought, were in the Ming
dynasty as decadent as painting, and in very similar ways. It seemed
that, on the whole, while refinement still predominated, power was
ebbing from the Chinese creative mind.

But although the Ming was not in itself a progressive era, it contained the germs of future history, both fortunate and unhappy. In this
sense it can be called a turning point in the development of Chinese
civilization.

To this period belong the great sea expeditions, sponsored by the
Emperor Ch'eng Tsu and undertaken on the most imposing scale.
Some few Chinese adventurers, and especially enterprising Buddhist
monks, had already ventured on the seas, but it was not until Ming
times that China began to make her name more widely known to
peoples of the Asiatic coasts, by grandiose and daring voyages on a
scale never equaled before or since. From then dates the preponderant
influence of China in the South Seas, whose lands are still largely col-
onized by Chinese men and women.

In earlier dynasties, contact had been made with Western Asia and

[1] Named from the town K'un-shan, near Shanghai, whence these tunes had originated.

even Eastern Europe for purposes of trade and profit, including the travels of the Polos in the thirteenth century. During the Ming dynasty an entirely new type of contact was effected: Christian missionaries from Europe arrived in China, bringing with them news of Western sciences. In their wake followed the foreign exploitation of China by the Great Powers which filled the history of the nineteenth century; and also the flood of modern learning, thought, and technical sciences which have been able to transform China into a modern nation, and to open up for her the possibilities of a new and glorious resurrection.

Another seed of future unrest was sown in the conflicts between China and Japan which broke out in the Ming dynasty. It was then that Japan first manifested an ambition to conquer her huge but enfeebled neighbor, and that the first major campaigns were fought on the continent of Asia.

In the Ming period too, closer contact was made with four other races, which were eventually to form a part of the Chinese Republic: the Mongols, the Manchurians, the Turkic Mohammedans or *Hui,* and the Tibetans.

In the chapters which follow, these four highly significant topics will be dealt with in order, and where necessary, some historical retrospect will be included.

XIX. SEA ADVENTURES

ALTHOUGH THE ROMANCES of the "Arabian Nights" only became known to the Chinese in recent years, through English translation, some of them have descriptions of Chinese merchants who traded with Arabia and who must have started out on their perilous journeys many hundreds of years ago.

The earliest Chinese record of an ambitious sea voyage comes from the Han dynasty (206 B.C.—A.D. 220). There is brief mention in the "Han History" (i.e. *"Han Shu"*) of a certain Chinese expedition, formed of officials and interpreters, which put to sea in 140 B.C. with a cargo of gold and silks. Its destination was *Huang-chih,* which we know was the Chinese name for Conjeveram, a town near Madras, and its business was to exchange the treasure it carried for "large pearls, crystals, and other precious stones." The writer describes the dangers of the passage—stormy seas and threatened attacks by pirates in the Malacca Straits. And indeed it must have been a hazardous and daring enterprise, for the Chinese are no seafaring people.

In a volume of another book, the "Later Han History" (i.e. *"Hou Han Shu"*), we read of a Chinese link with the Burmese states. In A.D. 120, according to the writer, the King of T'an (Burma) sent to the Emperor of China a band of Roman musicians and conjurers who could perform various magical tricks, swallow fire, dismember themselves, exchange the heads of animals, and other extravagant feats.

It is known that Buddhism was brought to China from India, somewhere in the beginning of the Christian era; and though we have no exact details about the earliest journeys of those Chinese monks who were ardent and adventurous enough to reach India and bring back copies of the Buddhist scriptures, it is probable that they followed a more ancient trade route. It is on record that Indian princes during the first century A.D. sent some of their more valued products to the Chinese Emperor—ivory, rhinoceros horn, and tortoiseshell, and even—miraculous as it seems in a time of oxen and camel transport—that these same Indian princes traded to China some of the rare and costly goods they had previously imported from Rome: linen, fur rugs, perfume, honey, pepper, ginger, and black salt! There is also specific mention of the Roman Emperor Antoninus in A.D. 166 sending gifts to the Han Emperor through the same port in South China. Thus did India form a link between two great civilizations, Western and Eastern, Roman and Chinese.

It seems fairly evident, then, that as early as the first century A.D. interchanges both of merchandise and culture took place between China and India, though we cannot be certain whether the Chinese merchants and scholars chose the overland route, with its vast mountain barriers and its huge stretch of wasteland, inhabited by barbarian tribes or only by wild beasts, or whether they rather chose the hazards of a sea voyage. At any rate, in the period following the Han dynasties, known historically as the period of the "Three Kingdoms," we hear of the Emperor of Wu Kingdom in the Southeast sending a naval expedition first to Japan, secondly to conquer Hainan Island, and thirdly—on a peaceful errand—to India. This expedition we know to have traveled by sea, by way of Cambodia, Siam, Borneo, and other islands of the Pacific, and to have landed at Ceylon.

Our belief that a sea route to India was known to the Chinese of very early times is further substantiated by the wanderings of the Chinese monk Fa Hsien, many accounts of which are preserved. Fa Hsien the Buddhist set out from Ch'ang-an, "the city of Lasting Peace," in A.D. 399 for India, the land of his Master. He did not return for fifteen years, and we know that at least two of them were spent at Tamluk, copying Buddhist scriptures (sutras) and sacred pictures. On his return, he boarded a merchant ship which was bound for Ceylon. He sailed for fourteen days under favorable winds until the island was reached. Fa Hsien's description of Ceylon, which he calls "the Lion Country," is recorded in his book *"Fo Kuo Chi,"* "Recollections of Buddha's Land." According to stories he heard from the inhabitants, the island had formerly been peopled by ghosts and dragons whose custom it was to bargain with any traders who landed there. They refrained from terrifying these visitors by their ghastly and ferocious appearance, but would leave in the market-places samples of the many precious goods that were to be found on the island, and—contrary to the unearthly nature of ghosts and dragons—would mark the prices upon them! The traders would examine them and make their choice, leaving the required sum of money in the place of their purchases. As the money always disappeared, it was assumed that the monsters came to fetch it, and nobody dared incur their anger by cheating!

But so warm, fruitful, and desirable a country could not be left indefinitely to the enjoyment of monsters: people of India and elsewhere, hearing about the delightful island with its cool sea breezes and fertile soil, immigrated and gradually built up a nation. Then Buddha, so it was told, mysteriously visited Ceylon, and as a symbol of his power left the imprint of his two holy feet, the one to the north of the present capital, and the other on a mountain top just beyond the city. Fa Hsien describes the pagoda which was built round the right footprint. It was four hundred feet high, painted gold and silver, and composed of costly materials. Beside the pagoda rose a great temple inhabited by five thousand Buddhist monks. In the huge central hall stood a jade image of Buddha, twenty feet high, encrusted with seven kinds of precious stones. Dazzling light seemed to radiate from the form, and its digni-fied mien was beyond the power of words to express. In the palm of the right hand lay a priceless pearl.

From Ceylon, Fa Hsien again boarded a large merchant ship which was sailing to the East Indies. The mild winds that first bore them along changed shortly into terrible gales and storms. The ship appar-ently sprang a leak, and the passengers had to throw their possessions overboard to lighten the weight, until the captain was able to rush the ship ashore upon an island and repair the damage. Fa Hsien, we imagine, was allowed to cling to his precious copies of Buddhist texts and paintings. After some days the ship resumed her course, but so formidable were the threats from pirates that in maneuvering to avoid them, she lost her way. For ninety days she tossed on the great chaos of seas, driven at the will of the winds, and with only the stars for guide. In the darkness of night, the passengers, we are told, were terrified almost to frenzy by the crashing waves and the vague forms of turtles, giant fishes, and sea monsters. At last their ordeal ended in a safe land-ing at Java.

Fa Hsien stayed in Java for five months: whether to recover his spirits before venturing once more upon the sea, he does not specify. The last stage of his journey, from Java to Canton, lasted eighty days, and the wretched monk was again tossed in perpetual storms. By the eightieth day, the whole crew were in the most despondent condition, for their store of fresh water was exhausted. By good fortune, however, the Chinese shore was just then sighted, and the ship put into port at Ch'ingchou on the coast of Shantung. Fa Hsien fell into the company of two huntsmen, and was conducted by them to the local prefecture. The prefect equipped him with a chariot and horses, and in this man-ner the adventurous monk returned to Ch'ang-an.

During the following centuries, in the later period of the Six Dynasties, there appears to have been considerable intercourse between both merchants and monks of India and China, though detailed records of their journeys are hard to find. At the end of the period, when one by one these short-lived dynasties collapsed and China once more came under the rule of a single imperial House—the Sui—a time of active development began. Besides the extension of the Great Wall, and the digging of the Imperial Grand Canal, wars were waged, a fleet launched, and envoys sent over the sea to make contact with neighboring countries. The official "History of Sui" gives, for instance, the colorful account of a journey to the King of Sumatra, undertaken by a Court official, Ch'ang Tsun, at the instigation of the Emperor Yang. This envoy, we are told, was welcomed on his arrival at the island by a convoy of thirty ships, while some kind of insignia, made of pure gold, was affixed to his own vessel. Bands were sent to the quay to escort the Chinese delegates to the King's palace, and before their audience Ch'ang Tsun and his retinue were brought to sumptuous lodgings, whither beautiful flowers in golden bowls, fragrant ointments in gold boxes, perfumed water in golden water jars, brilliant mirrors and white towels were carried, so that they might wash and adorn themselves. At dusk, two elephants, their canopies bedecked with peacocks' feathers, were sent to bear them to the audience hall; a hundred musicians, men and women, formed a procession around them. Having arrived in the King's presence, Ch'ang Tsun read aloud the Emperor of Sui's message which was graciously received. The palace orchestra was commanded to play Indian airs to charm the ears of the honored guests.

Several days later, the envoy and his retinue were invited to a royal banquet of vast dimensions. On the dining table, we read, was a dish made of leaves, fifteen feet square, and on it were arranged cakes of yellow, white, purple, and red coloring. A hundred other dishes contained beef, mutton, fish, turtles, pork, and every imaginable kind of meat and game. Wine was served in golden goblets, and lovely girls played native music while they dined.

On his return to China, Ch'ang Tsun was accompanied by a Sumatran prince, bringing presents and complimentary messages to Emperor Yang. These included a golden mallow crown and Borneo camphor—native products and great rarities for the Chinese. The writer tells how on the homeward voyage green flying fish were seen and marveled at. This journey was made in A.D. 610.[1]

---

[1] The Kingdom of "Red Soil," which Ch'ang Tsun visited, is also thought by some scholars to be within the boundaries of modern Thailand.

In the T'ang dynasty which followed Sui, and when every enterprise upon which the Sui Emperors had embarked was amplified, there seems to have been an increase in the sea traffic between China and her more western neighbors. Sea communications, we hear, extended to Arabia and Bagdad. Djerrarah on the coast of the Persian Gulf is described as having a pharos on which torches were hung to guide sailors on their course during the night.

A Buddhist monk of this period, by name I-ching, following the example of Fa Hsien, and indeed following his route fairly closely, records in his *"Ta T'ang Hsi Yu Ch'iu Fa Kao Seng Chuan"* ("Biographies of Learned Monks in the T'ang period who traveled to the Western Regions for Sutras") a description of his own journey to India. Financed by his patrons, devotees of the Buddhist faith, he set sail from Canton in 672. After a mere twenty days' sail he arrived at Sumatra, where he stayed for half a year and was much honored by the King. From Sumatra he proceeded to India, and set sail on the dangerous part of the journey—the passage of the seas which separated him from that land.

I-ching tells how his boat sailed past the shores of "the Island of Nude People," as he calls Nicobar, and how he sighted amazing forests of coco-palms and betel-nut trees. Natives leaped into their canoes at the approach of the ship, and paddled out in hundreds to do trade with its crew. They brought with them coconuts and bananas, rattan and bamboo furnishings which they bartered for metal. I-ching says that the rattan goods were of the finest quality that could be bought anywhere in the world. The men were completely naked, while the women wore only a leaf girdle. They would shoot poisoned arrows at any passers-by who refused to trade with them.

From the Nude People, I-ching sailed for half a month and reached Tamluk without further incident. He was well received by the Indians and managed to accumulate a huge number of Buddhist sutras— "enough to translate into a thousand volumes of Chinese," says I-ching. But on his return to China, his ship was set upon by pirates and he narrowly escaped with his life. The sutras were a great embarrassment to him, and he was reluctantly obliged to leave them in Sumatra, returning himself to Canton. However, a year later he was able to go back and fetch them. He brought the great library to Loyang in 689.

In the Sung and Yuan dynasties stories of trading and travel between China and her Ocean neighbors do not diminish. There is the report, for instance, of how Kublai Khan in 1292 sent a fleet of a thousand ships with many thousand sailors on board to attempt the conquest of

Java. A heavy naval engagement took place in which three thousand Chinese were killed, but the remainder took the King of Java prisoner and captured huge quantities of gold, precious perfume, and other costly and exquisite booty.

In the Ming period which followed, come the renowned exploits of Cheng Ho, indefatigable voyager in the service of Emperor Ch'eng Tsu, third and most ambitious of all the Ming sovereigns. Ch'eng Tsu was anxious to resume the foreign trade which had developed in the Yuan dynasty, but had been interrupted by civil wars. He also showed some of the love of grandeur and disregard of difficulties which is commonly associated with absolute monarchs. Expedition after expedition he sent on to the seas, full of unimaginable dangers as they must have been to the Chinese sailors of those days, partly to give a display of his own power, but mainly to extort tribute from the kings of the island countries—precious stones, pearls, coral, amber, gold, perfumes and ambergris, coconuts, medicinal herbs, giraffes and lions and zebras, panthers, ostriches, and white doves.

The eunuch Cheng Ho who led these various expeditions was a person of quite remarkable character and appearance. Son of a Mohammedan, and bearing the Mohammedan name of "Hadji," a contemporary writer describes him as being of great height and strength, with a neatly molded countenance and a set of exquisite teeth. When he walked he had the movements of a tiger, and when he spoke his voice thundered.

The first expedition set sail in 1405 at the sixth moon. It consisted of sixty-two ships with a complement of 27,800 men. This fleet sailed to Campa and Java and passed Sumatra on the return journey. The King of Palembang was summoned to confer with Cheng Ho. The former, who was also a Chinese sea adventurer, while formally consenting to the meeting, defied Cheng Ho's order, approached treacherously with his own ships, and offered battle. He was defeated and taken prisoner; five thousand of his men were lost, ten of his ships burned and seven captured. Cheng Ho returned to Peking with his trophies in the ninth moon of the year 1407.

But scarcely had he wiped the sweat of travel from his brow than he was dispatched once more—this time to Siam, Java, Cochin, and Calicut on the Indian border. On the return journey he landed at Ceylon, "the Lion Country," where in the name of his master, the Ming Emperor, he presented gold and silver furnishings, and banners embroidered with gold thread, to the famous Buddhist temple. He also had a monument built in Ceylon to record his own worshiping of Buddha there, and this is preserved to the present day in the Ceylon museum. The date of his return to China is 1409 in the second moon.

Only seven months later, Cheng Ho set out again for Ceylon, but this time with forty-eight ships. A battle had been fought between Cheng Ho's men and the King of Ceylon's troops. After a large part of Cheng Ho's following had landed by the King's invitation, the latter, we are told, sent an army of fifty thousand men to attack the ships, having first cut off the landing party by piling up logs in their rear. Cheng Ho sent word to the ships' commanders that they should engage the enemy and hold out at all costs, while he himself led the two thousand men of the landing party in an attack upon the capital. The daring action met with the fullest success: the town, being wholly unprepared, fell into the hands of the attackers, and the King with the royal family was taken prisoner. The huge army that had been sent against the ships now turned to meet Cheng Ho, but so invincible was this remarkable leader that with only one man to every twenty-five of the enemy, if we are to trust the records, he still carried off the victory! He returned gloriously to China in 1411, his ships laden with captives.

From this strenuous adventure, Cheng Ho took a little longer rest: his next journey was not attempted for three years, but it was an even more ambitious one. We are told he reached Hormuz in Persia, though we do not hear much either about the journey or the country itself. The narrator contents himself with describing an unimportant family quarrel which occurred in the royal household of Sumatra, an island which Cheng Ho visited on his return voyage. Apparently an old king of Sumatra had been assassinated by "the Tattoo-faced King" of a neighboring country, and his heir had been too young either to revenge his father or to take the throne. The queen then swore an oath that she would marry any man who would avenge her husband's death, and that she would share her kingdom with him. A simple fisherman came forward in the true fairy-tale manner, and with the Sumatran army to back him, proceeded to attack and kill the Tattoo-faced King. The queen remained true to her promise, and the fisherman became her consort and king. But he was not allowed to rule in peace: the Crown Prince in the course of some years grew up, and killing the fisherman, took what he considered his rightful place on the throne of Sumatra. The feud did not end here, however, for the fisherman's son escaped to the neighboring mountains, collected kinsmen and followers, and made constant raids upon the territory of the new king. It was against this importunate person that Cheng Ho was invited to exert his martial skill. Like an Eastern Hercules, Cheng Ho had little difficulty in capturing him after a single expedition, and so returned to China.

The fifth voyage, undertaken in 1417, seems to have had a peaceful intention: Cheng Ho was sent to sea, his holds crammed with Chinese embroideries and silks which he was to present to neighboring monarchs. He seems to have spent nearly three years on this voyage, returning in the seventh moon of 1419 with a variety of presents for the Emperor: lions, panthers, ponies from Hormuz in Persia, fast-running camels and ostriches from Brava, and a hundred other curious offerings.

On the sixth journey, by a supreme feat of seamanship he reached the east coast of Africa, but the glory of the achievement was somewhat dulled, for his Emperor Ch'eng Tsu died in 1424, before he could return to China. But with such a reputation and so great a thirst for the sea, it was not likely that he would be allowed to stay idly at home: six years after the succeeding Emperor came to the throne, Cheng Ho was dispatched once more to spread the glory of China beyond the China seas. He took with him nearly twenty-eight thousand men, including officers, soldiers, sailors, interpreters, clerks, doctors, engineers, and craftsmen of various sorts—an elaborately organized enterprise. This band was for three years at sea, and came as far as Persia, and we should like to know more of its adventures than the meager records tell us.

This seems to have been the last journey that he made, but his glory has not diminished in the five hundred years since his death, either among the Chinese themselves, who so far have not produced anyone to compete with him as a sea-adventurer, or among the islands he visited. The influence which Chinese merchants still have in the East Indies, and the great numbers of Chinese who have settled there, bear witness to the importance of Cheng Ho's enterprise, while in Java he is worshiped by the natives as a god to the present day. Every year, on the thirtieth day of the sixth moon, the anniversary of his first landing, Javanese throng to a temple which has been erected to him, and pay reverence to his memory.

XX. CHINA AND THE WESTERN POWERS
(1)—THE ARRIVAL OF CHRISTIANITY

ALTHOUGH CHINA ALWAYS LIKED to think of herself as the center of the world—the Middle Kingdom—self-supporting and self-sufficient, with a culture superior to all her neighbors, and a rich endowment of spiritual and intellectual gifts, it was inevitable that, sooner or later, she should open her doors to Western culture. The arrival of Western knowledge, which proved a blessing nourished with pain, came through Christian missionaries. The Nestorians were the first to arrive, making their way from Persia in the seventh century, and they were followed by the Jesuits from Europe in the sixteenth century. The former did no harm to the Chinese, while the latter brought many benefits in the form of Western science and educational principles. Unfortunately they were followed in the nineteenth century by other missionaries who propagated their doctrines side by side with political aggression, so that they marred the friendly, harmonious impression left on the Chinese by the honest-minded Jesuit Fathers.

The T'ang dynasty, which began its rule in China in the second decade of the seventh century, was a dynasty of cultivated, adventurous, generous-minded Emperors. They sent their envoys half across the world, and they exchanged not only tribute, but thought, with other countries. Religious doctrines were brought from India, Persia, and Arabia, and temples to the different deities were erected side by side in the T'ang capital of Ch'ang-an. All kinds of creeds, both "native" and foreign, were tolerated and even patronized by the early T'ang rulers.

Nestorian Christianity—the first form of the Christian faith to reach China—was so called from the founder of this sect, Nestorius, a Syrian priest appointed patriarch of Constantinople in A.D. 428. The doctrine spread in Syria, and especially in Persia—the country with which it came to be chiefly associated. After the Nestorians, with great evangelizing zeal, had founded bishoprics through Western and Central Asia, including India, a monk named A Lo Pen at last reached China in A.D. 638. He was welcomed by the Emperor T'ai Tsung, who even lodged him in the imperial palace and commanded him to build a church in Ch'ang-an. Failing to understand the real origins of Christianity, the Chinese called the church "the Persian Temple." These early missionaries were allowed to paint the picture of the T'ang Emperor on their church walls, and encouraged to translate the Bible into Chinese. The religion itself was called by the Chinese name "Ching Chiao" —"the Brightly Shining Teaching." "Persian Temples" were later erected in several other parts of China, and the religion continued to stand in imperial favor until, in 845, the Emperor Wu banned and persecuted all "foreign" religions. From that time the power of Christianity upon Chinese civilization practically died out until the arrival of the Jesuits in the sixteenth century.

After the fall of the T'ang dynasty in 907, communications between China and the continent of Asia were broken off. The Kitans and the tribes of Chin and Hsia hedged China in from the North and West, and attacked her continually. This may well explain why the zealous Nestorian missionaries failed to penetrate. Besides, Persia, the home of the Nestorian Church, was overrun by the Mohammedans early in the seventh century, and the great Sassanian empire vanquished in 652. The Nestorians were able, fortunately, to come to terms with the invaders, but their activities were undoubtedly curtailed. However, the great Italian traveler, Marco Polo, records that in his journey of 1274 across Asia, he saw Nestorian churches all along the trade route from Bagdad to Peking, which seems to indicate that during the Yuan (Mongol) dynasty the Nestorians were again tolerated by the rulers of China, though they were themselves mostly followers of the Lama religion. At the fall of the dynasty, Nestorian influence died out almost completely.

The arrival of the Jesuits in the Far East was an event of much greater significance than the visits of the Nestorians, for they brought with them from Europe all kinds of useful learning. The Order of Jesuits, or the Society of Jesus as it is rather beautifully called, is a branch of the Roman Catholic Church founded in 1539. Its members, bound by the vows of poverty, chastity, and obedience, were highly trained religious men, as famous for their learning as for their piety. At a time when European education had become pedantic and obsolete —a mere droning of Latin—the Jesuits founded free schools in which they taught from new, up-to-date textbooks, and with a fresh, attractive manner. For three centuries they were held to be the best schoolmasters in Europe.

With this equipment they began their missionary journeys, not only to China, but to India and to the native inhabitants of both the Americas. These far journeys were partly encouraged by circumstances: the Protestant Reformation in sixteenth- and seventeenth-century Europe weakened the power of the Catholics, and inevitably drove them to seek new converts in other lands. The way to the East was made easier by the advance of Portuguese, Spanish, and Dutch traders who found their way to the Pacific islands about this time, and presently to the mainland of China.

The first, and also the greatest of these Jesuit missionaries who came in the wake of the traders was the Italian Matteo Ricci. He arrived at Macao, the concession newly acquired by the Portuguese, in 1580. With enough wisdom to realize that the Chinese were still unsympathetic to foreigners, he won the confidence of his hosts by abandoning his own European habits and adopting their way of life. He dressed in Chinese robes, learned to speak Chinese, read Chinese books, and carefully studied the manners, the arts, and the learning which the Chinese most appreciated. He ate Chinese food, drank Chinese tea, and adopted a Chinese name—Li Hsi-t'ai. In fact, he respected the Chinese and their already ancient civilization, and refrained from thrusting his own way of thought at them as if it were superior.

With the same wise attitude of mind, he did not attempt merely to preach the Bible. How should he gain converts to so strange a doctrine unless he could demonstrate its practical as well as its spiritual value? Ricci began assiduously to teach Western sciences—arithmetic, geometry, geography, astronomy, and so on. He gave lectures attacking the Chinese belief that the sky is round and the earth square. He cured diseases and established a hospital at Nanking. In this way he gradually won the respect of the Chinese for the world he represented. They ceased to regard Westerners as barbarians, and were the more ready to receive the Christian faith—the faith of the Western world.

He rose to favor with people of high rank, who were astonished at his learning: at length he was allowed to come before the Emperor and plead for the recognition of his religion. He presented a memorial to the Ming Emperor Shen Tsung, together with pictures of Christ and the Virgin Mary, a copy of the Old Testament, a crucifix, two clocks, a harp, and—as a symbol of the "new" Western learning—a book of geography! It was a strange tribute, but evidently acceptable to Shen Tsung. Subsequently Ricci was allowed to build churches in Peking, the Ming capital, and even to give public lectures on the Christian doctrines. Through his sympathetic understanding he was able to convert several hundred people within a few years, among them the Minister of Rites, Hsu Kuang-ch'i, one of the earliest Chinese "scientists."

Not only did he translate books of European learning and religion, but he wrote some original works in Chinese: "World Geography with Maps," "The True Meaning of Christianity to Catholics," "On Friendship," "The Twenty-five Words"—in which he gives his view of Confucianism—and books on geometry and astronomy.

At his death he unfortunately left no disciples of the same ability and intellect, and reactionary movements against the Catholics broke out in Nanking. This oppression continued until, at the outbreak of war between the Ming rulers and the Manchus, the performance of the Portuguese cannon so impressed the Ming Emperor that Western scientists, merchants, and priests once more found favor. Some years later, the Emperor summoned four European scientists from Macao— the source of the miraculous cannon—and appointed them as high imperial officials for the designing of firearms. These were Jean de Rocha, Emmanuel Diaz, Jules Aleni, and François Sambiasi.

Shortly before the fall of the Ming dynasty, the famous German astronomer, Adam Schall, came to Peking. Although his learning was more concerned with stars than any technical contrivances, the Ming Emperor evidently thought that all Europeans must have knowledge of cannon building. Schall was therefore instructed to design and supervise the building of twenty cannon to repel the ever-increasing threats of the Manchus. Later he was allowed to do research work at the imperial observatory, where he produced a scientific work of the utmost importance—a new almanac.

The Chinese, since the Yuan dynasty, had used the Mohammedan calendar, but towards the end of the Ming period several inaccuracies were discovered. In 1610, an eclipse of the sun was miscalculated, and European scientists were thereupon invited to assist investigations at the observatory. Another eclipse in 1629 proved the Western calendar to be far more accurate, and the Ministry of Rites authorized Adam Schall, with three colleagues and some Chinese students of astronomy, to compile an almanac. The work, begun in 1629, took five years to complete, and seemed satisfactory to the scientists. But before it could pass into general use, the Ming empire fell, and the Manchu invaders marched into Peking.

As soon as the new Manchu dynasty was established, Schall presented a plea to the Emperor's uncle on behalf of his "Western" almanac, and this seems to have been well received. The Emperor graciously approved of Schall's labors, and the almanac was duly published. Schall himself was appointed Governor of the Peking Imperial Observatory, the equivalent of the English Astronomer Royal. His sun seemed to have risen, but it was to set all too soon: at the death of the first Manchu Emperor, whose friendship and patronage had protected him from the jealousy of rivals, Schall and his almanac were publicly challenged. A Chinese writer, Yang Kuang-hsien, included a bitter indictment of the new calendar in an essay called "Against the Heathens," holding it up to the Court as a sham, filled with mistakes. Schall and his colleagues, both European and Chinese, were thrown into prison. Five Chinese officials were sentenced to death, and twenty-five Europeans exiled to Canton. Schall died of a broken heart in 1666.

The second Emperor, Sheng Tsu (better known as K'sang Hsi), although he had not intervened to save Schall from prison, was nevertheless an admirer of Western science. A few years after the German astronomer's death, he sent for his Belgian friend, Ferdinand Verbiest, who was able triumphantly to vindicate the almanac. The controversy ended in the Europeans' favor, and Yang Kuang-hsien was dismissed from office. Verbiest, in collaboration with the Spanish scientist Pereird, also reconstructed the great telescope at Peking, which bandits had wrecked in the fighting at the fall of the Ming dynasty. The new instrument was fixed in a bronze stand, beautifully engraved with dragon designs, and the whole set on a marble foundation. The materials were solid and enduring.

When the Emperor made his periodical journeys over his dominions, these two Catholic scientists accompanied him, bringing with them machinery and assistants to make an accurate survey. The result was the first accurately drawn map of China with lines of latitude and longitude. Map designers up to the present day still use it as a basis.

All these scientists and their assistants were Jesuits, and though it is their scientific work which is chiefly remembered by the Chinese, they were also missionaries, teaching their doctrines to all those who respected their learning. Both Matteo Ricci and Adam Schall, it is told, brought sacred pictures to China which were a source of wonder to the Chinese of those days, unaccustomed as they were to the Western style of painting and laws of perspective. According to a Chinese writer of the late sixteenth century, one of the pictures Ricci brought shows "the Heavenly Lord, who is the ruler and Creator of the Universe and the myriad things. The Heavenly Lord is painted as a baby, at the bosom of a woman who is called the Heavenly Mother. The picture is drawn on bronze, and there are colors on it. The figures are alive."

From the terse language we can still read the author's amazement, both at the Heavenly Lord's humility and the lively touch of the painter.

It should be mentioned, however, that until very recent times Western forms of art astonished but did not inspire the Chinese, who regarded the application of perspective as mechanical and unimaginative. The Italian artist Castiglione spent most of his life working at the Court of the Manchu Emperor Ch'ien Lung, but failed to exercise any lasting influence upon Chinese art, while a Chinese man of letters from the same period, Tsou I-kuei, has left an uncompromising criticism of Western painting in general.

"The Western painters always make use of the rules of perspective in their pictures, which gives a vivid impression of depth and distance. . . . The frescoes representing buildings are so real that we are tempted to go in. Our students will be able to make a serviceable use of some small part of these methods, which are, however, quite lacking in a personal touch. Although these works bear witness to skill in drawing and conscientiousness in workmanship, they cannot be looked upon as true painting."

The early Catholics propagated their creed with tolerance and wisdom. They made no attempt to force converts into violating their own traditional customs. They were allowed to worship Confucius, for, argued the Jesuits, this worship was a form of veneration for a great teacher of morality. The worship of ancestors was equally tolerated, for it seemed to be no more than an expression of family affection, such as a man might show to his living parents. This, the Jesuits declared, was no idol-worship—no desire to be blessed by heathen spirits. Because of their sympathetic attitude, and their generous dispensation of Western learning, the Jesuits enjoyed the happiest relations with the Chinese. The arrival of Roman Catholic priests under the direct orders of the Pope had a very different result.

In 1704, the Pope, hearing that Catholic missionaries in China were actually tolerating the worship of ancestors, sent an envoy named Tournon to Peking with orders to stop the heresy. Tournon on his arrival was so moved by the sincerity of both the tolerant missionaries and their Catholic converts, that he felt very unwilling to intervene. After hesitating for the length of three years he published a portion only of the Papal Edict, and reluctantly declared that, on the authority of His Holiness the Pope, if any Catholic priest failed to obey the edict, he must withdraw from China.

The Chinese Emperor was enraged at the interference. Who was this "Pope" who dared to dictate the conduct of persons within the imperial dominions? He, the Emperor of China, should decide who was to come and who was to stay and on what conditions! Moreover, the priests were clever scientists and the Emperor required their practical services. The wretched Tournon was thrown into prison at Macao, under the control of the Portuguese. There he was kept in close and solitary confinement, and died miserably a few years later. In the meantime the Chinese Emperor even promulgated a counter-edict to the Papal Bull in which he declared that any Christian priests who did not follow the principles set out by Matteo Ricci would be banned from Chinese territory.

In the course of the eighteenth century, the spirit of antagonism grew between China and the West. The missionaries were no longer able to make themselves popular with the Chinese: orders were issued prohibiting them from owning lands in the interior, and compelling them to live only in the "treaty ports" at the coast. At the beginning of the nineteenth century many sacred books and pictures belonging to the missionaries were collected and burned. This attitude was maintained until the English and French armies and navies inflicted defeats on the Chinese, and compelled them at the point of the bayonet to grant every kind of concession to their nationals.

The reason for this change in relationship is not far to seek. The Jesuit Fathers who arrived in China during the latter part of the Ming dynasty had asked nothing from the Chinese; had demanded no special treatment; had not even vaunted their culture above that of their hosts. Rather they had offered their Faith and learning as disinterested gifts. The Catholic priests who succeeded the Jesuits in the Manchu dynasty adopted a patronizing and dogmatic behavior, antagonizing the Chinese. But even more significant was the attempt of the Western Powers at this time to exploit China commercially.

From the reports of European travelers and priests who had made their home in the Far East, but especially from the merchants trading in the Pacific, the governments of the great Powers learned that there were huge markets in which to sell their goods, and unlimited natural resources to tap for raw materials. As machinery and industry developed in the West, the demand for fresh markets became of increasing urgency, and trade agreements were eagerly sought at the Court of China.

China, for her part, was content to be her own world, and wished to ignore the "barbarians" from across the Ocean. The Chinese mind is naturally conservative and respectful to tradition; suspicious of innovation. And with their huge productive land, and their modest

standard of living, the majority were able to live in perfect contentment, working the land by the ancient traditions and producing simple
but beautiful goods without the use of machines. They had no desire
to trade with the foreigner, nor to learn his methods.

The Emperor at his Court in Peking, styling himself the "Son of
Heaven," was accustomed to think of himself as the highest being on
earth—the ruler of "The Middle Kingdom"—and though he was
pleased to receive envoys from the English King, and accept his presents, he saw no reason for entering into any closer relation. The
message sent to George III through his ambassador Lord Macartney
by the Manchu Emperor Ch'ien Lung, is a good illustration of the
Chinese attitude. It is perfectly courteous, but absolutely exclusive. "If
you assert that your reverence for our Celestial Dynasty," runs the
message, "fills you with a desire to acquire our civilization . . . our
ceremonies and laws differ so completely from your own that, even
if your envoy were able to acquire the rudiments of our civilization,
you could not possibly transport our manners and customs to your
alien soil. . . . As your ambassador can see for himself, we possess all
things. I set no value on objects strange or ingenious, and have no use
for your country's manufactures. This then is my answer to your
request to appoint a representative to my Court, a request contrary to
our dynastic usage which would only result in inconvenience to
yourself." [1]

Macartney, who came to Peking in 1793 on a diplomatic mission
from England, with a request for the opening of three more ports to
English traders, and the right to keep an envoy at the Chinese Court,
arrived at an unfortunate time. The Emperor was celebrating his
eightieth birthday, and although Lord Macartney repeatedly explained
that he had come expressly for trade negotiations, Emperor Ch'ien
Lung insisted on treating him as if he had traveled the great distance
from England solely to attend the celebrations! He was entertained
lavishly with feasts and given letters of greeting and gifts for King
George, but nobody would listen to his protests or discuss business.
Eventually he was obliged to return with the unsatisfactory answer
we have quoted.

The Chinese Emperors set great store by etiquette, while the English
envoys took no trouble to learn oriental good form. Lord Amherst,
who followed Macartney in 1816, was even less successful than his
predecessor. He took the liberty of landing at T'ientsin, which was the

[1] "Annals and Memoirs of the Peking Court," quoted by Mr. Hodgkin in "China
in the Family of Nations."

nearest port to Peking, instead of at Canton, which was then the only port open to foreigners. Because of this breach of agreement, he was refused an audience with the Emperor. He was brought sumptuous presents for the English monarch, but was directed to return by the proper route.

The Russian envoys had had a similar reception a century and a half earlier. Several times had they visited Peking with the intention of negotiating for trade, but seldom had they been received in person by the Emperor and allowed to conduct business satisfactorily. On the other occasions the envoys had refused to conform with Chinese ceremonial and "kow-tow" in the Emperor's presence. The Russians alone of the great Powers had been able to come to terms with the Chinese during those early years of contact between East and West. In 1689 a pact was signed defining the borders of Chinese Manchuria and Russian Siberia, and Russian merchants up to the limit of two hundred were allowed to come to Peking every three years, and to remain as long as eighty days to buy and sell.

All this time, through the seventeenth and eighteenth centuries, until the disastrous results of the Opium Wars awakened China from her dream of superiority, the Chinese had resolutely refused to know anything about Western civilization. The Emperor and his officials, in whose power it lay to admit Western science and inventions, believed that primitive guns, mechanical clocks, spectacles, and other quaint novelties of that kind, represented the core of Western culture, and rightly thought they could do without them. The scholars, who must to some extent have appreciated Western science, were too deeply rooted in tradition to take more than an academic interest in it. They had learned from a disciple of Confucius that "if a man wants to be mentally honest, he must first extend his knowledge to the utmost, and such extension of knowledge lies in the investigation of things." They were therefore ready to study the natural science of the West, but they always held it to be inferior to their native learning, and little was done to put it to a practical test for the benefit of their country.

The Chinese were later to pass from a contempt of the West to an almost abject admiration, and it is only within the last few years that they have really learned to appreciate both the good and the bad of the Western world; to adopt from it what was serviceable, and to preserve the best of their own civilization. Meanwhile, the seeds sown by the unsuspecting missionaries of the sixteenth and seventeenth centuries were to bear the bitterest of fruit.

XXI. CHINA AND JAPAN (1)—
THE FIRST CONTACTS

THE ORIGINAL INHABITANTS of the Japanese islands were the Ainu, or, as the Chinese historian calls them, "the Shrimp Tribes"—a people of very different appearance from the modern Japanese. They had profuse black hair and large eyes, and the men wore flowing beards. Tradition describes them as having descent from the youngest daughter of a king on the mainland of Asia, who eloped with her lover to the islands of Japan and there founded a tribe. The descendants of this race are still to be found in the extreme north of Japan, at Yezo and Sakhalin, where the climate is cold and bleak, having been driven there by the first Japanese.

The Japanese call themselves "the people of Nippon," Nippon being their term for "the land of the rising sun." The name may well have had a Chinese origin, for since the Japanese islands lie to the east of China, in Chinese eyes the sun would appear to rise out of them. Or we may read in it a reference to the Japanese myth about the beginning of the world. According to this story, little objects like the blades of rushes came down from Heaven and were transformed into gods and goddesses. Two of them stood on the Bridge of Heaven and stretched out their spears towards the sea. Water drops fell from their spear-heads and condensed into islands—the islands of Japan. Then the heavenly pair came down into the world and lived together. The goddess gave birth to the land, the mountains and the rivers, the grasses and the forests, and at last to the Goddess of Sunshine and her brothers. The Sunshine Goddess adopted a son from one of her younger brothers, and he was destined to be the ancestor of the first Emperor of Japan. This was Jimmu Tenno, "the Divine and Brave Heavenly Emperor." He became Emperor of Kiushiu, the western portion of modern Japan, and advancing eastward with his followers, he drove out the peaceful fishermen of the Shrimp Tribes and made himself master of all Japan. Japanese Emperors to the present day are supposed to be descended from Jimmu Tenno, and are worshiped as "divine" beings.

If we turn from myth to historical evidence, we are inclined to believe that the ancestors of the Japanese did indeed come from the West to conquer the Ainu, but from the continent rather than Kiushiu. Excavations have produced emeralds which must have had a Korean origin, also daggers with Korean design. The ancient Japanese custom of taking a cold bath before making a sacrificial offering to the gods seems to have originated in Malaya. Japanese fishermen to the present day tattoo their bodies in the belief that it protects them from "sea dragons," a superstition and custom that belong to the early days of Chinese history; while the tradition that the Goddess of Sunshine was a spinner of silk seems to connect her with China. From such indications as these, we may assume with some confidence that the Japanese race, like the Japanese culture and civilization, originated in the continent of Asia.

The first known contact between China and Japan occurred in the reign of the famous Chinese Emperor Ch'in Shih Huang Ti, builder of the Great Wall. In 219 B.C. he sent a delegate, Hsu Fu, to look for the "elixir of eternal life" in "the Islands of the Immortals." It is said that Hsu Fu put out to sea with some hundreds of Chinese boys and girls, that he came to Japan with his shipload of children, that he settled there and never returned. No doubt he knew that to return to China without the immortal medicine would cost him his life. Descendants of the Chinese are still to be found in Japan, though the notion that they were the first ancestors of the Japanese race, as some people believe, is a palpable error. Hsu Fu was buried honorably at Wahayama near Osaka, and his tomb is still visited. His name has been given to a kind of Japanese paper in use at the present day, so that he has himself achieved a kind of immortality!

The Han dynasty which succeeded the Ch'in won fame in all the surrounding lands. By trade and conquest a great Chinese Empire had been created. The Japanese across the sea had also heard of the Han achievements, and thirty envoys of various Japanese princes braved the dangerous passage to visit the Han Court. There is a seal, dating from the early Christian era and bearing the inscription "King of Wo, appointed by Han," which was evidently bestowed on one of these princes by the Han Emperor. We find another interesting note among the Chinese records, namely that in the year A.D. 200 the Japanese islands were first united under one ruler, the Empress Jingo, "Empress of Divine Merit."

The Han dynasty was followed by the confusion and strife of the Six Dynasties period, and at that time many Chinese families fled in despair to the peaceful refuge of Japan. In their wake came Buddhist scholars. We read in one record of a Chinese Buddhist, Ssu-ma Ta, arriving in Japan early in the sixth century and preaching Buddhism there. The Japanese called him "God of Korea"—a sign of the awe and reverence in which they must have held apostles of that Faith. There is a story of a Japanese envoy being sent to the Sui Emperor of China in 607 and addressing him as "Buddha Emperor West of the Sea," as if the Buddhist faith was a first attribute of Chinese majesty! There is, besides, evidence that Japanese monks were sent "west of the Sea" to study Buddhism, and that even at that early time Buddhist temples were built in Japan in imitation of the Chinese ones.

The envoy to the Sui Court was the first of many to visit China. It was a perilous journey for seafarers of those days, and the envoys who undertook it were held in especial honor. Before their departure they were promoted to high rank, and invited to banquets by the "divine" Japanese Emperor himself. The latter offered prayers for their safety on the sea, and composed poems of encouragement. Students always accompanied the delegation, and it is clear that the Japanese have venerated Chinese culture from the earliest days that they encountered it. During the reign of Emperor Hsuan Tsung—the T'ang Emperor under whom Chinese arts reached one of their loftiest peaks— five hundred Japanese students were sent to study in China. Some of them stayed as long as twenty or thirty years, and brought back to their own country knowledge of astronomy, geography, mathematics, medicine, literature, music, and painting. On their return they were usually appointed to high government positions, and in this way Chinese culture and science began to permeate the whole of Japanese society.

It is no exaggeration to say that all the Japanese culture of the present day is based on that of the Chinese in the T'ang dynasty. Even the Japanese writing was brought from China. In the early period of Japanese history, historical records were actually written in Chinese. Then, in the year A.D. 741 a Japanese student named Kibi returned to his own country after eight years' study in China and created a Japanese alphabet from a modification of Chinese characters. His was called the Katakana system. Shortly afterwards, a Japanese monk modified the Chinese running style of handwriting and so formed a second Japanese alphabetical system which was called the Hiragana. Both these alphabets are used in Japan today. The Japanese language itself proved too limited to express adequately every sort of idea, with the result that almost half the terms are borrowed directly from China. This explains the characteristic appearance of a Japanese book, with its mixed printing of Chinese words together with the more cursive outline of the Japanese characters.

In the realm of culture, relations between Japanese and Chinese in the T'ang dynasty were of the happiest and most amicable. Many poems have been preserved in which poets of these two countries capped verses with each other, and the story is told of a Japanese boy who went to China, loved the country so much that he became naturalized, and lived there for the rest of his life, adopting the Chinese name of Ch'ao Heng. He must have been the possessor of a fine intellect and a lovable character. He was first appointed adviser to the Emperor Hsuan Tsung, and then Governor of Annam. When he died at the age of seventy-two, his friend the great Chinese poet Li Po wrote in memory of him the graceful and moving lines,

> *The moon no longer returns to the sky,*
> *But sinks into the blue waves of the sea.*

While the scholars of the two countries lived in harmony and mutual admiration, their armies were embattled. Korea, the small but strategically important country over which so many wars were presently to be waged, was the present object of contention. The Chinese and Japanese armies met in 662, and the former won a decisive victory. Four hundred Japanese ships sank in flames. "Fire and smoke transfigured the sky, and the sea smelt rancid and seemed scarlet with blood!" Such was the mastery of the T'ang empire.

There were no more encounters between the warriors of Japan and her continental neighbor until both China and Korea had been swallowed by the Mongols and a Mongol Emperor occupied the Chinese throne. Supported by the Koreans, the Mongols attempted to add Japan to their colossal empire, but were met by horrible destruction. The first engagement took place in 1274, and at the second in 1281 four thousand battleships took part, carrying a hundred and fifty thousand men. The huge fleet was trapped beneath the Islands of the Five Dragons, and wiped out by a typhoon. The bodies of the drowned Mongol sailors were washed ashore in hundreds, so that they formed bridges for the victors to march over. The sea had defeated the hitherto undefeatable Mongols.

At the death of Kublai Khan, greatest and most ambitious of the Mongol rulers, the battles between Japan and China ceased for several hundred years. There was no feeling of neighborliness between the two countries, however, and the Japanese government prohibited its people from trading with the continent. But the proximity of so rich and fertile a country as China was a great temptation to the more adventurous and disreputable Japanese. Japanese pirates began to maraud the China coast. In the course of time they were joined in their plundering raids by Chinese criminals, and the looting became even more effective. Among them was the notorious Wang Chih, best known of all Chinese pirates. Formerly a trader in niter and sulphur with Japan and the East Indies, he had felt himself insufficiently supported by his government and had turned to the even more profitable occupation of piracy. It is said that he was absolutely fearless and would fight naked with a three-foot sword against all comers. In his new role he even had ships built for his followers, each capable of carrying two thousand men. They had a wooden tower amidships and decks upon which his cavalry might exercise their horses. With this strange armada, and a mixed following of Japanese and Chinese criminals and thieves, he attacked the China coast and brought his men up the lower Yangtzu where they took and plundered town after town on the river banks.

The pirate menace had become so grave that it called for drastic resistance. The molestation had already lasted for two hundred years when it was broken effectively by the Ming general Ch'i Chi-kuang. Ch'i first built up and trained a local militia which should deal effectively with pirates who landed at any points on the coast, and secondly had a special fleet constructed in three classes: ocean-going battleships that could crush the enemy's junks to splinters "like a wheel crushing a mantis," and two types of smaller vessel to fight on the inland rivers and lakes or for general purposes of patrol. Heavy naval engagements took place and the pirate fleet was utterly routed. By the year 1563 the whole force was dispersed, and from north to south the waters of China were free of marauders.

No sooner had China broken the Japanese pirate menace than she was threatened by an even more formidable force. There had risen to power in Japan an imperialist prime minister, Hideyoshi—probably the first of the many Japanese politicians who intended to conquer the world. He had first united all the sixty-six provinces of his own empire and brought their local governments under his personal control. Next he had asserted dominance over Siam and the Liukiu and Philippine Islands. China was to be the next ripe fruit which should drop into his greedy hand. He had believed the pirates' stories regarding the incompetence of the Ming troops, and had no doubt of the issue. China, he decided, under the inefficient Ming rulers, although a vast country, would be powerless against his own well-disciplined troops. He scoffed at Koreans who warned him that in attempting a conquest of China he would be "like a bee that tries to sting a turtle through its shell!"

Korea was the obvious stepping-off ground for a China campaign, especially as its government was now largely controlled by rather weak politicians. There was, besides, a strong opposition party which prepared the ground for a Japanese invasion. In 1592 Hideyoshi sent a force of two hundred thousand men to Korea. The capital fell almost immediately, and the Japanese armies made a steady advance across the country, the Korean troops falling back before them in confusion. They appealed to the Emperor of China for assistance. He responded by sending a few divisions of cavalry which were quickly routed. Hideyoshi's generals had ordered their men to conceal their faces behind devils' masks, and to give their horses' heads the appearance of lions. When the Chinese cavalry saw this appalling army bearing down upon them, their horses bolted and the riders were too terrified to control them!

Next year, the Ming Emperor determined to wipe out the ignominious defeat. He sent very strong reinforcements to Korea, which laid siege to the Japanese at the town of P'ingyang in the North. The Chinese commanding officer met cunning by cunning. He divided his troops into three sectors: one he sent north and one west of the city, while those who were to attack the southern gate he disguised in Korean uniform. The Japanese, having only contempt for the Korean troops, sent all their finest divisions to the northern and western sectors. When these were hotly engaged, the disguised Chinese regained their own uniforms and hurled themselves with all the force of their cannon and rockets against the southern wall. They broke through the south gate, which was but weakly defended, and though the swords and spears of the Japanese garrison "bristled like the hairs of a hedgehog," the Chinese battered their way in and took the city. This was the beginning of Chinese successes, and all Korean towns north of the Seoul River were recovered.

In the neighborhood of the Korean capital, the Chinese suffered a setback, and Hideyoshi, whose troops were now utterly exhausted, thought it a good opportunity for proposing an armistice and extracting favorable terms from the Ming Emperor. Unfortunately these terms, which were to include the return to Korea of her lost territory in exchange for a heavy subsidy, and improved relations with China through a royal marriage and trade agreements, were distorted by the interpreters. According to their version the Chinese Emperor understood that Hideyoshi wished to be nominated by him as "King of

Japan," and delighted at the easy terms, sent his envoys with the requisite document. Hideyoshi was outraged at the insult to his own Emperor, broke off negotiations, and resorted once more to arms. The war dragged on for years. Chinese reinforcements were continually sent up, but no decisive battle was won by either side. At last, in 1598, news was brought to the Japanese generals of Hideyoshi's death. Immeasurably thankful that their taskmaster could no longer drive them into the battlefield, they decided to retreat at once and return to their own land. This was not accomplished without heavy losses: when the armies had embarked and were making the perilous journey back to Japan, a section of them was cut off by the Ming fleet and destroyed.

The war had lasted for seven years. Korea had been utterly devastated, and Japan gained nothing. The only practical result was a bond of friendship between Korea and China which has lasted to the present day. At the time when the Ming empire was crumbling before the onslaughts of the Manchu invaders, the Koreans gallantly offered the help of their small army, and now in the great Sino-Japanese war, Koreans and Chinese are fighting shoulder to shoulder for the same object and against the same foe.

XXII. THE MANCHU DYNASTY OF CH'ING

A LARGE TRACT of country northeast of the Great Wall is familiar to Westerners under the name of Manchuria—"the Land of the Manchus" —and the tribe of Northerners who invaded China in the seventeenth century to establish their ruling House in place of the native Ming dynasty are known in history as the Manchus.[1] These people were, in fact, originally the Chin (Golden) tribe who occupied territory in Northern China during the twelfth and thirteenth centuries after the collapse of the Northern Sung dynasty. During the Mongol dynasty of Yuan (1277–1367) the Chins became Mongol subjects, but at the fall of this dynasty, and the accession of the Ming Emperors the Chins grew bold and started to expand south, east, and west. In 1616, the Chin chief, having seized a certain amount of new territory, declared his country to be the Empire of Ch'ing ("Purity"), and dubbed himself "Manchu Emperor."[2] Thus the tribe has gone down to history as the Manchus or Manchurians, and the dynasty, after the Ming had been defeated and a Manchu Emperor ruled over China, as the Ch'ing.

Three years later, in 1619, the "Manchus" fought a successful engagement against the Ming forces to the south of their so-called Empire, defeating, it is said, "a hundred thousand" imperial troops. Gradually all the land east of the Liao River was seized and put under Manchu domination. But at this point the Ming troops made a stand, armed, it is reported, with superior, modern equipment—cannon designed by the Portuguese! So, for the time being, the Manchu troops turned their attention westwards, to the Mongols who had been thrown back to the Northwest at the Ming conquest. By 1638 these Mongols were

[1] The Manchus originally occupied only the northern part of modern Manchuria. In the Ming dynasty, the southern portion formed the Chinese prefecture of Chienchou, the officials of which governed the ancestors of the Manchus, until the end of the Ming period. At that time, and after prolonged struggles, the Manchus were able to advance as far as the Shan-hai Pass on the borders of Hopei, and to occupy the whole of the modern Manchurian provinces.

[2] The name "Manchu" has various explanations. According to one source, it derives from the name of a Korean chief called Li Manchu; according to others it simply means "Grand Chieftain" or "Blessing."

completely overpowered by the audacious Manchu brigands, and the whole territory comprised in the modern provinces of Jehol, Chahar, Suiyuan, and Ninghsia ("Inner Mongolia") fell to the Manchu Emperor. Korea had already come under his sway.

Meanwhile, the Ming House was being undermined by local bandits, to the ultimate advantage of the Manchus. In the year 1635, a terrible famine occurred in Northwest China. The people were reduced to eating roots of grass and the bark of trees. When even these had been devoured, they ate earth. And still the Ming Emperor with the help of his officials continued to levy heavy taxes on the starving population, to pay for military operations against the Manchus. In the traditional Chinese fashion, many of these people rebelled and became bandits, keeping themselves and their families alive by plunder. The movement gathered force, and in a short time took on the form of a large, well-organized rebellion. The valleys of the Yellow River and the Yangtzu were first devastated, and this was followed by a march on the capital —Peking. Now, all the picked troops of the Emperor had been sent to the northeastern frontiers to hold off the Manchus, and Peking was almost without defenders. The Emperor armed his Court eunuchs as a desperate resort and sent them against the bandit hordes. This amateur army rapidly collapsed and the rebels poured into the beautiful city. The Emperor, filled with despair and remorse, hanged himself from a tree on a steep little hill overlooking Peking. It is called "the Radiant Hill," and the tree itself can be seen to the present day. In the belt of the dead Emperor, the bandits found a touching appeal, imploring them not to molest his people and taking upon himself the whole blame for the misfortunes that had overtaken his kingdom.

At this stage, a woman's beauty seems once more to have altered history. The bandit leader, Li Tze-ch'eng, could not feel himself secure until he had won over the imperial armies away in the North, who were still holding the Manchus at bay. The general in command, called Wu San-kuei, was possessed of a beautiful mistress, "a girl of the loveliest face and sweetest voice under heaven," and her Li Tze-ch'eng kidnaped and gave negligently to one of his lieutenants. He took Wu's father as well, thinking that out of fear for their safety, his enemy would surrender. Not so Wu. In a fury of indignation he called his father a craven for counseling terms, declared magniloquently that the man who killed his Emperor was his enemy, and whoever would kill that enemy should become his Emperor, and finally invited the Manchus to join with him to defeat the hateful Li who had stolen his lady!

* *Three armies weep bitterly and don white silk mourning,*
  The General's hair bristles with rage at the loss of his rosy one

wrote a poet about this strange order of events.

An invitation of this sort was beyond the dreams of the Manchus: they raised their standards and marched exultantly southwards. At the foot of the Great Wall, a little to the north of Peking, the armies of Wu and Li engaged. When the battle was hotly joined, the Manchu troops poured out on both the enemy flanks, spread confusion in all their ranks, and utterly routed them. Li retreated into Peking, hurriedly collected all the gold and silver articles he could lay hands on in the palace and in the houses of wealthy officials, had them melted down into "metal cakes," and fled with tens of thousands of them in his wagons towards the West, having first set fire to the palace and put Wu's father to death. The Manchus were now virtually masters of Northern China.

Some opposition still remained farther south. Prince Fu of the imperial Ming House had set up a government in Nanking, and was doubtlessly anxious to avenge the dead Emperor. The Manchu King professed to sorrow deeply over his dead rival, and sent assurances to Prince Fu that he had only come to restore order to the North, and had no intention of seizing territory. The tears and protests, however, both proved false: as soon as he had consolidated his position in the North, the Manchu King advanced towards the Yangtzu valley. Seven days' bitter fighting for the strategic city of Yangchou ended in the exhaustion of the heroic Ming garrisons: the Manchus entered the city and a ghastly massacre followed. The government of Prince Fu fell soon after and the Manchu King became Emperor Shih Tsu, Emperor of all China.

To the great mass of the people, changes of dynasty and political upheavals were matters of small importance: they were concerned with getting a living out of the soil, and it seemed that they could effect this as well under a Manchu Emperor as under a Chinese. However, with the arrival of the Manchus a major social crisis was precipitated over the question of pigtails. "John Chinaman" as he appears in the picture books and oriental plays of the West always wears a pigtail, and many Westerners are unaware that this is not a true Chinese fashion. The ancient Chinese wound their hair in a coil on top of the head, and it was only with the arrival of the Mongols that they were ordered to dress it in two pigtails. When the Mongol dynasty fell and the Chinese rulers were restored with the Ming dynasty, hair fashions reverted to the old native style. Now when the Manchus were masters of China, every Chinese was ordered, upon pain of death, to wear his hair in a single pigtail—the style of the conquerors. The people rightly felt this to be a stigma, a sign of moral surrender, and the usually docile working people rioted. "Your hair or your head!" was the Manchu slogan; "Our heads but not our hair!" came the stout Chinese retort. Some of the Southeastern provinces which had not yet been thoroughly subjugated by the invaders actually put up an armed resistance. The small town of Chia-ting, for example, held out for eighty days against the trained troops of the Manchus. When the town fell at last a "three days' massacre" was ordered as a warning to the obstinate. It is reported that 97,000 in the town itself and 75,000 in the suburbs died as a result of the brutal order. After this horrible occurrence, the Manchu troops were able to subdue the Southeast and Southwest without much formidable opposition, and the hated pigtail showed itself all over Shih Tsu's dominions, to gratify his sense of conquest.

The Manchu Emperors who followed Shih Tsu showed, on the whole, rather more tact and consideration, although they were stern enough in wiping out opposition or criticism. The second Emperor, the famous K'ang Hsi, bestowed high official positions upon the descendants of the Ming House, and even offered sacrifices at the tombs of the Ming Emperors. With a sincere respect for learning and good knowledge of Chinese literature, K'ang Hsi soon won favor with the intelligentsia by adding a special system of official examinations. Men of talent and scholarship who succeeded in passing them were given high places at Court. Emperor Ch'ien Lung, grandson of K'ang Hsi, was perhaps the most distinguished example of these "cultured" Emperors. Himself a poet of some talent in the Chinese manner, and an expert on Chinese painting, he instituted a work of the highest literary importance. Scholars of the first rank were assembled and the plan unfolded to them. An anthology was to be compiled: the most immense anthology that had ever existed. It was, in fact, to contain all the books of serious value that had been written in Chinese! Books and manuscripts were bought or borrowed from public and private collections throughout the country; editions were collated, and the whole colossal undertaking, comprising some 36,000 volumes, was copied out, seven times, by hand. It was known as "The Four Treasuries," so called because it was divided into four sections, the Confucian Classics and their commentaries, philosophy and science, histories, and literature. The seven copies, each in itself a complete library, were distributed throughout the Empire, and were lodged in seven of the most beautiful and honorable spots—the imperial palace of Peking, the "Round and Bright Park" (the imperial summer residence in the suburbs of Peking), the libraries of Feng-t'ien, Jehol, and Yangchou, the "Golden Hill Temple" of Chen-chiang, and the Sheng-yin Temple on the shores of the "Western Lake" in Hangchou.

This apparent veneration for the native Chinese letters was only one side of the Manchu policy: while appearing as patrons of literature, the Manchu officials, at the command of the Emperor, exercised the strictest possible censorship over writers, publishers, even book collectors, whose books displayed the least criticism of the Manchu regime. Believing, like the ancient tyrant Ch'in Shih Huang Ti, that by destroying tendentious books he could wipe out the spirit of criticism from his subjects' hearts, Ch'ien Lung had hundreds of volumes which were supposed to inspire anti-foreign feeling committed to the flames. Anyone who was found in the possession of "prohibited" books would be put to death. On one occasion, seventy people were executed for their part in a "History of the Ming Dynasty," which was privately printed, and contained an account of the Manchu conquest, doubtlessly couched in terms that showed more regret than gratification, and revealing facts which the reigning House would have liked forgotten. As the actual author of the reprehensible parts had already died, his body was dug up and dishonored. A poet of the time lost his life for two lines of verse,

> Oh pure wind, you don't know how to read—
> Why throw my pages into confusion?

The Chinese word for "pure" is the same as the name of the Manchu dynasty, and the officials were not long in discovering its implication.

In spite of these petty tyrannies, the early sovereigns of the Manchu dynasty ruled with considerable talent and wisdom. They and their entourage had a proper respect for the ancient Chinese culture, studied and practiced the arts of the land they had conquered, and in general so adapted themselves to Chinese life that they almost ceased to appear "alien." Under their rule the country grew strong and prosperous. However, many of the Chinese still nourished in their hearts a resentment against the interlopers, while there still hung from their heads the hated pigtail. They only waited for a sign of weakness in their rulers in order to start rebellions. One of these occurred under the premiership of a certain Ho K'un, a rascally Manchu who by illegal means had amassed so huge a fortune that he was reputed even richer than Louis Quatorze of France. The revolt was organized by a dubious

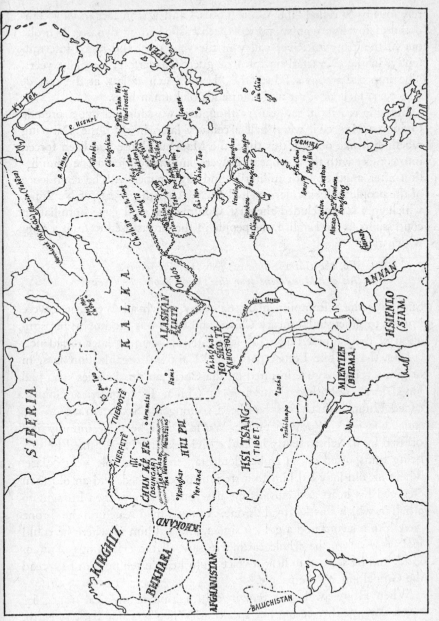

The Ch'ing (Manchu) Period (*cir.* A.D. 1760)

religious body called "the White Lotus," and was in fact mainly composed of loyalists who supported the banished Ming dynasty. It broke out in the Yangtzu River valley in the year 1793, and raged intermittently, in the characteristic form of guerrilla warfare, for eight years. The imperial troops subdued the "Lotus" men at last, at the cost of 20,000,000 taels of silver and thousands of human lives.

But this rebellion, sanguinary though it was, formed but a prelude to approaching civil wars: half a century later, in 1850, the T'ai-p'ing rebellion broke out. By this time, the Manchu House had been forced into contact with the European Powers, and had suffered one humiliation after another, both militarily and diplomatically. The confidence of the people in their rulers melted away. After the Treaty of Nanking, which in 1842 concluded the first Opium War and gave humiliating concessions to the English, the people in the streets used to hum a song which ran,

> *We, the Chinese masses, fear our Mandarins,*
> *But our Mandarins fear the Devils from the Ocean!*

Such was the uncomplimentary name by which all Westerners were known to nineteenth-century China, and such was the impossible situation of the Chinese under the Manchu House in its later decadence.

Like the "White Lotus" party, the T'ai-p'ing organization was, in origin, a religious sect, inspired by the Christian missionaries who had long since established themselves in China. Its founder, a Chinese called Hung Hsiu-ch'uan, had been reading a Christian tract—so the story goes—"A Warning to the World," and been profoundly impressed by it. Subsequently he had a vivid dream. He dreamed he was being transported on an embroidered tapestry to a resplendent palace. There an old lady led him to a stream to be washed, and an old man changed his heart and entrails for new ones. He was then brought to a hall in which stood a royal throne. An aged man seated on the throne gave him a sword and a golden signet, and led him to where he could look down over the whole earth. He saw all the evil-doings of mankind, and he seemed to hear a voice from heaven telling him to spread the Gospel among the people.

When Hung awoke, he remained in a kind of mystical trance for seven days, neither eating nor speaking. When he came back to earth, he declared he had seen the God of the Christians! God had summoned him and told him that a great calamity would befall mankind unless the people turned from their idols and worshiped Him. Hung began teaching the Bible to the Chinese, and insisted on the destruction of Buddhist idols and the images of ancestors.

It is difficult for us now to judge of Hung's sincerity, but we may perhaps believe that at the outset he really felt himself ordained to rescue the Chinese from disaster. But it was not long before he became involved in politics and the vexed question of the ruling House.

At a time when the rulers and their officials were pitiably weak and corrupt, secret societies and pseudo-religious sects sprang up all over the country, their somewhat strange characteristics being due, no doubt, to the influx of Western ideas, which were not yet properly understood. Among them was a sect called "God's Party," led by one who claimed descent from the imperial Ming family, but proved to be a survivor of the "White Lotus" party, playing on the religious sentiments of the people, and also on their hatred of the Manchu rulers, to gain political power. His career was, however, cut short by certain government officials who had him seized and executed. The dreamer Hung was offered the leadership of the party, and accepted it.

It is recorded that Hung's eloquence brought thousands of converts into "God's Party," but the confusion of politics and religion became even deeper. The "God's Party" members dispensed with the pigtail and wore their hair in the fashion of the Ming period. They called each other "brother" and "sister," and declared that Jehovah was their Heavenly Father, while Jesus Christ was His first Son, and Hung— such was the waywardness of their thought—His second. Hung's following increased to such an extent that in the year 1850 he established the "T'ai-p'ing T'ien Kuo"—the "Heavenly Kingdom of Peace"—in a small town of Kuangsi province, and declared himself the "Heavenly King." He evidently saw in himself the representative of God, establishing His Kingdom on earth to save the people from the wickedness of the Manchus. At this point the Crusade began: the troops of the "Heavenly King" marched.

In three years of far from "bloodless" victories, the "Heavenly King" brought most of the Yangtzu River valley under his sway, and established his capital—the "Heavenly Capital"—at Nanking. He built an altar in the city from which he used to preach in the manner of a Pope. A new order was declared. A new system of government was inaugurated, based on the ancient Chinese models of the great Han and T'ang dynasties. Opium smoking was forbidden, and an agreement was reached with the commander-in-chief of the English naval forces at Shanghai to stop imports of opium. Drink was also prohibited, and the punishment for adultery was death. Girls were no longer allowed to have their feet bound, and equality between the sexes was encouraged. The "Heavenly King's" regime seems to have aimed at a combination of the traditional Chinese form of government as opposed to the Manchu, and the rules of a Christian community. But it was unfortunately not without charlatanism, and the actions of its members were aimed more at temporal than spiritual power.

From 1857 till 1861, the Manchu House was again at war with England and France. The imperial standing army was cowardly and feeble. The soldiers bravely fired their cannon from a distance, but in hand-to-hand fighting they took to their heels. Wherever they went, gambling houses and opium dens were opened; rape and rapine followed. The generals, who were paid a gross sum by the government for the wages of their men, preferred to let their armies diminish and pocket the money, rather than replace the killed and wounded. As for their own conduct, it is said that they ran for their lives as soon as "the wind from the enemy blew towards them."

This situation seemed to the T'ai-p'ing leaders an ideal one for their own purposes: they made overtures to the French and English consuls, to whom their "Christianity" must certainly have appealed, and who could not be averse from military assistance against the Manchu opponent. At the same time they renewed their efforts to draw the Chinese masses to their banner. "Trust in God," they exhorted, "and throw the Manchu Emperor out of Peking!" An era of peace would follow in which these civil and foreign broils would cease.

Perhaps the divine envoys were bad diplomats. They seem, at any rate, to have bungled the situation in some way. The foreigners in Shanghai apparently sensed a danger to their interests, should the "Heavenly King" succeed in mastering the whole of China. Financed by the Shanghai merchants, who were naturally the most nervous, an American adventurer, Frederick Townsend Ward, organized an army of Chinese and Filipinos, including some American officers, and with it was able to "protect" Shanghai from capture by the troops of the "Heavenly King." This was the first check to the latter's series of victories.

Ward, a leader of fearless spirit, had come to China as a young man in search of adventure, and joined the Chinese merchant navy. In 1859, despite the charges of his consul who accused him of violating United States neutrality, he offered his services to the imperial army. He was given the command of a small force which he so drilled and trained that a year or two later it formed the backbone for that large international force known in history as the "Ever-victorious Army." With the confidence and support both of the Manchus and the foreign authorities at Shanghai, Ward soon had the country cleared for a radius of thirty miles around the port. In September of 1862, however, in an attack on Tzuchi, ten miles from Ningpo, he was shot and mortally wounded.

Meanwhile, in 1861, the second Opium War was concluded, and the Peking Pact signed between the Manchus and the English and French allies, in favor, as usual, of the European Powers. Britain and France now decided that it would profit them more to support the Manchus, who, albeit painfully and under protest, would agree to any concessions that the Westerners demanded. The "Heavenly King," on the other hand, as many foreigners had already realized, would make no compromise, and was set on total power. Accordingly they gave official sanction to the voluntary enlistment of their subjects in the Manchu armies. Ward's "Ever-victorious Army" was now put under the command of the English general Charles George Gordon, and battle was joined in earnest between the hosts of the "Heavenly" and the earthly kings. Gordon's army remained true to its name, and in three years of continuous victory, fifty towns had been recovered for the Manchus. At the end of the three years, however, Gordon resigned, having disagreed, it is said, with the Manchu commanders because they killed their prisoners of war.

But by now the tide had turned against the "Heavenly King." In the last resort, racial feeling against the Manchus was not so strong as traditional loyalty for the crowned Emperor, deeply implanted in Chinese minds at least since the days of Confucius. The discipline of the crusaders declined, the leaders quarreled among themselves, while hundreds of their followers, in disillusion, deserted for the opposite camp. In 1864, Nanking was recaptured by the Manchu troops, and the "Heavenly King," seeing his cause to be lost beyond recovery, put an end to his remarkable career by poison. It took another two years of conflict before the whole territory was won back, for in the course of their exploits the T'ai-p'ing troops had taken more than six hundred towns. By 1866 the "Heavenly Kingdom of Peace" had ceased to exist.

It cannot be said that the T'ai-p'ing movement brought any profit to the Chinese as a whole; rather it hampered the Manchus in their effort to resist Western pressure. But it set a precedent for revolution, which the weakness, folly, and stupidity of the decadent Manchu rulers further precipitated. This was the true People's Revolution, led by Dr. Sun Yat-sen, that was presently to rise and bring the tottering dynasty to an end.

A leading figure in the final degradation of the Manchu House was the notorious Empress Dowager Tzu Hsi. This blindly ambitious woman, whose name means literally the "Kind and Blessed Queen," having entered the royal family as a concubine of Emperor Wen Tsung, succeeded in becoming Regent to his grand-nephew, the ill-fated Teh Tsung, in 1875. In her lust for absolute power, she murdered the innocent and intrigued against her own relatives: under her short-sighted, selfish administration, China suffered one diplomatic defeat after another in its relations with the Western Powers. The prestige of the Celestial Empire reached its lowest depths. She it was who sponsored the Boxers' Rebellion, an event which wrote one of the horrible pages in China's history, though the foreign imperialists against whom it was directed must carry their share of blame. But this story remains to be told more fully in a later chapter.

Goaded to desperate means, a "Reform" party of the more progressive elements at Court plotted to get rid of the discreditable old woman, but the plot was destroyed by the double-faced Yuan Shih-k'ai who later became first President of the Republic. The young Emperor Teh-tsung was implicated, and virtually imprisoned. He died eleven years later in mysterious circumstances, while Tzu Hsi herself was found dead the following day. P'u-i, present "puppet" ruler of the Japanese-created "Manchukuo," succeeded to the throne, but the dynasty was beyond saving: it did not long outlast his accession.

XXIII. MONGOLIA, SINKIANG, AND TIBET

ALTHOUGH THE HISTORY of the Manchu dynasty is filled with conflicts against the Western Powers—conflicts in which the Chinese were consistently the losers—the imperial armies were also at war with border tribes, and in those fields won many victories. These tribes were no longer the "Huns" or the Turks, but Mongols, Huis, and Tibetans, the latest inhabitants of China's northern and western borders.

When the Republic came to birth in 1911, the first Republican flag bore the design of five different-colored bars, symbolizing the five main races of which the present Chinese population is composed: the Han—the "Chinese proper"—the Manchurians, the Mongols, the Hui, and the Tibetans. The homes of the last four bordered those of the ancient Han, and are what we now call Northern Manchuria, Mongolia, Sinkiang, and Tibet. When they were strong they quarreled with the Chinese and pillaged their towns: when they were weaker, they negotiated and traded with them. But strong or weak, willing or unwilling, they all inherited the Chinese civilization, which was once the greatest and noblest not only in the East, but probably in the whole world.

The empires of the Mongols and the Manchus swelled at one time to vast dimensions, and they both, for a period, conquered and ruled the Han race, but the Hui and Tibetans were conquered by them and became subject races. Time and the developments of history alter the relations between peoples. After the Republic had been founded, the representatives of these five races acknowledged their brotherhood, and agreed to live on equal terms. This chapter will give briefly the history of the Mongols, the Hui, and the Tibetans, and how they became incorporated with the Han, especially in the decisive period of the Manchu dynasty.

The Mongols, who had achieved a conquest of China in the first half of the thirteenth century, and had established a dynasty which they called the Yuan, were driven out little more than a hundred years later by Chinese revolutionary forces. The Mongol Emperor and his entourage fled from Peking towards the mountains north of the Great Wall,

237

while the revolutionists set up a new dynasty—the Ming. The descendants of the last Mongol Emperor made repeated and furious attempts to regain their lost empire, but were always repulsed by the loyal Ming troops. Eventually they abandoned the hopeless struggle and made a permanent settlement north of the Wall. They divided into two main bodies, the Oirats and the Tartars. The former lived in the West and the latter in the East, in the present Mongolia and the northern part of Sinkiang.

After a time, the Oirats resumed their aggressive operations and even succeeded in capturing one of the Ming Emperors. But they were not able to follow up this victory, and as a result of internal squabbles, so weakened themselves that in the second half of the sixteenth century they became subject to the Tartar chieftain, the masterful Tayen Khan. The whole Mongol territory was divided in three after his death, and that part which had formerly come under the suzerainty of the Oirats passed eventually to Tayen's grandson—that battle-loving Anta who proved himself the bitterest enemy of the Ming Emperor. Beginning from 1549, and for fifteen years, Anta's forces constantly invaded the Ming empire until Romance and Religion most unexpectedly intervened and brought the two powers into a happy relationship.

Anta had arranged the betrothal of his grandson to a young girl of astonishing beauty, but even in his old age had fallen in love with her himself, and made her his wife. The young man, enraged at being cheated of his bride, ran away from the Tartar Court and impulsively took refuge with his grandfather's greatest enemy—the Ming Emperor at Peking!—probably hoping to avenge himself in battle. The girl, distressed for her lover's safety, wept day and night, until the old Kahn was moved by her sorrow. He had also in the meantime been converted to the Lama religion, a branch of the merciful Buddhist faith, and in his old age a peaceful spirit overcame his bloodthirsty nature. Anta appealed to the Ming Emperor to return his grandson, and promised that there should be peace between them thereafter. Friendship was sealed between the two powers, and even after Anta's death it was not broken. His beautiful widow married two successive rulers of the Oirat territory, and out of gratitude to the Ming Emperor kept the flame of peace alive as long as she lived.

It may be apposite here to explain something of the role played by Lamaism, to which Anta and many of his countrymen were converted, and which has exercised a very marked influence on the relations between China proper and the peoples of Mongolia, Sinkiang, and Tibet. Lamaism is not, as many Europeans believe, a distinct religion: it is merely a branch of Buddhism, having all its fundamental tenets in common with that great Faith. Its first home was Tibet, the junction of the Indian civilization which had given birth to Buddhism, and the Chinese which had adopted it. Later it spread northwards into Mongolia and North China itself. In origin, it was doubtlessly as noble and "spiritual" a faith as its progenitor Buddhism, but like the Catholic Church of the Middle Ages, its leaders strove for temporal power; and from the time that Anta was converted and all through the seventeenth century, the heads of the Lama faith exercised the same sort of authority in Tibet and parts of Mongolia as at one time did the Pope over Christendom. They organized military campaigns and joined in the political struggle for supremacy, bringing much discredit on their religion among the true believers. In later times it became even more debased through other causes—immorality among the monks and priests, superstitions, and the multiplication of images to the detriment of the spiritual elements.

Lamaism was first fully developed in Tibet during the eighth century, when the Tufans [1] inhabited that land. It was during this century that a famous Indian monk Padāmkara was invited to Tibet and the first Lamaist monastery was established, a little to the southeast of Lhasa. Fifteen years later, in 764, a native Tibetan was made abbot of the monastery, thus becoming the first "Lama" (literally, "Superior One"). It was at this time too, when the T'ang dynasty ruled in China proper, and there was an interchange first of blows and then of trade and culture between the two peoples, that Lamaism was introduced to China, and the first converts made.

Lamaism took root and spread rapidly among the Tufans, and it is even probable that its teachings of peace and compassion had some effect upon their natural inclination for battle. At all events, the campaigns against neighboring countries decreased and the tribe, powerful so long as it remained united, split into groups and became ineffective as an aggressive force. At the same time, the power of the Lama priesthood was greatly augmented until the main temporal power lay in its hands. Then came the whirlwind of Mongol conquests in the thirteenth century, when the mighty Jenghiz Khan, and Kublai Khan, brought the greater part of Asia under Mongol rule.

But such was the force of the Lama faith at that time that the all-powerful Kublai was mastered by it. He was converted by the abbot of a monastery called Sas-kya, and in return for crowning him "Emperor

[1] See Chapter XIV.

of China" Kublai appointed this Sas-kya Lama "temporal ruler of
Western Tibet." It was a remarkable triumph for the Lama priesthood.
The Sas-kya "Papacy," as it might be called, maintained political supremacy for several generations, and oppressed its rival sects. Very
bitter strife broke out between the various monasteries, chiefly over
political questions, and the Lama religion was much discredited until
at the beginning of the fifteenth century a monk named Tsung Ke Pa
started a reform movement. His followers wore a yellow hat and robe
to differentiate themselves from the monks of the old cult who were
dressed in red. They came to be distinguished afterwards as the "Red
Lamas" and the "Yellow Lamas."

The Yellow Lamas, although reforming the discipline of the Lama
Church, by no means denied themselves temporal power. In the course
of five generations the sect achieved, and retains to this day, the priest-
kingship of all Tibet. Tsung Ke Pa's successor, one of his pupils, became the first of these priest-kings known as the Dalai Lama—the
Grand Lama—and since celibacy was one of the rules of the reformed
order, the succession was based on a theory of reincarnation. The spirit
of the dying abbot was held to be reincarnated in the body of a new-
born child—born in the hour of the abbot's death. The fifth Grand
Lama has declared that both he and the first Yellow Lama abbot were
reincarnations of the ancient King Srong-btsan. He in his turn was
said to have been the earthly reincarnation of the Compassionate Spirit
of the Mountains, who gave heavenly food to the Tibetans' progenitors,
and thus transformed them from monkeys to men!

It was in the time of the third Dalai Lama that the Mongol Khan
Anta was converted to the Lama faith. Partly through the influence of
religion, as we have seen, Anta formed ties of sincere friendship with
the Chinese Emperor, and in the year 1579 he introduced the Dalai
Lama to the Chinese Court, thus forging a new link between Tibet and
China. About the same time, a deputy of the Dalai was established at
Urga in Outer Mongolia, becoming head of the Lama Church in that
country. He was known as the "Mongolian Living Buddha." Under
Anta's influence there began that intervention of the Mongols in Tibetan affairs which was destined to develop very markedly in the
following century.

Some of the remnants of the Red Lamas held authority over a part
of Tibet, and in 1643 a powerful minister of the Yellow Lamas, Sang
Chieh—a crafty prelate—invited a Mongol chieftain, Ku-shih Khan, to
exterminate their power. Sang Chieh soon intrigued with another
Mongol chieftain to destroy Ku-shih Khan. This chieftain, Ke Er Tan,

who had already made himself master of the Mongol territory north of the Great Wall, speedily made conquest of Tibet, and theoretically offered it to the Dalai, while remaining himself its actual ruler. Having so much of the bordering lands under his control, Ke Er Tan turned his attack upon the imperial forces of the Manchus, who were now ruling in China in succession to the Ming, and only after three years of bitter fighting was he defeated. The great Khan ended his ambitious career by suicide, in 1697.

His nephew Ts'e Mang took up the struggle for power in the West. In 1715, he rushed his troops into Tibet, occupied Lhasa, and took the Sixth Dalai prisoner. His methods were cruder than his uncle's. A three-cornered struggle began, for the Manchu rulers were patrons of the Lama religion and felt Tibet with its Grand Lama to be under their "protection." Their armies forthwith descended upon Tibet and evicted those of the Mongol Ts'e Mang. They elected a new Sixth Dalai, and returned home.

The new Dalai was ungrateful. Only a few years later he joined forces with the rascally Ts'e Mang in support of a revolt which was then breaking out northeast of Tibet, against the Manchu empire. Again the Chinese acted quickly, launching a surprise attack on the rebellious Mongols in early spring "before the pastures were green and the enemy's animals duly fed with new grass." The Chinese cavalry rushed down upon the tents of the Mongol and Tibetan armies, and would have taken the Mongol chief prisoner had he not speedily escaped on a white camel in the disguise of a woman. The importance of this Chinese victory lies in the fact that the district known as Ch'ing-hai—"the Blue Sea"—in which the revolt had taken place was now incorporated for the first time into the Chinese Empire, and remains to this day one of the western provinces of the Chinese Republic.

The Mongol power was not yet waning. Ts'e Mang died only three years after the disaster at Ch'ing-hai, and was succeeded by his equally ambitious and capable son, Ke Er Tan Ts'e Ling, who, subduing all his rival Mongol chieftains, was able for some time to offer a powerful and united front against the would-be invasion of Chinese forces. But in later years he could not withstand the Chinese onrush. Victorious first, his armies were presently thrown into confusion and fled before the imperial troops "like ravens darting to their nests." They retreated into Northern Sinkiang, the ancient home of the Oirats.

From this time on, the glory of the Mongols, former rulers of almost a whole continent, faded rapidly. Civil wars, Chinese invasions, and epidemics of smallpox combined to decimate their population. By the middle of the eighteenth century, forty per cent. had been killed by pestilence, thirty by wars, and twenty had fled to Russia, leaving only a tenth in their old territory, and this remnant never recovered its strength and prosperity. For the first time Mongolia, including the northern part of Sinkiang, was brought completely under the domination of the Chinese Court. Tibet had long ceased to be an independent country, and the large western province of Ch'ing-hai had been incorporated permanently into Chinese territory.

Sinkiang, vaguely described by ancient Chinese historians as "the Western Regions," and referred to by European and American writers as "Chinese Turkestan," is geographically split by the great range of T'ien Shan—the "Heavenly Mountains"—which stretches right across it, west and east. That part north of the mountains was inhabited, as we have learned, by the Mongolian tribe of Oirats. The southern portion was the home of the Hui tribe.

The Hui are of three racial types, and are differentiated into Ch'an Hui, Han Hui, and Kazaks. The Ch'an or "Turbaned" Hui, so called from the head-dress of their men—a cap beautifully embroidered in gold thread and in winter bordered with sable or otter fur—live to the west of Sinkiang province, centered in the town of Kashgar. They seem to be of a very different origin from the inhabitants of China Proper. In the districts where they live, there are very few Chinese, and the usual accompaniments of "Chinese" life—the wine shops, the characteristic groceries, the pig markets, and so on, are "nowhere to be found." The Han Hui ("Chinese" Hui), on the other hand, had probably migrated at some time from the Chinese province of Kansu. They live in the Chinese manner, and can speak the language, though their natural language is Arabic. Like their "turbaned" kinsmen, they are faithful worshipers of Mohammed; they are honest and reliable in business, and self-respecting members of a well-organized community. The Kazaks are nomads, coming from the stock of the Kirghiz people. They live chiefly in the Altai mountains, round the town of Illi, so much coveted by imperial Russia. All three branches of Hui have a mixed origin, though they are mainly of Turkish extraction.

The name "Hui" was given to them by the Chinese because of their relations with a branch of the ancient Uigurs, called by them Hui-he. The Hui-he established a kingdom in Central Asia during the ninth and tenth centuries and were converted to Mohammedanism. They sent expeditions to Sinkiang, to their fellow-tribesmen who had remained there, and these too became followers of Mohammed. The

Chinese then began to call Mohammedanism "the Hui Religion," and those who practiced it in Sinkiang, "the Hui People."

For some centuries, the Hui kept their independence, though they foolishly weakened themselves by religious schisms. The two main sects, known as the White Mountain and the Black Mountain cults, did not come together until the middle of the eighteenth century, when for urgent political reasons their followers united and joined with the Mongols in their struggle against the imperial armies of the Manchus. A few years later, the Hui troops invaded Chinese territory, trapped the advance forces of the Manchu army on the banks of the Black River, and tried to starve them into surrender. When the besieged men had reached the extremity of cooking their horses' saddles for food, reinforcements arrived, and the Hui were severely defeated. The two Holy Descendants—supposedly descended from the prophet Mohammed himself—who had led the army, fled to a friend for refuge. He had them both beheaded and sent their heads to the victorious general. As a result of this disaster, Southern Sinkiang now came under Chinese rule, and has remained part of the Chinese territory ever since.

The history of Mongolia, Sinkiang, and Tibet in more recent times is no longer one of contest with imperial China. The day when China could call herself a "Celestial Empire," and her Emperor "Ruler of all under Heaven," had passed. In the second half of the nineteenth century, she was forced to contend with the Western imperialists, and those border territories in the North and West by which China had expanded her empire in the past were now looked upon with lustful eyes by Tsarist Russia on the one hand, and Victorian Britain on the other. In the year 1876 Russian forces had advanced into Central Asia and conquered Kokand, on the very borders of Sinkiang, and the next year Queen Victoria proclaimed herself Empress of India. The three powers of China, Russia, and Britain were drawing towards each other with their rival claims, and conflict seemed inevitable.

China being in no condition to resist the Western Powers, rights, privileges, and territory began to pass out of her hands. A local rising in Sinkiang first gave the Russians an excuse for encroachment. They occupied the border town of Illi, calling it a matter of "voluntary protection," yet when the disturbance was put down, by the effort of Tso Tsung-t'ang, one of the ablest ministers, the Russians refused to withdraw. The Manchu government, at that time utterly exhausted by the Opium War with Britain and France, and by the T'ai-p'ing rebellion, had now the choice of declaring war on Russia or agreeing to all her demands. Negotiations were opened, as a result of which Russia planted her foot firmly in Sinkiang. She was allowed to trade there without paying taxes, and to open consulates in several important towns.

As far as Tibet was concerned, it was well known that the British Viceroy of India coveted that "Secret Land." Now, the Lamas who formed the principal ruling class in Tibet held the important trade monopoly of tea. They bought Chinese tea in bulk and sold it to the population at very considerable profit. These worldly priests had thus a good reason to fear the opening of communications between India and Tibet: Indian tea would be rushed in and their main source of revenue would vanish! Accordingly they strongly supported the Manchu Court in its effort to shut off Tibet from communication with the outer world—an effort that was assisted by the geographical situation of the country.

In 1879, British forces took Afghanistan under their protection, and in 1885 they annexed Burma. They were creeping up to Tibet from both south and west. Meanwhile the Russians bit by bit extended their sphere of influence into Tibet from the north. They appeared to abandon their Christian religion and to become faithful Lamaists. They pretended to be sympathetic to the Tibetans disturbed and assailed by the ambitious British. The latter were furious at the success of their rivals, and when, in 1904, war broke out between Russia and Japan, the British lost no time in marching their troops into Lhasa, the Tibetan capital. The Dalai Lama fled to Ch'ing-hai. Three years later, after protracted discussions, the British struck a bargain with the Manchu Court, whereby several treaty ports in Tibet were to be opened to their trade, and all the fortifications from Lhasa to the frontiers would be destroyed. The British imperialists had gained their ends.

Cheated of Tibet, the Russians now turned their attention to Mongolia. Since Mongolia had become part of the Chinese Empire in 1697 the Manchu Court had exercised no positive policy towards it, save that of keeping their Chinese subjects out of it. Mongolia borders on Manchuria, and the Manchus were naturally apprehensive that if the Chinese settled there in great numbers, they would vent their rancor on Manchuria, the home of their conquerors. Even Chinese merchants who traveled in the country for trade must produce passports, and no Chinese was permitted by the Manchu government to buy land or to settle there for more than one year at a time.

The Mongolians themselves, however, had other ideas. They were mainly cattle breeders and no agriculturists. They found it, therefore, very much to their advantage to rent the land to Chinese farmers who managed by one means and another to evade the restrictions. In difficult times, they not infrequently mortgaged their fields to the immigrants, and as they were not always able to pay their debts, the land passed into the hands of the Chinese.

The Russians over the border were quick to notice the infiltration, and ironically accused the Manchu Court of conspiring against them by sending aggressive Chinese into Mongolia! As a counter measure, they began to offer extensive loans to the Mongol nobility, asking for them to be repaid not in money but in lands. By this means, they gradually came to exercise a dominating influence in Mongolia.

The Russo-Japanese war of 1904-5, which had given the British an opportunity to consolidate their influence in Tibet, also resulted in the expansion of Japanese control in the Chinese northeastern provinces, formerly coveted by Russia. The discomfited Russians now redoubled their efforts to become masters of Mongolia. They addressed a stern memorandum to the Manchu Court, requesting free immigration of Russian subjects into Mongolia and Sinkiang, the right of Russian merchants to trade in China free of taxes, and the opening of many new treaty ports.

The Manchu Emperor was in no condition to deal with demands of this sort. His throne was already tottering, and before any conclusions were reached the Emperor fled before the Chinese revolutionary forces. Seizing this golden opportunity, the Russians inspired the Lama "Living Buddha" of Urga, virtual ruler of Outer Mongolia, to declare the independence of his government. The Russians then used this government as a pawn and entered into negotiations with Republican China. In November 1913 a pact was signed by which Russia recognized Chinese suzerainty in Mongolia, and China acknowledged the autonomy of Outer Mongolia. The Chinese government also accorded Russia certain privileges in the whole Mongolian territory.

Then came the Russian Revolution. The automatic regime of the "Living Buddha" in Outer Mongolia, losing Russian financial support, collapsed like a bubble. In November 1919 an appeal was sent to the Chinese Republican government that Outer Mongolia might return to the Motherland. But before China could receive her erring child, Soviet Russia intervened. The remnants of the imperial Russian troops had fled into Mongolia with the Red Army hot on their heels. There the imperial troops were practically annihilated, and the Soviet army set up a new government in Outer Mongolia, calling the State the Republic of "Mongolia." It was presently incorporated into the Soviet Union, while Soviet Russia still recognized Chinese suzerainty over Outer

Mongolia. A very similar agreement had been reached over Tibet between the Chinese and the British. By the pact of April 1914, Great Britain acknowledged Chinese suzerainty over Tibet, while China recognized the autonomy of Anterior Tibet, bordering on India.

Thus, for the time being, relations had been established between the three powers of China, Russia, and Britain in their struggle for domination on the western borders of the Chinese Republic. Mongolia was divided, by foreign suggestion, into "Outer" and "Inner." The Outer division is usually referred to in textbooks simply as "Mongolia," while the Inner division comprises the four Chinese provinces of Jehol, Chahar, Suiyuan, and Ninghsia. Outer Mongolia is chiefly occupied by Mongolian-speaking peoples, but in the four provinces of Inner Mongolia the population is largely Chinese-speaking, the ancestors of the present inhabitants having left their homes in the interior of China and settled there some thousands of years ago. In the great province of Sinkiang too, Chinese-speaking people form the majority, with a sprinkling of the old Hui inhabitants. Most of them are Mohammedans, and the zeal with which they followed their religion has infected the adjacent provinces of China. In Kansu and Ch'ing-hai especially, many thousands of Chinese are faithful to the teachings of Islam.

The future of these peoples, after the present desperate struggle is over, cannot be exactly predicted, but it may be prophesied. The European War of 1914-18 both brought to a peak and terminated the imperialism and territorial intrigues of the previous century, while the theories propounded at Geneva after the Peace Treaty, and some hints given out by the Russian Revolution, combined to awaken the consciences and minds of the Chinese themselves. Following the laws of tradition and the bonds of treaties, they felt that these non-Chinese-speaking peoples of Mongolia, Tibet, and Sinkiang belonged to China, and ought not to be separated from them. Nevertheless, a new sense of justice and idealism, slowly awakening all the world over, refused to admit the right of a stronger people forcibly to incorporate a weaker one. We Chinese realize that we should allow our fellow-beings the Mongols, the Hui, and the Tibetans to make their own choice of government—of freedom or dependence. We should, however, guide and assist them to reach a true independence, and to live in good-neighborliness. We should make sure that no other power annexes them by force, or under the pretext of exercising a merciful policy: no other power, whether it cries "Imperialism" or "Socialism."

XXIV. THE OPIUM WARS

UP TO THE CLOSE of the eighteenth century, which marked the end of the long reign of Ch'ien Lung, the Emperor who refused George III's diplomatic overtures, the Manchu empire had been a powerful one. European envoys had been obliged to choose between "kow-towing" before the oriental sovereign or being refused any communication. For the preceding century and a half, Chinese history had been a tale of conquests. As we have seen, the Mongols, Hui, and Tibetans all fell before the Manchu armies; in addition, Korea, Annam, the Liukiu islands, and Burma became Chinese "Protectorates."

But the nineteenth century brought a tide of ill fortune to the Chinese. Civil wars broke out in 1813, culminating in the T'ai-p'ing rebellion which wasted so many thousands of lives and laid China open to attack from without. The Opium War of 1840 waged against the English, and later against the allied armies of England and France, was in part, at least, the fruit of these civil disturbances. It brought low the ancient prestige of China, and initiated a hundred years of foreign invasion which at the present day has reached its climax in China's deadly struggle against the Japanese.

Opium-smoking is specially associated with the Chinese in the minds of Westerners, among whom it is regarded with not a little contempt. And yet the habit was not native to China, and for a long time after the drug had been introduced by European traders the poppies were not grown on Chinese soil.

As early as the thirteenth century, opium was imported into China for purely medicinal purposes. The Chinese called it the *"fu-shou-kao"* —"the happiness and longevity gum." But it was not until three centuries later, when the Portuguese traders arrived in the Far East, that the Chinese were persuaded to smoke it for pleasure. Still only wealthy, self-indulgent Chinese traders and some effete young men abandoned themselves to what De Quincey called "the chronic pleasures" of opium, but with the founding of the British East India Company in the seventeenth century, and its exploitation of Indian natural resources, opium began to be imported into China from that country on a grand scale. Then all classes of Chinese fell before its deadly power, from the mandarins to the coolies; the physique and morale of the whole country began to be affected.

The English merchantmen, their holds stacked with crates of this poisonous drug brought from India, would weigh anchor at a good distance from the shore, beyond the jurisdiction of Chinese law. Chinese smugglers on the South China coast would paddle out to them in small junks under cover of darkness, and bring ashore the contraband. Both merchants and smugglers made a roaring trade. The Chinese people quite lost their heads over the opium: money that should have been spent on building up the military strength of the country to resist foreign encroachments poured out to pay for this degenerate form of indulgence. It is said that in the year 1838, at the port of Canton alone, 30,000,000 taels of silver were expended on the purchase of opium.

That the price of silver rose as a result, while that of copper coins fell, was only one of the attendant evils. Farmers and merchants had to pay their taxes to the government in silver, so that their burden was made even heavier than before. It was evident that measures must be taken against the insidious poison. In 1838, one of the Emperor's ministers presented a memorandum to him under the heading of "A Petition for Strict Measures against Economic Leakage and for the Nourishment of the National Strength." Its contention was that the existing penalties for opium smoking were far too lenient: a hundred strokes of the whip and three years' penal servitude—the punishment usually awarded to offenders—were much less painful to a hardened opium-smoker than to give up his smoking. But if the death penalty was imposed, even the most enslaved would hardly risk their lives for it, and the habit might be exterminated. The petition concluded by suggesting that a year's moratorium should be granted, during which smokers could gradually cure themselves of the craving. If after a year people still clung to opium, the government could have them put to death without any injustice.

The Emperor gave the memorandum his approval, and sent copies to the governors of all the provinces for consideration. A certain governor Lin Tse-hsu, who controlled two large provinces of Central China, took up the purge enthusiastically. In a short space of time he had collected and destroyed 3,500 opium pipes, and opium gum to the weight of 12,000 taels. Thankful wives embarrassed him with their gratitude: now that their husbands could no longer smoke, the women declared, they had thrown off their physical weakness, were saving money for their families, and becoming once more mannerly, good-natured house-mates.

After this lively success, Lin was sent to the south coasts to investigate the root of the evil, namely, the English merchantmen with their forbidden cargoes. Immediately on his arrival he ordered defenses to be built and manned along the cliffs and shores. This done, he dispatched a peremptory message to the English consul in which he demanded the delivery within three days of all stores of opium owned by the English merchants. Lin was not diffident in pointing out the reprehensible conduct of these merchants, who had been freely granted every facility in trading with the Chinese and who in return were poisoning their customers.

The request was refused with equal decision by the English consul, whereupon Lin ordered a blockade of the English residents in that district. Faced with the starvation of his nationals, the consul was obliged to submit. Bags and boxes of opium poured in until the unimaginably great weight of two million catties had been delivered!

Lin decided to dramatize its destruction so that the ordinary people should never forget the lesson. Between the twenty-second day of the fourth moon in that year of 1838 and the fifteenth day of the fifth moon, the melting of the opium took place on the seashore of Kuangtung province. Two huge pools, each 150 feet square, were dug on the beach and lined with marble slabs. Pipes were fixed leading down into the sea to carry away the dregs, and water reservoirs were constructed in the rear. When all this was prepared water was let into the pools from the reservoirs, and salt added to it. Then the opium gum, cut into small pieces, was thrown in. Lastly, pieces of lime were added from time to time to keep the water boiling. On little bridges constructed over the pools, workmen stood with long poles, constantly stirring the huge caldron until every particle of the evil stuff had been dissolved. At the turn of the tide the sea pipes were opened and the liquid flowed away into the waters of the Pacific. The pools were cleansed once more with pure water so that not a single grain of the opium should remain on Chinese soil. The impressive ceremony was then complete.

Lin was satisfied with the results of his energetic measures. However, he was not the man to rest in his efforts, and he now suggested to the Court that if foreigners were found still carrying opium cargoes they should be hanged. In those provinces over which he himself had jurisdiction, he lost no time in issuing the order: normal trading with Western merchants would be very welcome to the Chinese, but if any foreign trader were found carrying opium contraband, he would be put to death and his ship and cargo confiscated.

The English traders evidently took the order in bad part, and their relations with the Chinese grew increasingly strained. An English crew landing at Hong-Kong had a sailors' brawl with some Chinese, and in the fight which developed a Chinese was killed. The local government demanded the surrender of the assassins, but was curtly refused by the the English consul. At this, Lin immediately issued the edict that no Chinese were to trade with the English. Such a situation was impossible. In the early summer of 1840 fifteen English warships steamed into Macao, with some fifteen thousand troops on board. The first "Opium War" was declared.

The English opened operations by shelling the southern port of Canton, but as Lin's defenses already covered this region, the enemy was unable to effect a landing. The warships moved farther north and began to attack strongholds immediately below the mouth of the Yangtzu. Several islands and towns were taken, and the Manchu Court in Peking was seized with terror. Looking for a scapegoat, the Manchu officials pounced on Lin; they declared that his tactless and aggressive attitude to the English was bringing disaster on the whole empire. He was forthwith relieved of his post, and a Manchu official, Ch'i-shan, sent to discuss terms with the English consul.

In order to make a suitable background for the peace talks, the foolish Ch'i-shan wiped out all Lin's coastal defenses without even consulting the Court. Then he obsequiously approached the English consul and asked for terms. Before hostilities could cease, came the consul's reply: Hong-Kong must be ceded to England, Canton made a "Treaty Port," and an indemnity of six million Chinese dollars be paid to the English merchants in payment for the seizure of their opium cargoes. Ch'i-shan, whose one idea was "to make peace," accepted everything on behalf of the Emperor without hesitation or diplomatic argument.

For this abject acceptance of humiliating terms, Ch'i-shan had no authority from the Emperor, and they were promptly repudiated when news of them reached Peking. Hostilities were renewed with even greater violence. Now that Lin's defenses had been destroyed, the English troops soon broke through the Chinese lines in the South, capturing five hundred cannon in the action. It was a formidable loss to an army of those days. The following month the great city of Canton fell to the English.

In the seventh moon of the same year, the victorious English armada moved northwards and took Amoy and other coastal towns. Shanghai fell, and the English, having brought their warships up the Yangtzu, were threatening Nanking with their guns. The Chinese Court was again in panic, and the first modern unequal treaty was accepted and signed, to the great misfortune of the country. By the Treaty of Nanking, the Chinese were to pay an indemnity of six million dollars for the expenses of the war, as well as another nine million to the English merchants for their loss of trade during the war and for their opium contraband. Hong-Kong was to be ceded to England and five coastal towns opened as treaty ports.

Amoy, Foochow, Ningpo, and Shanghai were duly opened to English traders, but the people of Canton, traditionally bold and independent, refused to admit any encroachment on their sovereignty or to allow the English consul to enter the city. When the latter attempted to rush his gunboat up the Pearl River into the heart of Canton, he found himself facing the armed threats of tens of thousands of Cantonese militia, who crowded along both banks. He was obliged to withdraw, and it was not until nine years later, in 1856, that the gallant resistance of Canton was overcome.

The second Opium War began with another trivial incident. A boat named "Arrow," owned by Chinese illegal traders but registered in England and flying the English flag, was sailing into Canton harbor. The commander of a Chinese patrol vessel, having observed the approach of the ship, sent his men aboard to arrest thirteen of the crew and tear down the English flag. The English consul protested at the action, demanded the restoration of the boat's crew and the offering of an official apology.

The Chinese governor Yeh, to whom the note was addressed, was a somewhat naïve politician, more interested in books and paintings than in diplomatic wrangles. He read off the protest with a smile and saw no harm in handing back the crew. The English consul, however, insisted that the officer responsible for ordering the English flag to be hauled down should be heavily punished. Yeh thought the demand excessive, and promptly sent the crew back to jail. He hoped and believed that the whole affair would then blow over.

But to his disappointment, the roar of English guns began to rend the air, and news was brought of an English troop landing. He still refused to be alarmed and told his own forces to hold their fire and let the foreigners make as much clamor as they liked. He was evidently relying on the Chinese proverb that "it takes two porcelain bowls to make a clash," and thought the domineering behavior of the English would be put to shame by his gentlemanly reception. The English troops naturally enough landed and, amazed at the simplicity of the operation, marched into Canton.

The arrival of English soldiers enraged the populace, and a riot broke out. The local authorities were quite unable to control the more violent elements, who deliberately set fire to all foreign property in the western suburbs, irrespective of nationality. In reprisal, the English soldiers fired all the small dwelling houses of the Cantonese on the city's outskirts. Nor was this the end of the disaster: American and French property had suffered, and the French, under the administration of the ambitious Napoleon III, made an alliance with the English and dispatched a fleet to the Far East.

The governor Yeh, incapable of learning from events, neither attempted to open negotiations with the enemy nor made any military preparations. He did not even discuss the situation with his military advisers. He just waited, imperturbably, for whatever fate might bring.

The rumble of war soon sounded. In the autumn of 1857 the allied navies opened fire on Canton. "Cannon roared like a million thunderclaps, and flaming streets lit up the sky," wrote an historian. The local militia organized a defense and were able to resist the invaders for two days, but on the third day French and English soldiers fought their way into the city. Red flags were hoisted on every fortress in Canton to signify its fall.

Governor Yeh was taken prisoner. He was placed in a dignified sedan chair, wearing his Court dress, and with a peacock's feather and his official button in his hat. In this manner he was carried to prison in Hong-Kong. But even this personal disgrace and the defeat of his people appeared not to affect him: while in solitary confinement he continued to paint pictures and to compose elegant pieces of calligraphy for the English connoisseurs who had heard of his skill! Such a person was obviously too foolish to execute and too harmless to imprison. He was accordingly sent to spend the rest of his days in Bengal, taking with him his military attaché, his hairdresser, and two servants. He died there two years later in "the Hall where the Sea is Pacified," and his body was brought back to his native land with all honor for burial. A ballad was composed about him, and passed from mouth to mouth in Canton, preserving his memory for longer than it deserved. It runs:

> *You neither fight,*
> *Nor make peace,*
> *Nor prepare defense.*

You neither die for your duty,
Nor surrender,
Nor flee to safety.

It is a minister's generosity,
And a governor's liberality
Which find no example in ancient
Nor an equal in modern history!

Next year, the English and French fleets sailed north and made an unforeseen attack upon T'ientsin. This constituted a very serious menace to the capital, and the Chinese Court sent an appeal to the allied command that they should make a temporary withdrawal of their troops, so that an armistice might be considered. When this was conceded, the Chinese hastened to build strong defenses in that area, to bring up heavy cannon, to block the river mouth, and to send up their "crack" Mongol and Manchurian cavalry divisions.

As no negotiations appeared to be forthcoming, the enemy fleet once more approached the river mouth, broke through the barricades, and after a heavy bombardment managed to land troops. But they now met with a formidable and unexpected resistance, and were completely routed. Four of their warships were sunk by Chinese fire.

The Chinese officials were triumphant. They thought they had turned the tables on the foreigners, and that the enemy would immediately plead for peace! With oriental tact, they cleared away all the defense works in that region as a sign that they would gladly welcome the English and French negotiators, and even ordered their troops to withdraw. Alas for their plans! The enemy did not take the hint, but benefiting by the undefended positions, landed their armies and bore down upon the unsuspecting Chinese! The famous cavalry divisions mustered and attempted to check the advance, but they were mown down "like walls collapsing" as soon as they came within range of the gunfire. The Chinese, to their chagrin, felt obliged to ask for terms, but as these were too outrageous, battle began again, the enemy advancing almost to the outskirts of Peking. The Manchu Court seemed still to live in a dream of its invincibility, and to have no sense of the enemy power. The Manchu general Sheng-pao, who now led his troops against the allied armies, was decked out in his brilliant Court uniform, and rode into battle with a red button in his hat and a yellow jacket! He naturally offered a target for the enemy bullets: he was shot in the face, and fell from his horse. After he was carried from the field, his army retired in confusion.

The Manchu Emperor took fright and decided to make "an autumn tour of inspection" at his summer residence in Jehol, and took the imperial family with him, leaving the peace negotiations to a Manchu prince. The Russian minister offered to act as arbitrator between the two parties, and in 1860 the notorious Peking Pact was signed in that city. By this treaty the Chinese agreed to pay a huge indemnity to both England and France and to lease to England the Peninsula of Kowloon, opposite Hong-Kong. Eight more treaty ports, including Kiukiang and Hankow, were to be opened to the English and six to the French. In addition, the customs on English and French merchandise were to be reduced. The unjust system of extraterritoriality was brought into force. This meant that English and French nationals who acted against the law in Chinese territory were subject only to the judgment of their own consuls. French and English missionaries were allowed by the treaty to preach in the interior, and French Catholics were even permitted to buy and own lands there for their churches.

The Russians, who had done the Chinese the great service of acting as go-between in this discreditable pact, soon insisted on a pact of their own. In 1861, the Chinese, who were quite powerless to oppose any suggestion, were obliged to cede "voluntarily" the land north of the Black Dragon River and east of the Ussuri River—lands which then came to form the Russian "Maritime" province and the province of Amur.

The significance of the Peking Pact does not lie only in the losses which China sustained. It was the first occasion when she was forced to surrender part of her sovereign, independent rights to a foreign power. Increasing pressure was put on her in the years that followed, by the Russians and Japanese as well as the French and English, and the country would have fallen into a state of utter slavery had the incompetent Manchu rulers not been driven from the throne.

The huge sums of money that had to be squeezed from the groaning people as indemnities to the wealthy Europeans brought the Empire to the verge of bankruptcy. Through the low customs duty and preferential tariffs accorded in the treaties to the industrial nations of the West, foreign, machine-made goods poured into China, and not only ousted native goods, but effectively prevented the development of a national industry. In the settlements and concessions owned or leased by foreigners, extraordinary rights were extended to all the inhabitants, so that these places became a sanctuary for common criminals of all nationalities, including Chinese; for scurrilous Chinese politicians, traitors, and war-lords. Chinese justice was thus impaired, and evils that should have been exterminated continued to poison the State from a safe shelter.

It was at this time too, that Christianity in China began to have very marked political reactions. Priding themselves on being superior to their "heathen" brethren, the Chinese who had adopted the "religion from across the Ocean" took on some of the overbearing ways which the foreigners themselves used towards the native inhabitants, and much bitter feeling resulted.

The most grievous of all consequences was that the Chinese lost faith in themselves and their nation: they relaxed their endeavors at reform and development; they were over-impressed by the scientific inventions and war machinery of the Westerners so that they began to despise their own ancient civilization, and servilely to imitate the foreigners. As the years passed, hostilities broke out unceasingly between China and the Western Powers. There were wars with France in 1884, with Japan in 1894, and with eight powers in 1900, all of them provoked by the Westerners who wanted to extort concessions from the Chinese and impose their trade upon them without any regard for the country's needs or wishes.

China with her ill-equipped, old-fashioned army invariably suffered defeat, and in the treaties that followed she had to surrender protectorates, lease naval bases and strategic military positions; she had to destroy her own fortifications, and give up concessions and settlements. "Spheres of interest," the rights of railway building and mine digging, the compulsory employment by the Chinese of foreign advisers, decreased even further the Chinese control of their own land. Even their rivers were opened up to patroling foreign battleships and the interior to foreign agents. Indeed, it was no longer a conflict between China and the Western Powers, but a squabble between the rival powers over the powerless body of the Chinese Empire.

People of the present day who are witness to the struggle of the weaker nations in Europe to maintain or regain their independence must sympathize with China in her own struggle which has no other object than the restoration of her sovereignty and the right to live as a free, independent nation among the other nations of the world.

XXV. CHINA AND THE WESTERN POWERS (2)—THE "PARTITION" OF CHINA AND THE BOXER REBELLION

THE FIRST ARMED CONTACT with foreigners in the Opium War of 1840-42 gave a rude jolt to the Chinese *amour propre,* and the series of disastrous wars with Western Powers that followed shattered it altogether. At this stage in her history, China was bound to acknowledge the usefulness of Western science. It was clear, for instance, that the clumsy Chinese war junks, dependent on wind and tide, could not hope to match the steam-driven English warships. Gradually her people began to realize the scope of the world; that China was only one of the many nations East and West; and even that Western civilization was not necessarily inferior.

Forcibly roused from her phlegmatic dreams of the past, China now believed her prestige might be restored if she mastered this strange Western learning. Scholars who knew foreign languages began feverishly to translate books on physics, optics, thermo-dynamics, electricity, magnetism, and acoustics. Sound, light, power, and heat were eagerly discussed, in place of the old literary controversies, while the officials began to envisage a new up-to-date army and navy, and a network of railway lines across the length and breadth of the country.

An English priest, Timothy Richard, played a preliminary part in this act of the Chinese drama. Like Matteo Ricci, he had a real respect and affection for the people he lived among, was very well learned in Chinese culture, and offered his hosts practical knowledge as well as spiritual wisdom. As may be supposed, he found many a ready ear among the scholars and officials, for he brought information of the coveted Western science.

Presently he left his missionary work in the interior and came to Peking, where he joined the "Society for the Diffusion of Christian and General Knowledge," a society founded by the Western missionaries. Many scientific books were published under its auspices, as well as a magazine known as the "International Review." Richard was soon made editor of the magazine, and in this capacity he brought to the knowledge of his Chinese readers their first exact information about the political and economic structure of the Western nations. He even translated into Chinese editorials from prominent European newspapers, commenting upon current events. The magazine leaped to popularity.

In a short time, many Chinese scholars who admired Richard's ideas set to work with equal zeal for the scientific education of China. A second paper, called "Chinese Daily," was issued, and another society founded—the "Society for National Development." A shipping bureau was opened. Electric cables were laid in the large towns and the first railways were built. Most important of all for the ultimate direction of Chinese affairs, many Chinese students were sent to study in the West. It was from this band of Western educated young men and women that the seeds of revolution and the foundations of the new Republic were destined to spring.

This eager desire for Western knowledge was not without opposition: the more reactionary members of the aristocracy and Court officials, who probably sensed a danger to themselves in the break-up of the old order, spoke fiercely and bitterly against the new learning. A prominent member of the cabinet at that time declared that he would rather see the whole nation wiped out than adopt any reformation according to foreign political principles. In evidence of his indignation, he always went out through his back gate because his residence faced a foreign Embassy! He was, moreover, largely instrumental in liquidating the "Society for National Development" when it had existed only for four months.

But while this internal controversy raged in a somewhat academic manner, the Western Powers decided that China had too valuable a market to be allowed to pursue her own destiny without their participation. A fierce struggle between their imperialist ambitions and the natural independent growth of China was initiated, and lasted until the fall of the Manchu dynasty in 1911.

This disastrous phase of China's history began with the defeat of the Chinese forces in the Sino-Japanese war of 1894-95. By the Treaty of Shimonoseki which concluded the war, China was obliged to recognize the independence of Korea, and to cede to Japan the Liaotung Peninsula including Port Arthur, a base of vital importance commanding the entrance to the Yellow River and offering an immediate threat to Peking.

The advance of Japan towards the nerve-center of China greatly

alarmed the Western Powers, who hastened to lodge a stern note with
the Japanese government. They stoutly refused to recognize the cession
of the Liaotung Peninsula, and in face of their combined protests the
Japanese withdrew their claim. The way was now open for the seizure
of Port Arthur by Russia, and for the Russo-Japanese war of 1904
which ensued. The Russian defeat which startled the world sealed the
death warrant not only of the Tsarist regime in Russia but of the
Manchu dynasty, as we shall see in another chapter.

Meanwhile, after forcing Japan to give up what she had won by
battle, the powers proceeded to make a nominal division of China
among themselves, and so to balance their respective "sphere of influence" that they might not come to blows with one another over their
booty. Germany was the first to move. In 1897, two German missionaries were murdered in Shantung, and the German government made
the incident an excuse for occupying the port of Ts'ingtao for use as a
naval base, and for exacting mining rights in the rich coal district of
Chiao-chou in Shantung. Russia now stepped forward and proposed to
take under her wing the much-disputed Port Arthur. By bringing up
a number of warships, their decks cleared for action, the Russians were
able to persuade the powerless Chinese Court to fall in with their
wishes. In order, as they said, to keep the balance of power on this
northeast coast of China, strategically so important both in relation to
Japan and to the Chinese capital, the English government applied for
the lease of Weihaiwei and received it without protest. It was at this
time, too, that Manila in the Philippine Islands and the Islands of
Hawaii were annexed by America, who thereby firmly planted her
stake in Pacific affairs.

After the cession of these coastal towns came the virtual mortgaging
of land in the interior, through the ceding of railway rights. The Chinese treasury was too far impoverished by wars and ruinous indemnities to undertake the construction of railways, and her method was to
borrow from the powers and to allow them to build the railways themselves. The railways served as a pledge for the credits, and their administration was freely given to the creditors without argument. The
profits gathered in by the railway companies were supposed in time to
repay the loans. Through this unbusinesslike arrangement, not only the
railways themselves, but the property attached to them became mort-
gages to foreign companies.

The scramble for railway rights on the part of the Western Powers
can readily be understood, but in order to avoid open conflict they
concluded agreements among themselves, without any consultation

with China, as to their respective areas. The upshot of the disreputable bargaining was that Russia was allowed to build railways north of the Great Wall, that is, principally in Manchuria; Germany in the Yellow River districts; France in South China, and Britain in the Yangtzu River valley. British influence extended presently into the Southwest, and the recent construction of a line from Burma to the Chinese frontier has been of value to China in her present war.

America now appeared on the scene as the champion of China's rights. In 1899, she addressed a memorandum to the governments of Great Britain, France, Russia, Japan, Germany, and Italy, in which she demanded that the integrity of Chinese territory be respected, and that the "Open Door" policy be fairly applied. China was unable to close her doors to the foreigners, but they had closed her doors for her from within. America demanded that the powers should renounce their privileges within their own "sphere of influence," and have no reduced customs and transport rates in those areas.

China was in a nightmare. It was not within her power to open or shut her doors, and the country was at the mercy of foreign depredations. She was drifting into chaos. The ruling House, now represented by the blind and incompetent Empress Dowager, Tzu Hsi, had grown so feeble that the foreign diplomats almost disregarded its existence. Like all women tyrants, Tzu Hsi was interested only in her own pleasure and power, and was incapable of caring for her country. The money voted for constructing a strong navy to protect the national interests, she commandeered for an extravagant pleasure park, and the only ship which appeared was one of marble that lay beside the lake and on which she held her imperial tea parties.

But the germ of revolution was already beginning to stir like yeast in the Chinese masses. The defeat by Japan in 1895 was a great education to them: it showed that a comparatively small country, but one having a constitutional government and an up-to-date state machinery, could conquer a great nation ruled by despots who were blind to the outer world. The cry for reform rang through China.

The leaders of this movement came, naturally enough, from South China. The Cantonese, who for years had traded with Hong-Kong and had mixed with the foreign merchants and administrators, were accustomed to comparing their businesslike methods with the old-fashioned inefficiency of their own government. In addition, many of the Cantonese students had traveled to Japan, to Singapore, to Australia, and even to Western America, and there had seen popular government in action. Sun Yat-sen, founder of the Chinese Republic, and its revolutionary leader, was born and educated in the southern province of Kuangtung, and at the close of the nineteenth century had already started his activities, but his great day was still to come. Meanwhile, another Cantonese, K'ang Yu-wei, was attempting to initiate reform within the old framework.

K'ang was a man of traditional learning, a Confucian scholar, and a writer of talent. His books on the reforms of the Japanese Emperor Meiji, and on those of the Tsar Peter the Great of Russia, made a great impression on the Chinese Emperor. He was supported in his views by a younger disciple, Liang Ch'i-ch'ao, founder of the journal *"Shih Wu Pao,"* and a pioneer of the new literature movement. Liang's most famous writings were his studies on the reconstruction of modern Italy, and the fall of Poland. His easy, subtle, yet powerful style made him, perhaps, the most popular and influential writer of the day. Following the lead of K'ang and Liang, many scholars began to translate the works of European thinkers and philosophers, including Charles Darwin and Herbert Spencer, Johannes Müller, Adam Smith and David Hume, Jean-Jacques Rousseau, Voltaire, and Montesquieu. The public mind was being prepared for violent changes.

The fame of K'ang Yu-wei's works eventually reached the ears of the young Emperor Têh Tsung, who was by now a ruler in his own right. In 1898 he received a memorandum from K'ang setting out the proposals for constitutional government, together with copies of his books on the Japanese and Russian reforms. We hear that he was profoundly impressed, that he sent for K'ang and his pupil Liang Ch'i-ch'ao, and that he entrusted to them the working out of a complete system of reform for China.

From the fifth to the seventh moon of that year, the enlightened decrees poured out, but unfortunately the Empress Dowager, who had been safely out of the way in her gorgeous summer palace, got wind of them, and sensed a threat to her power. She returned suddenly and declared that the reformers were plotting against her life. She ordered their immediate execution, and six of the most brilliant leaders were beheaded a few days later. K'ang Yu-wei was secretly warned by the Emperor, and escaped to the protection of the International Settlement at Shanghai, and thence to Hong-Kong, while Liang Ch'i-ch'ao fled to Japan.

The helpless Emperor had to endure an undignified scolding from his royal aunt, and was then made prisoner on the beautiful "Immortals' Island" in the "Southern Sea" lake of the Peking Imperial Park. "He needs a little rest to recover from his indisposition," declared his loving aunt, who now took the affairs of government back into her own hands and hastened to annul all the recent innovations.

The Empress Dowager's rage against the reform party now extended to the interfering foreigners who had planted these ridiculous ideas of "constitution" and "popular government" in the minds of her country-men. Moreover, the foreign legations had saved the young Emperor from assassination, had declined to recognize his forced "abdication," and had refused to deliver up the two main "conspirators," K'ang Yu-wei and Liang Ch'i-ch'ao, to her avenging hand. Besides having her personal grievances, she felt it essential to find some outlet for popular discontent: a furious persecution of the "foreign devils" seemed a very appropriate policy.

The instrument was ready to her hand. North of the Yangtzu, secret societies were adding their disturbances to the general confusion, the most influential among them being the *"I-ho Ch'uan,"* "the Society of Righteous and Harmonious Boxers." They were the descendants of the "White Lotus" men who had once raised their troops against the Man-chu Court. Now they wandered about the country, living like gypsies, and earning a precarious livelihood by street exhibitions of boxing and sword dancing. They were glad to welcome "converts," but more as members of a secret political society than as followers of a religion. They do not seem now to have had any fervent political beliefs, but were ready to make mischief against any party when it served their ends.

Their chief center of activity had orginally been Shantung province, in Northeastern China, but when Yuan Shih-k'ai (the future first President of the Chinese Republic) was made governor of that province, he undermined their organization and drove them out. They wandered northwards, inland, and arrived presently in the vicinity of Peking.

At the capital, they found a strong atmosphere of racial hatred against the foreigner, nourished and incited by the formidable Empress Dowager. Nothing could be more to their taste, and they proceeded to fan the flame to white heat, under the grateful patronage of the Court. "Back the Court and damn the Foreign Devils!" was their new watch-word. They declared that their talismen were proof against the vaunted foreign bullets, and by spreading extravagant rumors of miracles, gained some credence for their claims. The Empress Dowager, a vain old woman intoxicated with hatred, readily believed any superstitious story that came to her ears, and her weakness was encouraged by the section of the Court whose anger against the foreigners was as hot as hers. One claimed to have had a spirit message from Kuan-kung, the

Chinese God of War, to the effect that the foreigners were about to be annihilated. Another said that news had come of five dragons guarding the mouth of the Taku River: any foreign warship that dared to defy them and attempted to steam up-river would be sunk outright!

In a word, China had been driven mad by the oppressions of foreign imperialists for many years, and now that the clear-headed statesmen and the young scholars, who alone had a realistic view of the modern world, had been driven out, the country was at the mercy of one proud, ignorant, flattery-besotted woman.

In 1900 the storm broke. The Boxers, in their characteristic red turbans, broke into the homes of Chinese Christians and massacred them by the hundred. Some foreign missionaries were also assaulted and murdered. The inventions of the hated foreigner—railway tracks, electric cables, telephone wires, post offices—were torn up, mutilated, or set on fire.

The movement spread and lost all control. The Empress Dowager, urged on by reactionary nobles, ceased merely to give covert support to the Boxers. She openly joined in the hunt and ordered that "all foreigners in China be put to death"—an order that was seized upon by the mob with frenzied delight.

Many of the foreigners and some Chinese Christians took refuge in the legations. On the twentieth of June in the same year, the Empress Dowager sent an ultimatum to the legations, ordering them to leave Peking within twenty-four hours. Upon the rejection of the ultimatum she declared war on them, and for eight weeks they were ferociously besieged until the armies of the eight allies—England, France, Russia, Germany, Japan, U.S.A., Italy and Austria—reached them.

As these armies marched towards Peking, no God of War and no five dragons intervened to save the Chinese. The imperial troops collapsed after a brief resistance, and the evil Tzu Hsi escaped from Peking in disguise, carrying the Emperor off with her, having first had his favorite concubine drowned in a well.

The lovely city of Peking was left to the mercy of the victorious allied soldiers, who burned, looted, plundered, raped, and destroyed even more savagely than the Boxers had done. It was not a reputable page in the history of either East or West.

By the peace terms which were concluded in 1901, the leaders of the anti-foreign movement were to be put to death, and all the fortifications from the sea coast to T'ientsin, just east of Peking, were to be abolished. This was in order that foreign troops could march into the capital at any time should such a movement ever break out again. Finally, so huge an indemnity was demanded—450 million taels (about 325 million dollars)—that until 1940 the Chinese people remained under its burden.[1]

Even after the treaty had been signed, Russia did not cease hostilities; her troops were already in Manchuria, and by a secret agreement subsequently concluded with China she virtually annexed these huge northern provinces, and was given permission to connect Port Arthur with the trans-Siberian railway. By this act, the inevitable conflict between Russia and Japan moved a step nearer. War broke out between them three years later.

Tzu Hsi's sun was setting. The humiliating peace terms with the foreigners, the contemptible opposition which the army had put up, and the general confusion of public affairs, served to turn the people's hatred against the Court. Their sense of nationalism, already roused by anti-foreign propaganda, reminded them of the fact that their ruling House was "foreign" too. The Manchus must be driven out!

Subversive literature—papers, periodicals, books—began to roll off the printing presses of the foreign concessions at Shanghai, Hong-Kong, and Macao, beyond the reach of the Empress's prohibition. Many of them contained criticism of the Manchu dynasty, the conduct of their nobles and rulers; others described the battles, massacres, and oppressions which had taken place when the Sung and the Ming dynasties fell before the pressure of the Mongols and the Manchus. Revolutionary articles began to appear. The stage was set for Sun Yat-sen's revolutionary movement, and the Manchu dynasty did not long outlast Tzu Hsi's death, which occurred in 1908.

---

[1] In 1907 the U.S.A. agreed to remit a part of the indemnity unconditionally to China, and in her gratitude the Chinese government decided to spend this upon scholarships to American Universities. The Tsing Hua College, until the outbreak of the present Sino-Japanese war in Peking, was also built largely with these funds. The flow of Chinese students to America had a profound and decisive effect upon Chinese history. It virtually sealed the fate of dynastic government in China.

XXVI. CHINA AND JAPAN (2)—THE KOREAN CAMPAIGNS AND THE PRELUDE TO MANCHURIA

SIDE BY SIDE with the attempt of Western nations to "monopolize" the Chinese market, and to extort by war or diplomacy special privileges for themselves on her territory, came a new wave of encroachment from China's eastern neighbor. Towards the end of the nineteenth century, Japan resumed her offensive against Northeast China, especially Korea, which the military despot Hideyoshi had first attempted during the Ming dynasty. And now it was as a "modern" power that Japan advanced with her armies.

Japan's earliest contact with the Western world had, like China's, been through the Christian missionaries, who at first brought useful learning, but subsequently began to meddle in politics and to pave the way for the imperialist ambitions of the countries they represented. Hideyoshi at the end of the sixteenth century already recognized the danger, and ordered a general expulsion of the missionaries and a persecution of their Japanese converts. His successor continued the policy, accompanying it with crucifixions, ear and nose cuttings, immersions in pools of sulphur, and other brutalities more than worthy of the Spanish Inquisition. Finally, in the year 1637, after a formidable rising had occurred among some Japanese Christian peasants, the government decided to close the country to all intercourse with other nations.

For more than two centuries, Japan retired from the world like a recluse, until in July 1853 a strange event startled her from her dream of self-sufficiency. Matthew Calbraith Perry, an American commodore, arrived in Japanese waters with four warships. He dropped anchor, came ashore, and requested an interview with the leaders of the government. Complaining that some shipwrecked American sailors had been maltreated by the Japanese, Perry demanded the right to purchase raw materials and to trade at certain ports. Having staked his claim, he steamed back to America, promising to return the following year for the Emperor's answer.

The Japanese had been terrified at the sight of self-propelling warships, and the peasants took them to be a kind of sea-monster. The Emperor prayed to Heaven for assistance, but no help came. Next year the monsters returned in even greater number, and with humiliation and anger the Japanese were obliged to open treaty ports to American merchants.

This event, which changed the whole course of Japanese history, almost coincided with the accession of Japan's greatest Emperor—the Emperor Meiji. America forced Japan into contact with the modern world; Meiji broke the power of rival factions within the island empire, and introduced a modern form of government. The result was that within a matter of two generations Japan passed from a civilization typical of the Middle Ages, to that of a modern twentieth-century power, capable among other things of challenging and defeating the huge Russian Empire.

With the accession of the Emperor Meiji in 1867, Japan's internal strength, and consequently her ambitions, grew by leaps and bounds. Her industries and armies modernized, she joined the imperialist powers, and took part in their intrigues at China's expense. The first stage of her continental policy, enacted during the decadent period of the Manchu dynasty, took form of a plot to seduce from China her protectorate and ally Korea. This was finally accomplished in 1910, and from that time onwards Japan began steadily to exert her power over Northeastern China. By bribe and threat she insinuated herself into the confidence of Chinese administrators and war-lords, until she was able, in 1931, to occupy the whole Manchurian territory, thus opening the door for a large-scale invasion of China. Fully to understand the present struggle in East Asia, it is essential to know something of these preludes.

The initial move against Korea took place in 1875. Japanese warships of a new model slid up the the Seoul River, looking for trouble. The Korean garrisons immediately opened fire, and the Japanese commander hastened to lodge an indignant protest with the Chinese officials. China at that time had no Foreign Office. The body responsible for the management of her foreign policy was called the "General *Yamen* for controlling Foreign Affairs," and was staffed by bureaucrats entirely ignorant of their business. On being interrogated by the Japanese naval commander, the *Yamen* spokesman responded vigorously that Korea was indeed a Chinese Protectorate, but when a complaint against the Korean garrison was deposited, and compensation required, the *Yamen* hastened to wash its hands of the whole incident, declaring that it never interfered with the foreign or internal affairs of that country.

No reply could better have pleased the Japanese, who lost no time in pressing the Koreans to accept their demands. When her Protectorate had been compelled, under the watchful eyes of Japanese warships, to proclaim its "independence," the Chinese officials realized too late how ill-advised had been their declaration. The wily Japanese had won the first move in their game of conquering Korea and advancing upon China.

Japan then began her famous policy of *"divide et impera,"* which she later used in China with such disastrous effects upon her victim. There was in Korea at that time a section called the "Innovation Party" which desired to emulate the political innovations recently effected in Japan. It was an easy matter for the Japanese to give both overt and covert support to this party, and to intensify the internal conflicts, so as to weaken the government's authority.

One of the mischief makers was a certain Japanese general who had been invited to act as military adviser in the formation of a more up-to-date army. He soon provoked a quarrel in the barracks which led to rioting, and in the course of it the general himself was killed.

The Japanese were secretly delighted. To atone for the assassination of a worthless general, they were allowed to station troops in the Korean capital! In 1884, these Japanese soldiers urged some truculent elements of the population, including members of the "Innovation Party," to make an assault upon their "reactionary" rulers. They led an attack on the palace, where the Queen was seized and put to death. The country trembled on the edge of a grave civil war, while the Japanese armies across the water waited anxiously for the moment when they might pounce upon their entangled prey. The Korean government, however, promptly applied to China for help, and Japan was obliged to look on with chagrin while Chinese forces put down the rebellion which she had just been at such pains to provoke.

Next year, Japan lodged a protest with China, rebuking her for the interference, and reminding her of Korean "independence." A pact was then concluded by which both powers agreed to withdraw their troops, and not to respond to any appeal from the Korean government without notifying the other signatory.

The pact was not long in bearing fruit. In 1894 another group of Korean malcontents, calling themselves "Partisans of Oriental Studies," raised an armed rebellion and began to spread destruction in the south. The Korean government appealed once more to China, who hastily dispatched troops and quelled the revolt, even before the angry Japanese were able to embark an army.

The Japanese ministers were furious. Why had China given no notice of her intention to send troops? Had she forgotten her pact with Japan? The officials of the *"Yamen* for Controlling Foreign Affairs" were genuinely astonished. Of course they remembered the agreement, but they had merely given a helping hand to the Korean government: China had gained nothing from the exploit, and was about to withdraw her troops once more. Would not Japan agree to withdraw her protest—and her troops too?

Japan would do neither. For some years now she had been preparing for open conflict with China, and while the Chinese Court hesitated and vacillated, Japan attacked her forces on Korean territory. China had never imagined such a situation, and was ill-prepared. Before she had properly mustered her forces, enemy troops had fallen upon them, driven them back well beyond the boundaries of Korea, and occupied a large part of Chinese territory, while the Japanese navy had simultaneously destroyed the Chinese fleet off the former British base of Weihaiwei.

The Chinese Court was so alarmed that it hastily offered to negotiate. In the third moon of 1895, the notorious Treaty of Shimonoseki was concluded—notorious because by its terms Japan was able for the first time to fasten her claws into the continent of Asia. Besides paying a huge indemnity, China agreed to cede Formosa to Japan, to open four treaty ports to her, and to allow Japanese warships to sail inland on the Chinese rivers.

Before the negotiations were concluded, China had, in addition, agreed to hand over a part of Southern Manchuria known as the Liaotung Peninsula, including the vital base of Port Arthur. Now, Manchuria was regarded by Russia as her "sphere of influence," and she would not tolerate the proposal. Backed by Germany and France, she refused to countenance Japan's so-called "legally" acquired prize, and under very strong pressure, Japan, exhausted by war, was obliged to restore it to China in return for a large subsidy. From this moment, Japan began to foster thoughts of revenge against the Russian giant.

After the Boxer Rising, which was put down in 1901 by a combination of eight powers, including Russia, the disputed part of Southern Manchuria which had been wrested from Japan passed virtually into Russian control. Moreover, without any act of war, Russia was gradually extending her influence over Korea! Japan knew that with Korea in Russian hands, not only would she be driven out of China, but her own independence would be threatened. She decided to open hostilities with her mighty neighbor, before that neighbor could base its warships on Korean ports.

Strengthened by an alliance with Great Britain, who also viewed with some dismay the Russian expansion, Japan demanded the monopoly of Korea, while acknowledging Russia's special interest in Southern Manchuria. The Russian militarists, contemptuous of the Japanese gnat, and quite unconscious of the deadly nature of its sting, did not hesitate to reject the proposal. In February 1904, the Russo-Japanese war was declared.

The new Japanese navy left port, and in a short time the Russian warships stationed in Eastern waters were swept from the sea. Then the armies met. The battles were fought out on Chinese soil, while the feeble Chinese government proclaimed its "strict neutrality," and uttered never a protest. A decisive engagement was fought on the first of January, 1905: 850,000 men took part in it, and the Russians were soundly defeated. Two months later, the famous Russian Baltic fleet, having made a tremendous journey by the Cape of Good Hope, arrived in the Pacific and engaged the Japanese navy. To the astonishment of the whole world, the proud Russian fleet had sailed to utter destruction: twenty-one warships were sunk and seven captured within a few hours! By April of 1905 the Russians were suing for peace.

The American President, Theodore Roosevelt, offered to act as arbitrator, and the peace treaty was signed at Portsmouth, U.S.A., in August of 1905. By its terms, the southern half of Sakhalin Island, one of the greatest fishing centers in the world, which Russia had previously acquired from China, now passed into Japanese hands. The important naval bases of Port Arthur and Darien were also made over to Japan, while the southern section of the Chinese Eastern railway, which ran through Manchuria, and had been built by a Russian loan, became the property of Japan, and she was allowed to station her troops along it. Finally, Russia agreed to recognize Japanese predominance in the political, economic, and military affairs of Korea. China, as may be imagined, found herself in a strange situation: her own territory and rights were being transferred from one power to another without even a consultation!

Japan, on the other hand, had secured the position she had dreamed of, and quickly proceeded to strengthen her hold upon the eastern edge of the continent. Her first move was to set up a "Southern Manchurian

Railway Joint Stock Company," to serve as a political and economic agent in China. She followed this by establishing powerful army units —known as the Kuantung Army—in those Chinese coastal towns formerly leased to Russia and now given away to Japan. It was the clever co-operation of this army with the Manchurian railway which to a great degree facilitated the seizure of Manchuria and Jehol in 1931 and 1932. In 1910, despite her former pledges, she annexed the whole of Korea.

Having once established herself on the continent and brought to a successful end the first phase in her plan of Asiatic domination, Japan prepared for new acts of aggression. Her opportunity came in 1914, at the outbreak of war in the West: she declared war on Germany and made Chiao-chou, the German concession in Shantung province, her first objective. With the support of British troops, she captured the town, and proceeded thence along the railway westwards for at least a hundred miles. China protested fruitlessly: her neutrality was no more respected than it had been during the Russo-Japanese war.

When every German soldier had left Chinese soil, the Chinese government proposed to the allied forces of Japan and Britain that their troops should be withdrawn and the territory restored to China. The British troops reasonably complied, and withdrew from Chiao-chou, but the Japanese called the suggestion "insulting," and instantly submitted a counter-proposal—the famous "Twenty-one Demands."

The Demands were contained in five sections. Under the first, China was required to recognize Japan's inheritance of all the former German rights and concessions in Chinese territory, as well as permit her to build railways in Shantung. The second section consisted of new Japanese claims upon Southern Manchuria and Eastern Mongolia. The third demanded the right to participate in the working of China's largest iron foundry, iron deposits, and coal mines. The fourth directed China not to cede any ports, bays, or islands along the entire China coast to any third party, while the fifth—most invidious of all—insisted on the employment of Japanese "advisers" in Chinese political, economic, and military organizations.

The Chinese government was at that time under the control of the treacherous Yuan Shih-k'ai, who not only lacked the military support for rejecting Japan's humiliating demands, but possibly even the will to do so. On the twenty-fifth of May, 1915, the agreement was signed with only a few modifications. The Japanese menace was creeping like a cancer into the body of China! When, in 1917, the Chinese government decided to enter the European war on the side of the Allies, she was doubtlessly actuated by a number of motives. But it seems likely that, with the participation of America, she was reckoning on a German defeat, and wished to have a seat at the Peace Conference, where she might discuss Japan's claims to her territory on an equal footing. She hoped for a Japanese withdrawal from Shantung and Southern Manchuria.

But her hopes were doomed to disappointment. When the nations met to draw up the Versailles Treaty, despite President Wilson's initial support of China's claim to her own land, the German rights in Shantung were granted to Japan. The protests of the Chinese delegation were overruled, and in anger and disappointment it withheld its signature from the treaty.

China's cause had been betrayed at Versailles, and the powers were not unaware of it. It was mainly in order to make some atonement that the Washington Conference was called in 1921, at the suggestion of America. Nine powers took part: China, Japan, Great Britain, France, Italy, Portugal, Holland, Belgium, and U.S.A., and in February 1922 all these powers, including Japan, put their signatures to a treaty which promised

"to respect the sovereignty, the independence, and the territorial and administrative integrity of China."

The treaty also contained clauses to the effect that China should be given the fullest opportunity "to develop and maintain for herself an effective and stable government." In accordance with the treaty, Japan was, at long last, obliged to withdraw from Shantung, and also to renounce some of the "Twenty-one Demands."

But although the Western Powers had admitted China's right to work out her own salvation, there was as yet no government holding real authority in the country. Since the fall and death of Yuan Shih-k'ai in 1915, the North had split into factions under rival war-lords, quite in the evil old imperial style. The South, under the leadership of Sun Yat-sen and the Kuomintang ("The National People's Party"), was feeling its way towards a modern republican government, but its authority was still limited. At last, with Chiang Kai-shek at its head, the Kuomintang army began its victorious march through China, subduing, unifying, and finally overthrowing the regimes of the war-lords —a story which must be told in a later chapter. Japan, on the pretext of "protecting her nationals in Shantung," sent troops to the North, who, disguised in the uniform of the war-lords, were able for a short time to hold up the advance of the Chinese patriots. But this civil war in North China, fermented and sponsored by the Japanese, was finally broken when Chang Tso-lin, a powerful general who controlled the Peking government, and former confederate of the Japanese, unexpectedly made his peace with the Kuomintang.

Japan could no longer fail to realize that a free, united Republican China was in the throes of birth, and that in the course of time it would grow to powerful manhood. There was no moment to be lost if she was to keep her grip upon the continent and fulfill the destiny she dreamed of. Intrigue and diplomacy were powerless now, and she therefore resorted to force. In September 1931 she invaded Manchuria with a considerable army, and within a few months had brought the whole of it under her domination. This was the spark which kindled the present war in the Far East.

XXVII. DR. SUN YAT-SEN, FATHER OF THE CHINESE REPUBLIC

In the flank of the Purple-and-Golden Hills, on the outskirts of Nanking, stands a marble mausoleum, in which lies the body of a much-loved Chinese patriot. It is the memorial hall of Sun Yat-sen, Father of the Chinese Republic.

At a time when the Chinese nation was suffering more grievously than ever before in her history, when her rulers had forfeited all the respect and affection of their subjects, when Japan and the powers from the West were doing their best to tear her in pieces and to seize the juiciest morsels, Sun Yat-sen appeared to direct the unrest of the Intellectuals towards a reasonable political theory, and eventually to lead the masses in armed revolt against their reactionary rulers. To his inspiring leadership is due the rise of the New China—the China which, with still diffident hands, is building a great destiny.

He seems to have been born to rebellion. It is recorded that unlike the customary docile Chinese children, he frequently defied his teacher, and was soundly beaten for it. This defiance he soon carried into the wider world outside the school gate. Even as a young boy, he looked with the utmost contempt upon the respected bourgeois householders of the neighborhood who gave themselves superior airs but were worldly enough to keep a number of frivolous concubines! He hated the government officials: he saw them extorting unreasonable taxes from his honest, hardworking farmer friends, and he noticed that they were powerless to restrain the pirates who attacked the coastal village where he lived, and burned down the little cottages.

Eventually he came to hate the ruling House as well. An old man to whose stories he would listen with shining eyes and rapt attention was a veteran of the T'ai-p'ing rebellion. He would tell over and over again the fascinating story of that daring revolt against the Manchu rulers which had ended just three years before Sun's birth, until the seed of racial hatred against the Manchu conquerors was sown deeply in the young boy's heart.

As he grew older, his bright imagination and adventurous spirit longed for new scenes and new ideas. He wanted to leave the atmosphere of tradition in his family circle. An elder brother had already established himself as a farmer in Honolulu, and now, at the age of thirteen and against the wishes of his parents, Sun decided to join him and to start a new life in the new world.

At first, he worked with his brother, helping him with the sale of his produce, but presently, as he showed signs of remarkable intellectual qualities, he became a student at the University of Hawaii. During his course there, he adopted the Christian religion, much' to his brother's displeasure. Sun the elder felt that the young man was being swept off his feet by the attractive culture of the West, and would come to despise the wisdom of the Chinese sages. Accordingly he removed him from the university and sent him home.

In 1884, at the age of eighteen, Sun found himself once more in the Fatherland, full of alarming ambitions and modern ideas. One of his first actions was to insult the local god. In his village there stood a temple to the powerful deity "Pei Ti"—the Northern Heavenly Emperor—an object of veneration to all the inhabitants, including his own relatives. Sun, with his Christian training and Western education, looked upon this practice as an ignorant superstition, and entering the temple one day, in a mood of rebellious anger he dealt the image such a smashing blow upon the cheek that he broke his own fingers! The act appeared to the villagers as unpardonable blasphemy, and they waited in terror for the god's vengeance. For fear of being lynched, Sun was obliged to flee to the sanctuary of Hong-Kong.

At Hong-Kong the young man began to develop a political consciousness, and the following year, 1885, marked a vital phase in his mental development. The cession of Annam to France by the disheartened Manchu Court, although it had suffered no military defeat at the hands of the French, stirred a rumble of complaint through the all too acquiescent masses, and as a result of this shock the conception began to form in the mind of the student Sun, that China's salvation must come through revolution, and that this revolution was imminent.

To organize a revolutionary party, however, under a despotic government, was neither a safe nor an easy matter. Weak as the Court was in its relations with foreign powers, it was strong enough to handle the unarmed people, and could be expected to put down a conspiracy with the utmost brutality. Moreover, if any agent of the Court got wind of such a plot, it would mean death and torture not only for the conspirators, but for their families, relations, and friends. Sun, accordingly, decided to work with caution, and under the guise of respectability. He would study medicine, and as a doctor would have ample opportunity of mixing with all types of people and of spreading his doctrine wherever the ground appeared fruitful. At the age of twenty-one he became a student at the Yale-in-China medical school at Hong-Kong, where he and three of his closest acquaintances earned the nickname of "the Four Great Bandits." In 1892 he obtained his doctor's degree, and proceeded to open a chemist's store in Canton, where he sold his political ideas to his customers, together with his prescriptions.

Two years later, China suffered an ignominious defeat at the hands of Japan in Korea, and at the Treaty of Shimonoseki was obliged to make humiliating concessions. The Chinese masses, whom an autocratic government kept deliberately uneducated, heard little of all this, except that even heavier taxes were levied on them to pay war indemnities to Japan. But the students and intellectuals, especially those of the South who had studied in missionary schools and colleges, and had made enough contact with Western learning to realize the backwardness and inefficiency of their government, now began to organize themselves into secret political societies. This military defeat at the hands of their puny neighbor "spurred the sides of their intent": the same year they attempted to set up a revolutionary government in Canton, but the rising was premature, and was instantly quelled by government troops.

Dr. Sun, meanwhile, had returned to Honolulu, where, in his old university circle, he organized a political society under the name of the *"Hsing Chung Hui"*—"Resurgent China." These supporters were outside the jurisdiction of the Manchu officials, and ran no risk of capture. It proved later that the backbone of the whole revolutionary movement, both in men and money, was to come from the Overseas Chinese—inhabitants of Malaya, of the Pacific Islands, and of Australia, as well as more distant countries.

Next year, the revolutionists advanced one step nearer: headquarters of the "Resurgent China Society" were set up in Hong-Kong, territory still under the protection of Western law. It was now that the national flag, under which the people of Free China are still fighting for their rights and liberty, was first designed. It shows a white sun on a plain blue field, representing the sky, and symbolizes the qualities of "purity" and "brightness." It was with the establishment of this society in Hong-Kong that the movement for revolution was inexorably set in motion: from now on it gathered force and momentum until, in 1911, it burst upon the country like a flooding river.

From Honolulu, Dr. Sun began a more extensive tour: he traveled first to the United States, and thence to England. There was in Sun's character a remarkable combination of the visionary and the realist. While he dreamed of a People's Government, under which a reign of perfect justice, charity, and contentment would begin, he also saw that before China could throw off the hated domination of foreign powers and stand on an equal footing with them, she would have to learn the rules of the Western game, as Japan had done.

"Chinese aspirations," he wrote once, "can be realized only when we understand that, to regenerate the state . . . we must welcome the influx of foreign capital on the largest possible scale, and also must attract foreign scientists and trained experts to develop our country and train us."

It was in order to win the sympathy and ultimately the financial and technical support of the American and British governments, that he undertook the journey. But soon after his arrival in London, he was kidnaped by the Chinese Embassy! The ambassador at that time was a Mandarin, who evidently planned to win the eternal gratitude of his Emperor by sending the revolutionary leader to his death. The plot was foiled by an Embassy porter who brought news of the arrest to Dr. Sun's former teacher, Sir James Cantlie. Next morning, the news flashed across all the headlines, and a protest dispatched from the Foreign Office secured his instant release. The little room at 49 Portland Place, where he was secretly detained, is preserved as it was, to the present day, in memory of that strange incident.

The following year, 1897, was another critical one in Chinese affairs. The occupation of Chiao-chou by the German fleet, on a trumped-up excuse, was instantly followed by demands on the part of the other powers for similar naval bases. The carving up of China into "spheres of influence" for the rival Western Powers had begun. Dr. Sun returned from Europe. He dared not risk capture by landing in China, but went to Japan where he organized secret revolutionary societies, especially among Chinese students at the universities. He had the tireless, ever-welling energy of the political reformer, and for the next few years he traveled incessantly between Japan, Hong-Kong, and Annam, founding societies, issuing orders, consulting, encouraging, planning.

Another revolutionary attack on Canton in 1902 was a failure, and a rising in Hunan in 1904 was quickly put down. In 1905, Japan, realizing the implications of Sun's influence upon Young China, began a persecution of Chinese students in her country. For the sake of the future, Sun could not afford to risk his life, but removed his headquarters to Annam. In 1907 and 1908 there were further failures in military operations, and in 1909 Dr. Sun had to travel once more to Europe to appeal for financial help. The movement was in desperate need of funds if it was to break the back of the imperial armies.

Despite all these reverses, persecutions, and rebuffs, despite the fact that financiers abroad continued to regard him as a wild visionary and preferred to stake their money upon the decadent Manchus, Sun Yat-sen hoped, believed, and toiled. And the winds of revolution were rising. There were mysterious assassinations of Manchu nobles; there were sporadic rebellions in every quarter of the country; the doctrine of revolution passed from lip to lip.

The Emperor drafted "new armies" to defend his throne; young revolutionaries volunteered and secretly spread their propaganda among the soldiers. It was not long before the new army was a solid body of revolutionists! The battle for Canton was reopened by this very army in 1910, and though, owing to the death of its brilliant leader, the revolutionists again scored no success, their day was almost at hand. In March of 1911 seventy-two young partisans, "the flower of the party," fell in bitter fighting round the city, and were buried at Yellow Flower Hill in the suburbs. Their tomb is still visited by thousands of their grateful countrymen. This was the last failure.

In October of the same year, the great revolution broke in earnest and spread beyond the control of the government forces. Sun's "visions" were justified. The government's misguided policy over the railway rights offered the occasion, though the roots lay broader and deeper. A branch of the Great Peking-Hankow-Canton railway system was to be built in Ssuch'uan, and was to be financed by a loan raised among the inhabitants of the province. After capital had been invested and the construction was already in progress, the Peking government, feebly yielding to foreign pressure, handed the building rights over to the bankers of Germany, Great Britain, France, and U.S.A.

The Ssuch'uanese were disappointed and angry. Their own railway in which they had invested their savings, and the very soil of their own country, were being sold over their heads to the interfering foreigner. They began to organize for rebellion. A "Society for the Protection of Railway Rights" was formed, and under its auspices thousands of angry citizens rallied in the provincial capital for a demonstration, bearing with them the ancestral tablet of the last Emperor, Teh Tsung "the Virtuous," who had treated them with fairness and generosity. The movement quickly caught fire: the ordinary townspeople were supported by the merchants and students of the whole province, hun-

dreds of whom went on strike and brought the normal life of Ssuch'uan
to a standstill.

The provincial governor, nicknamed "the Butcher," temporarily
subdued the rising with the utmost brutality. He ordered his cavalry-
men to charge the demonstrators, and at least forty were killed and
many more injured in the mêlée. But the Ssuch'uanese did not suffer
and die in vain: their act and its bloody sequel served as the cue for
rebellious deeds and voices all over the country.

About a month later, a plot to assassinate the governor of a neighboring province—Hupei—was discovered, and a precious book containing a register of the revolutionists fell into the governor's hands! There
was only one way to avert a wholesale execution—immediate action.

Next night, the fateful tenth of October, the first shots were fired
on the governor's house at Wuch'ang, and the governor took to his
heels under cover of darkness. The revolutionists had, as yet, no competent leader, and accordingly they devised the ingenious plan of
capturing one by force! While one of their bands attacked the governor's house, another visited the house of a celebrated army officer,
and dragging him out of bed, compelled him at the pistol's butt to act
as their military commander. This was Li Yuan-hung, a man of such
easy-going temper that he had the nickname of "Goddess of Mercy Li."

Under Li's nominal leadership, the revolutionary army occupied
the three neighboring towns of Wuch'ang, Hankow, and Hanyang—
the very heart of China in the center of the Yangtzu valley. From this
spark, flames leaped up in all corners of the vast country. Within fifty
days fourteen provinces had declared for the revolutionists; the governors appointed by the Court had been driven out, and revolutionary
forces, formed of local militia and volunteers, were organized to keep
order. The nuclei of local revolutionary governments were formed.
Even in the vicinity of Peking there was underground revolutionary
activity.

The Court, now thoroughly alarmed, dispatched a powerful army
to Hankow under the ambitious and treacherous Yuan Shih-k'ai, till
now a keen supporter of the Emperor. Yuan's army was more than a
match for the inexperienced revolutionary forces: Hankow fell, and the
city was burned almost to the ground. Having given a demonstration
of his power, Yuan held his hand, hoping to strike a favorable bargain
with the revolutionaries. Meanwhile, Dr. Sun Yat-sen had been hastening back from Europe to direct the movement, and on arriving in
Shanghai, agreed to become temporary president of a Chinese Republic.
But although the acknowledged leader and initiator of the revolution,

and already greatly beloved in his circle of supporters, Sun was still little known to the masses. Moreover, Yuan Shih-k'ai stood at the head of a powerful army, and it seemed clear to Sun that if the revolution was to succeed, terms must be reached with his opponent. He therefore privately approached Yuan and offered him the presidency if he would loyally support the revolution.

Now Yuan was an ambitious politician before everything, and to become the country's leader would fulfill his most extravagant dreams. Without more ado he gave solemn assurances to Sun Yat-sen, his old enemy, and, abandoning the cause of the Court he had so long upheld, addressed a memorandum to the young Emperor, expressing his own sympathy with the opinion of the masses, and advising that he should abdicate "like the ancient Sage-Emperors Yao and Shun."

Deserted by their most powerful and able statesman, the Emperor and his supporters realized that their hour had come. The Emperor abdicated; the Republic was given birth; the country belonged to the people!

A People's Parliament was called, though it cannot be claimed that it was, as yet, representative of the nation. There was no system of universal suffrage, nor would it have been practical until the masses, who had hitherto been deliberately kept in ignorance of public affairs, received some political education. The parliament which now "elected" Yuan Shih-k'ai first President of the Chinese Republic was formed principally of representatives of the revolutionary forces. Sun Yat-sen's own political party—the original "Resurgent China Society," subsequently reformed into "The China League"—was once more reorganized, and given its present name of "Kuomintang"—"The National People's Party." Dr. Sun himself, with the zeal and self-immolation of the true reformer, made no attempt to appropriate a high position in the new regime. Declaring his aim of bringing China into line with the modern civilizations of the West, he departed to Japan, in order to study their methods of industry, and especially railway building.

In his absence, Yuan Shih-k'ai proceeded to give full rein to his ambitions. An inner voice began to tempt him with the notion of declaring himself Emperor and founding a dynasty for his descendants. It is certain that the inner voice was supported, if not promoted, by the Japanese, who saw in the birth of a Republic, and the strong, modern, industrialized nation which might grow out of it, the death blow to her hope of dominating the continent of Asia.

Yuan's first treacherous act was to dissolve the Kuomintang in 1913, which was tantamount to removing the whole Opposition. A year later, he dispensed wth parliament altogether. Dr. Sun, though disappointed, never despaired. He reassembled the Kuomintang in Japan, renaming it the "Chinese Revolutionary Party," and declared he would organize a movement to depose Yuan—he would bring about a new and better revolution!

Meanwhile, in Peking the idea was sedulously fostered that only by a return to the monarchy could China recover her failing power. Dr. Frank Goodnow, American adviser to the President, was reported to have offered his opinion that "the monarchical system is better suited to China than the Republican system," and this, possibly casual, observation formed the basis of a great propaganda drive by Yuan's agents. A society was formed, called the *"Ch'ou An Hui"*—the "Society for Promoting Security"—whose main object was the restoration of the monarchy. The provincial governors, war-lords who owed their position to the President, enthusiastically invited Yuan to mount the throne. At the "Packed" elections of December 1915, the majority declared in favor of monarchy. The Council of State thereupon formally invited Yuan to receive the imperial crown. A rebellion immediately broke out in the South, and Yuan's courage began to ebb. He postponed the enthronement; and in March of the following year renounced his claim. A few months later, death cut short his failure and humiliation.

From Yuan's death in 1916 till the second revolution in 1926, China was at the mercy of contending rulers. In the North, officers of Yuan's "Northern Ocean Army"—the powerful army which he had organized for the defense of the Manchu Court—fought a series of civil wars with one another for almost twenty years. During Yuan's five years of power, their quarrels had been kept within reasonable bounds, but they now broke out into ferocious conflicts which devastated the country and solved nothing. A few of these war-lords were generals of strength and personality, but for the most part they were vain, illiterate men. They had little knowledge of their own country, and still less of international affairs. They surrounded themselves with the scum left behind by the Manchu Court. They gambled and indulged in food, wine, and passion. They levied impossible taxes on the peasants within their jurisdiction, and they falsely administered the law, invoking the death penalty at their pleasure. Their undisciplined soldiers were a terror to their subjects. When their forces were destroyed by rivals, they fled to the protection of the foreign concessions or settlements.

Their public administration was as worthless as their personal behavior. Education was entirely neglected; industry, so sorely needed by the country, was discouraged. Most of the schoolmasters and employees in public utility services remained unpaid. All the money that could be drained from the unfortunate people was deposited in foreign banks against the time when their influence would collapse, and they would be obliged to become "gentlemen of leisure." The war-lords were immeasurably rich.

In the South, Dr. Sun had returned to Canton and reorganized the Chinese revolutionary party which he had formed in Japan into the "Chungkuo Kuomintang"—the Chinese National People's Party. In 1921 he set up a revolutionary government in the city and was elected extraordinary president. It was at this stage that the influence of Russia played an interesting and profound part in the direction of the revolution. Although Dr. Sun never believed in the application of Communism to Chinese society, he could not fail to be roused by its achievements in replacing the Tsarist regime. Already, in 1920, the first Communist organization had appeared in China in the form of a scientific society "for studying Socialism and Marxism." At the Third Plenary Assembly of Socialist Youth, held in 1924 at Canton, it was decided to form this society into a branch of the Third International, and to call it the Chinese Communist Party. At this time, the membership was between five and six hundred.

Meanwhile, in 1923, a joint declaration had been issued by Russia and the Canton government, announcing the cordial and friendly relations which were to exist between the two countries. Russia then sent two very able advisers to Canton—Borodin and Galens. The former was well experienced as a revolutionary organizer, while the second was an able militarist, capable of supplying that drive and organization which the Chinese revolutionaries so badly needed. It was under his guidance that a Military Institute was established at Whampoa (or Huang-P'u)—an island opposite Canton—and here, under the supervision of China's future leader, Chiang Kai-shek, and with Russian instructors, a conquering military weapon was forged. Borodin, for his part, had strongly urged the creation of an institute for training propagandists, the essential of every popular movement, and he persuaded Sun Yat-sen to compile, publish, and propagate his revolutionary principles. The book which resulted is the famous *"San Min Chu I"*—the "Three Principles of the People"—which became a sort of Bible to the whole Chinese nation, and is known by heart by every school and college student of the present day.

It was also due to Borodin's influence that Dr. Sun agreed to admit Communists to membership of the Kuomintang. During the military conquest of the North by the armies of Chiang Kai-shek, these Communist members supplied very valuable assistance, and their good relations gave promise of a national unity which was still far from existing.

In 1924, the head of the Peking government was overthrown by two enemy generals, who now invited Dr. Sun to Peking to discuss the establishment of a central government. Dr. Sun's semi-Communist government in Canton had been on the verge of disaster from a revolt of Cantonese merchants; he was also gravely ill with cancer. Probably these two factors influenced him to accept the invitation, unpalatable as it must have been to Comrade Borodin. Soon after his arrival in Peking, and before the conversations could start, Dr. Sun died, on the twelfth of March, 1925.

He died disappointed, but not despairing. He knew that much had been achieved, but that the revolution was not fully accomplished. He left a courageous and moving Testament to his comrades, in which he declared:

"For forty years I have devoted myself to the revolutionary cause. My aim is to obtain for China freedom and equality. From my forty years' experience I perceive that to carry out this aim we must rouse the whole nation, and we must ally with those nations which will treat China on an equal footing. Then let us all rise and fight together! The revolution is not yet! Let my comrades follow the policy I have prescribed in my books. . . . Let them continue to strive and struggle till final victory. Let them carry out my latest policy of calling a People's Congress, and of abolishing the unequal treaties. This must be achieved speedily. Such is my Will!"

A great leader was lost, but the revolutionary movement which Dr. Sun had swung into motion abated nothing of its force with his death. It followed the path he had measured for it until it was fully consummated. But the debt of modern China to its Father remained incalculable: without his energy, imagination, and inspiring guidance, China might never have become a solid, living unity, capable of standing, as she does today, against the Japanese armies. It is said of Dr. Sun that despite his visionary schemes, so powerful was his eloquence that his dreams became realities for his audience while he spoke. He himself never doubted the successful end of the Republic. In the gravest crises, he held the chosen band together with that spirit of *"ta wu wei"* —"the great undauntedness"—which was a favorite phrase in his writings. After his death, an aura of divinity seemed to grow around him; and until the rise to glory of the Generalissimo Chiang Kai-shek,

Dr. Sun was the object of adoration with almost every Chinese throughout the world. In most Chinese houses at the present day, a picture of Sun Yat-sen hangs from the wall of the living room; the "father" looks down on his great family with kindly eyes. By the side of the portrait are generally reproduced two lines of his handwriting,

> "The Revolution is not achieved yet,
> My comrades must struggle now as in the past!"

The *"San Min Chu I"*—"Three Principles of the People"— may sound neither remarkable nor new to Western ears, to whom the Rights of Man is already an old story, but to China at the beginning of the twentieth century they were something to marvel over. The three principles were those of Nationalism, Democracy, and Livelihood. The principle of Nationalism was to unite the five sub-races which compose the modern Chinese people, and to give them political, economic, and social equality. It aimed at overriding the traditional and limited loyalties of family and clan by the wider loyalty to a united nation. It also declared that China should be freed from foreign pressure so that she stood as an independent nation among the modern nations of the world.

The principle of Livelihood dealt with the protection of the workers from unjust laws, the control and limitation of capital, the regulation of land ownership, the development of peasants' and workers' movements, and their political education. Under the principle of Democracy were classed all those "rights" which are now a commonplace in the West—"a state belonging to all the people, a government controlled by all the people, and rights and benefits for the encouragement of all the people."

Dr. Sun divided the building of the new China into three stages— military operations, political tutelage, and constitutional government. During the first stage, the revolutionary army would have to fight for the unification of the country, though wherever the forces went they would disseminate the Three Principles of the People, and explain the aim of their leader. In the second stage, members of the Kuomintang with special training in organization and propaganda would be sent into every district that the army had occupied, and there would train the people in self-government. When a province had completed its training, representatives of every district would be convened, provincial laws promulgated according to the local traditions, and a provincial governor elected by popular vote. When more than half the provinces in the country had thus set up their new provincial laws, a People's

Congress would be summoned and a National Constitution created. This congress would usher in the third and final stage—Constitutional government—"by, of, and for the people."

The three stages have not been worked out as their great designer hoped. The destruction of the war-lords was hardly achieved before a break between Kuomintang and Communists ushered in a new period of civil hostilities, and no sooner had these two revolutionary parties united than Japan launched her undeclared war on the whole country. It seems that since Dr. Sun's death until the present time, there has been no pause in "Military Operations."

Despite these adverse circumstances, however, the second and third stages had been given a tentative trial. During the years of war between the Communist and Kuomintang armies, both parties promoted political activity among the masses—an activity which in some measure conformed with Dr. Sun's idea of "Political Tutelage." Moreover, the union of the two parties immediately before the outbreak of war has given the people a chance to exercise their constitutional rights, and to exert some influence upon government policy. A People's Council has been set up alongside the administrative and executive organizations which allows the people at least a nominal voice in the direction of national affairs.

It cannot be admitted that China is yet politically educated, and even less that her present government is "constitutional" in the sense understood by the Western democracies, but we can truly declare that the revolution is working towards this end, and the complete fulfillment of Dr. Sun's ambition for his countrymen.

XXVIII. CHINA AND THE WESTERN POWERS (3)—THE EUROPEAN WAR AND THE "NEW CIVILIZATION MOVEMENT"

AT THE TIME when the young Chinese Republic struggled to birth, the foreign powers had nicely adjusted their "spheres of influence" in China, and were at pains to see that no one of them enjoyed greater rights or larger territorial concessions than the rest. But with the outbreak of the European War of 1914–18, this balance was shaken to pieces. Germany, Russia, Great Britain, France, Belgium were all too deeply involved in their own deadly struggle to be able to safeguard their interests in China, while Japan, the Villain of Asia, was free to seize her golden opportunity, and to assert her long-desired domination of the Far East by every means, fair or foul, that lay in her power. The United States, it is true, remained outside the European conflict until the final year, but her heart and ultimate interests lay with the Western democracies. From time to time she attempted to intervene in the Far East and to restrict Japan's predatory movements, but her actions were on the whole ineffective, since the Japanese felt sure she would not resort to arms.

At the outset of the Great War, China decided to remain neutral, and proposed that hostilities should be excluded from her territory, including that leased by the belligerent foreign powers. Japan, however, declared war on Germany, while loudly asserting that she had done so in fulfillment of obligations to her ally, Great Britain, and that she had no territorial ambitions in China at all. This well-known prevarication deceived nobody: an attack upon the German property in China was both expected and delivered. In little more than a month, the German garrisons capitulated and Japan became master of Chiaochou, an important district of Shantung province. China, of course, as a "neutral," had not interfered, beyond protesting, quite ineffectively, that Japan had extended her operations beyond the former German territory.

The acceptance of the shameful "Twenty-one Demands," which fol-

lowed on this Japanese success in Shantung, must be laid at the door
of President Yuan Shih-k'ai; but for China's entry into the European
War, Yuan's pro-Japanese lieutenant, the Premier Tuan Ch'i-jui, was
responsible. No doubt the Allies had exerted considerable pressure
upon the Chinese government to take this step, partly in order to re-
cruit Chinese labor and partly to gain control of enemy shipping
interned in Chinese ports. Moreover, as we have noted, Tuan's government counted on an allied victory and hoped by participation to better
China's position vis-à-vis Japan. But Tuan's own motives were far
from disinterested. His private plan in declaring war was to announce
a huge war budget, and on the strength of it to borrow heavily from
the Japanese. The loan would not be used to support the forces of
democracy: on the contrary, it would be of splendid service to his own
reactionary government in fighting the revolutionary forces of the
South!

Japan had no illusion about Tuan's integrity. But it suited her own
plans to nourish civil wars in China, for in that way the country would
be weakened and laid open to her predatory armies. She accordingly
invested her money in the unhappy Chinese wars, and it is on record
that from August 1917, when the government at Peking declared war
on Germany, till his fall in 1920, Tuan borrowed from Japan sums
amounting to no less than five hundred million Chinese dollars. As a
reward for these favors, Tuan's representatives offered Japan the much
disputed rights of railway building in Shantung, former German
"sphere of influence."

This small gift proved to be its donors' ruin. Under the Treaty of
Versailles, by which China expected to regain full sovereignty of her
own territory, including Shantung, Japan was allowed to retain almost
all the rights formerly enjoyed by Germany. It was discovered (to the
convenience—let us admit—of the Western nations) that in Tuan's
pact with Japan the Chinese government had courteously expressed its
"pleasure" in handing over the railway rights, and what had been done
with "pleasure" could hardly be called "compulsion," argued the
powers. In vain did the Chinese delegation—which was composed of
representatives from both Northern and Southern governments—plead
with the Conference. The decision could not be reversed.

When the delegation returned to China, and news of its defeat spread
among the people, a long-suppressed disgust and anger at the government's dishonesty, felt especially by the young intellectuals, broke out
with a fury that swept all before it. It is called in history the "May the
Fourth Movement," and from this memorable fourth of May, 1919,

dates not only the growing power of the revolutionary forces under the Kuomintang, but a phenomenon of immense significance to China's future—a cultural renaissance!

The Movement broke out in Peking, under the organization of Kuomintang agents, and the agitators consisted almost entirely of school and university students. In each university or secondary school, a students' union was formed, with the seriousness and character of a political party. Each union was composed of a committee of representatives, who discussed and made decisions like a parliament, and a committee of wardens who in the role of cabinet executed the decisions. All the members were elected by vote, and the members in turn voted among themselves for representation on the Peking students' union—the supreme organization in the new political movement. Thus began that participation of present-day students in serious politics which has been so remarkable a feature of modern Chinese life. It was no casual outburst on the part of some hot-headed youngsters, but a systematic movement which continued and still continues at the present time. The fact that in the present Sino-Japanese war the Japanese have deliberately tried to bomb and wipe out the main centers of education in China is a great tribute to the determined opposition offered them by the Chinese students.[1]

The May the Fourth incident began with an assault upon the foreign minister Chang Tsung-hsiang, who had been responsible for signing the ignominious pact with Japan. Armed with wooden clubs, iron bars, and cans of petrol from their laboratories, some three thousand students marched through the streets of Peking to the minister's house. Chang was away from home, but was tracked down to the house of a colleague, where he was holding consultations with a circle of his pro-Japanese partisans. The party broke up and fled in consternation at the approach of the agitators. Only Chang himself was caught and ignominiously beaten. The house was smashed up and set on fire, and a number of students were arrested for their part in it.

The students' indignation was not exhausted by this act of violence: a widespread strike was organized, both as a protest against the arrest of their members and against the diplomatic policy of the government. The Peking students led the way, and were quickly supported by the shopkeepers of the city. The merchants followed suit. In a short time students and retailers all over the country began to come out on strike,

[1] The movement was not strictly an innovation, but rather the revival of an old Chinese tradition, alive in the Han, Sung, and Ming periods, when students and intellectuals formed an active opposition to corrupt governments.

and when the railwaymen announced their intention of taking similar action, the government yielded. Chang and all the other ministers responsible for signing the pact with Japan were removed from office. It was an unbelievable triumph!

The success of the students' movement stirred the whole nation. The educated classes, who till now had taken their main guidance, both in public and private conduct, from the writings of Confucius, began to realize that they had been living in a classical dream of the past. The Sage's teachings, which had been of value to the society of several hundred years ago, had in later generations been so adulterated and explained away by the sophisticated that there was no longer any blood in them. Ceremony, propriety, forms remained, but they had ceased to have much significance.

New times produce their own prophets. Confucius had lived some five hundred years before Christ, when China was already "civilized," when modern Europe had not even been born, and America was an undiscovered continent. Now, after more than two thousand years, the Western Powers had shown only too clearly their lordship over the earth, while China appeared to be passing into an abyss of stagnation. Some fundamental change seemed imperative. A change in government from an enfeebled monarchy to a somewhat diffident republic had evidently not been enough to regain for China her honorable position among the world powers. K'ang Yu-wei and his "reform party" had been right: China must accept the Western heritage of learning and thought, from which Europe's mastery appeared to spring.

Thus, side by side with the political movement among the students, there came into being that great cultural movement of modern China known as the Literary Renaissance, or more aptly—as the "New Civilization Movement." In its early stages, very little creative work appeared. Its sponsors confined themselves to attacking the old idols —chief among them Confucius—and to producing a great flood of translations from the works of eminent European and American writers. Tolstoy, Ibsen, de Maupassant, Byron, Shelley, Kropotkin, Marx, Engels, Poe and Irving were among the writers and thinkers whose works were invited to the altars of Chinese literature and philosophy. An American professor, John Dewey, was once extolled, in a speech given by the president of the National Peking University, as being a greater thinker than Confucius! The young intellectuals quite lost their heads over the New Culture.

The leading personality in this literary movement was Dr. Hu Shih, a prominent scholar and iconoclast. His name is connected not only with the introduction of Western literature, but especially with a parallel development—the creation of a popular literature, written in the ordinary spoken language of ordinary people. The significance of this in the education of the nation can hardly be emphasized enough. Up till now, the Chinese written language had been substantially the same as that used by Confucius; the common people understood it as little as English children of the present day would understand the archaic language of Chaucer. To write in words that everybody spoke and anybody understood, was indeed a revolution, and one that might have imponderable consequences. It would mean that the new ideas of the Western world would become available to the whole population.

Nor was it the people only who benefited: Chinese literature was enriched and refreshed. Dr. Hu Shih and his followers spoke contemptuously of works written in the classical style as "dead literature." The words were fossils—preserved but lifeless. But to write books in the language of living people was to bring back life and reality to literature itself. The old ballads, novels, folk-tales, and plays, which had long been neglected by the intellectuals, because of their "vulgar" language, were unearthed and given new places of honor. These were alive; they were real. Presently, the young intellectuals began to write stories, novels, and poems in this "vulgar" (*pai hua*) vocabulary, still keeping very much to the old forms. At a later stage they imitated European models, and finally produced works of genuine originality and imagination. New magazines and literary periodicals poured off the Shanghai and Peking presses. New life, and an abundance of it, was animating the soul of young China.

It was the time for the young. They had seized political power for themselves out of the hands of the old-fashioned bureaucrats, and from the dry-as-dust literati they had taken the authority to create literature. The day of the conventional "Mandarin" was passing, together with arm-chair politics and the writings of scholars who had learned all their skill from old books, and hardly looked outside their own study walls. China was filled with hope and young endeavor.

Among the first to benefit by the new conceptions now animating Chinese society were the girls. Any Westerner who has read such old Chinese novels as the "Dream of the Red Chamber," which has an abridged version, or such modern books as Lin Yu-tang's "Moment in Peking," can picture the life of unnatural seclusion to which Chinese girls have been subjected all through their history. They rarely saw or spoke to a man, except the members of their own family, until they married. Indeed, they were hardly allowed outside the gates of their houses. A normal education was denied them: few could read or write, though they were skilled in cooking, needlework, music, and embroidery. At the time of the Students' Movement, some of the more up-to-date families already allowed their girls to attend the modern schools and colleges, but they were still strictly segregated from the boys, and did not even join with them in social activities. On the tide of the great political movement, however, the girls boldly rose to assert their rights. Flaunting tradition, they began to work with the boys in the same studies and libraries; they joined the same political organizations; they walked openly in the streets and felt no shame for it. This was the beginning of the participation of Chinese women in national life—a step that is bearing great fruit at the present time. In the war against Japan, they have taken the men's places in factories; they have formed bands for the entertainment of the soldiers, and also for war propaganda among the illiterate peasants. Many of them are nurses, and some doctors. They have organized refugee and Red Cross centers. Some have even undertaken guerrilla activities with the utmost courage.

The ferment caused by the entrance of the young into politics, and the unrest brought about by the introduction of so many schools of Western thought, some of them mutually contradictory, had to find outlet in a practical forward movement. The new political leaders had learned much, both from a study of Western history and from the past experience of the revolutionaries, especially in the period of Yuan Shih-k'ai's dictatorship. They realized, perhaps with reluctance, the necessity for force if the reactionary Peking regime was to be abolished, and the country united under a truly popular government. Even more vividly did they realize that if the movement was to succeed, to convert the educated classes was not enough: the masses must be mobilized. Up till now, the movement had remained far too theoretical: no serious appeal had been made to the industrial workers or peasants—for whose rights the revolutionaries were ultimately struggling—to organize, much less to offer armed resistance. All this must alter.

In 1924, the Kuomintang, the main revolutionary party, struck a truce with the Communist party, so that both might co-operate in the supreme task of throwing out the reactionary government. Under their guidance, workers' movements in the industrial towns and peasant movements throughout the countryside rapidly developed. The emancipation of the workers was not achieved without bloodshed, and as in every other country, some pioneers had to endure martyrdom for the benefit of those who came after. There was, for example, a serious incident in June 1925, which almost led to an international clash.

Eight employees of a Japanese firm in Shanghai made representations to their employer on behalf of all the factory workers on questions of hours and wages. The factory manager was so incensed at this insubordination and impudence that he drew his revolver, shot the head of the delegation, and called in English police to put the remainder under arrest. The Shanghai students thereupon organized a demonstration and marched along the main thoroughfare of the English Settlement in protest again so flagrant an abuse of workers' rights. They were dispersed by the police, and seven of them were shot by orders of the English chief constable.

The story of this crime spread throughout the country. A great anti-British and anti-Japanese movement sprang up. Demonstrations took place in many of the large cities, despite the experience of the Shanghai agitators. At Canton, an even more shameful incident was enacted: the warships of Japan, Great Britain, France, and Portugal, who by special treaty rights were allowed to drop anchor in the Pearl River, fired upon the demonstrators in Canton, causing serious casualties. The friction between British and Chinese, which originated from the incident at the Japanese spinning factory, did not die down until two years later, when two further clashes between Chinese and British sailors at Hankow and Kiukiang ended in negotiations between the two powers. Great Britain restored certain "concessions" to China, and the Kuomintang leaders felt they had achieved a victory of sorts.

The Communist party, however, strongly disapproved of any conciliation with the "imperialist" powers. Moreover, there had been many other causes of friction between the two parties before this incident, and during the course of that year, 1927, their relations were broken off. Hostilities followed, and for nearly ten years Chinese blood and endeavor were wasted on inconclusive campaigns launched by the Kuomintang forces against the Red armies. The Kuomintang gradually drifted into a policy of friendship with the Western democracies, England, France, and America, while rejecting any alliance with Soviet Russia. The Communists would only associate themselves with the U.S.S.R. And so the internal conflict continued in the face of a national peril—Japanese invasion.

The break between Kuomintang and Communists in 1927, unfortunate as it was politically, acted in other ways as a stimulus and brought about an important literary development. The Communists being thrown more and more into the arms of Soviet Russia, began to study and imitate its culture. A movement for creating proletarian literature was set on foot, first in Shanghai, then in Peking, and subsequently in every important Chinese town where a Communist group secretly existed. Books of the new Russian writers, as well as American proletarian novels, were translated and published with indiscriminate zeal. The works of Lenin, Trotsky, Pukhalin, Plikhanov, Bogdanov, Upton Sinclair were warmly welcomed by young Chinese students, while original novels and stories with working-class themes began to pour from their pens. It seemed to be a logical development from the original literary movement. From writing in the *language* of ordinary people, it was only one more step to write about their lives.

This new movement in literature had the effect of bringing many of the younger generation into the Communist party. Its novelty appealed to their youth, and its basic principle to their humanity. Many who did not actually join the party sympathized with its aims, in opposition to the Kuomintang, which was by now the legally constituted government of China. For some time, the latter remained unaware of this development, but when the inherent danger of the movement was brought to its notice, it acted ruthlessly. Certain bookshops were closed by government order; many publications were banned; some "dangerous" writers were arrested or forced to escape from the country. Many of them found temporary refuge in Japan. The proletarian movement in literature was half-stifled, though not entirely killed, very soon after its birth, while the central government called into being a countermovement—the "Three People's Literature," representing more orthodox views, and supported by writers of the Kuomintang party.

The Communists had also been experimenting in social reforms in the territory under their control. All the most advanced and humane developments of the time seemed to emanate from them. If the central government was to hold its own and prevent the whole nation from turning Communist, it must offer some counter-attractions to the people. Some idea like this must have been in Chiang Kai-shek's mind when he devised and inaugurated his "New Life Movement." It is significant that the movement was started at Nanch'ang, the provincial capital of Kiangsi—province where the Communists had once set up an entirely new order of society. The New Life Movement was a practical, rational movement, based on old ideals of conduct, but with modern applications. It was intended to promote, as General Chiang said, "a new national consciousness and mass psychology"; to instill in the masses of the people a sense of order, responsibility, and honesty in public and private dealings.

The four cornerstones of the movement, upon which the people

were invited to build their lives, were the moral virtues of right behavior (etiquette), justice, integrity, and honor mentioned in the work
of a Sage even older than Confucius.[1] But these virtues were to be applied in everyday affairs "such as food, clothing, shelter, and action."
Opium smoking, for instance, and even cigarette smoking were discredited; public dancing was later forbidden; the homes of the poorer
people were inspected and cleaned up; education was promoted;
women were encouraged to dress with simplicity; the notorious corruption of officials was to a great extent eliminated. Discipline and
promptness in public service; frugality, orderliness, and good taste in
the home; patriotism and productivity throughout the country—these
were the aims of the movement, by means of which China was to grow
strong.

The "New Life Movement," and even more the establishment of a
strong and stable central government under Chiang Kai-shek, brought
comparative peace and a more reasonable standard of living, so much
desired and deserved by the Chinese people. Educational institutes of
every kind, from modern primary schools to research laboratories and
institutes, were founded, and some of the latter have contributed important scientific knowledge to the world. Among the best known are
the *Academia sinica* (sponsored by the government), the National Library of Peiping (Peking), the Geological Survey, and the Chinese
Architectural Society, all of which have produced valuable publications.

Today, China is fighting for her life, and the whole population is
mobilized: men and women, boys and girls. In contrast with the old
days of the Empire, when the chief conception of loyalty was to the
family, or at most, to the local officials, the Chinese people now have a
broad conception of the nation as a whole, and are prepared to endure,
work, and suffer for its salvation. China wants to live, for she realizes
that a great future lies ahead of her if she survives the present tide of
war. Her young people are full of energy and hope. Because of their
unshakable faith in the future, nothing can daunt the people of the New
China. Only such a faith could have sustained hundreds of students,
who, carrying a large part of their libraries with them, trekked on foot

---

[1] The English equivalent of the Chinese terms *"Li," "I," "Lien,"* and *"Ch'ih"* is
difficult to give accurately. In a booklet published by the Association for the Promotion
of the New Life Movement, written by General Chiang himself, and translated into
English by his wife, the following definition is offered:

"Li" means a regulated attitude (mind as well as heart).

"I" means right conduct (in all things).

"Lien" means clear discrimination (honesty in personal, public, and official life).

"Ch'ih" means real self-consciousness (integrity and honor).

and by small rowing boat from Peking hundreds of miles to the safety of the mountainous Southwest, there to carry on their work and prepare themselves for the leadership of the future. Only such a faith could have enabled courageous factory workers to load their machinery on to hand barrows and to wheel or drag them away from the Japanese-controlled cities to the interior, there to continue their production for the national war effort. The stories of heroism and endurance are numberless, and some of them are almost incredible. China's hope for the future lies in this newly found self-realization, unity, and communal effort.

XXIX. GENERALISSIMO CHIANG KAI-SHEK

Dr. Sun Yat-sen, "Father of the Republic," greatly loved in his life-time by all who felt his personality, has, since his death in 1925, been worshiped almost as a Saint. Chiang Kai-shek, his disciple and successor, is trusted and respected by nearly every one of China's four hundred and fifty million people. They look to him as the only man who can keep them from enslavement to the Japanese. His name Kai-shek (in standard romanization "Chieh-shih") means "Firm-as-a-Rock," and his people know he can be trusted to strike no compromise with the enemy, but will fight for complete freedom, to the death. So remarkable are his qualities of leadership that he has won the out-spoken admiration even of his enemies. The Japanese author of his biography, Ishimaru Totaro, has confessed, "Chiang Kai-shek is really great. He is greater than the two European dictators. Although he is the leader in resisting Japan, and in recovering Manchuria, and thus offers an obstacle to the advance of Japanese influence, no Japanese could refuse to acknowledge his greatness!"

He was born in 1887 at Feng-hua, in the province of Chekiang. This is a southern coastal town of great beauty, backed by rocky hills and facing a quiet inlet of the blue Pacific. It is a fertile province, and Feng-hua is rich in wildflowers of unusual fragrance. Waterfalls tumble down the hills, and at dawn and dusk the traveler will be brought into a mood of calm by the gentle tinkle of bells from many Buddhist temples perched on the heights. It is a place for poets to dream in; and yet it bred Chiang Kai-shek, supremely a man of action—one of the most brilliant generals and ablest statesmen!

A great part of the population at Feng-hua is composed of ferrymen. Loading goods at the port, they carry them up-river, to trade with the inhabitants of the broad Yangtzu valley, till their cargoes are exhausted. Then they sail merrily down-stream and back to their home port, to reload and sail out once more. These bare-footed, dark-skinned sailors, as they waited for a favorable tide, used to congregate in the tea-shops, and in their rough good-humored voices exchange tales of their experiences. Unlike Chinese peasants and workers, who rarely venture, at most, beyond a neighboring town, these men had seen something of the world, and had experienced many forms of danger and adventure. Welcome guests at the tea-houses, they kept the company shouting with laughter, or open-mouthed with amazement, until the bugle of the tide-watchers rang out, and the ferrymen made off to their boats in a whirlwind of haste to catch the tide.

Chiang Kai-shek during his boyhood used to love the company of these good-humored, naïve wanderers, and it is said that from them he acquired not only stories about other parts of the Eastern world, but also an adventurous spirit and a deep sympathy for working-class people. This early unconscious teaching was to have a remarkable influence upon his future career.

Chiang was not a patrician. His father had been a modest tradesman who died when his son was only nine years old. His mother brought him up devotedly, and paid for his education by selling her own embroideries. Unlike most of the women in her district, Madame Chiang was a person of some education. She taught her son to read, and answered with intelligence all the questions of life and learning posed by the inquiring mind of a young child. Such was her zeal and love for him, that on his fiftieth birthday, in 1936, a day of universal celebration, Chiang confessed to his countrymen how "great" a woman his mother had been, and how all his career had been inspired by her.

At nine he was sent to school, where he received the regular classical education, based on the Confucian books. The Manchu regime had not yet fallen, and modern education, inspired by the methods of the West, had been introduced only at a few centers. But he had determined on a military rather than an official career. At eighteen he passed into the Paoting Military School—one of the comparatively modern military schools established by Yuan Shih-k'ai. Something of Yuan's character has already been described—his shrewd realism, his personal ambition, his intrigues. From his contact with Yuan at Paoting, Chiang Kai-Shek learned a great deal about the latter's plans, the conspiracies of his henchmen, as well as the corruption of the Manchu Court. At Paoting the truth was borne in upon him that if the people and the country were to be saved, a revolution was inevitable.

From 1907 till 1910, he continued his military studies in Japan, where methods were already far more up-to-date than in China. He then joined a Japanese brigade and trained as a cadet. He left Japan at a dramatic moment in Chinese history, and, we may believe, not without premonitions of the part he himself was destined to play in that great modern drama. In after years, the Japanese brigadier who had trained him wrote, "When the Chinese Revolution broke out in 1911, Chiang Kai-shek was about to leave for his own country, and we had arranged a farewell feast for him. It was snowing, and I said to him and his friends, 'Gentlemen, if you won't drink my wine, at least have a cup of plain water!' Now, according to our code of chivalry, to drink water at a farewell feast is the sign of a man's determination to die for his career. So saying, I offered a cup of plain water to Chiang, and he drank it at a draft. 'Sir,' he exclaimed, 'I have determined to die for my career!' and his face as he said this was flushed with excitement. However, I did not realize at the time how great a part he was to play in the future." The story is a very living one, and brings a picture of the young man vividly before us—the excitement of leave-taking, the dreams and the resolve, the embarking on a career at one of the most critical moments in the whole history of his country.

On arriving in China, he joined the revolutionists immediately, and on the strength of his military training was appointed commander in the fifth brigade of the revolutionary army. He fought in his home province of Chekiang, and succeeded in mopping up all the opposing forces in Shanghai. Shortly afterwards, however, the whole army suffered a general reverse, and Chiang's brigade, fighting against heavy odds, was dispersed by the army of his former teacher, Yuan Shih-k'ai.

Chiang continued to fight loyally for the revolutionists. Ten years later, in 1921, having set up a government in Canton, Sun Yat-sen sent for the young officer and appointed him commander of his personal bodyguard, his adviser on military matters, his secretary, and deputy at social functions. It was a signal honor for so young a man. Chiang served Sun with a mixture of practical zeal and worship. He revered him as his father and teacher. He learned from him the experience, wisdom, and spirit of a great revolutionary leader that were to stand him in good stead in after years.

It was none too soon for Chiang to learn these lessons. Although Dr. Sun was not an old man, his health was failing. Himself a trained physician, he probably recognized the cancer from which he was suffering, and knew its deadly nature. In 1922, the year after Chiang had become his confidential adviser, a treacherous lieutenant in the revolutionary army, named Ch'en Chiung-ming, started a revolt and raided Dr. Sun's presidential office at Canton, evidently with the intention of assassinating him. Protected by Chiang Kai-shek's men, Sun was able to escape and board a ship on the Pearl River, which brought him through the bay to Hong-Kong. Later he made for the greater safety of the International Settlement at Shanghai.

Canton had become a center of unrest. In 1924 a rising of Cantonese merchants threatened to destroy the whole revolutionary movement there. And Dr. Sun was by now a very sick man. Just at this time, the Northern war-lords had broken the power of General Wu P'ei-fu, most formidable opponent of the revolutionists, and there seemed a possibility of reconciliation between the North and South. Accordingly, Dr. Sun, we may believe not without inner misgivings, went to Peking to discuss the formation of a united government. But before the discussion had materialized, he died. As he lay on his death-bed, Chiang Kai-shek was staunchly fighting the rebels in the South. Many rumors about the fighting reached Peking, and among them, that Chiang had been killed. When Dr. Sun heard this, the tears poured from his eyes and he exclaimed, "Alas! I would rather have lost a hundred thousand troops than this Kai-shek of mine!" Meanwhile, Chiang was very much alive, and in a short time had crushed the revolt with his small band of picked "student troops."

These so-called "student troops" were students of the Whampoa (Huang-p'u) Military School, virtually Chiang's own creation, though under the supervision of Russian advisers, and newly opened in June of 1924. The success of the Soviet-Russian revolution had much impressed Dr. Sun, and from it he had learned the necessity of supporting a revolutionary doctrine with an efficient armed force. He had sent Chiang to Moscow in 1923 to study military conditions there, and on the latter's return to Canton in the following year, he was authorized to found an up-to-date military school at Huang-p'u, a suburb of Canton (in Western textbooks the name usually appears as Whampoa). The early students of this school became the army leaders of later years—men who helped destroy the Northern war-lords and enabled Chiang to unite the country under the Nationalist government. Subsequently they formed the kernel of the Chinese central army, and many of the ablest generals at the present time are old students of the Whampoa school.

In the spring of 1925, Dr. Sun had died at Peking. In the following year, a meeting of the People's Government was held in Canton, and Chiang Kai-shek was appointed to take command of the People's Revolutionary Army. The period known as the Second Revolution began. At the same meeting, two guiding principles for the new revolutionary phase were laid down: to fight for the independence and freedom of China against the foreign imperialists, and to destroy the power of the war-lords, bureaucrats, usurers, and plutocrats. The first of these was obviously a concession to the Communist members, whose fury against foreign imperialism was tremendous. In order to bear out the two principles, the government proposed four main tasks: the formation of a people's army; the establishment of a fair and equitable government; the protection of the national industry; and the development of peasants' and workers' organizations.

No time was lost in putting precept into practice: in July the new revolutionary army, under Chiang's command, began to march northwards. Within a few months he had occupied the two provinces of Kiangsi and Hunan which bordered Kuangtung province to the north.[1] He pressed on into Hupei, and there, near the important city of Hankow, for four days and nights without respite, he engaged the forces of Wu P'ei-fu, who at that time held the dominant military power in the Yangtzu valley provinces. Wu's army was practically wiped out. By April of 1927, all important towns south of the Yangtzu, which roughly divides China in two, had fallen to the revolutionaries.

Meanwhile, in 1927, had begun that tragic split between the two great revolutionary parties, the Communists and the Kuomintang, which was outlined in the last chapter. Differences in ideals and beliefs engendered hatred between brother and brother, father and son. Some of the nation's most promising youth was destroyed in civil feuds. One catastrophe followed another for years: terror raged through the country. It may be advisable here to trace in more detail the origins of the conflict, and to show how the course of the quarrel and its final liquidation influenced the development of the revolution. The relation between these two parties was, and to some extent remains, one of the major problems of Chiang Kai-shek's political career.

The relationship of Kuomintang and Communists can very easily be understood by English people if they substitute "British Labor Party" for "Kuomintang." During the nineteen-thirties, when the British Communist Party first became a serious political body, with a considerable membership, the right wing of the Labor Party declared itself the most bitter enemy of Communism, and despite the growing threat of Fascist domination throughout Europe, stubbornly refused to unite with "the Reds." The Labor left wing, however, under such men as Aneurin Bevin and George Strauss, vehemently urged the formation of a "Popular Front" of all Left Parties—Liberal, Labor, and Communist.

In China, the Kuomintang was also composed of left and right wing elements, and at the first plenary session of the People's Government, summoned by Dr. Sun in 1924, the more moderate Kuomintang members tried to oppose the acceptance of Communists into the govern-

---

[1] Kuangtung is the province of which Canton is the chief city, and was therefore already loyal to the revolutionaries.

ment. They were unsuccessful, and as long as Dr. Sun lived, his tact, statesmanship, and persuasive personality held the intransigent members of both parties in harmony. As soon as the great man died, however, private grumbling turned to public action. Chiang Kai-shek, although he had proved himself an able militarist, had yet to earn general recognition as a political leader. The parties momentarily lost their central control. At this point, the Kuomintang right wing members began to raise petulant voices that China was the country of Confucius, and should on no account be laid open to the conspiracies of Soviet Russia, who would effect horrible changes and destroy every valued Chinese tradition. The Communists for their part, with the support of the left wing Kuomintang, without Dr. Sun's restraining hand, and under the influence of Soviet advisers, behaved indiscreetly, and with marked lack of moderation.

The young leader, Chiang Kai-shek, found himself in a difficult position. Since his visit to Russia in 1923 on the orders of Dr. Sun, he was probably not without sympathy for the Communist political ideal. On the other hand, the right wing members of the Kuomintang had declared themselves the only faithful supporters of Dr. Sun Yat-sen's policy. Chiang could hardly, it seemed, for the sake of the movement, decline to support them. Moreover, Communist intrigues showed signs of undermining the Kuomintang itself, and it was clear that in the event of a split in the two parties, he must inevitably take action against the Communists.

In Chiang's victorious northward march, his armies had occupied Hankow, together with the adjoining cities of Wuch'ang and Hanyang, in October of 1926. Now, this triple city, known under the collective name of Wuhan, was the largest industrial center in the whole of China, excepting only Shanghai. The iron works at Hanyang were the largest in the country. To the Communists, this city with its thousands of industrial workers seemed an ideal center from which to propagate their political faith. And so, while Chiang Kai-shek was pursuing his military campaign farther down the Yangtzu valley, certain left wing members of the Kuomintang, headed by Wang Ching-wei, were able to move the government from Canton to Hankow, and to announce the establishment of a National Government at Wuhan, in November 1926.

Meanwhile, though not blind to the significance of this move, Chiang was rapidly bringing his forces up for the attack on Shanghai, according to plan. The security of the foreign settlements at Shanghai with their foreign police and extraterritorial rights, had attracted Chinese merchants and bankers in huge numbers: the greatest reserves of wealth in the country were probably accumulated in that city. Mastery of Shanghai would bring with it control of the rich and fertile Yangtzu valley, with its great towns, at least as far west as Wuhan. In March 1927 the city fell to Chiang's forces, and in the same month they occupied Nanking. At the latter, Chiang established the national capital, as desired by Dr. Sun Yat-sen in his lifetime. The government at Wuhan hastily convened its central executive committee and recorded its decision to annul the "dictatorship" of Chiang Kai-shek. From this month, March 1927, there were two popular governments in China, in addition to the various local governments of the war-lords; the revolutionary influence was sharply split in two. A less able leader than Chiang might well have despaired of ever bringing this huge country, with its contending, warring, and mutually antagonistic factions, into a unity.

But all was not proceeding smoothly on the Upper Yangtzu. The Communist element in the Wuhan government was overstepping the wishes of its Kuomintang supporters. Incessant strikes and peasant demonstrations kept the central provinces in a constant state of tension, while reprisals taken by the People's Court, under Communist auspices, against old enemies such as the usurers and plutocrats, were so drastic that they destroyed the people's confidence in Communist justice. The army of Hunan province, the government's chief military support, began to complain about the disruptive influence of the "Reds," and went so far as to put down by force a peasant demonstration for which the latter had been responsible.

Relations between Wang Ching-wei and his supporters on the one hand, and the Communists with their Russian advisers on the other, grew increasingly strained as the months passed. It seemed clear that their political aims differed fundamentally, and that a split could hardly be avoided. Some members of the government suspected the Communists of being in the pay of the Soviet Embassy; there were hints of a plot to destroy the Kuomintang and to replace it by a Communist regime.

Numbers of the Communists were arrested; some of the leaders escaped to Moscow, and the Wuhan government repudiated the Russian alliance. The way now seemed clear for a reconciliation between the right and left wings of the Kuomintang. To facilitate this, Chiang Kai-shek accepted a suggestion to resign his position as commander-in-chief and head of the Nanking government. In August 1927, he retired to Japan, and the next month a united "National" government was established at Nanking.

In December of that same year, Chiang returned to Shanghai, where a significant union was solemnized. Chiang was married to Mei-ling Soong, youngest sister of Sun Yat-sen's wife. Mei-ling was then only twenty-five, and her husband forty. She had studied at an American university, and was a fitting representative of modern Chinese womanhood. The union has proved of the greatest value to China as a whole. Madame Chiang was a Christian, and by her persuasion her husband was also baptized. She had the highest admiration for Western culture and the democratic system, as well as a love of the old Chinese civilization. There is no doubt that Chiang, who was brought up on Confucianism, and on a background of pure Chinese culture, obtained a better understanding of the Western mind through the influence of his wife, and that this understanding was of great service to him as he strove to rebuild China into a World Power.

Madame Chiang is a woman of sincere, unpretentious character, and although she learned to admire the American political and educational systems, was never captivated by the luxury and superficial brilliance of modern New York. She dresses like a simple and modest Chinese wife, and as one of the leaders in the "New Life Movement" she has given an example to the women of China to dress plainly, live frugally, and abjure those new-fangled frivolities which are quite out of keeping with their dignified Chinese traditions.

When operations were in progress against the Communists, Madame Chiang accompanied her husband to the front. And now that China is at grips with Japan, she is still to be found at her husband's side, wherever the danger is greatest. She seems absolutely fearless. She is the adopted mother of every Chinese wounded soldier in the hospitals, and her husband's "diplomat" in interviews with important foreign guests. She also acts as Chiang's private secretary, and for a time was personally responsible for the promotion of the air force. She is not only beautiful and intelligent, but a patriot of tireless energy and a selfless servant of struggling China.

While Chiang Kai-shek and his newly wedded wife remained in Shanghai, the Nanking government discovered it could not dispense with his services. Chiang was the inevitable leader of the People's Government, and was soon recalled to his old position. His honeymoon was cut short while he launched a new attack against the armies of the Northern war-lords, and by the beginning of 1928 his troops had obtained control of almost all the provinces of China Proper.

Peking still held out, largely through the machinations of the Japanese, who feared their interests in Northeast China (Shantung and

Manchuria) would be jeopardized. At the beginning of May 1928, three Kuomintang armies began to move up from south and west, but a strong Japanese force was meanwhile landed at Ts'ingtao, the port of Shantung, and proceeded inland along the railway to Peking. A little south of the city, a clash occurred between the two forces, resulting in the temporary withdrawal of the Chinese southwards. Very shortly after this setback, Chang Tso-lin, the pro-Japanese war-lord then controlling Peking, in the hope of coming to favorable terms with the Kuomintang, deserted his former ally and withdrew into Manchuria with his army. As his own train crossed the border, it was blown up, obviously the work of Japanese agents. His son, Chang Hsueh-liang, despite repeated warnings from the Japanese, made an alliance with the Nanking government. In July, Peking fell to the armies of Chiang Kai-shek: Manchuria, under the rule of Chang Hsueh-liang, already flew the new flag of the Chinese Republic. The whole of China was united, nominally at least, under General Chiang's sole leadership.

But while the Nanking or "Nationalist" government was strengthening its position, the Communists were also consolidating theirs. After their split with the Kuomintang in 1927 they had established headquarters in Kiangsi province in the central Yangtzu valley. In 1928, the year of Chiang Kai-shek's northern victories, the Communists founded their "Red Army," with a membership of two thousand men. It was put in the command of Chu Teh (the present leader of the Eighth Route Army in the war against Japan), and under this excellent organizer of guerrilla warfare, the "workers' and peasants' irregulars" were inaugurated. Within two years, the "Red Army" had multiplied its members ten times, and become a formidable weapon, its members being politically educated as well as thoroughly trained in military affairs. In 1931, a "Chinese Soviet Republic" was established, with its government at the town of Jui-chin, on the southeastern border of Kiangsi.

Even before this, in July 1930, the Communist forces had invaded their old stronghold of Hunan and invested the capital city. They were launching drives in several directions with the hope of theatening Nanking. Chiang Kai-shek now realized that the Communists were offering a definite challenge to the Kuomintang's power, and that he must meet it with concentrated force. China could not be effectively united while such a large body of the population remained in aggressive opposition.

Between the years 1930 and 1934, Chiang used his utmost endeavor to crush the Kiangsi "Reds." In all, he employed about six hundred thousand men, and launched six general offensives. Still he could reach no decisive victory against their guerrilla tactics. Finally, his forces tried to blockade them, and a lack of food and salt eventually brought the Communists to the edge of starvation. But they did not surrender. With belief in their political faith, and with spirits of the utmost courage and endurance, they decided to evacuate Kiangsi in November 1934, and to begin their "Long March" of eighteen thousand *li* (nearly six thousand miles) to the Northwest. This almost incredible feat, so vividly described by Edgar Snow in his "Red Star over China," culminated in the re-establishment of the Chinese Soviet Republic in Kansu, out of the immediate reach of the Nationalist armies.

These inconclusive civil wars seemed to Japan an excellent opportunity for making mischief on her own account. In 1931, when Chiang Kai-shek was heavily engaged in Kiangsi, the Japanese occupied Manchuria. Chiang had put his trust in the League of Nations. The great Western Powers were strong; the Chinese Republic was very young, and still weak like a child. The League's failure to intervene on China's behalf over the Manchurian question was a bitter disillusion to him, while the reproaches of his own people at allowing their national sovereignty to be violated without striking a blow convinced him that immediate measures must be taken to recover the lost territory. At the same time as he fought the Communists for the sake of internal unity, he began to forge a strong military weapon which might be used in the course of time against the enemy from without.

His first task was to improve and enlarge the National Central Army, and to bring the provincial troops, which up till now had been recruited and controlled by local leaders, and knew no obligation except to defend their own district, under a central command. They were to be "nationalized" and taught to defend the whole country against the foreign aggressor. Compulsory military service, a law which had lapsed since the thirteenth century, was reinstated. With the help of European and American military advisers, he was able to build a vast modern army. Communications were opened up with a view to facilitating troop movements within the country. Railways were extended and huge schemes for road construction put in motion. Industries to feed the military machine were encouraged and subsidized by the government.

Generalissimo Chiang is the founder of the Chinese Air Force. By his orders a "Three Years' Plan" was inaugurated for the development of aviation. Foreign-built planes were purchased, and pilots trained to fly them. In front of one of the Chinese schools of aviation stands a monument with the pilots' oath inscribed on it: "Let our bodies and machines be destroyed together with those of our enemy!"

To build a great army and a competent air force; to reorganize or build up afresh sufficiently powerful industries to feed the war machine; to solve unemployment problems, improve the nation's financial structure, and multiply the export trade; to educate the people politically—not all this could be achieved in a short time. Chiang Kai-shek showed both forbearance and foresight in refusing to be rushed into war, either by the reproaches of his own people or the threats of his enemies the Japanese. "We are still a weak people," he said repeatedly in his speeches before the party executive, "and we dare not provoke a war. But if we are forced to fight, we shall not stop until the last man has fallen, or until we are victorious."

Conscious of his country's unpreparedness for such an encounter, Chiang frequently offered to negotiate with Japan. In 1936, no less than seven conversations were held between the Japanese and Chinese diplomats, but without any agreement being reached. Hirota, who was then Foreign Minister of Japan, insisted on his famous "Three Principles," and these were quite unacceptable to China. They were: (1) all public or private anti-Japanese organizations should be dispersed, and "the policy of playing the Western Powers against Japan" should be abandoned for good; (2) China should acknowledge "Manchukuo" (i.e. should acknowledge Manchuria and the province of Jehol as an "independent" State, under Japanese control), and (3) the Japanese army in China should co-operate with the Chinese in suppressing the "Communist-bandits."

All these discussions broke off inconclusively, and a clash between the two powers seemed to draw inexorably nearer. This same year, 1936, proved to be a crucial one, both in the career of Generalissimo Chiang and in the history of modern China. It will be remembered that Chang Hsueh-liang, or "the Young Marshal" as he was called, had succeeded his father, the old war-lord of Manchuria, Chang Tso-lin, and having sworn loyalty to the Nationalist cause, had been put in command of troops in the northeastern provinces.

Now, a large part of the "Young Marshal's" soldiers were from Manchuria: their homes had been seized by the Japanese, and they were hungry for revenge. But instead of sending them to fight their natural enemies, the Government gave orders that they should march west against the Communists. Kansu was like a foreign country to them and they felt profoundly homesick. They were resentful at being forced to kill their own countrymen instead of the invader. Moreover, in their contact with the Communists, they began to feel the force of the Communist doctrine, and instead of fighting, an amicable interchange of political views began to take place! The "Young Marshal's" followers found that the "Reds" were not the murderous bandits they had been led to believe, but people with a sane, intelligent outlook, who appeared to put the interests of China before personal conquests.

Indeed, since the Japanese invasion of Manchuria, the Chinese Communists had very much altered their tactics. Formerly, their anger had been vented on the Kuomintang, on the one hand, and the landowning, moneyed classes on the other. But from 1931 onwards they had changed their slogan from "Down with the Kuomintang!" to "Unite with us to fight the Japanese aggressor!" History had taught them that civil wars had never solved the problem of conflicting ideologies, but had only brought whole nations into slavery, and in many cases betrayed them into the hands of some foreign power. The tragic truth of this belief has been illustrated again in recent years, when the bitterly waged civil wars in Spain from 1936–38 ended, not in any compromise between the Left and Right, but in a virtual loss of national sovereignty to the German and Italian dictators.

The Chinese Communists were waiting for a chance to express their loyalty to Chiang Kai-shek: they hoped to persuade him into a united resistance against the Japanese invader. To the "Young Marshal" it seemed that his opportunity had come to mediate between the two great parties.

Meanwhile, General Chiang, at Nanking, could not understand the stagnation of the Kansu operations, and in December he decided to make a personal visit to the front. At Sian, the "Young Marshal's" headquarters, he learned the true facts of the situation, and was so disturbed at what he heard that he left the city immediately to spend a few days in undisturbed thought somewhere in the outskirts. He retired to the beautiful Hua-ch'ing Lake, beside which rose the famous Black Horse Hill. Here Ch'in Shih Huang Ti, creator of the Great Wall, had laid out his extravagant imperial park, and Emperor Hsuan Tsung of the T'ang dynasty had wantoned with his beautiful and ill-starred concubine, Yang Kuei-fei. Next morning at daybreak he rose, dressed, and having bathed in the nearby hot springs, was reading in his room. A sudden clamor arose at the gate, and crowds of shouting people broke through and poured into the courtyard. There could be no doubt of their malignant intentions, and with some presence of mind, Chiang escaped through the back of the house and climbed up the historic Black Horse Hill. But he was pursued by the rebels, seized, and carried back to Sian, where he was made a virtual prisoner. Many of the generals who had accompanied him from Nanking were made prisoner at the same time.

The method, called by the Chinese "armed persuasion," for influencing a leader is a traditional one of very long standing. The story is told of an official serving the Duke of Ch'u in the sixth century B.C. whose reasonable advice to his master was repeatedly neglected. At last, for the good of the State of Ch'u, and his master's reputation, the official thought fit to threaten the latter with his sword. Thereupon the Duke accepted his advice. The worthy official now declared, "Although I have served my Lord well in this, I have threatened him with my sword, and ought to punish myself." Thereupon, he struck off his own legs! The "Young Marshal," who went immediately to visit the Generalissimo in his confinement, found him in such a state of mental suffering, that tears broke from his own eyes. He expressed sincere sorrow that he had lost control of his followers, and declared himself willing to take any punishment his leader thought fit after an agreement had been reached.

At the same time, he felt obliged to put the proposals of his officers and soldiers before the Generalissimo. These were: reconciliation with the Communists, reorganization of the National Government, and resistance to Japanese aggression. Although realizing that his very life might be in danger, Chiang courageously refused even to consider such proposals since, he declared, to negotiate in such circumstances was illegal. After this, he refused even to grant an interview to the "Young Marshal." Madame Chiang, despite the warnings of her friends, took a plane from Nanking, and flew to join her husband, to live or die with him.

It was a hard winter, and snow was falling everywhere in China. The people's hearts were heavy. Some thought Chiang Kai-shek was dead; others expected a fresh outbreak of civil war when the Nanking armies would be sent against Sian to release the Generalissimo and avenge the indignity. A cloud of gloom and tragedy overhung the whole country for many days. But on the twenty-fifth of December, several planes, escorted by fighters, flew from Sian to Nanking, and landed in brilliant sunshine. The occupants were Chiang Kai-shek, his wife, and the imprisoned generals! Their faces were all smiles, and as the news spread, smiles broke from the face of every Chinese citizen. That night, fireworks were let off in every town, bands marched through the streets; the people were almost delirious with joy!

From that day on, China has been truly united. China belongs to the whole people and not to any privileged party. There are no more Soviets on Chinese soil, and no Red Army. Communists and Nationalists have joined forces for the common good. There is only one slogan for all: "Fight for Existence!" In the birth of this unity, Japan saw the death of her hopes in China, and did her best to prevent its fruition. Only a few months after the Sian "incident" she launched her undeclared war. It has proved a bitter and costly struggle, but beyond the war, China foresees a great future for herself, and draws strength and consolation from that vision.

XXX. CHINA AND JAPAN (3)—THE INVASION OF MANCHURIA AND NORTH CHINA

As THE TWENTIETH CENTURY entered its third decade, a period of unrest and distress began for a large part of the world. The Economic Crisis, starting in Europe, and spreading very shortly to the Americas, involved both conquering and conquered of the World War, and cast heavy shadows of privation, unemployment, bankruptcy over the so-called Great Powers of the West. The rise of Fascism and Nazism and its outcome—the attempt of the Dictators to dominate the world by force—have been the monstrous progeny of those fateful years. Meanwhile, in the Far East a fresh storm was blowing up, and seemed about to burst over Eastern Asia. The Manchurian crisis of 1931 was the first intimation, and its logical outcome is the major war now being fought out between China and Japan, and of which the whole vast territory of China forms the battleground.

In the China of 1930, General Chiang Kai-shek's government had reached only the semblance of an equilibrium. The Second Revolution had just been completed; the northern provinces, including Manchuria, had been brought into line by the Nationalist armies, and a central government established at Nanking, intrusted with the administration of the whole country. But great as this achievement was, it did not imply that a golden age of peace and prosperity was being ushered in, or that China's problems were, even temporarily, at an end.

It has been shown in the last chapter how the power of the Communists in Kiangsi and the regions south of the Yangtzu had, at that time, been steadily increasing, and how, in 1931, they had established their own Soviet and mobilized a large "Red Army." The failure of Chiang's campaign against them in that same year had constituted a serious blow to his authority.

Nor was this the only source of disunity: there were personal jealousies and dissensions within the government ranks. Chief among Chiang's rivals was that double-faced Wang Ching-wei, who in 1927 had organized the semi-Communist Wuhan government, and who in 1939 swung over to Fascism and was later appointed head of the Japanese-sponsored government at Nanking. Wang now assembled round him a group of political malcontents, and started what he called an "anti–Chiang Kai-shek campaign." Meanwhile, in the North, two leading generals who were nominally loyal to the central government, but who secretly clung to the old war-lord attitude of regional control, and who resented their loss of independence, joined forces with Wang Ching-wei's clique. A serious rebellion broke out in the North. It was put down eventually by Chiang Kai-shek's forces. Also in the extreme South, the military leaders of Kuangtung and Kuangsi continued to differ with certain aspects of the central government's policy for some years to come, and were often on the verge of organizing a revolt.

Japan had been watching the progress of these internal dissensions with the greatest interest, and had even spitefully meddled in them. She was waiting across the Sea of Japan, like a wary tiger, ready to pounce on her victim when the best occasion offered. Especially did she lust after those three provinces of Northern China, Heilung-chiang, Chilin (Kirin), and Liaoning, to which foreign journalists had given the name of "Manchuria," and over which she had covertly been extending her influence for many years.

This great tract of northern pasture land, only partly exploited, had formerly been the bait for the eastward advances of Russia. Not only would it have provided a new and fertile colony for her peasant farmers, but also a much-coveted ice-free port in the Liaotung Peninsula. But Japan's unexpected victory over the Russian imperial forces in the war of 1904–5 had resulted in the handing over of Russian railway rights in Manchuria to Japan, and the reluctant withdrawal of Russia from that part of Eastern Asia.

Japan lost no time in spreading her tentacles over the new booty. By "treaty rights," she stationed troops along the whole length of the South Manchurian railway and instituted her own officials. She also acted as a colonizer. The familiar Japanese plea for *lebensraum* has been shown up in all its falsity over the development of Manchuria. Although she was free to settle her superfluous millions in these three large provinces, the proportion of Japanese to the total population was indeed negligible. The main settlers in the three provinces of Manchuria from Japan were fortune-hunters. Consequently their numbers could not possibly be large. The inhabitants of a temperate island found the severe climate of the mainland hard to endure. Nor were the Japanese peasants fitted for the heavy agricultural work entailed in developing a raw country, being habitually gardeners rather than farmers.

The soil of these three Manchurian provinces is very fertile. The country is rich with natural resources. In the meantime, the northern part of China, especially Hopei, Shantung, and Honan, has been suffering from over-population. In the years of famine, Chinese peasant families from the border provinces, in the hope of finding new and better lands to cultivate, poured over the Wall into Manchuria and settled there. Between 1905, when the Japanese began to take control, and 1931, the population of Manchuria was almost doubled.

At the same time as Japan extended her influence over Manchuria, she also employed a form of espionage—a familiar device of the totalitarian States. The mass movement of German and Italian "tourists" as the vanguard of invasion has become a sickeningly familiar sight in Europe. Japan had used a similar though even more dastardly method in North China many years before. Some of their own free will, others by encouragement of their government—prostitutes, criminals, bandits, tramps, and general good-for-nothings, scum that the great Japanese Empire cast up from its shores, poured into China to make their fortunes. Most of them settled in Manchuria; others in the shadier districts of Shanghai. With them came smuggling, the ever-increasing sale of opium and other narcotics, and venereal diseases. The physique and character of the Chinese within the Japanese-controlled areas were thus grievously undermined.

This was, however, by no means the only service rendered by them to their Motherland. As time went on, those of them with more wits than the rest were appointed "advisers" to the Japanese army, and in that capacity were able to move at will in Chinese official circles. Protected by those extraterritorial rights enjoyed by all Japanese subjects, they could travel about the whole country without any special permit or any hindrance. They drew up maps, made reports, conferred with high officials, both Japanese and Chinese, and by every possible means prepared to betray the country which had given them hospitality.

The harm done by these rascals is incalculable. Not only did they give the greatest assistance to the Japanese in their impending military operations, but they ruined forever the possibility of a Sino-Japanese understanding. Their knowledge of Chinese affairs was, to be sure, a very thorough one, but their lack of education and training led them to misinterpret and misunderstand at every point. So that, although Japan had planned long ago the economic conquest of China, the tactics she adopted were largely governed by the shortsighted advice of these "China Experts." A flagrant example is provided by the present war. Japan still referred to this major conflict, which had already lasted more than four years at the time when she started attacking the Western Powers on December 7, 1941, and had cost her hundreds of thousands of lives, as "the China Incident." Owing to the failure of her "China Experts" to recognize the growth of a new and powerful national spirit, Japan expected to complete her subjugation of China in a few months.

However mistaken was Japan's entry into the present conflict, her timing of the knockout blow against Manchuria was well calculated. Not only were operations against the Communists in Central China fully occupying the Chinese national armies, but by a cruel stroke of Nature, both the Yellow and the Yangtzu rivers rose higher than at any other time recorded in history (1931). The valleys of these two rivers are as densely populated as any areas in the world, and the hundreds of thousands of families drowned were only a fraction of those destined to starve in the following winter from the destruction of crops. In the autumn, Japan arranged one of her notorious "incidents" and her armies were set in motion.

On the evening of September 18, 1931, a bridge on the South Manchurian railway, just outside Mukden, provincial capital of Liaoning, blew up. The Japanese hastened to assert that this had been perpetrated by "some Chinese soldiers commanded by the bandit General Chang Hseuh-liang, son of the late bandit General Chang Tso-lin." Japanese forces attacked the Chinese garrisons as they slept in their barracks, and wiped them out before any resistance could be organized. The city of Mukden fell immediately.

The true source of the explosion is beyond question. Ameleto Vespa, an Italian eye-witness, in his remarkably revealing book "Secret Agent of Japan," has pointed out the premeditated nature of the whole affair. "The Japanese troops stationed at Liaoyang, Yingkow, and Fenghuangch'eng had, on the day before the incident, received their orders to advance on Mukden at 3 P.M. on September 18. Seven hours *before* the alleged explosion they had already started towards their destination. By 4 A.M. of the nineteenth, only six hours after the alleged explosion, thousands of printed posters had already been pasted on the walls of Mukden and in these it was said that the Manchurian government was discredited, since 'it had ordered an attack on the Japanese railway.' The people were advised to remain calm. It would have been a physical impossibility to have ascertained the facts and to have drafted, printed, and distributed so many official notices in only six hours." [1]

[1] See "Secret Agent of Japan," Chapter II, pp. 19-28.

The Chinese airdrome on the outskirts of Mukden was immediately occupied by the Japanese, and five hundred planes passed into their hands without a shadow of resistance being offered. Next day, Japanese troops occupied as many as eighteen towns, a fact that in itself points to a carefully prearranged plan. Within less than a fortnight, more than half the towns of Liaoning and Chilin, the two southernmost provinces of "Manchuria," passed into Japanese hands.

Still the Chinese government made no move. The provincial troops were ordered to retreat and to avoid a collision with Japanese forces at all costs, while the central government hastened to put its case before the League Council, then in session, and of which both China and Japan were members. Japan, for her part, disclaimed any intention of annexing Manchuria, while at the same time her armies continued to advance unresisted, and the Chinese waited patiently for their case to be judged.

The League Council hesitated fatally. Some of its leading members were obviously unwilling to go to war with Japan: she was their "traditional ally" and had, moreover, important economic relations with them. The United States offered to send warships into the Pacific in support of China's just cause, if the British would do the same. The British government refused. There was some talk of Japan withdrawing her troops from the railway, and of the establishment of an "International Zone." Japanese troops marched on. Finally, at the instigation of the offending party, Japan, a Commission was appointed under Lord Lytton to investigate the matter at first hand, and report back to the League.

While Lord Lytton's Commission was making its pleasant sea voyage, Japan was pressing north into the third province, Heilung-chiang. Here she met some resistance from provincial regulars and local volunteers, but without reinforcements they were unable to stem the Japanese onrush. Most of them retreated into the mountains, or over the Russian frontier. Japan thus roughly occupied all three provinces of "Manchuria," and was already setting up local "puppet" governments when the Commission arrived at Harbin, the Japanese headquarters in Chilin province, early in May 1932.

Lord Lytton's reception was very carefully arranged by his Japanese hosts. Elaborate precautions were taken to prevent any true information reaching the Commission. Even the hotels where the delegation lodged were guarded by detectives; special maids and valets were installed who could be trusted to keep their mouths shut, and accept no bribes. Many Chinese were put under arrest for suspected communication with the

Commission; moreover, it was announced that any such illegal communication would be punished with the death penalty.

It can therefore be well understood that the Lytton Report was not entirely unbiased owing to the circumstances. The Japanese had skillfully prevented its members from obtaining a true picture. The Report, however, whether a true or false interpretation of the facts, proved a fruitless undertaking, for when asked to fulfill her obligations as a League member, Japan walked out. Once she had ceased to be a member, the League was no longer under any compulsion to deal with her affairs!

Manchuria had been a test case, and the League had failed. Henceforward, aggressor nations did not hesitate to exercise force whenever it suited their ends. The series of "unprovoked aggressions" which followed in Europe was the immediate fruit of the League's failure to act in support of China.

Meanwhile, in January of 1932, Japan had committed a fresh act of aggression in Shanghai. The people's reactions to the Mukden incident of September 18, and the government's phlegmatic attitude, had been very violent. The boycott of Japanese goods was intensified, shops refused to sell provisions to Japanese customers, and bankers refused financial transactions with Japanese firms. There were fierce student demonstrations. The anti-Japanese feeling reached its height in Shanghai, and it was here that the storm broke.

Some street fracas had occurred between a few Chinese and a group of Japanese immigrants. Whether the incident was prearranged or not, the reprisals taken were quite disproportionate. A furious Japanese mob attacked a commercial firm known as the "Three Friends Industry Association," and smashed it up. The choice of this particular victim was apparently from Japan's malicious jealousy, for the goods produced by the Association were taking the place of similar Japanese products in the Chinese markets. It was a brutal retort to the boycott. In the course of the regular battle that developed, Japanese warships took care to train their guns upon the general store of the Commercial Press, the most important book company in China, and also upon the "Eastern Library," where the largest collection of ancient Chinese printed books was stored, together with many precious and irreplaceable examples of handwritten MSS. dating from the ninth to the thirteenth centuries. The whole contents was mercilessly destroyed.

No sooner had news of the original "incident" reached the Japanese authorities, than a part of the fleet sailed into Shanghai. The commander announced his intention to "perform my duty in the protection of Japanese immigrants." At the same time, the European and American legations in Shanghai received notice that a Japanese landing party would occupy the city within four hours.

Japan was unable to fulfill her boast. While the central government still waited for League mediation, the nineteenth army, backed by the voices of the people, refused to retreat before the enemy. Three times the Japanese commander-in-chief was changed, and reinforcements were repeatedly sent both from North China and Japan. A furious battle raged in the district of Chapei, on the north side of the Nanking-Shanghai railway, and not until the Japanese eventually managed to land a force at Liuho, north of Shanghai, on the south bank of the Yangtzu, did the Chinese garrisons retire to avoid being outflanked. Since neither government intended a major war to develop in this part of the country, the mediation of an English envoy in Shanghai brought about a Sino-Japanese peace pact. Japan withdrew her troops under the surveillance of a neutral Commission.

While this fierce but pointless conflict had been raging in Central China, Japan took the opportunity of renewing her fruitful activities in the North. The province of Jehol, immediately north of the Wall, and adjoining Liaoning to the West, was her next objective. The Chinese governor of the province, a worthless war-lord, first swore to shed his last drop of blood in defense of his native land, only to escape with his harem and treasures loaded on to two hundred military lorries at the approach of the Japanese vanguards. The Japanese occupied the whole province with very little loss.

The aggressor was triumphant at the success. Now seemed the moment to found an autonomous State north of the Wall, and to break these provinces, in form as well as in fact, away from China. Japan was confident that many survivors of the "Mandarin" class—families who had served at Court in the past, and who looked back with nostalgia on the old days, still existed in the Northern regions. Relying on these elements of the population, she now proclaimed the three provinces of Manchuria and Jehol to be an independent kingdom—"Manchukuo," or "the Kingdom of the Manchus." To give her puppet State the appearance of sovereignty, she duly enthroned a puppet Emperor, Mr. Henry P'u Yi, the young Manchu Emperor who had abdicated before the revolutionary armies in 1911. Till now he had been carefully treasured in the Japanese Settlement at T'ientsin. His second enthronement did him little good, for the government of China refused to recognize his so-called "Kingdom," nor has he ever enjoyed more than nominal power, being entirely under the Japanese thumb.

Since they had solidly established themselves north of the Wall, the Japanese now moved south, broke through the Wall, and invaded Hopei province from east and north, in January of 1933. They were met with brilliant resistance by the twenty-ninth army—the "Big Sword" troops [1] whose battle slogan "We are waiting for you at the Front! We shall die first, but you will follow us!" made a profound impression upon the rest of the country. The population took heart and strengthened its resolve. But the central government still hoped to settle its differences with Japan by negotiation, and on the thirtieth of May an armistice was signed by order of Nanking. Japan now occupied Chinese territory to the east of Peking.

It was a cruel blow to the whole nation. Although Peking was no longer the capital city, it was the loveliest in all China; it was an ancient home of kings; it enshrined some of the most valued historic associations, and nearly all the most splendid art treasures of the nation, accumulated through centuries. It meant to Chinese what Paris means to Frenchmen.

And yet the central government did not offer the other cheek, time and again, without good reason. When the first aggressive move was made against Manchuria, Chiang Kai-shek, in common with many other world statesmen, had sincerely believed in the efficacy of the League of Nations, and even when this potential peace instrument had failed to hinder the Japanese, he hesitated to act. On the one hand, he was still under the influence of Wang Ching-wei, whose opinion now carried considerable weight in the Kuomintang, and who consistently advocated appeasement with Japan. On the other hand, the Communist opposition in Central China had grown so formidable that Chiang was unable to move his armies North and engage the Japanese in a battle of very doubtful issue, for in so doing he would leave the southern part of China in even greater confusion. "To resist foreign aggressors, China must first be unified"—this was his constant argument. Such an attitude, reasonable though it was, could not be shared by the whole population, especially by the younger, more hot-headed elements. During these years of the Japanese advance, numbers of brilliant young men and women joined the Communists, thus increasing the central government's problems.

Meanwhile, the Japanese appetite for Chinese territory continued to grow. Her next plan was to split off the five Northern provinces of Hopei, Shantung, Shansi, Chahar, and Suiyuan from China, and or-

[1] So called from their deft use of an ancient form of sword, ornamented with scarlet tassels. The wild appearance of these weapons terrified the Japanese.

ganize them into a "North China Autonomous State" similar to "Manchukuo," and like that "puppet" State, entirely under Japanese control. She hoped to achieve this without fighting. Playing upon the personal grievance of some Northern militarists against the central government, she approached a certain General Sung Cheh-yuan, with the bribe of personal power. If he would break away from Nanking, Japan declared, she would put him at the head of the new Autonomous State and support his position with her armies. General Sung, however, proved unexpectedly patriotic, and his attitude was upheld by all his officers and soldiers. Nothing daunted by the rebuff, Japan was content to bide her time and await a more favorable chance.

Opportunity was not long in coming. In 1935, the two great Chinese rivers were again in flood, bringing such misery to so much of the population that the people had no heart for resistance. Moreover, the Abyssinian War was distracting all eyes from the Far East. Japan could exercise a free hand in China without rousing the attention of any but her victim. With little opposition she set up the bogus State of East Hopei, a small piece of territory to the east of Peking, having first won over a national traitor, Yin Ju-keng, to be its ruler.

This ushered in a heyday for Japanese smugglers. Yin Ju-keng declared the independence of the customs houses within his "territory," and as there was no fixed boundary between his bogus State and the rest of Hopei, smuggled Japanese silks, clothing, sugar, drugs, and narcotics poured into many parts of China. In the short period between February and November 1936, the income of the Chinese Customs had fallen by about $75,000,000 through this source. Since November until the outbreak of the present war, the losses were steadily mounting. Officials sent by the general Customs House to investigate the trouble were seized and even murdered by Japanese smugglers or secret agents. So serious did this illicit traffic become that even European and American merchants were affected, while a fresh irritant was offered to the already exasperated Chinese people.

With the opening of 1936, a fateful year had dawned for China. It was a year of significant events; of testing, both for the leaders and the people; the year when the first real unity was achieved, and when the Chinese nation as a whole turned resolutely at bay to face the Japanese hunter. In the course of this year, it became apparent to the Chinese leaders, though not to the thick-headed Japanese agents, that something new had come to birth. It was a national spirit. Party prejudices, local loyalties, personal ambitions, jealousies, and dissensions were at last beginning to give way before the larger spirit of patriotism and national pride. The influence of the central government began to be felt even in the provinces most remote from Nanking, while the personality of the leader, Chiang Kai-shek, having developed through fifty fateful years, was becoming the focal point of the people's loyalty. The Chinese Republic was growing up.

Although Japan failed entirely to recognize the nature of this new spirit, she could not fail to notice the growing authority of the Chinese government, and the expansion of its armed forces. Accordingly, in 1936, she made repeated overtures to the Generalissimo, offering peace in exchange for economic co-operation and the destruction of the "Communist bandits."

Chiang refused any compromise with the enemy, and Japan now demanded that he should resign, so that she might enter into peaceful negotiations with a more accommodating government. One may believe that Chiang would have conceded this, had he thought that by so doing he could have saved the country from war. But this was not to be imagined. The Japanese attacks on the person of Chiang merely had the effect of strengthening the people's confidence in him. It even caused numbers of the Chinese Communists to swing round in his favor. Japan was forging the weapons of her own discomfort.

Three major events still remained to be played out in the crucial year of 1936, before a real and complete unification could be achieved: the Liang-Kuang revolt in June, the Japanese invasion of Suiyuan in November, and the Sian incident in December.

"Liang-Kuang" is a term used for the two southern provinces of Kuangtung and Kuangsi. It may be remembered that the leading generals of these two provinces were always somewhat uncertain supporters of the Nanking regime. There can be no doubt that Japanese suggestions and bribes, offered in the desperate hope of stirring up a civil war before the central government became too strong, activated these two military leaders in their revolt of June 1936.

The general commanding the Kuangtung army was Ch'en Chi-t'ang, a type of old war-lord, and prodigiously wealthy. The atmosphere prevailing in Kuangtung military and political circles was admittedly corrupt, and the substantial sums of money which passed into Ch'en's pocket from the Japanese, together with the bait of personal power, must have persuaded him without much difficulty to raise the revolt. The case was different with Li Tsung-jen, commander of the Kuangsi army and military governor of the province. Under his administration, Kuangsi had become one of the most progressive provinces in China. Many of the leading men, while not belonging to the Communist party, tended to sympathize with the latter's call for resistance, rather than with the central government's policy. General Li himself was a clever soldier and a brilliant strategist. In the present war against Japan, it was he who led the forces at T'aierchuang in February 1938, where the Chinese won a glorious and historic victory.

His object now in marching against the government troops was to force the central government into resisting the Japanese advance in the North, and under this battle-cry these two very divergent characters, Ch'en Chi-t'ang and Li Tsung-jen, joined their armies and began to march towards Hunan and Kiangsi. It was afterwards discovered that the Kuangsi leaders had been supplied with war material by Japanese agents on condition that they would start a mutiny against the central government, no matter in what name.

It is even now not clear how serious was the intention of the two leaders to start a large-scale civil war—an event that would have inevitably laid the country open to a disastrous Japanese invasion. The new spirit of national loyalty in the people, and even in these two armies, together with the personality and assurances of Chiang Kai-shek himself, brought the revolt to a rapid conclusion. A divisional commander of the Kuangtung army declared his loyalty to the central government, and refused to lead his men against it, while General Li of the Kuangsi army, having been persuaded to meet Chiang Kai-shek in conference, was so sincerely convinced of the latter's intention to resist Japan at the appointed moment, that he immediately transferred his support to the central government together with the services of his men—and the Japanese ammunition!

Thus were the Japanese machinations foiled in China. She now returned to her old quarry in the North, where she had hitherto won such easy successes. Since, however, she had failed to tempt the northern leaders into deserting the central government and forming a "North China Autonomous State," she turned her attentions to the Northwest, with the object of building a Japanese-sponsored Mongol empire. If she could achieve this, she dreamed of penetrating even farther west and south, and of creating a Japanese-sponsored "Mohammedan Empire" on the huge, undeveloped Chinese provinces of Sinkiang, Ch'ing-hai, and Kansu. In this way Central China would be practically encircled from east, north, and west, and the path would be opened for Japan's advance into Asia.

The leading figure in the opening stages of this plot was the Mongol nobleman Prince Teh. Prince Teh had some personal grievance against the Chinese government, and accordingly offered a very willing ear to

Japanese agents with their whispers of a new Mongol empire, of which he would be crowned Emperor. Already in May of 1936 he was persuaded to send his small army, considerably augmented by Chinese bandits, deserters from the Jehol campaign in 1932 and armed by the Japanese, into the vast plains of Northern Chahar. There Japan created a "Mongol Military Government." With this as a base, Japan hoped to advance and overrun the two adjacent provinces of Suiyuan and Ninghsia.

In order that her operations might not be too greatly hindered, Japan ordered her ambassador in China to hold "peace talks" with the Nanking government. The Chinese northern garrisons were therefore instructed to act only on the defensive, for fear of hindering negotiations. The Japanese forces were thus able to retreat in perfect safety wherever they suffered a local set-back, and advance steadily whenever the chance occurred. However, in the second attack on Suiyuan, in which the Japanese were rebuffed, the Chinese forces took the matter into their own hands, and not only pursued the retreating enemy, but recaptured two strategic points that had long since fallen into enemy hands. This unexpected victory of the Chinese called a halt to the Suiyuan campaign late in November, and so the situation remained until the outbreak of the Sino-Japanese War.

A month later came the incident at Sian, which has already been fully described. In the solution of this crisis, the Communists agreed to relinquish their extreme policy, such as the appropriation of land and wealth, while the central government expressed its determination to protect the integrity of China at all costs. All the progressive elements had been united at the desire of the people, and at a time of national crisis.

Japan was seriously alarmed, and with good reason. These events spelled the end of her tricks and conspiracies, with their object of dividing the country against itself. And the unification of four hundred and fifty million people provides a formidable challenge to any neighboring country conscious of its guilty past.

China has been frequently accused by Japan of "provoking" a war. No Western reader can hold any doubts nowadays of the true aggressor. Even though China had strengthened herself in a remarkable way, she was still, militarily, far weaker than Japan, and had no possible reason to provoke an invasion. It would be just as ridiculous to suppose that Abyssinia, Albania, Czechoslovakia, or Poland had madly driven Italy and Germany to war against them through the menace they offered to these two strongly armed powers!

Incidents, quarrels, cases of missing Japanese subjects were innumerable in the year or two before the outbreak of war. Japan was always hopeful of making some one of them a cause for opening hostilities. But the truth about them came embarrassingly to light, supported by photographs and signed documents. There was, for example, the interesting case of the Japanese Vice-Consul Muramoto at Nanking, who mysteriously disappeared in 1935. The government at Tokyo declared he had been murdered by the Chinese and threatened immediate reprisals. It seemed that the loss of this diplomat was about to start a major war. However, an exhaustive search resulted in his being discovered among the "Purple-and-Golden Hills," in the suburbs of Nanking. On being questioned by the police, he confessed to having received secret orders from his government to commit suicide, so that the Japanese war machine might proceed to action. He had heard that wild animals—wolves and leopards—haunted these hills, and had made up his mind to let himself be devoured by them! Such were the naïve devices which Japan employed to ensnare her would-be victim.

The first clash at the Marco Polo bridge, outside the town of Wanp'ing, near Peking, which set China ablaze and ushered in the present national war between China and Japan, was itself clearly engineered by the Japanese, as will be disclosed in the chapter that follows.

XXXI. THE WAR AND THE FUTURE

THE GREAT WAR between China and Japan which broke out in July of 1937 sprang from one of those many "border incidents" taking place between free Chinese territory and the Japanese occupied areas in North China, of which Japan herself was the instigator. For some time past, she had illegally stationed a garrison in Hopei province, very close to the barracks of the Chinese twenty-ninth army. This was the army commanded by General Sung Cheh-yuan which had held out so gallantly against the Japanese invasion of East Hopei in 1933. It was an army of patriots to whom the proximity of foreign troops was both irksome and odious. The Japanese soldiers encamped nearby behaved with characteristic insolence, and treated the Chinese like an enemy already beaten on the field. The Hopei provincial authorities, having adopted a policy of conciliation towards Japan, forced these patriots to endure every humiliation without retort. The army nursed its anger but was unable to smother it.

On July 6, 1937, the Japanese troops held a military maneuver outside the town of Wanp'ing, not far from Peking. On returning at dusk, they found one of their force was "missing," and immediately declared that he had been kidnaped by the Chinese soldiers. Although the "missing" man duly reported himself some hours later, the Japanese insisted on forming a Committee of Chinese and Japanese delegates "to settle the permanent disturbances between the two armies." The Japanese delegates then demanded the withdrawal of the Chinese garrisons from Wanp'ing—an order that was properly refused. The Japanese forces thereupon opened fire on the strategic bridge leading to Wanp'ing, the marble bridge of Marco Polo or the Lukou Ch'iao (the Ditch-of-Weeds bridge). The Chinese garrisons returned fire in good earnest. The long expected war had begun!

It was very clear that the whole "incident" had been arranged by Japan: that the soldier had purposely been ordered to absent himself, and that deliberately unacceptable demands had been laid before the committee. The central government, quickly realizing that this was the start of a major war, ordered General Sung Cheh-yuan to evacuate

Peking, with his forces, and to proceed to Paoting, a little to the south along the railway. He was to direct military operations from there. Sung hesitated, but in order to save the ancient capital from becoming a battleground he retired on the night of July 29. The enemy marched in quietly, "without inflicting any war damage on this most civilized city of China."

Peking, capital of the former Manchu dynasty, was of strategic importance as the railhead of the first railway systems to be established in China. Once in possession of the city, the Japanese armies began a drive in three directions, following the main lines. The first push was along the Peking-Suiyuan railway towards the provinces of Chahar, Suiyuan, and Shansi; the second along the Peking-Hankow railway towards Shansi and Honan; and the third along the T'ientsin-P'ukow railway towards Shantung and Kiangsu. The final objectives of the three movements were the important cities of Sian, Hankow, and Nanking respectively.

The drive west towards Chahar made easy and rapid progress. In the initial stages, Japan reaped the fruits of her long and patient labor to detach the Northern generals from the central government. General Liu Ju-ming, Chairman of the Chahar Provincial Government, having received the specious offer of Japanese "friendship," opened a vital Pass, leading from Hopei into Chahar, to the advancing armies. Japan marched on unimpeded, occupied Kalgan and other strategic towns in Chahar, then turned south, still following the railway, into Shansi province. The important town of Tat'ung, a city famous throughout the world for its Buddhist sculpture, dating from the third century, fell with hardly a struggle. Meanwhile, a second large force, which had proceeded due south from Peking along the Peking-Hankow railway, turned off at Chengting on to a branch line leading west into Shansi. The pincer movement effected by these forces in collaboration with the forces holding Tat'ung resulted in the seizure of the Shansi capital of T'aiyuan.

The third prong of the Japanese fork, moving east from Peking into Shantung province, also scored an initial success. Shantung was defended by the army of a national traitor, Han Fu-chu. He too was offered Japanese "friendship," and steadily withdrew his troops, allowing Japan to occupy Northern Shantung without opposition. Han's treachery, however, was discovered: he was arrested by a deputy of the central government, sent to Hankow, court-martialed, and shot. The blood of Han Fu-chu wrote the last page in the history of the Chinese war-lords and the Japanese intrigues with Chinese militarists.

In addition to this Northern campaign, Japan started a central battle-front by attacking Shanghai on August 13 of the same year. She accompanied the action of her troops with heavy and ruthless bombardment of civilians on the usual Fascist model. The Chinese forces put up a tough and heroic resistance, but heavily outnumbered, especially in planes and mechanized divisions, they were obliged to withdraw after two months' fighting. The Japanese army proceeded up the Yangtzu valley, and a month later occupied Nanking, the Chinese government having previously withdrawn to the safety of Chungking. In China's modern capital, Japanese soldiers committed the foulest atrocities that have yet been recorded in the annals of modern warfare.

From Nanking, a part of the Japanese army turned northwards along the Peking-P'ukow railway, and there they met their first smashing defeat at the battle of T'aierchuang, on the borders of Shantung and Kiangsu provinces. These divisions were later reinforced, and effected a junction at Hsuchou, an important town where the Peking-P'ukow and Lunghai railway systems joined. Another part of the forces occupying Nanking proceeded westward up the Yangtzu to attack the last large city in Central China, the important industrial center of Hankow.

In the South, Japan had formerly hesitated to strike for fear of becoming involved with the British authorities at Hong-Kong, and the British fleet patrolling its waters. The great city of Canton, separated from Hong-Kong by only a small stretch of water, controlled one of the remaining vital arteries for the defense of Central China: the Canton-Hankow Railway. However, the Munich Conference of September 1938 allayed Japan's immediate fears. Believing that Britain, in the steadfast pursuit of appeasement, would offer no hindrance to Japan in the Far East, Japan sent her fleet into Bias Bay and captured Canton—the prize of the South.

Hankow, already within fire of the Japanese guns on the Yangtzu, could not hope to hold out now that reinforcements might no longer be brought up from the South. Chiang Kai-shek accordingly ordered the evacuation of the city, to avoid the useless destruction of his armies.

After this series of comparatively easy victories, and the fall of almost every large city, Japan declared triumphantly that Chinese resistance had "collapsed." On the contrary, since the occupation of Hankow, the Japanese have made no more important advances, while the Chinese fighting power has steadily grown, and with it the confidence of the nation. The only notable gains since Hankow were Nanch'ang and Ich'ang in Central China, and Nanning in the South, the last of which, however, has since been retaken by Chinese forces. On the other hand,

Japan has suffered blow after blow in every sector, her heaviest losses being in the surroundings of Ch'angsha and Nanning.

Ever since the outbreak of war, the Chinese General Staff knew that in order to conquer the enemy, hostilities must be made to last the longest possible time. The Japanese armies must be drawn deeper and deeper into the country, farther and farther from their sources of supply; they must be lured beyond the limits of the railways and the good main roads; they must be dispersed, enticed into the mountains, there to be harassed and demoralized by Chinese guerrilla fighters. They must be made to spend money, men, and instruments of war until they grew bankrupt of one or all of them. The Chinese therefore avoided fighting in the plains and river valleys. Although their armies had more men and better spirit, they lacked the tanks and heavy guns essential to open warfare. In particular, the guns of the Japanese warships, easily brought up the lower reaches of China's great rivers, wrought fearful havoc on the many riverside towns. To have attempted to hold the large towns, situated as most of them are on the sea coast or along the Yangtzu River, would have proved too costly, and would ultimately have availed the Chinese little. The evacuation, therefore, of one city after another in the first phase of the war was simply a matter of strategy, and although it seemed at the time a cause for dismay, we now realize the wisdom of it.

It will have been observed from this brief outline of the first and most spectacular phase of the war, that Japan's rapid advance from one province to another was only possible for her through gaining control of the railway lines. Although China had been busily extending her communications in the few years before the outbreak of war, she had, relative to the area of the country, very few railways, and these all connected with the most important towns. But on the other hand, mere possession of a long strip of metal, and the few centers with which it is punctuated, does not imply the conquest of an almost immeasurably great country like China. The Japanese are certainly learning the truth of this. Although they have attempted to set up their own administration in every supposedly "conquered" province, very rarely have they been able to maintain one. Mysterious assassinations and disappearances occur among the higher officials, who are no match for the hatred and self-sacrifice of Chinese patriots. And it is well known that the Japanese garrisons are afraid to venture more than a mile or two from each bank of the railway on which they are stationed, for fear of meeting the Chinese guerrilla bands. It is manifestly impossible to conquer China in this way: the country is too large!

It seems also that China is too populous for Japan to swallow. She has five times the population of her opponent, and even if she loses five men to every one of the enemy, the balance has still not turned against her. If the proportion of losses is more equal, Japan can hardly win. In point of fact, although the Chinese casualties in the Shanghai battle were appallingly high, since the fall of Hankow the losses of both belligerents became almost equal—a fact that obviously weighs very heavily in China's favor. It has even been reported that in a certain period of guerrilla fighting in Shansi province, the losses were fourteen to one against the Japanese! From these observations it will be seen that time, space, and man-power are all working in favor of the Chinese arms.

Chiang Kai-shek once declared that the war in China would be waged in three phases. The first phase, ending with the evacuation of Hankow, would be of a defensive character. It was, in fact, a period of repeated withdrawals from certain selected areas for strategic reasons, and to save unnecessary loss. The second phase, said the Generalissimo, would consist in guerrilla fighting. The guerrilla bands would be formed of the local peasantry, irregulars, and also parts of the regular army: their operations would be controlled from headquarters and their objectives selected. During this phase, increasingly heavy losses would be inflicted on the Japanese, who would be prevented everywhere from consolidating their gains, and would be forced to spend a great deal of man-power and war materials without making any appreciable progress. Moreover, the morale of the Japanese soldiers, who fight well in a sharp engagement but have none of the patient endurance of the Chinese, would gradually break down. In the third phase, the Chinese armies, having built up their strength, especially in the mechanized divisions, would turn against the weakened and dispirited invader, and thrust him back into the sea.

Hostilities during the second phase can be neither decisive nor spectacular, but they are unquestionably effective. From those cities which the Chinese prepared to evacuate, industrial plant, machinery, and factory equipment were removed to the interior beforehand, according to plan. When the city had been emptied, communications and important buildings were systematically destroyed, so that nothing of any significance was left for the invading hordes. After the evacuation of Hankow, for example, Chinese sappers began a methodical destruction of communications which might be used by the advancing enemy. Sections of road were blown up, foot-paths across the fields were dug over and camouflaged. Outstanding trees were hewn down and set up in different places, artificial hills were thrown up, traps and hidden trenches dug. The natural scenery all the way from the mountains west of Hankow to the sea east of Hangchou, in the areas through which the Japanese armies would travel, was mysteriously changed by the hand of man! This is a part of what is called the "scorched earth policy"—a policy which naturally included the more obvious expedient of burning down crops and homesteads to deprive the enemy of food.

The main characteristic of this phase—guerrilla fighting—is a form of warfare in which the Chinese with their comparative lack of modern equipment, their knowledge of the country, their ingenuity and endurance, have particularly excelled. And in this field, the former "Red Army" reorganized into the Eighth and the Fourth Route armies, and working under a central control, has played a valuable part. The Eighth Route Army, operating from its former headquarters in the Northwest, moved into Shansi province early in the war and engaged the Japanese forces there, winning several major battles. The defense of Shansi proved to be of the utmost importance: it prevented the enemy from pushing on westward to capture Sian—a movement that would have laid the Chinese wartime capital of Chungking open to attack from the North. Having gained a substantial foothold in Shansi, the Eighth Route Army extended its guerrilla activities eastward towards the Yellow Sea and Manchuria, and northward towards the borders of Outer Mongolia. Thus in the North, where Japan had formerly met with the weakest resistance, and where she had hoped to establish her influence permanently, she found her position even more tenuous than in other parts of the country. In Central China, the Fourth Army once waged guerrilla warfare over the vast area between Hankow and the seashore to the east.

As time went on, the great peasant population of China became roused to organized resistance and assisted the armies in irregular fighting. In this fact lies one of China's main hopes for victory. The Japanese, indeed, have mainly themselves to thank for this new and sharp thorn in their side. To have stirred a naturally phlegmatic, easygoing, and largely uneducated section of the people into a furious opposition, points to brutality, vandalism, and inhuman conduct on the part of the Japanese soldiery. The Chinese peasants were a peace-loving people. In their hearts they hated the war; they dreaded the overrunning of their fields by the opposing armies, and the added hardships of a wartime existence. They loved their homes; they loved their small plots of land—the "good earth" which their forefathers had tilled before them.

At the outbreak of war, thousands of these little homesteads passed into the Japanese-occupied area. Still, if their new overlords had left them unmolested to continue their inoffensive activities of raising crops and tending cattle, the peasantry might have felt no bitterness against the invader. But the Japanese behaved with an insane brutality. The peasants saw their beloved cottages needlessly set on fire, their fields devastated, their granaries robbed, their cattle slaughtered. With horrified eyes they were obliged to look on while their mothers, wives, sisters, and daughters were shamelessly violated. The true Chinese values the chastity of his women above everything else, and this was not the first time in Chinese history that wholesale violation had led to the offenders' downfall. Nine hundred years before, this same crime committed by the Liao officials on the women of the Chin tribe in North China had caused the young men of Chin to rise and overthrow the Liao empire. A century later, the Chins repeated the same error against the Mongolian women, and their empire was in turn overthrown by the rising Mongols. In the present war for freedom, the unrestrained license of the invader has been the best possible instrument of propaganda in uniting the masses against the common enemy.

Hundreds of ingenious and heroic guerrilla exploits could be recorded. In general the guerrilla troops do not encourage villagers to leave their homes: for this type of fighting the men need the food and shelter which the villagers can best provide. By staying quietly at home, they can also supply valuable information about enemy movements. Heroic stories from the main battle-fronts are also too numerous to start recounting. There was the general who shot himself rather than fall into enemy hands; there were pilots who, having baled out and found themselves surrounded by the enemy, have fought with only a pistol until they themselves were killed, rather than surrender. There are also many records, made by eye-witnesses, of the famous "human shells"—suicide soldiers who have wrapped themselves in explosives and rolled themselves in the path of advancing enemy tanks. In the bitter defense of Nankow Pass, northwest of Peking, ten thousand soldiers gave up their lives rather than fall back before the enemy's mechanized columns. Such is the spirit of the Chinese today.

Japan had made repeated peace overtures, all of which China had steadfastly rejected. Japan attempted once more to set the Chinese against each other. Unfortunately, it seems that Quislings will be found in any country, to play the traitor at times of national crisis. During 1937, Japan was able to set up a puppet government in the North under Wang K'e-min, with headquarters at Peking, and another in Central

China at Nanking, under Liang Shih-i, nicknamed "the Mammon." Both traitors were notorious remnants of the old war-lord regime of Peking. A little later, Japan decided that to unite these two governments under a single head would present a more impressive picture of a strong and stable Japanese-controlled regime operating over a large part of China. The old General Wu P'ei-fu, former bitter opponent of Chiang Kai-shek, who had once governed important regions of the North and the Yangtzu valley, and whose name was known and respected by the population, seemed the most suitable candidate. But Wu proved himself a true patriot, and stood adamant against bribe and threat. He died soon after, poisoned, it is said, by the Japanese, but he lives in the gratitude of his fellow-countrymen.

In contrast with this patriotism of an old soldier who was once a war-lord, stands Wang Ching-wei, an original member of the Revolutionary Party, and former idol of the young revolutionaries. He it was, to his eternal infamy, who resolved Japan's anxieties. After a million of his countrymen had fallen in the struggle for national freedom, Wang Ching-wei—"the Old Fox" as he was nicknamed—fled from the Chinese government at Chungking to Annam, and thence to Hong-Kong and Shanghai. Eventually he agreed to set up a government at Nanking. He signed a pact with Japan to the effect that all the resources of the country should be exploited by the conquerors to develop the economic bloc of Chung-Jih-Man (China-Japan-"Manchukuo"), and that Japan might co-operate with the Chinese puppets to wipe out "Bolshevik influence" from China. It is strange to reflect that this Wang Ching-wei was once leader of the Communist-supported Wuhan government, and that Japan had expressed her extreme gratification at a pact with Russia!

Wang Ching-wei's treacherous act has done very little to alter the general situation; it has certainly not affected in any way the determination of the Chinese people under Chiang Kai-shek's leadership to fight the war to a finish. To come to terms with our mortal enemy would spell death for us as a nation, and entail the domination of all Eastern Asia by a brutal militarist power. I need only quote two authoritative statements made by Japanese spokesmen in support of this assertion. The first is from the famous Tanaka Memorandum, drawn up in 1927 and presented to the Japanese Emperor by Baron Tanaka, then Prime Minister of Japan. Some extracts from it run:

"Evidently Divine Providence wishes me to assist Your Majesty in ushering in a new era for the Far East, and in developing a new continental empire.

"If we succeed in conquering China, all other Asiatic countries in the South Seas will capitulate before us, and the world will then understand that Eastern Asia is ours, and will not dare to encroach upon our rights. . . .

"Having the resources of China at our command, we shall proceed to conquer India, the Archipelago, Asia Minor, Central Asia, and even Europe.

"Our seizure of control in Manchuria and Mongolia is the first step."

The second interesting quotation is from the book "Japanese Agent in China," by the Italian writer who signs himself "Ameleto Vespa." "Vespa" had worked for fifteen years in Manchuria before the Japanese occupation of 1931, and subsequently became, against his will, a Japanese agent. He managed finally to escape to Shanghai, where he wrote his authoritative book, bringing to light the black nature of the Japanese. This is what a high Japanese official told him:

"Our culture is sacred, and likewise sacred is everything Japanese. We have no intention of imparting our civilization to the people whom we have conquered or shall conquer. They will simply disappear. The Koreans will be eaten by vice; the Chinese will be the victims of opium and narcotics; the Russians will be ruined by vodka. They will all be annihilated."

So much for Japan's much-vaunted "civilizing mission" in Asia. And how closely it resembles the utterances of the "Aryan" Dictator, in its arrogance, its insane racial pride, its pagan boasting! It was not, however, a baseless vaunt on the part of the Japanese official, as facts have proved. In the countryside of occupied China, the Japanese have persuaded Chinese farmers to plant opium instead of their normal, healthy food of kaoliang and millet. In the towns, Chinese children have been compelled to learn Japanese script, and to study forged history, while their parents are induced to spend their time in public houses smoking opium, taking narcotic injections, gambling, drinking, and whoring. Such a life will gradually destroy their bodies and souls.

It is clear that China must fight Japan in order to survive. It is unfair, therefore, for those few writers in democratic England to protest, against the opinion of their more understanding countrymen, that Japan's invasion is justified on the plea of *lebensraum*. There is no truth in the assertion. Between 1895 and the outbreak of the present war in 1937, Japan had already filched from China, Korea and the Liukiu protectorates, the provinces of Formosa, Liaoning, Chilin, Heilung-chiang (the three provinces of Manchuria), Jehol, and parts of Hopei and Chahar, with their virgin soils and forests, their world-famous production of soya beans, their ideal pastureland for cattle, their gold, iron, coal, sugar, rice, and other yet unexploited treasures. In addition, the Japanese had won from Russia half the island of Sakhalin with its world-famous fishing ports, and by the League of Nations had been intrusted with the mandate of several strategic islands in the Pacific. All these territories put together, and including Japan, are equal to prewar France, Germany, Italy, and Great Britain put together, and they are much richer in natural resources than these great European countries! It can hardly be argued that Japan is being deprived of the fruits of the earth, or that her people have no room to live.

It is not yet possible to prophesy when and in what manner this war will end, but I can express my sincere belief in the final victory of freedom-loving people over the dictator countries. The four powers, America and Britain, Russia and China, in alliance with the other democratic peoples can end the war triumphantly and build a brave new world. Faith and honesty, understanding and unselfishness are the foundations of permanent friendship between individuals, as well as between nations. The whole world is looking to us, and we must not fail.

China, as a nation of a most ancient and a very young spirit, has a history that deserves attention. From it we may judge that the Chinese form of culture will enrich future humanity, and that for China herself great hopes lie ahead. There are also grave obstacles to overcome: the reconstruction of the country on the ruins of war, and various deep-rooted doctrinal controversies. Nevertheless, we Chinese are a tolerant people. Our ancestors received many different faiths from foreign lands such as Buddhism, Mohammedanism, and Christianity; our open-minded acceptance of all kinds of foreign beliefs has been unrivaled in the world. Shall the present generation be any less tolerant of political faiths? Any doctrine that will be a blessing to the nation will be supported by the people, and what is supported by the people in a democratic way must be adopted by the nation. We naturally look abroad for collaboration with our friends and allies. Britain and Russia are our great neighbors on land, and the American people, with whom throughout our history we have maintained friendship, cannot be separated from us even though the mighty Pacific Ocean rolls between!

NOTE.—The Wade System of transcription of Chinese names is used in the Appendices. But in the text I have omitted, for the convenience of readers, some of its complicated signs.

APPENDIX I

TABLES OF DYNASTIES

1. "The Five Sovereigns (*)."

Dynastic Title	Accession B.C.
*Huang Ti (The Yellow Emperor)	2697
Shao Hao	2597
*Chuan Hsü	2513
*Ti K'u	2435
Ti Chih	2365
*Yao (T'ang Yao)	2357
*Shun (Yü Shun)	2255

2. The Hsia Dynasty, 2205–1766 B.C. Family name: Shih.

	B.C.
Yü, The Great	2205
Ch'i	2197
T'ai K'ang	2188
Chung K'ang	2159
Hsiang	2146
Shao K'ang	2118
Ch'u	2057
Huai	2040
Mang	2014
Hsieh	1996
Pu Chiang	1980
Chiung	1921
Chin	1900
K'ung Chia	1879
Kao	1848
Fa	1837
Chieh	1818

3. The Shang or Yin Dynasty, 1766–1122 B.C. Family name: Tzŭ. Capitals: Po, Nao, Yin.

	B.C.
T'ang	1766
T'ai Chia	1753

Dynastic Title	Accession
	B.C.
Wu Ting	1720
Ta Kêng	1691
Hsiao Chia	1666
Yung Chi	1649
T'ai Wu	1637
Chung Ting	1562
Wai Jên	1549
Ho T'an Chia	1534
Tsu I	1525
Tsu Hsin	1506
Wu Chia	1490
Tsu Ting	1465
Nan Kêng	1433
Yang Chia	1408
P'an Kêng	1401
Hsiao Hsin	1373
Hsiao I	1352
Wu Ting	1324
Tsu Kêng	1265
Tsu Chia	1258
Lin Hsin	1225
Kêng Ting	1219
Wu I	1198
T'ai Ting	1194
Ti I	1191
Shou (Chou Hsin)	1154

4. THE CHOU DYNASTY, 1122–255 B.C. Family name: Chi. Capitals: Fêng (1122–771), Loyang (770–255).

	B.C.
Wu Wang	1122
Ch'êng Wang	1115
K'ang Wang	1078
Chao Wang	1052
Mu Wang	1001
Kung Wang	946
I Wang	934
Hsiao Wang	909
Yi Wang	894
Li Wang	878
Hsüan Wang	827
Yu Wang	781
P'ing Wang	770

Dynastic Title		Accession
		B.C.
Huan Wang	. . . .	719
Chuang Wang	. . . . . .	696
Hsi Wang	. . . .	681
Hui Wang	. . . .	676
Hsiang Wang	. . . . . .	651
Ch'ing Wang	. . . . . .	618
K'uang Wang	. . . . . .	612
Ting Wang	. . . . . .	606
Chien Wang	. . . . . .	585
Ling Wang	. . . . . .	571
Ching Wang	. . . . . .	544
Ching Wang	. . . . . .	519
Yüan Wang	. . . . . .	475
Chên Ting Wang	. . . .	468
K'ao Wang	. . . . . .	440
Wei Lieh Wang	. . . .	425
An Wang	. . . .	401
Lieh Wang	. . . . . .	375
Hsien Wang	. . . . . .	368
Shên Ching Wang	. . . .	320
Nan Wang	. . . . . .	314
Tung Chou Chün (Duke of Eastern Chou)	.	255

5. THE CH'IN DYNASTY, 255–206 B.C. Family name: Ying. Capital: Hsien Yang.

		B.C.
Chao Hsiang Wang	. . . . .	306
Hsiao Wên Wang	. . . .	250
Chuang Hsiang Wang	. . . .	250
Shih Huang Ti	. . . . . .	246
Erh Shih Huang Ti	. . . .	209
Tsŭ Ying	. . . . . .	207

6. THE HAN DYNASTY, 208 B.C.–A.D. 220. Family name: Liu. Capitals: Ch'angan (208 B.C.–A.D. 25), Loyang (A.D. 25–220).

Dynastic Title	Accession	Title of Reign and Its Adoption
	B.C.	
Kao Ti (Liu Pang)	206	
Hui Ti . .	194	
Kao Hou (Empress Lü, of Kao Ti) .	187	
		B.C.
Wên Ti . .	179	Hou Yüan . . 163

Dynastic Title	Accession B.C.	Title of Reign and Its Adoption	B.C.
Ching Ti . .	156	Chung Yüan	149
		Hou Yüan	143
Wu Ti . .	140	Chien Yüan	140
		Yüan Kuang	134
		Yüan So	128
		Yüan Shou	122
		Yüan Ting	116
		Yüan Fêng	110
		T'ai Ch'u	104
		T'ien Han	100
		T'ai Shih	96
		Chêng Ho	92
		Hou Yüan	88
Chao Ti . .	86	Shih Yüan	86
		Yüan Fêng	80
		Yüan P'ing	74
Hsüan Ti . .	73	Pên Shih	73
		Ti Chieh	69
		Yüan K'ang	65
		Shên Chüeh	61
		Wu Fêng	57
		Kan Lu	53
		Huang Lung	49
Yüan Ti . .	48	Ch'u Yüan	48
		Yung Kuang	43
		Chien Chao	38
		Ching Ning	33
Ch'êng Ti . .	32	Chien Shih	32
		Ho P'ing	28
		Yang So	24
		Hung Chia	20
		Yung Shih	16
		Yüan Yen	12
		Sui Ho	8
Ai Ti . . .	6	Chien P'ing	6
		Yüan Shou	2
	A.D.		A.D.
P'ing Ti . .	1	Yüan Shih	1
Ju Tzŭ Ying . .	6	Chü Shê	6
		Ch'u Shih	8
(*Hsin* Mang) .	9	Chien Kuo	9
		T'ien Fêng	14
		Ti Huang	20

Dynastic Title	Accession A.D.	Title of Reign and Its Adoption	A.D.
(Huai Yang Wang)	23	Kêng Shih	23
Kuang Wu Ti .	25	Chien Wu	25
		Chung Yüan	56
Ming Ti . .	58	Yung P'ing	58
Chang Ti . .	76	Chien Ch'u	76
		Yüan Ho	84
		Chang Ho	87
Ho Ti . . .	89	Yung Yüan	89
		Yüan Hsing	105
Shang Ti . .	106	Yen P'ing	106
An Ti . . .	107	Yung Ch'u	107
		Yüan Ch'u	114
		Yung Ning	120
		Chien Yüan	121
		Yen Kuang	122
Shun Ti . .	126	Yung Chien	126
		Yang Chia	132
		Yung Ho	136
		Han An	142
		Chien K'ang	144
Ch'ung Ti . .	145	Yung Chia	145
Chih Ti . .	146	Pên Ch'u	146
Huan Ti . .	147	Chien Ho	147
		Ho P'ing	150
		Yüan Chia	151
		Yung Hsing	153
		Yung Shou	155
		Yen Hsi	158
		Yung K'ang	168
Ling Ti . .	168	Chien Ning	168
		Hsi P'ing	172
		Kuang Ho	178
		Chung P'ing	184
Shao Ti . .	189	Kuang Hsi	189
		Chao Ning	189
Hsien Ti . .	189	Yung Han	189
		Chung P'ing	189
		Ch'u P'ing	190
		Hsing P'ing	194
		Chien An	196
		Yen K'ang	220

7. SAN KUO (The Epoch of The Three Kingdoms), WEI, A.D. 220–265; SHU-HAN, A.D. 221–264; WU, A.D. 229–280. Family names: *Wei*, Ts'ao; *Shu-Han*, Liu; *Wu*, Sun. Capitals: *Wei*, Loyang; *Shu-Han*, Ch'êngtu; *Wu*, Nanking.

Dynastic Title	Accession A.D.	Title of Reign and Its Adoption	A.D.
Wei Wên Ti	220	Huang Ch'u	220
Shu-Han Chao Lieh Ti	221	Chuang Wu	221
Wu Ta Ti	222	Huang Wu	222
		Huang Lung	229
		Chia Ho	232
		Ch'ih Wu	238
		T'ai Yüan	251
		Shên Fêng	252
Shu-Han Ssŭ Ti (Hou Chu)	223	Chien Hsing	223
		Yen Hsi	238
		Ching Yao	258
		Yen Hsing	263
Wei Ming Ti	227	T'ai Ho	227
		Ch'ing Lung	233
		Ching Ch'u	237
Wei Fei Ti	240	Chêng Shih	240
		Chia P'ing	249
Wu Fei Ti	252	Chien Hsing	252
		Wu Fêng	254
		T'ai P'ing	256
Wei Shao Ti	254	Chêng Yüan	254
		Kan Lu	256
Wu Ching Ti	258	Yung An	258
Wei Yüan Ti	260	Ching Yüan	260
		Hsien Hsi	264
Wu Mo Ti	264	Yüan Hsing	264
		Kan Lu	265
		Pao Ting	266
		Chien Hêng	269
		Fêng Huang	272
		T'ien T'sê	275
		T'ien Hsi	276
		T'ien Chi	277

8. THE TSIN (CHIN) DYNASTY, A.D. 265–420. Family name: Ssŭ-ma. Capitals: Ch'angan and Loyang (265–316), Nanking (317–420).

Dynastic Title	Accession A.D.	Title of Reign and Its Adoption	A.D.
Wu Ti . . .	265	T'ai Shih	265
		Hsien Ning	275
		T'ai K'ang	280
		T'ai Hsi	290
Hui Ti . . .	290	Yung Hsi	290
		Yung P'ing	291
		Yüan K'ang	291
		Yung K'ang	300
		Yung Ning	301
		T'ai An	302
		Yung An	304
		Chien Wu	304
		Yung Hsing	304
		Kuang Hsi	306
Huai Ti . . .	307	Yung Chia	307
Min Ti . . .	313	Chien Hsing	313
Yüan Ti (*E. Tsin*)	317	Chien Wu	317
		T'ai Hsing	318
		Yung Ch'ang	322
Ming Ti . .	323	T'ai Ning	323
Ch'êng Ti . .	326	Hsien Ho	326
		Hsien K'ang	335
K'ang Ti . .	343	Chien Yüan	343
Mu Ti . . .	345	Yung Ho	345
		Shêng P'ing	357
Ai Ti . . .	362	Lung Ho	362
		Hsing Ning	363
Ti I (Hai Hsi Kung)	366	T'ai Ho	366
Chien Wen Ti .	371	Hsien An	371
Hsiao Wu Ti .	373	Ning K'ang	373
		T'ai Yüan	376
An Ti . . .	397	Lung An	397
		Yüan Hsing	402
		Lung An	402
		Ta Hsiang	402
		Yüan Hsing	403
		I Hsi	405
Kung Ti . .	419	Yüan Hsi	419

9. THE SOUTHERN DYNASTIES, A.D. 420–589. Family names: *Sung*, Liu; *Ch'i*, Hsiao; *Liang*, Hsiao; *Ch'ên*, Ch'ên. Capitals: Nanking (420–589), and Chiang Ling (502–589).

Dynastic Title	Accession A.D.	Title of Reign and Its Adoption A.D.	
Sung Wu Ti	420	Yung Ch'u	420
Shao Ti	423	Ching P'ing	423
Wên Ti	424	Yüan Chia	424
Hsiao Wu Ti	454	Hsiao Chien	454
		Ta Ming	457
		Yung Kuang	465
Fei Ti	465	Ching Ho	465
Ming Ti	465	T'ai Shih	465
		T'ai Yü	472
Fei Ti (Ts'ang-wu Wang)	473	Yüan Hui	473
Shun Ti	477	Shêng Ming	477
Ch'i Kao Ti	479	Chien Yüan	479
Wu Ti	482	Yung Ming	483
Yü-Ling Wang	493	Lung Ch'ang	494
Hai-Ling Wang	494	Yen Hsing	494
Ming Ti	494	Chien Wu	494
		Yung T'ai	498
Tung Hun Hou	498	Yung Yüan	499
Ho Ti	501	Chung Hsing	501
Liang Wu Ti	502	T'ien Chien	502
		P'u T'ung	520
		Ta T'ung	527
		Chung Ta T'ung	529
		Ta T'ung	535
		Chung Ta T'ung	546
		T'ai Ch'ing	547
Chien Wên Ti	549	Ta Pao	550
Yü-Chang Wang	551	T'ien Chêng	551
Yüan Ti	552	Ch'êng Shêng	552
Chêng-Yang Hou	555	T'ien Ch'êng	555
Ching Ti	555	Shao T'ai	555
		T'ai P'ing	556
Ch'ên Wu Ti	557	Yung Ting	557
Wên Ti	560	T'ien Chia	560
		T'ien K'ang	566
Lin-Hai Wang	567	Kuang Ta	567
Hsüan Ti	569	Ta Chien	569
Hou Chu	583	Chih Têh	583
		Ch'êng Ming	587

10. The Northern Dynasties, A.D. 386–581. Family names: *Northern Wei*, Toba and "Yüan"; *Western Wei*, Toba; *Northern Ch'i*, Kao; *Northern Chou*, Yü-wên; *Eastern Wei*, Toba. Capitals: Tat'ung (N. Wei, 386–493) and Loyang (N. Wei, 493–535); K'aifêng (E. Wei, 534–550); Yeh (N. Ch'i 550–577); Ch'angan (W. Wei and N. Chou, 535–581).

Dynastic Title	*Accession* A.D.	*Title of Reign and Its Adoption*	A.D.
N. *Wei* Tao Wu Ti	386	Têng Kuo	386
		Huang Shih	396
		T'ien Hsing	398
		T'ien Tz'ŭ	404
Ming Yüan Ti .	409	Yung Hsing	409
		Shên Jui	414
		T'ai Ch'ang	416
T'ai Wu Ti . .	424	Shih Kuang	424
		Shên Chia	428
		Yen Ho	432
		T'ai Yên	435
		T'ai P'ing Chên Chün	440
		Chêng P'ing	451
Wên Ch'êng Ti .	452	Hsing An	452
		Hsing Kuang	454
		Hsiao Chien	454
		Ta An	455
		Ho P'ing	460
Hsien Wên Ti .	466	T'ien An	466
		Huang Hsing	467
Hsiao Wên Ti .	471	Yen Hsing	471
		Ch'êng Ming	476
		T'ai Ho	477
Hsüan Wu Ti .	500	Ching Ming	500
		Chêng Shih	504
		Yung P'ing	508
		Yen Ch'ang	512
Hsiao Ming Ti .	516	Hsi P'ing	516
		Shên Kuei	517
		Chêng Kuang	519
		Hsiao Ch'ang	525
Lin-T'ao Wang .	528	Wu T'ai	528
Hsiao Chuang Ti .	528	Chien I	528
		Yung An	528
		Kêng Hsing	529
T'ung-Hai Wang .	530	Chien Ming	530
Chieh Min Ti .	531	Chin T'ai	531

Dynastic Title	Accession A.D.	Title of Reign and Its Adoption A.D.	
An Ting Wang .	531	Chung Hsing	531
Hsiao Wu Ti .	532	T'ai Ch'ang	532
		Yung Hsing	532
		Yung Hsi	532
E. *Wei* Hsiao			
Ching Ti .	534–550	T'ien P'ing	534
		Yüan Hsiang	538
		Hsing Ho	539
		Wu Ting	543 (–550)
W. *Wei* Wên Ti .	535–551	Ta T'ung	535
N. *Ch'i* Wên			
Hsüan Ti .	550–559	T'ien Pao	550
W. *Wei* Fei Ti .	552–553	. . .	
W. *Wei* Kung Ti .	554–557	. . .	
N. *Chou* Hsiao Min			
Ti .	556–557	. . .	
N. *Chou* Ming Ti .	557–560	Wu Ch'êng	558
N. *Ch'i* Fei Ti .	560–560	Ch'ien Ming	560
N. *Ch'i* Hsiao			
Chao Ti .	560–561	Huang Chien	560
N. *Ch'i* Wu			
Ch'êng Ti .	561–564	T'ai Ning	561
N. *Chou* Wu Ti .	561–578	Pao Ting	561
		T'ien Ho	566
		Chien Têh	572
N. *Ch'i* Hou Chu	565–577	T'ien Tung	565
		Wu P'ing	570
		Lung Hua	576
N. *Ch'i* An-Têh			
Wang . .	577–577	Têh Ch'ang	577
N. *Ch'i* Yu Chu	577–577	Ch'êng Kuang	577
N. *Chou* Hsüan Ti	578–580	Hsüan Ch'êng	578
		Ta Ch'êng	579
N. *Chou* Ching Ti	580–581	Ta Hsiang	580
		Ta Ting	581

11. THE SUI DYNASTY, A.D. 581–618. Family name: Yang. Capitals: Ch'angan and Loyang.

	A.D.		A.D.
Wên Ti . .	581	K'ai Huang	581
		Jên Shou	601
Yang Ti ("The			
Shady") .	605	Ta Yeh	605

Dynastic Title	Accession	Title of Reign and Its Adoption
	A.D.	A.D.
Kung Ti Yu . .	617	I Ning	617
Kung Ti T'ung .	618	H'uang T'ai	618

12. THE T'ANG DYNASTY, A.D. 618–907. Family name: Li. Capital: Ch'angan.

	A.D.		A.D.
Kao Tsu . .	618	Wu Têh	618
T'ai Tsung ("The Great") .	627	Chên Kuan	627
Kao Tsung . .	650	Yung Hui	650
		Hsien Ch'ing	656
		Lung So	661
		Lin Têh	664
		Ch'ien Fêng	666
		Tsung Chang	668
		Hsien Hêng	670
		Shang Yüan	674
		I Fêng	676
		T'iao Lu	679
		Yung Lung	680
		K'ai Yao	681
		Yung Shun	682
		Hung Tao	683
Chung Tsung .	684	Ssŭ Shêng	684
Jui Tsung . .	684	Wên Ming	684
Wu Hou (Empress)	684	Kuang Tsê	684
		Ch'ui Kung	685
		Yung Ch'ang	689
		'I'sai Ch'u	689
		T'ien Shou	690
		Ju I	692
		Ch'ang Shou	692
		Yen Tsai	694
		Chêng Shêng	695
		T'ien T'sê Wan Sui	695
		Wan Sui T'ung T'ien	696
		Shên Kung	697
		Shêng Li	698
		Chiu Shih	700
		Ta Tsu	701
		Ch'ang An	701
Chung Tsung .	705	Shên Lung	705
	(Restored)	Ching Lung	707

Dynastic Title	Accession A.D.	Title of Reign and Its Adoption A.D.
Jui Tsung .	. 710 (Restored)	Ching Yün 710
		T'ai Chi 712
		Yen Ho 712
Hsüan Tsung .	713	Hsien T'ien 713
		K'ai Yüan 713
		T'ien Pao 742
Su Tsung .	. 756	Chih Têh 756
		Ch'ien Yüan 758
		Shang Yüan 760
		Pao Ying 762
Tai Tsung .	. 763	Kuang Têh 763
		Yung T'ai 765
		Ta Li 766
Têh Tsung .	. 780	Chien Chung 780
		Hsing Yüan 784
		Chên Yüan 785
Shun Tsung .	. 805	Yung Chên 805
Hsien Tsung	. 806	Yüan Ho 806
Mu Tsung .	. 821	Ch'ang Ch'ing 821
Ching Tsung .	. 825	Pao Li 825
Wên Tsung .	. 827	T'ai Ho 827
		K'ai Ch'êng 836
Wu Tsung .	. 841	Hui Ch'ang 841
Hsüan Tsung .	. 847	Ta Chung 847
I Tsung .	. 860	Hsien T'ung 860
Hsi Tsung .	. 874	Ch'ien Fu 874
		Kuang Ming 880
		Chung Ho 881
		Kuang Ch'i 885
		Wên Têh 888
Chao Tsung .	. 889	Lung Chi 889
		Ta Shun 890
		Ching Fu 892
		Ch'ien Ning 894
		Kuang Hua 898
		T'ien Fu 901
		T'ien Yu 904
Chao Huan Ti (Or Ai Ti) .	. 904	T'ien Yu 905

13. Wu Tai (The Epoch of The Five Dynasties), A.D. 907–960. Family
names: *Later Liang,* Chu; *Later T'ang,* Li; *Later Tsin,* Shih; *Later
Han,* Liu; *Later Chou,* Kuo. Capitals: K'aifêng (i.e. Pien) and
Loyang (907–923); Weichou and Loyang (923–936); Loyang and
K'aifêng (936–946); K'aifêng (947–960).

Dynastic Title	*Accession*	*Title of Reign and Its Adoption*	
	A.D.		A.D.
L. Liang T'ai Tsu .	907	K'ai P'ing	907
		Ch'ien Hua	911
Kitan T'ai Tsu .	907	Shên Ts'ê	916
		T'ien Tsan	922
		T'ien Hsien	925
L. Liang Mo Ti .	913	Chên Ming	915
		Lung Tê	921
L. T'ang Chuang Tsung . .	923	T'ung Kuang	923
L. T'ang Ming Tsung	926	T'ien Ch'êng	926
		Ch'ang Hsing	930
Kitan (Liao) T'ai Tsung . .	926	T'ien Hsien	926
		Hui T'ung	937
		Ta T'ung	946
L. T'ang Min Ti .	933	Ying Shun	934
L. T'ang Lu Wang	934	Ch'ing T'ai	934
L. Tsin (Chin) Kao Tsu . .	936	T'ien Fu	936
L. Tsin Ch'u Ti .	942	K'ai Yün	944
L. Han Kao Tsu .	947	T'ien Fu	947
		Ch'ien Yu	948
Kitan (Liao) Shih Tsung . .	947	T'ien Lu	947
L. Han Yin Ti .	948	Ch'ien Yu	948
L. Chou T'ai Tsu .	951	Kuang Shun	951
Liao Mu Tsung .	951	Ying Li	951
L. Chou Shih Tsung	954	Hsien Têh	954
L. Chou Kung Ti .	959	Hsien Têh	959

14. The Sung Dynasty, A.D. 960–1279. Family name: Chao. Capitals:
K'aifêng (i.e. Pien 960–1126), Hangchou (1127–1279).

	A.D.		A.D.
T'ai Tsu	960	Chien Lung	960
		Ch'ien Têh	963
		K'ai Pao	968

Dynastic Title	Accession A.D.	Title of Reign and Its Adoption	A.D.
Liao (KITAN)			
Ching Tsung	968	Pao Ning	968
		Ch'ien Heng	978
T'ai Tsung . .	976	T'ai P'ing Hsing	
		Kuo	976
		Yung Hsi	984
		Tuan Kung	988
		Shun Hua	990
		Chih Tao	995
Liao Shêng Tsung	983	T'ung Ho	983
		K'ai T'ai	1012
		T'ai P'ing	1021
Chên Tsung . .	997	Hsien P'ing	998
		Ching Têh	1004
		Ta Chung Hsiang	
		Fu	1008
		T'ien Hsi	1017
		Ch'ien Hsing	1022
Jên Tsung . .	1022	T'ien Shêng	1023
		Ming Tao	1032
		Ching Yu	1034
		Pao Yüan	1038
		K'ang Ting	1040
		Ch'ing Li	1041
		Huang Yu	1049
		Chih Ho	1054
		Chia Yu	1056
Liao Hsing Tsung	1031	Ching Fu	1031
		Ch'ung Hsi	1032
Liao Tao Tsung	1055	Ch'ing Ning	1055
		Hsien Yung	1066
		Ta K'ang	1074
		Ta An	1083
Ying Tsung . .	1063	Chih P'ing	1064
Shên Tsung . .	1067	Hsi Ning	1068
		Yüan Fêng	1078
Chê Tsung . .	1085	Yüan Yu	1086
		Shao Shêng	1094
		Yüan Fu	1098
Hui Tsung . .	1100	Chien Chung Ching	
		Kuo	1101
		Ch'ung Ning	1102
		Ta Kuan	1107

Dynastic Title	Accession A.D.	Title of Reign and Its Adoption A.D.	
		Chêng Ho	1111
		Ch'ung Ho	1118
		Hsüan Ho	1119
Liao T'ien Tsu Ti	1101	Ch'ien T'ung	1101
		T'ien Ch'ing	1110
		Pao Ta	1119
Chin (GOLDEN) T'ai Tsu . .	1115	Shou Kuo	1115
		T'ien Fu	1115
Chin T'ai Tsung	1123	T'ien Hui	1123
Liao Têh Tsung	1125	Yen Ch'ing	1125
		K'ang Kuo	1126
Ch'in Tsung . .	1126	Ching K'ang	1126
Kao Tsung (S.Sung)	1127	Chien Yen	1127
		Shao Hsing	1131
Chin Hsi Tsung	1135	T'ien Hui	1135
		T'ien Chüan	1135
		Huang T'ung	1141
Liao Kan T'ien Hou . .	1136	Hsien Ch'ing	1136
Liao Jên Tsung .	1142 (–1154)	Shao Hsing	1142
Chin Hai-Ling Wang . .	1149	T'ien Têh	1149
		Chên Yüan	1153
		Chêng Lung	1156
Chin Shih Tsung	1161	Ta Ting	1161
Hsiao Tsung .	1162	Lung Hsing	1163
		Ch'ien Tao	1165
		Shun Hsi	1174
Kuang Tsung .	1189	Shao Hsi	1190
Chin Chang Tsung .	1190	Ming Ch'ang	1190
		Ch'êng An	1196
		T'ai Ho	1201
Ning Tsung .	1194	Ch'ing Yüan	1195
		Chia T'ai	1201
		K'ai Hsi	1205
		Chia Ting	1208
Chin Wei-Shao Wang .	1209	Ta An	1209
		Ch'ung Ch'ing	1212
		Chih Ning	1213

Dynastic Title	Accession	Title of Reign and Its Adoption	
	A.D.		A.D.
Chin Hsüan Tsung	1213	Chên Yu	1213
		Hsing Ting	1217
		Yüan Kuang	1222
Chin Ai Tsung .	1224	Chêng Ta	1224
		T'ien Hsing	1232
		K'ai Hsing	1233
Li Tsung . .	1224	Pao Ch'ing	1225
		Shao Ting	1228
		Tuan P'ing	1234
		Chia Hsi	1237
		Shun Yu	1241
		Pao Yu	1253
		K'ai Ch'ing	1259
		Ching Ting	1260
Chin Mo Ti .	1234 (–1234)	Shêng Ch'ang	1234
Tu Tsung . .	1264	Hsien Shun	1265
Kung Ti . .	1274	Têh Yu	1274
Tuan Tsung . .	1276	Ching Yen	1276
Ti Ping . .	1278 (–1279)	Hsiang Hsing	1278

15. THE YÜAN (MONGOL) DYNASTY, A.D. 1206–1368. Family name: Ch'i-O-Wên. Capitals: Holin (Karakorum) and Peking (Tatu).

	A.D.		A.D.
T'ai Tsu (Jenghis)	1206		
T'ai Tsung (Ogotai)	1229		
Ting Tsung (Kuyak)	1246		
Hsien Tsung			
(Mangu) .	1251		
Shih Tsu (Kublai)	1260	Chung T'ung	1260
		Chih Yüan	1264
Ch'êng Tsung .	1294	Yüan Chên	1295
		Ta Têh	1297
Wu Tsung . .	1307	Chih Ta	1308
Jên Tsung . .	1311	Huang Ch'ing	1312
		Yen Tu	1314
Ying Tsung . .	1320	Chih Chih	1321
T'ai Ting Ti . .	1323	T'ai Ting	1324
		Chih Ho	1328
Yu Chu . .	1328	T'ien Shun	1328
Ming Tsung . .	1328	T'ien Li	1328
Wên Tsung . .	1329	T'ien Li	1329
		Chih Shun	1330
Ning Tsung . .	1332		

Dynastic Title	*Accession*	*Title of Reign and Its Adoption*	
	A.D.		A.D.
Shun Ti . .	1333	Yüan T'ung	1333
		Chih Yüan	1335
		Chih Chêng	1341

16. THE MING DYNASTY, A.D. 1368–1644. Family name: Chu. Capitals: Nanking (1368–1402), Peking (1403–1644).

	A.D.		A.D.
T'ai Tsu (Chu Yüan-			
chang) .	1368	Hung Wu	1368
Hui Ti . .	1398	Chien Wên	1399
Ch'êng Tsu .	1402	Yung Lo	1403
Jên Tsung .	1424	Hung Hsi	1425
Hsüan Tsung	1425	Hsüan Têh	1426
Ying Tsung .	1435	Chêng T'ung	1436
Tai Tsung .	1449	Ching T'ai	1450
Ying Tsung			
(Restored) .	1457	T'ien Shun	1457
Hsien Tsung .	1464	Ch'êng Hua	1465
Hsiao Tsung .	1487	Hung Chih	1488
Wu Tsung . .	1505	Chêng Têh	1506
Shih Tsung . .	1521	Chia Ching	1522
Mu Tsung . .	1566	Lung Ch'ing	1567
Shên Tsung . .	1572	Wan Li	1573
Kuang Tsung .	1620	T'ai Ch'ang	1620
Hsi Tsung . .	1620	T'ien Ch'i	1621
Ssŭ Tsung (I Tsung,			
Huai Tsung, or			
Chuang Lieh			
Min Ti) .	1627	Ch'ung Chên	1628

17. THE CH'ING (MANCHU) DYNASTY, A.D. 1583–1912. Family name: Gioro (Ai-Hsin-Chieh-Lo). Capitals: Liaoyang (1621–1643), Peking (1644–1912).

	A.D.		A.D.
T'ai Tsu (Nurhachu			
or Nu-er-ha-			
ch'ih) . .	1583	T'ien Ming	1616
T'ai Tsung (Huang			
Taichi) .	1627	T'ien Ts'ung	1627
		Ch'ung Têh	1636
Shih Tsu . .	1644	Shun Chih	1644
Shêng Tsu . .	1661	K'ang Hsi	1662

Dynastic Title	Accession	Title of Reign and Its Adoption	
	A.D.		A.D.
Shih Tsung .	. 1723	Yung Chêng	1723
Kao Tsung .	. 1735	Ch'ien Lung	1736
Jên Tsung .	. 1795	Chia Ch'ing	1796
Hsüan Tsung	. 1820	Tao Kuang	1821
Wên Tsung .	. 1850	Hsien Fêng	1851
Mu Tsung .	. 1861	T'ung Chih	1862
Têh Tsung .	. 1875	Kuang Hsü	1875
(P'u Yi) .	. 1908	Hsüan T'ung	1909

18. THE REPUBLIC, A.D. 1911–
    Capitals: Peking (1911–1916), Nanking (1916–1937), Chungking
    (1937–   ).

APPENDIX II

GREAT EVENTS OF THE LAST 100 YEARS

1838. Lin Tzê-hsü appointed Viceroy of Liang-kuang (Kuangtung and Kuangsi), to deal with the Opium Case.

1839. Viceroy Lin Tzê-hsü confiscated and burned opium in Canton.

1840. The blockade of Canton and the attack on Ningpo by the British.

1841. Chih-ying appointed Imperial Representative to negotiate peace with the British. The British Navy attacked Ting-hai.

1842. British Fleet seized Chênchiang. Anglo-Chinese Treaty signed, October 8.

1843. British Commercial Treaty signed, October 8.

1843. Shanghai opened as a Treaty Port, November 17.

1844. First American Treaty with China signed, July 3.

1847. The Mutiny of the Mohammedans started in Shensi and Kansu.

1847. Clashes between Cantonese and British inhabitants in Canton.

1849. Portuguese expelled Chinese Customs officials from Macao, March 5.

1850. The Rising of the T'aip'ingists.

1851. Hung Hsui-ch'üan, the T'aip'ing leader, declared himself the Heavenly King of the T'aip'ing Heavenly Kingdom.

1853. Nanking captured by the T'aip'ingists and made their capital.

1854. Agreement for foreign administration of Customs at Shanghai, June 29.

1856. T'aip'ingists suffered a reverse in Wuch'ang.

1856. The "Arrow" incident occurred at Canton between the Chinese and the British, October 8.

1857. Rising of the Cantonese against the foreigners; Canton captured by British and French, December 29.

1858. T'ientsin Treaties with America, Britain, France, and Russia signed in June.

1859. The British and French suffered a defeat at Taku, June 25.

1859. Frederick T. Ward, an American soldier, entered the service of the Chinese Government against the T'aip'ingists.

1860. British and French troops entered Peking, October 13. Yüan Ming Park (the old summer palace) burned down by the invaders.

1860. British Convention signed at Peking, October 24; French Convention signed, October 25.

1861. Establishment of a "General Controlling Yamên of Foreign Affairs" (Tsung Li Kê Kuo Shih Wu Ya Mên).

1863. Robert Hart appointed Inspector-General of Customs.

1863. Colonel Gordon, an Englishman, succeeded Ward on March 25, the latter having been killed in a battle at Tsŭch'i in September of the preceding year.

1863. The Government bought seven modern steamers from abroad.

1864. Gordon disbanded his men on May 31.

1864. Nanking was recovered by the governmental troops, and Hung Hsui-ch'üan committed suicide.

1865. The first levy of the "likin" tax, by which Chinese commodities were taxed at every interior port while foreign goods were exempted by virtue of the protection of the treaties.

1866. T'aip'ingists completely quelled.

1866. Mohammedan revolt in Ili.

1867. American Fleet visited Korea in January.

1867. A School of Mechanics was opened by the Shanghai Manufacturing Bureau (Shanghai Chih Tsao Chü). A Navigation Manufacturing School was established in Foochow.

1867. Three provinces of Cochin China occupied by the French in June.

1868. American Berlingame Treaty re Chinese Immigration signed in Washington, July 28.

1868. Chinese students first sent to study in America in July.

1868. First building of steamers by the Mamoi Factory in Foochow, September.

1869. Land-trading Pact with Russia signed.

1870. Birth of Dr. Sun Yat-sen, November 12.

1871. Russian occupation of Kuldja and Ili.

1871. Cable system between Shanghai and Hong-Kong opened by a British firm, June 3.

1872. Shên Pao, the first Chinese newspaper, published in Shanghai.

1873. Shensi-Kansu Mohammedan revolt completely suppressed.

1873. Diplomatic Corps received in audience for the first time.

1876. Chefoo Treaty signed, and Ich'ang, Wuhu, Wênchou, Pekhoi opened as treaty ports, September 13.

1876. Japanese-Korean Treaty signed, February 26.

1876. Railway between Woosung and Shanghai started to operate.

1877. The Woosung and Shanghai railway purchased and destroyed by the Chinese, after a protest that the construction of the railway brought into existence a "sphere of influence."

1877. Consuls sent to foreign countries where there were Chinese immigrants. First Chinese envoy arrived in London.

1877. Ssŭch'uan Munition Factory established in Ch'êngtu.

1878. Mohammedan revolt in Chinese Turkestan suppressed, January.

1878. Establishment of a Woolen Factory in Lanchou, Kansu Province.

1878. First Chinese envoy to U.S.A. arrived, October 28.

1878. K'aip'ing Coal Mine opened.

1878. Chinese postage stamps first printed, December.

1879. Japanese annexation of the Chinese colony in Liukiu Islands, March.

1880. Peiyang (Northern Ocean) Navigation School established in T'ientsin, January.

1880. American-Chinese Immigration Treaty and American Commercial Treaty signed, November 17.

1880. Land telegraph lines sanctioned, November.

1881. Sino-Russian Pact signed in St. Petersburg, February 24. Kuldja and Ili restored to China.

1881. The "Chinese Rocket" (locomotive) made its first trip from K'aip'ing Colliery to the Canal, June 9.

1881. Shanghai-T'ientsin telegraph line opened, December 1.

1882. The Linen-spinning Machine-shop opened in Shanghai.

1882. Demarcation Treaty with Russia signed, for the regulation of the northwestern frontiers.

1883. The establishment of Sinkiang Province in Chinese Turkestan, January.

1883. Mr. Chu Ta-ch'un invested a hundred thousand Chinese dollars for the establishment in Shanghai of the Yüan-ch'ang Metals Factory, the first modern Chinese firm run on the capital of a Chinese citizen.

1884. Franco-Chinese war over Annam commenced.

1884. T'ientsin Military School opened, being the first Chinese organization for military training.

1885. Chinese-Japanese Convention regarding Korea signed at T'ientsin, April 18.

1885. Franco-Chinese Treaty of Peace signed at T'ientsin, June 9. Concession of Annam Protectorate to France.

1886. Franco-Chinese Convention re frontier trade signed, April 25.

1886. Anglo-Chinese Convention re Burma and Tibet signed, July 24. Concession of Burma Protectorate to Britain.

1887. Building of T'ientsin-Taku Railway commenced.

1887. New Franco-Chinese Convention re frontier trade signed, June 26.

1887. Birth of Chiang Kai-shek.

1887. Portuguese-Chinese Treaty signed, December. Macao yielded to the latter.

1888. Railway between T'ientsin and T'ongshan opened, August.

1888. Pciyang (Northern Oceans) Naval Forces established, December.

1890. Anglo-Chinese Convention re Sikkin and Tibet signed in Bengal, March 17.

1890. Hanyang Iron Works opened.

1891. Peiyang, Nanyang (Southern Oceans), Kuangtung, and Fukien Naval Forces reorganized or established; Port Arthur made the base for the Peiyang Fleet.

1893. I-ho Park (the new summer palace), begun in the spring of 1888, now completed, January.

1893. Peking-Shanhaikuan Railway completed.

1893. Early restrictions for overseas trading by individuals now abolished by an imperial edict.

1894. Anglo-Chinese Convention re Burma and Tibet signed, March 1.

1894. American-Chinese Treaty prohibiting immigration of Chinese laborers for ten years signed, March 17.

1894. Tunghsiao (Oriental Studies Party) Rebellion started in Korea, March-May.

1894. Sino-Japanese War declared, August 1.

1895. Peace Treaty with Japan signed in Shimonoseki, April 17.

1895. Franco-Chinese Convention re frontier trade signed, June 20.

1895. Japan advised by Russia, France, and Germany to retrocede the Liaotung Peninsula, April.

1896. Post Office officially opened for the first time.

1896. General Railway Company established by the Government.

1896. Russo-Chinese Agreement re the Chinese Eastern Railway, September 8.

1897. Franco-Chinese (non-alienation) Convention signed, by which China promised France not to lease Hainan Islands to any "third Power," and to allow the French to prolong the Lungchou Railway and dig mines in Kuangtung, Kuangsi, and Yünan provinces, March 15.

1897. Ts'ingtao and Kiaochou (Chiaochou) seized by Germany, November 14.

1898. Declaration as to non-alienation of Yangtzŭ Valley, February 11.

1898. Promise to Great Britain of Inspectorate-General of Customs, February 13.

1898. Lease of Kiaochou to Germany for 99 years.

1898. Lease of Kuantung Peninsula (Darien [Talien] and Port Arthur included) to Russia for 25 years, March 27.

1898. Declaration as to non-alienation of Southern Provinces.

1898. American Contract for Hankow-Canton Railway made.

1898. Kuangchouwan (Bay of Canton) seized by the French, April 22.

1898. Anglo-Chinese Convention for lease of Kowloon hinterland to Britain for 99 years signed, June 9.

1898. Sino-Japanese Convention signed, declaring non-alienation of Fukien Province, April 26.

1898. Anglo-Chinese Convention for lease of Weihaiwei for 25 years signed, July 1.

1898. Reformation of Emperor Têh Tsung, April.

1898. Yüan Shih-k'ai appointed special commissioner for the training of the Peiyang (Northern Oceans) Army, from which the later Peiyang War-lords came into being.

1898. The Empress Dowager seized power again, imprisoned the Emperor Têh Tsung, and liquidated the Reformation Movement, September 22.

1899. Anglo-Russian Agreement signed re interests in the Manchurian provinces and the Yangtzŭ Valley, April 29.

1899. Lease of Kuangchouwan to France for 99 years.

1899. Secretary Hay of the U.S.A. declared the Open Door Policy in China, September 6.

1900. The Boxers, backed by the Empress Dowager, attacked the Legation Quarter in Peking. The Empress Dowager declared war against "all foreigners in the world." (June 20) Southern Governors concluded separate neutral treaties with the Powers.

1900. The Allied Forces of eight nations entered Peking, August 14. The imperial Court fled to Shansi and then to Shensi.

1900. Peace Treaty signed at Peking, September 7.

1901. Office of General Controlling Yamên of Foreign Affairs reorganized into Ministry of Foreign Affairs (Department of Diplomacy).

1902. Intermarriage between the Han and Manchurian peoples first sanctioned by an imperial edict.

1902. The Court returns to Peking, January 30.

1902. The Russian Trans-Siberian Railway completed.

1902. The British Commercial Treaty signed.

1904. Russo-Japanese War opened on Chinese territory of Liaotung district, February 8.

1904. British troops marched into Lasha; Dalai escaped to Urga, August 8.

1905. Russia and Japan signed peace treaty at Portsmouth, America, September 5.

1905. China made to agree to transfer to Japan of all Russian rights in Manchurian provinces, December 22.

1906. Anglo-Chinese Treaty re Tibet signed, April 27.

1906. Imperial edict issued in preparation for Constitutional Government, September 1.

1907. First Municipal elections under new order introduced.

1907. Anglo-Russian Agreement re Tibet, August 31.

1908. Dalai attended the imperial Court and received new nomination to his post.

1908. Death of Emperor Têh Tsung, November 14.

1908. Death of Dowager Empress, November 15.

1909. Peking-Hankow Railway redeemed from foreign bankers.

1909. Provincial assemblies met, October.

1910. Provincial National Assembly met, October 3.

1911. Canton attacked by revolutionists, 72 of whom were killed and buried in the Yellow Flower Hills.

1911. Four-Power Group signed contract re Hukuang (Hu-Kwang) railways, May 20.

1911. Imperial edict declared nationalization of all Chinese railways, May.
1911. Outbreak of revolution at Wuch'ang, October 10, soon followed by many other provinces.
1911. The Living Buddha, Hut'ukêt'u, declared himself "Emperor of Outer Mongolia," December 28.
1912. Sun Yat-sen installed as Provisional President of Republican China.
1912. Abdication of the Manchu Emperor, P'u Yi, February 12.
1912. Yüan Shih-kai installed as Provisional President, March 10.
1912. Announcement of the Provisional Constitutional Law of Republican China, March 11.
1912. Russian occupation of Ili, June.
1912. China League reorganized into Kuomintang.
1913. The Living Buddha of Mongolia concluded a pact with Russia for the latter's support, January.
1913. The Rebellion of the Tibetans, backed by British influence, March.
1913. The Living Buddha's forces attacked the Republican forces, April.
1913. First Session of the Chinese Parliament, April.
1913. Formal recognition of the Chinese Republic by the U.S.A., May 2.
1913. Russo-Chinese Convention re "Outer Mongolian affairs" signed, by which Chinese suzerainty in Outer Mongolia is recognized by Russia and the autonomy of Outer Mongolia by the Chinese, November.
1914. Yüan Shih-kai dissolved Parliament, January.
1914. Japanese and British forces captured Ts'ingtao from Germany, November 7.
1914. Wedding of Dr. and Mme. Sun Yat-sen, November 25.
1915. Japanese presented to Yüan Shih-kai the Twenty-one Demands, January 18.
1915. Japanese Ultimatum to China, May 7.
1915. Yüan Shih-kai accepted treaties based on the Twenty-one Demands, May 9.
1915. Russo-Chinese Convention re "Outer Mongolia" signed; the Living Buddha renounced his imperial title and received nomination from the Chinese Government, June.
1915. Yüan Shih-kai declared himself Emperor; General Ts'ai O declared the independence of Yünan Province, December 25. Troops were sent to fight Yüan.
1916. Yüan Shih-kai renounced his imperial position, March 22.
1916. Yüan Shih-kai died, June 6. Li Yüan-hung, the Vice-President, succeeded him as President.
1917. The American Government invited China to break relations with Germany, February 2.
1917. China agreed to the American proposal, February 9.
1917. Secret Agreement between Japan and Britain concerning Shantung, February 16.

1917. Secret Agreement between Japan and France re Shantung, March 1.

1917. Secret Agreement between Japan and Russia re Shantung, March 5.

1917. China broke off relations with Germany, March 14.

1917. Li Yüan-hung, President of the Republic, forced by the military leaders to dissolve Parliament, June.

1917. China declared war on Germany, August 14.

1917. Dr. Sun Yat-sen elected by the Extraordinary Parliament in Canton as C.-in-C. of the Chinese Navy and Army, and declared his wish to protect the Constitutional Law.

1917. The military leaders broke into two groups under Tuan Ch'i ju and Wu P'ei-fu: Anfu and Chihli schools.

1918. Tuan Ch'i-ju became Prime Minister of Peking Government, March.

1918. Red Russian troops invaded Outer Mongolia, May.

1918. Secret Agreement between Peking Government and Japan re Shantung signed, September 24-28.

1918. Tuan Ch'i-ju resigned his post as Prime Minister. Hsü Shih-ch'ang became President of China, October.

1919. Peace negotiated in Shanghai between the Canton Revolutionary and Peking Governments, February.

1919. Great Demonstration of students in Peking, May 4.

1919. Chinese Delegation to Peace Conference declined to sign the Treaty of Versailles, June 28.

1919. Chinese Delegation signed only the Austrian Pact (part of the Treaty of Versailles), September.

1919. Reorganization of Kuomintang, October 10.

1919. Denunciation of Russo-Chinese Convention concerning "Outer Mongolia," November.

1920. China formally accepted as a member of the League of Nations, June.

1920. Forces of Tuan Ch'i-ju utterly defeated by those of Wu P'ei-fu, July.

1920. Soviet Russia declared to China her willingness to give up all the extraordinary rights acquired from China by the Tsar's Government through unequal treaties, November.

1921. Dalai sent an envoy to Peking to express his loyalty, January.

1921. Mongolian bandits and White Russians captured Urga, February.

1921. Dr. Sun Yat-sen was elected President of the Republic by the Extraordinary Parliament Assembly in Canton, May 5.

1921. Mongolian lords in Outer Mongolia expressed their loyalty to the Republic, September.

1921. Washington Conference for the settlement of Pacific affairs opened, November.

1921. Liang Shih-i ("the Mammon") became Prime Minister of the warlords' regime in Peking.

1922. Nine-Power Treaty relating to territorial integrity and independ-

356 A Short History of Chinese Civilization

ence of China, and resumption of the "Open Door" policy in China. Washington Conference concluded, February 6.

1922. War broke out between the military leaders Wu P'ei-fu and Chang Tso-lin, heads of Chihli and Fêngt'ien war-lords; the latter defeated, May.

1922. Dr. Sun Yat-sen's Northern Expeditionary Army entered Kiangsi province, May 6.

1922. Ch'ên Chüng-ming, Dr. Sun's general, revolted in Canton and the Northern Expeditionary Army was recalled to engage the rebels, June.

1923. Ts'ao K'un, supported by Wu P'ei-fu, succeeded in the presidential election in Peking, October.

1923. Communist Party members were accepted by Kuomintang.

1924. First Plenary Session of Kuomintang representatives opened in Canton; co-ordination with the Communist Party recognized, January.

1924. Soviet Russia recognized by China; Russo-Chinese Treaty signed, May 31.

1924. Huang-p'u (Whampoa) Military School established in Canton, May.

1924. Second major war broke out between Wu P'ei-fu and Chang Tso-lin. This time Wu crushed, September.

1924. Ts'ao K'un resigned, October 25.

1925. Dr. Sun Yat-sen died at Peking, March 12.

1925. The British and Japanese in the International Settlement of Shanghai shot and killed many Chinese civilians (May 30), which led to the boycott of British goods.

1925. Chinese National Government inaugurated in Canton, with Wang Ching-wei as chairman of the Government, June 1.

1925. British and Portuguese shot and killed many Chinese civilians in Shachi, Canton, June 23.

1925. Wu P'ei-fu in alliance with another war-lord, Sun Ch'uan-fang, crushed Chang Tso-lin's influence in the Yangtzǔ provinces, October 10.

1926. Chiang Kai-shek became Commander-in-Chief of the Northern Expeditionary Army, July 9.

1926. Fêng Yü-hsiang registered as a member of Kuomintang.

1926. Great victory of the Northern Expeditionary Forces leads to the capture of Wuch'ang in the Upper Yangtzǔ valley, October 10. T'ang Shêng-chih with his troops assigned the responsibility of clearing out the remnants of the enemy in this district.

1927. Revolutionary forces occupied British Concession at Hankow after a clash between British bluejackets and Chinese civilians, January 26.

1927. Northern Expeditionary Forces captured the city of Shanghai, March 20.

1927. Northern Expeditionary Forces took Nanking, March 24. Clash between Chinese soldiers and foreigners. Nanking bombarded by British and American warships.

1927. Soviet Bank at Peking adjoining Russian Embassy raided by Chinese police; important documents seized, April 6.

1927. United States, Great Britain, France, Italy, and Japan sent identical notes of protest concerning Nanking incident, April 11.

1927. Great purge of Communists by Kuomintang, led by General Chiang Kai-shek, April 12.

1927. Yen Hsi-shan joined Kuomintang; elected member of the National Government and appointed Commander-in-Chief of Northern Revolutionary Army, June 6.

1927. Communist Party and part of Kuomintang members under Wang Ching-wei broke off relations with Nanking Government under Chiang Kai-shek, and organized the Wuhan Government. T'ang Shêng-chih, in their support, began his Eastern Expedition against Nanking, July 1.

1927. The Central Government troops, having defeated the Communists, occupied the triple-cities of Wuhan, November 11.

1927. Uprising of laborers at Canton, December 11.

1927. Kuomintang withdrew its recognition of the Government of Soviet Russia, December 15.

1928. Chiang Kai-shek resumed his post as Commander-in-Chief of the Northern Expeditionary Forces, January 9.

1928. General offensive against the war-lords taken by the Northern Expeditionary Forces, April 9.

1928. Japanese openly gave military assistance to the retreating war-lords by the occupation of Tsinan (Chinan). Chinese civilians massacred, May 3. A Kuomintang deputy and twenty of his assistants tortured to death by the Japanese soldiers.

1928. Japan warned China no "disorders" will be permitted "in Manchuria," May 18.

1928. Chang Tso-lin retreated from Peking to his Manchurian home and was killed on the way by an explosion laid by the Japanese at the Huang-ku T'un Station, June 4.

1928. Yen Hsi-shan's forces marched into Peking, June 8.

1928. Japan warned General Chang Hsüeh-liang "not to raise the Kuomintang flag in Manchuria," August 10.

1928. The Central Bank established in Shanghai, November 17.

1928. Chang Hsüeh-liang cabled the Central Government expressing his loyalty and was elected a member of the Government, December 29.

1929. Clash between Chinese and Japanese police at Têhling, September 23.

1930.   Weihaiwei returned to China by the British Government, October 1.

1930.   Wang Ching-wei, Yen Hsi-shan, and Fêng Yü-hsiang set up a government in Peking (Peiping) against the Central Government in Nanking, February; fighting continued from May to September.

1930.   Communist forces raided Ch'angsha, capital of Hunan province.

1931.   Riots in Kirin and Korea over the release of Wanpaoshan on the borders of China and Korea, April–August.

1931.   Li Tsung-jên set up a rival government in Kuangsi, May 28.

1931.   The National Conference on Aviation met at Nanking, April 20.

1931.   The People's Constitutional Convention assembled at Nanking, May 5. Provisional Constitution adopted, May 12.

1931.   Floods in the Yangtzŭ, Yellow, and Huai River valleys brought disaster to sixteen provinces; forty million people affected. July–August.

1931.   Japanese garrisons on Chinese territory along the Southern Manchuria Railway launched a surprise attack against Mukden and took the city at midnight, September 18.

1931.   Eighteen Chinese towns and mining cities seized by Japan without a declaration of war, September 19.

1931.   League Council urged Japan and China to refrain from acts that might aggravate the situation, September 22. On the same day the Japanese seized the important town of Liaoyang.

1931.   General Ma Chan-Shan and troops were withdrawn from Heilungkiang (Heilungchiang), which fell into Japanese hands, December.

1932.   One hundred thousand Chinese troops under the command of Jung Chên withdrawn from Chinchou. Japanese completed occupation of Manchurian provinces, January 3.

1932.   Mr. Stimson, American Secretary of Foreign Affairs, sent a note to Japan stating that the American Government would not recognize any de facto situation, January 7.

1932.   The Commission of Inquiry of the League of Nations to Manchuria, headed by Lord Lytton, formed, January 7.

1932.   The signatories to the Nine-Power Treaty of 1922 decided to stand up for the territorial and political inviolability of China, January 7.

1932.   Japan, without declaration of war, attacked the Chinese garrisons in Shanghai, January 28.

1932.   Shanghai Chinese garrisons were withdrawn to new positions, March 3.

1932.   P'u Yi installed as Emperor of the puppet Manchukuo Government by the Japanese, March 9.

1932.   Assembly of League of Nations agreed upon a three-point proposal for the settlement of the Sino-Japanese affair, March 10.

1932.   Japan attacked Jehol province, July.

1933. The Japanese seized Shanhaikuan ("Mountain and Sea Pass"), January 3.

1933. T'ang Yü-lin, Governor of Jehol, withdrew from the capital, Ch'êng-têh, March.

1933. Japan attacked Hopei province from the Great Wall, and met with resistance from the Chinese twenty-ninth army, March–April.

1933. Japanese completed occupation of districts east of the Luan River in Hopei province, April 19.

1933. Armistice Pact with Japan signed in T'angku, May 30.

1934. The Japanese-sponsored Mongolian Local Automatic Political Committee set up, April 23.

1934. Japanese Government declared her policy in China, stated her objection to foreign assistance in China, and announced a "China Monroism policy," April 23.

1935. Japanese action in Mongolia, January 30.

1935. Doihara visits Kuangtung province, April.

1935. Japanese commander of Northern China Garrison sent demands to Nanking, including the resignation of Yü Hsüeh-chung, chairman of Hopei Provincial Government, and removal of the Government from T'ientsin to Paoting, May 9.

1935. Japanese forces occupied Northern Chahar province, July.

1935. Communist Party surrendered to Kuomintang, urging co-operation to check the Japanese aggression, July.

1935. Chinese Soviet Government and the Communist Central Committee issued a declaration to the people of China, urging union to check the Japanese menace, August 1.

1935. Guerrilla leaders fighting in Manchuria responded to the Communists' suggestion, giving full support, October 11.

1935. Nanking tendency for co-operation with Japan soon after Wang Ching-wei's return to the Government was shown by the preparation to send an economic mission to Japan, August.

1935. Discussion between China and Japan over the Hirota Three Principles; no conclusion reached, August.

1935. Chinese Government announced the abandonment of silver bases of currency, and put into effect a system of controlled currency, November 4. Sharp Japanese protest, November 9.

1935. Wang Ching-wei, challenged by a patriot for treachery, was shot at and received three bullet wounds, November.

1935. Great demonstrations of Chinese students in Peking, protesting against autonomy of five Northern provinces, planned by Japanese agents and General Sung Chêh-yüan's deputy; clashes between students and police, December 9 and 18.

1935. Hopei-Chahar Political Committee set up, Sung Chêh-yüan being appointed chairman with Japanese approval, December 18.

1935. Yin Jü-kêng installed head of the puppet Eastern Hopei Government by Japanese agents, December.

1936. Five-year Plan by Chinese Government for additional construction of 5,300 miles of railway after 1936.

1936. Suiyüan Mongolian Political Committee established as isolated from the Japanese-controlled Peilingmiao Mongolian Political Committee, February 13.

1936. Prince Têh, superintended by Japanese agents, established the Mongolian Military Government in Chiapussü of Chahar Province, May 12.

1936. Japanese reinforcements poured into Hopei, May.

1936. Liangkuang "rebellion" starts, June 8.

1936. The forces under Prince Têh and Wang Ying, a bandit, in cooperation with Japan, attacked the eastern borders of Suiyüan and were repulsed, June–August.

1936. Japanese reconnaissance machine flies over Chinese posts in Suiyüan; great enemy forces concentrated in Shangtu, Chahar province, November.

1936. General offensive against Chinese forces launched by Prince Têh's forces, November 13.

1936. Japanese-sponsored offensive against Hungkêêrt'u of Suiyüan province routed, November 15.

1936. Chinese forces entered Peilingmiao (November 24), leading to the mopping up of Japanese influence in Suiyüan.

1936. German-Japanese Anti-Comintern Agreement signed in Berlin by Japanese Ambassador Count Muskakoji and Von Ribbentrop, German Ambassador to London, November 25.

1936. Sian Incident. General Chiang Kai-shek was kidnaped by Chang Hsüeh-liang's army, which urged a war with Japan, December 16.

1936. General Chiang Kai-shek was released and flew to Nanking, December 26.

1937. Lukouch'iao Incident. Japanese forces attacked Chinese forces in the suburbs of the town of Wanp'ing, Hopei province, July 7.

1937. American Secretary of State, Mr. Cordell Hull, issued a general statement of principles about international affairs, July 26.

1937. The bogus Peiping (Peking) Safety Preservation Committee set up under Japanese sponsorship, July 7.

1937. The bogus T'ientsin Safety Preservation Committee set up under Japanese sponsorship, August 30.

1937. Kalgan fell, August 5.

1937. Shanghai War started, August 13.

1937. The British Ambassador to China, Sir Hughe Montgomery Knatchbull-Hugesson, machine-gunned by Japanese plane on the way from Nanking to Shanghai, August 26.

1937. Tat'ung fell, September 13.

1937. Paoting and Ch'angchou fell, September 24.

1937. The Advisory Committee of the League of Nations condemned the Japanese bombings of defenseless Chinese towns, September 28.

1937. President Roosevelt of the U.S.A. in a Chicago speech strongly condemned the aggressor nations, October 5.

1937. The American State Department accused Japan of violating the Kellogg Pact and the Nine-Power Treaty, October 6.

1937. The League of Nations adopted a resolution upholding the American attitude, October 6.

1937. Shihchaichuang fell, October 12.

1937. T'aiyuan fell, November 9.

1937. The Eighth Route Army defeated the Japanese in P'inghsing Pass, September 25.

1937. Shanghai city fell, November 11.

1937. Wuhu fell, December 10.

1937. Nanking fell, December 13.

1937. Wang K'ê-min, employed by Japanese agents, set up a bogus government in Peking, December 14.

1937. Chinese troops began to destroy textile mills and other Japanese property, valued at 250,000,000 yens, in Ts'ingtao, December 18.

1937. Tsinan fell, December 27.

1937. Hangchou fell, December 24.

1937. Autonomous Mongol State headed by Prince Yün established, October.

1937. The U.S. gunboat "Panay" and a Standard Oil tanker were sunk by Japanese bombs in the Yangtzŭ River. Three Americans killed. December 12.

1937. The British warships "Ladybird" and "Bee" were shelled by Japanese shore batteries at Wuhu, December 12.

1938. Chinese victory at Lini, Shantung province, March 4.

1938. Chinese smashing victory at T'aierchuang, Shantung province, April.

1938. Hsüchou fell, May 19.

1938. The League of Nations authorized its member states to apply sanctions against Japan as aggressor in the Far East War, September 30.

1938. The American Government presented three requests to Japan. Japan answered vaguely, October 6.

1938. A Chinese mail plane was shot down by Japanese fighters near Hong-Kong, August 24.

1938. Japanese landed at Bias Bay, October 12.

1938. Canton fell, October 25.

1938. Chinese forces withdrew from Hankow, October 25.

1938. General Chiang Kai-shek proclaimed that fighting was to go on, November 1.

1938. Arita, Japanese Foreign Minister, rejected the request for the opening of the Yangtzŭ River by the British, American, and French Governments, November 14.

1938. Prince Konoi, Japanese Premier, declared his principles, December 28.

1938. Wang Ching-wei left Chungking secretly by plane, December.

1938. Great Chinese victories in the North; East Hopei guerrillas penetrated into most of the districts and attacked the T'ientsin-Mukden Railway.

1939. Japanese landed at Hainan Island, February 10.

1939. Nanch'ang fell, March 27.

1939. Chinese general offensive, to consolidate their positions. More than 70 towns retaken, April.

1939. Japanese offensive in Upper Yangtzŭ against Hsiangyang districts routed, May.

1939. More than 16 Japanese divisions in the north of Lunghai Railway attacked Chinese in East Hopei. Japanese lost 7,000 men. July.

1939. Seven Japanese divisions, in an attempt to occupy the plateau of East Hopei and secure the north bank of the Yellow River, were driven back by Chinese Central Army, July.

1939. Japanese advanced towards Ch'angsha and suffered a smashing defeat, September–October.

1939. Japanese invaded Pekhoi, November 15.

1939. Nanning fell, December.

1940. American-Japanese treaty abrogated, February 3.

1940. Chinese counter-offensive in Nanning section; K'unlun Pass retaken; Japanese garrison smashed, February.

1940. Japanese made serious demands on Portuguese authorities at Macao, including the evacuation of Lappa and Wantsai islands; armed Japanese penetrate into the town of Macao, March 30.

1940. The British Ambassador to Tokyo made a speech which caused a bitter impression among the Americans, who feared a "Far East Munich," March 30.

1940. Wang Ching-wei installed by Japanese army as head of the new bogus Nanking Government, March 30.

1940. Mr. Cordell Hull, U.S. Secretary of State, condemned Wang Ching-wei's organization in Nanking, March 30.

1940. The Japanese-sponsored North China Autonomous Government, the Peking Provisional Government, and the bogus Nanking Reformed Government dissolved. The Japanese-controlled "Central Government of China" formed in Nanking. April 6.

1940. British-Japanese talks resumed. Sir Robert Craigie spoke on improved Anglo-Japanese relations, April 6.

1940. Chinese army recaptured Nanning, April 6.

1940. 150,000 Japanese troops routed at Tsaoyang, May.

1940. Anglo-Japanese agreement on Burma Road. The Road was closed. July 27.
1940. Yonai's Cabinet of Japan resigned, succeeded by Prince Konoi's Government, July 27.
1940. Japanese troops began to evacuate Kuangsi, November 16.
1940. Japanese-U.S.A. agreement reached on Shanghai International Settlement. French Courts in Shanghai handed over to the Japanese-controlled Nanking Government. Japanese-Nanking agreement signed, November 16.
1940. Burma Road reopened by the British Government, November 16.
1940. Japanese-Dutch East Indies oil agreement signed, November 30.
1940. British Government announced £5,000,000 loan to China, December 10.
1940. By the end of the year about 1,700 Chinese Societies of Industrial Co-operation produced about $30,000,000 of agricultural goods. Conditions were rapidly improving.
1941. Soviet-Chinese Barter agreement reached: Soviet to buy $6,000,000 of Chinese tea, wool, and mineral products, January 13.
1941. Japanese launched offensive in the Han River area; repulsed, January 18.
1941. Laughem Currie, President Roosevelt's Administrative Assistant, sent at the head of a mission to Chungking, February 7.
1941. Chinese military success at Honan, April 19.
1941. Chinese troops repulsed Japanese offensive in the Yangtzŭ valley, April 19.
1941. Chinese fourth army disbanded by order of the Central Government, April 19.
1941. Japanese started a "five-year plan" for exploiting coal and agricultural products in North China, April 19.
1941. Japanese-Russian Pact concluded, April 26.
1941. American $200,000,000 loan to China announced, April 26.
1941. British £5,000,000 loan to China announced, May 10.
1941. Dr. John E. Baker appointed to take charge of the dispatch of American traffic along the Burma Road to China, June 20.
1941. Owen Lattimore appointed as special political adviser to the Chinese Government in Chungking, on the recommendation of President Roosevelt, June 28.
1941. Chinese-Burmese frontier agreement concluded, June 28.
1941. China withdrew her diplomatic representatives from Berlin and Rome, July 5.
1941. The Axis countries recognized the puppet Nanking Government, July 5.
1941. A Chinese Mission to Malaya arrived, July 5.
1941. Japanese troops launched Yellow River offensive, July 12.

1941.   Mr. Cordell Hull issued a statement renouncing extraterritorial rights in China, July 12.

1941.   The Chinese Government announced a three-year economic plan, July 12.

1941.   Japan-Indo-China agreement concluded on Japanese occupation of Indo-China, July 26.

1941.   Britain froze Japanese assets, July 26.

1941.   U.S.A. froze Japanese assets, August 9.

1941.   Dutch East Indies froze Japanese assets, August 9.

1941.   Mongol-Manchu frontier delimited by the Japanese-Soviet Legations, August 23.

1941.   Prince Konoi sent a letter to President Roosevelt, August 30.

1941.   China accepted Atlantic Charter, August 25.

1941.   China broke off diplomatic relations with Germany and Italy, October 11.

1941.   Japanese big defeat in Ch'angsha, October 11.

1941.   Chinese victory in Ich'ang area, October 11.

1941.   British mission, headed by Sir Otto Niemeyer of the Treasury, arrived in China, October 11.

1941.   General Magruder, American adviser, arrived in Chungking, October 12.

1941.   Lt.-General Tojo became Japanese Prime Minister, October 25.

1941.   Kurusu, the Japanese "expert," arrived in America, November 25.

1941.   Japanese attacked the American Pacific bases, December 7.

1941.   United Kingdom and U.S.A. at war with Japan, December 8.

1941.   CHINA DECLARED WAR ON JAPAN, GERMANY, AND ITALY, AND BECAME FORMALLY A MEMBER OF THE ALLIED NATIONS IN THE WORLD WAR, DECEMBER 9.

APPENDIX III

BIBLIOGRAPHIES

I. WORKS OF PRE-CH'IN AND CH'IN PERIODS

Confucius. *Shih Ching,* or "The Book of Poetry," *Ch'i Yüeh, P'u T'ien, Ta T'ien, Mien, Shêng Min, Kung Liu, Hsüan Niao.*

Confucius. *Shu Ching,* or "The Book of History," *Yao Tien, Yü Kung, T'ang Shih, Chiu Kao.*

Confucius. *I Ching,* or "The Book of Changes," *Ch'ien, Chi Chi, Hsi Ts'ŭ.*

Lun Yü, or "The Analects" by Confucius and his students, recorded by the latter, Books III, IV, V, VI, VII, VIII, XI, XII, XV, XVI, XVII, XVIII.

Li Chi or "The Records of Rites" by the students and early followers of Confucius, *Wang Chih, K'ao Kung Chi, Ta Chuan, Ta Hsiao, Chung Jung.*

Tso Ch'iu Ming. *Tso Chuan,* or "Tso's Commentary on Confucius's 'Spring and Autumn Annals,' " texts for the 24th year in the reign of Duke Hsi; the 7th and 24th year in the reign of Duke Chao; the 10th year in the reign of Duke Ting; and the 14th year in the reign of Duke Ai.

Tso Ch'iu Ming. *Kuo Yü,* or "History of Nations."

I Chou Shu, Ming T'ang P'ien.

Shan Hai Ching, or "The Book of Mountains and Seas," Books XVI, XVII, XVIII.

Mencius. *Mêng Tzŭ,* or "The Book of Mencius," Books I, II, III, V, VI.

Hsun Ch'ing. *Hsun Tzŭ,* or "The Works of Hsun Ch'ing," Book XIII.

Li Er. *Leo Tzŭ Tao Têh Ching,* or "The Way and Waygoer," etc.

Chuang Chou. *Chuang Tzŭ,* or "The Works of Chuang Chou," Books II, IV, VI, XVII.

Lieh Yü-k'ou (ascribed). *Lieh Tzŭ,* or "The Works of Lieh Yü-k'ou," Books V, VII.

Kuan Chung (ascribed). *Kuan Tzŭ,* or "The Works of Kuan Chung," Books XXIII, XXIV.

Mo Ti. *Mo Tzŭ,* or "The Works of Mo Ti," Books IV, V, VI, VIII.

Han Fei. *Han Fei Tzŭ,* or "The Works of Han Fei," Book XIX.

Chu Shu Chi Nien, or "Chronicles inscribed on the Bamboo Slips."

Mu T'ien Tzŭ Chuan, or "The Biography of Emperor Mu."

Lü Pu-wei. *Lü Shih Ch'un Ch'iu,* or "Critical Essays of Lü," Books I, XVII.

Ch'ü Yüan. *Li Shao* and *T'ien Wên* in the anthology *Ch'u Tzŭ.*

II. WORKS OF THE HAN PERIOD (206 B.C.–A.D. 219)

Ssŭ-ma Ch'ien. *Shih Chi,* or "Historical Records," Vols. I, III, IV, V, VI, VII, VIII, X, XLIV, XLV, XLVII, XLVIII, LIX, LXV, LXVII, LXXXIV, CVI, CX, CXI, CXXIII.

Pan Ku. *Han Shu,* or "The History of Han," Vols. IV, XIX, XXI, XXIV, XXXVI, XL, XLIX, LIII, LXI, LXXXVIII, XCVI, XCIX.

San Fu Chiu Shih, or "Ancient Events in Three Suburbs of the Capital," in Chang Shu's *Er Yu T'ang Library* Edition.

Hsü Chêng. *San Wu Li,* or "The Chronicle of the Three Lords and Five Sovereigns," quoted by the editor of *T'ai P'ing Yü Lan* in Vol. II.

Hsiang Chün. *Shih Hsiao P'ien,* or "The Primary Studies," quoted in *T'ai P'ing Yü Lan,* Vol. LXXVIII.

Wei Hung. *Han Kuan Chiu I,* or "Ancient Etiquette of Han Officialdom," quoted by Ssŭ-ma Chên, Commentator of *Shih Chi,* in Vol. LV.

Kui Tsang I (pseudo—?), quoted by Hung Hsing-tsu, Commentator of the poem *T'ien Wên* in the anthology *Ch'u Tz'ŭ,* or "Poetry of Ch'u States."

K'ai Shih (pseudo—?), quoted by Kuo P'u, Commentator of *Shan Hai Ching,* in Vol. XVII.

Tun Chia K'ai Shan T'u (pseudo—?), quoted by the editor of *T'ai P'ing Yü Lan* in Vol. LXXVIII.

Ch'un Ch'iu Wei (pseudo—?), quoted by Ssŭ-ma Chên in *Pu Shan Huang Pên Chi,* or "The Chronicle of the Three Lords. An Appendix to *Shih Chi.*"

Yü Lung Ho T'u (pseudo—?), quoted by Chang Shou-chieh, Commentator of *Shih Chi,* in Vol. I.

Liu An. *Huai Nan Tzŭ,* or "Essays of the Prince of Huai-nan," Vols. III, IV, VI, XIX.

Chia I. *Hsin Shu,* or "The New Book."

Chia Shan. *Chih Yen,* or "Words of Significance."

Wang Fu. *Ch'ien Fu Lun,* or "Essays of a Retired Man," Vol. XII.

Liu Shang. *Lieh Nü Chuan,* or "Biographies of Distinguished Ladies."

Kuo Hsien. *Tung Ming Chi,* or "The Records of Mysterious Events."

Chang Hêng. *Hsi Ching Fu,* or "Western Capital, a *fu* Poem," in the anthology *Wên Hsüan,* Vol. II.

Hsü Shên. *Shuo Wên Chieh Tzŭ Hsü,* or "Preface to 'The Book of Etymology.'"

III. WORKS OF *San Kuo* AND THE SIX DYNASTIES PERIODS (A.D. 220-588)

Ch'ên Shou. *San Kuo Chih,* or "The History of the Three Kingdoms," *Wu Chih* II, and Vols. XXX, CCXXX, and CCXLII.

Fan Yeh. *Hou Han Shu,* or "The History of the Later Han Dynasty," Vols. LIII, LXVIII, LXXVII, XC, XCIV, XCVII, CIX, CXV, CXVI, CXVIII, CXIX, CXX.

Shên Yüeh. *Sung Shu,* or "The History of Sung," Vol. XCV.

Wei Shou. *Wei Shu,* or "The History of Northern Wei," Vols. VII, CIII, CXIV.

Wang Su. *K'ung Tzŭ Chia Yü,* or "Anecdotes of Confucius," Vols. III, V, VIII.

Huang-fu Mi. *Ti Wang Shih Chi,* or "Chronicles of Emperors and Kings."

Huang-fu Mi. *Kao Shih Chuan,* or "Biographies of Hermits."

Liu I-ch'ing. *Shih Shao Hsin Yü,* or "New Anecdotes of the World."

Ch'ang Chü. *Hua Yang Kuo Chih,* or "Geography of the Country of Hua Yang," Vols. I *(Pa Chih)* and III *(Shu Chih).*

Shêng Hung-chih. *Ching Chou Chi,* or "Records of Ching County."

Kê Hung. *Hsi Ching Tsa Chi,* or "Miscellaneous Records of the Western Capital."

Tsung Lin. *Ching Ch'u Sui Shih Chi,* or "Records of the Local Customs of Ching-ch'u District."

Fa Hsien. *Fo Kuo Chi,* or "Recollections of Buddha's Land."

Chang Hua. *Po Wu Chih,* or "Notes on Curious Things."

Wang Chia. *Shih I Chi,* or "The Collection of Some Neglected Stories."

Jên Fang. *Shu I Chi,* or "Stories of Wonders."

T'ao Ch'ien (ascribed). *Hou Shou Shên Chi,* or "A Supplement of 'The Search for Immortals.'"

Shih Ch'ung. *Wang Ming Chün Tz'ǔ,* or "The Lady Bright, a Poem," in the anthology *Wên Hsüan,* Vol. XXVII.

Tso Ssǔ. *Wu Tu Fu,* or "The Capital of Wu, a *fu* Poem," in *Wên Hsüan,* Vol. V.

Yüan Chi. *Yüan Ssǔ Tsung Chi,* or "The Works of Yüan Chi," with the commentary of Wang Shih-hsien of the Ming Period.

Liu Ling. *Chiu Têh Hsüng,* or "A Eulogy on the Virtue of Wine," in the anthology *Wên Hsüan,* Vol. XLVII.

IV. WORKS OF THE SUI AND T'ANG PERIODS (A.D. 589-905)

Fang Hsüan-ling. *Tsin Shu,* or "The History of Tsin," Vols. XLV, XLIX, LV, CVIII, CXII.

Ling-hu Tê-fên. *Chou Shu,* or "The History of the Northern Chou Dynasty," Vol. L.

Yao Ssǔ-lien. *Liang Shu,* or "The History of Liang," Vols. XLVIII, LIV.

Wei Chêng. *Sui Shu,* or "The History of Sui," Vol. LXXXII.

Li Yen-shou. *Nan Shih,* or "The History of the Southern Dynasties," Vols. VI, VII.

Li Yen-shou. *Pei Shih,* or "The History of the Northern Dynasties," Vols. XCIV, XCVI, XCVIII, XCIX.

Ssŭ-ma Chên. *Pu San Huang Pen Chi,* or "The Chronicle of the Three Lords, a Supplement of *Shih Chi.*"

Chang Shou-chieh. *Shih Chi Chêng I,* or "Commentary on *Shih Chi,*" text of *Shih Chi* IX referred.

Yen Shih-ku. *Han Shu Chu,* or "Commentary on the History of Han," Vol. XCVI.

Yen Shih-ku. *Ta Yeh Shih I Chi,* or "Reminiscences of the Events of the Ta Yeh Period."

Han Wo. *K'ai Ho Chi,* or "The Making of the Canal."

Han Wo. *Hai Shan Chi,* or "Records of the Lakes and Rocks."

Liu Su. *Ta T'ang Hsin Yü,* or "New Anecdotes of the Great T'ang Period."

Yüan Chiao (or Yang Chü-yüan?). *Kan Tz'ê Yao,* "Ballads of the Fair Rain."

Hsüan Chuang. *Ta T'ang Hsi Yü Chi,* or "Memoirs of the Western Regions."

I Ching. *Ta T'ang Hsi Yü Ch'iu Fa Kao Sêng Chuan,* or "Biographies of Learned Monks in the T'ang Period Who Traveled to the Western Regions for Sutras."

Hui Ssŭ (ascribed). *Ta Shêng Chih Kuan Fa Mên,* Vols. II, III. (Taisho Issaikyo, Vol. XLVI.)

Fa Tsang. *Chin Shih Tzŭ Chang,* or "On the Golden Image of a Lion." (Taisho Issaikyo, Vol. L.)

Li Po. *Li T'ai Po Shih,* or "Poetical Works of Li Po," with Commentary by Wang Ch'i, Vol. XXV, *K'u Ch'ao Ch'ing Hêng.*

Tu Fu. *Tu Shih Ching Ch'üan,* or "Poetical Works of Tu Fu," with Commentary by Yang Lun, *I Hsi, Li Jên Hang, Hsi Ping Ma, Ai Wang Sun.*

Wang Wei. *Wang Yu Ch'êng Chi,* or "Poetical Works of Wang Wei," with Commentary by Chao Tien-ch'êng, Vol. II, *Sung Mi Shu Ch'ao Chien Huan Jih Pên Kuo.*

Po Chü-i. *Po Hsiang Shan Shih,* or "Poetical Works of Po Chü-i," with Commentary by Wang Li-ming, Vol. XII, *Ch'ang Hên Ko.*

Ch'ên Hung. *Ch'ang Hên Chuan,* or "The Story of Everlasting Lamentation," quoted by Wang Li-ming in *Po Hsiang Shan Chi,* Vol. XII.

Li Shang-yin. *Yü Hsi Shêng Shih,* or "Poetical Works of Li Shang-yin," with Commentary by Fêng Hao, Vol. VI, *Sui Kung.*

P'i Jih-hsiu. *P'i Jih Hsiu Shih,* or "Poetical Works of P'i Jih-hsiu," Vol. IV, *Ch'a Chung Tsa Yung.* (In the Imperial Edition of *Ch'üan T'ang Shih,* "A Complete Library of the T'ang Poets," Vol. XXIII.)

Ching Ching. *Ta Ch'in Ching Chiao Liu Hsing Chung Kuo Pei,* "A Tablet recording how the Radiant Religion from the Great Ch'in has been Promulgated in the Middle Kingdom."

V. Works of the Wu Tai and Sung Periods (A.D. 907–1276)

Liu Hsü. *Ch'iu T'ang Shu,* or "The Old History of T'ang," Vols. XXIX, CC.

Ou-yang Hsiu. *Hsin T'ang Shu,* or "A New History of T'ang," Vols. LXXVI, CXCII, CCXV, CCXXI.

Ou-yang Hsiu. *Hsin Wu Tai Shih,* or "A New History of the Five Dynasties," Vols. VIII, XXIX, LXXII.

Ssŭ-ma Kuang. *Tzŭ Chih T'ung Chien,* or "The General Mirror for Administration," Vols. LXV, CV, CXIII, CXXIV, CXXVI, CLXXX, CLXXXIII, CCI.

Wang P'u. *Wu Tai Hui Yao,* or "A Summary of the Political and Social Systems of the Five Dynasties Period."

Hsü Mêng-hsin. *San Ch'ao Pei Ming Hui P'ien,* or "A Collection of Diplomatic Records during the three Successive Reigns (of the Emperors Hui Tsung, Ch'in Tsung, and Kao Tsung) with the Northern Peoples."

Yü-wên Mao-chao. *Ta Chin Kuo Chih,* or "Records of the Great Golden Empire," Vols. I, XIV, XV.

Li Fang. *T'ai P'ing Yü Lan,* or "An Imperial Reader for Peaceful Times," Vols. II, LXXVIII.

Lo Pi. *Lu Shih,* an ancient history, *Ch'ien Chi,* Vol. II.

Pêng Ta-ya and Hsü T'ing. *Hei T'a Shih Lüeh,* or "A Brief Record of the Affairs of the Black Tatars."

Chao Kung. *Mêng T'a Pei Lu,* or "Notes on the Mongol Tatars."

Wang Ch'êng. *Tung Tu Shih Lüeh,* or "A Brief Account of the Affairs in the Eastern Capital."

Mêng Yüan-lao. *Tung Ching Mêng Hua Lu,* or "Visions of the Eastern Capital."

Wu Tzŭ-mu. *Mêng Liang Lu,* or "Records of a Dream."

Chêng Wên-pao. *Chiang Nan Yü Tsai,* or "Reminiscences of the Affairs of South of the Yangtzŭ River," Part II.

Ch'iu Ch'u-chi. *Hsi Yu Chi,* or "A Journey to the West."

Chou Ch'ü-fei. *Ling Wai Tai Ta,* or "A Guide Book for Districts beyond the Mountain Ridge."

Chou Mi. *K'uei Hsin Tsa Shih,* or "Miscellaneous Notes written in the House on K'uei Hsin Street."

Chou Mi. *Ch'i Tung Yeh Yü,* or "Talks of a Rustic in Eastern Ch'i."

Wang Shao. *Pi Chi Man Chih,* or "Miscellaneous Records written in the House on Green Chicken Street," Vol. III.

Chou Shan. *Pei Yüan Lu,* or "Traveling to the North."

Yeh Mêng-têh. *Shih Lin Yen Yü,* or "Talks on Leisure by Shih-lin."

Wei Chuang. *Huan Hua Chi,* or "The Poetical Works of Wei Chuang," Vol. IV.

Su Hsün. *Chia Yu Chi,* or "The Works of Su Hsun," Vol. III, *Liu Kuo Lun.*

Wang An-shih. *Wang Ching Kung Chi,* or "The Works of Wang An-shih." *Yü Tsêng Kung Li Shu* ("a letter to Tsêng Kung-li").

Chu Hsi. *Chu Tzŭ Wên Chi,* or "The Essays of Chu Hsi," Vol. XLVI, *Yu Liu Shu Wên Shu* ("a letter to Liu Shu-wen").

Tsêng Chao. *Yao Fu Ya Tz'ŭ,* or "Refined Verses from Musical Songs," Part I.

Kuo Mao-ch'ien. *Yao Fu Shih Chi,* or "An Anthology of the Poems for Musical Songs," Vol. XXXVIII, Part I.

Shih Hao. *Mao Fêng Chên Yin Man Lu,* or "Miscellaneous Memoirs of a Real Hermit in Mao Mountain," Vol. XLVI.

Hsieh Fang-têh. *Tieh Shan Chi,* or "The Works of Hsieh Fang-têh," Vol. II, *Sung Fang Po Tsai Kuei San Shan Hsü.*

Sung Hui Tsung (ascribed). *Hsüan Ho Hua P'u,* or "Criticism on Paintings collected in the Hsüan Ho period," Vol. II.

Lü Ta-lin. *Po Ku T'u,* or "Illustrations of Curiosities."

Hung Hsing-tsŭ. *Ch'u Tz'ŭ Chu,* or "The Commentary on 'Chu Poems.' "

VI. Works of the Yuan and Ming Periods (A.D. 1277-1643)

T'o K'ê T'o. *Sung Shih,* or "The History of Sung," Vols. I, CLXXIII, CCCLXV, CDLXXI, CDLXXXV, CDLXXXVI, CDXCII.

T'o K'ê T'o. *Chin Shih,* or "The History of Chin (Golden Race)," Vol. I.

T'o K'ê T'o. *Liao Shih,* or "The History of Liao (Kitans)," Vol. XXXVII.

Sung Lien. *Yüan Shih,* or "The History of Yüan (Mongols)," Vols. V, XXXIX, XLIII, CV, CXXXI, CXLVI, CLXII, CCII, CCV, CCX.

Ming Shih Lu, or "True Records of the Ming Court," Vols. CXVI, CCCLVI.

Shêng Hsi-ming. *T'u Hua K'ao,* or "A Study of Painting," Vol. III.

Ma Hüan. *Ying Ya Shêng Lan,* or "The Beautiful Views at the Boundary of the Immortals' Ying Island."

Fei Hsin. *Hsing Ch'a Shêng Lan,* or "The Beautiful Views seen from on Board a Log-boat towards Stars."

Yüan Chia-ku. *T'ien I,* or "Interpretations of Affairs of the T'ien Region," Vol. VIII.

Yüan Chung-ch'ê. *Ku Chin Shih Chien,* or "Fortune-telling for the Ancients and the Moderns."

Chiang I-k'uei. *Yao Shan T'ang Wei Chi,* or "Memoirs of the Owner of Yao Shan Studio."

Chu Yung-ming. *Ch'ien Wên Chi,* or "Anecdotes."

Hsü Ju-k'o. *Hsü Nien Yang Kung Chi,* or "The Works of Hsü Ju-k'o," in the series of *Ch'ien K'un Chêng Ch'i Chi,* or "Essays on the Right Spirit in the Universe," Vol. XXIX.

Shên Ch'üeh. *Nan Kung Shu Tu,* or "The Correspondence and Memoranda of Shên Ch'üeh," in the series of *P'o Hsieh Chi,* or "Essays Denouncing Heretics," Vol. I.

Huang Po-lu. *Chêng Chiao Fêng Pao Chi,* or "Records of the Right Religion receiving Imperial Patronship."

Yang Kuang-hsien. *Pu Têh I,* or "I am obliged to Speak."

Ch'ien Ku. *Wu Tu Wên Ts'ui Hsü Chi,* or "Supplements to 'Selected Essays of Writers from the Wu Capital,'" Vol. XX.

Ku Ch'i-yüan. *Kê Tsuo Tsui Yü,* or "Table-talk with the Guests."

Tsou I-kuei. *Hsiao Shan Hua P'u,* or "Essays on Painting by Hsiao Shan."

Chiang Shao-shu. *Wu Shêng Shih Shih,* or "A History of the Unsung Poetry."

VII. Works of the Ch'ing Period (a.d. 1644–1911)

Chang T'ing-yü. *Ming Shih,* or "This History of Ming," Vols. V, VI, VII, CCXII, CCXXXI, CCXXXVIII, CCXXXIX, CCCIV, CCCV, CCCIX, CCCXXII, CCCXXVII.

Pi Yüan. *Hsü Tzŭ Chih T'ung Chien,* or "Supplement to Ssŭ-ma Kuang's 'General Mirror for Administrations,'" Vols. I, XV.

Hsü Wên Hsien T'ung K'ao, or "Supplement to Ma Tuan-lin's 'General Study of Documental Records and Oral Traditions,'" Vol. CCXIV.

Ch'ing Chien I Chih Lu, or "An Easy Study of the History (Mirror) of Ch'ing," *Chêng P'ien,* Vols. VI, IX.

K'o Shao-min. *Hsin Yüan Shih,* or "A New History of Yüan (Mongols)," Vol. I.

Li Yüan-tu. *Kuo Ch'ao Hsien Chêng Shih Lüeh,* or "Brief Biographies of the Elders of the National Dynasty," Vol. XIV.

Wei Yüan. *Shêng Wu Chi,* or "The Sacred Heroism," Vol. III.

Chiang Liang-chi. *Tung Hua Lu,* or "Material from the Cabinet Documents in the Library near the Tung Hua Gate of the Imperial Palace," for the ninth year of the K'ang Hsi period.

Ta Ch'ing I T'ung Chih, or "The Geography of the Great Ch'ing Empire, covering the Universe," Vol. CLX.

Yang Chou Shih Jih Chi, or "Ten Days in Yangchou."

Chia Ting T'u Ch'êng Chi, or "The Massacre of Chia Ting."

Wu Wei-yeh. *Wu Shih Chi Lan,* or "The Poetical Works of Wu," with Commentary by Chin Jung-fan, Vol. VII, Part I, *Yüan Yüan Ch'ü.*

Chu I-tsun. *Ching Chih Chü Shih Hua,* or "Talks on Poetry in the Peace-in-Mind Studio."

Liu O. *T'ieh Yün Ts'ang Kuei,* or "T'ieh-yün's Treasures of the Turtle Shells."

Lo Chên-yü. *Yin Hsü Shu Ch'i Ch'ien P'ien* and *Hou P'ien*, or "inscriptions on the Turtle Shells from the Mounds of Yin, the Former Part," Preface, and "The Latter Part," Vol. II.

VIII. MODERN PUBLICATIONS AND MAGAZINES

Mao Ssŭ-ch'êng. *Min Kuo Shih Wu Nien I Ch'ien Chih Chiang Chieh Shih Hsien Shêng,* or "Chiang Kai-shek, before 1926."

Chiang Kai-shek. *Hsi An Pan Yüeh Chi,* or "Half a Month in Sian," 1937, Nanking (Chêng Chung).

Tso Shun-shêng. *Chung Kuo Chin Po Nien Shih Liao Ch'u P'ien* and *Hsü P'ien,* or "Historical Matter of the Recent Hundred Years in China": an Anthology. Shanghai (Chung Hua).

Chou Yü-t'ung. Kuo Ch'ü Liao Tê Wu Ssŭ 1937. Shanghai (K'ai Ming leaflet).

An Yang Fa Chüeh Pao Kao, Reports of the Excavations at Anyang, made by the Central Research Academy, Nos. I and IV (1929 and 1933). Shanghai (Commercial Press).

Bulletin of the Geological Society, China, Vols. V, VI, VIII, XI, XIV (1923, 1924, 1930, 1931, 1935). Peking.

Bulletin of the Geological Society, China. Memoirs Series A, Vol. V, 1925.

Palaeontologia Sinica, Series D, Vol. VII, Fasc. 2, 1931.

INDEX

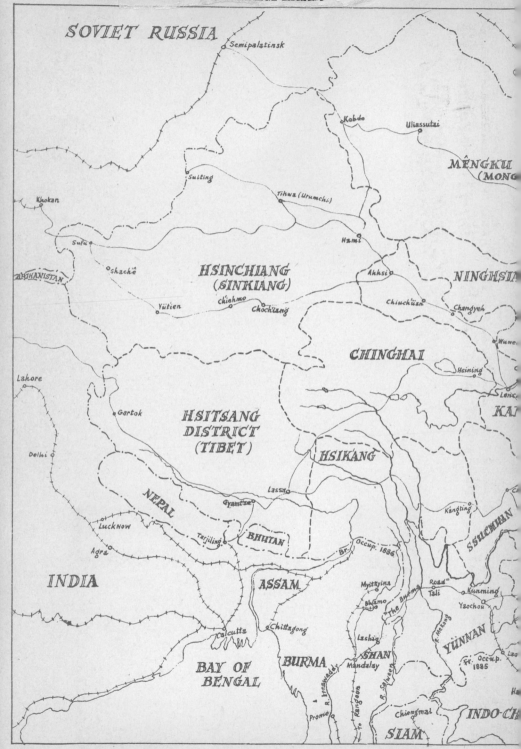